WITHDRAWN

FATEFUL TRANSFORMATIONS
THE FOUR YEARS' PARLIAMENT
AND THE CONSTITUTION OF MAY 3, 1791

BY
JANUSZ DUZINKIEWICZ

EAST EUROPEAN MONOGRAPHS, BOULDER
DISTRIBUTED BY COLUMBIA UNIVERSITY PRESS, NEW YORK

1993

EAST EUROPEAN MONOGRAPHS, NO. CCCLXV

Copyright © 1993 by Janusz Duzinkiewicz
ISBN 0-88033-265-4
Library of Congress Catalog Card Number 93-79569

Printed in the United States of America

in memoriam

Jadwiga Duzinkiewicz
(1907–1991)

Contents

Preface	ix
Introduction	1
1. The Four Years' Sejm in Historical Perspective	14
2. The Scope of the Constitution of May 3, 1791	40
3. Parliamentary Procedures and the Four Years' Sejm in Light of Stanislawian Antecedents	90
4. Some Glimpses at Parliamentary Behavior	120
5. Sejm and Country	161
6. Constitution and Country: Complications, Elaborations, and Explanations	188
7. Political Groupings	230
8. Concluding Considerations	254
Notes	267
Glossary of Foreign Terms	302
Bibliography	306
Index	319

List of Tables

1	Noble Privileges Bestowed by Polish Kings	19
2	Major Noble Rights Passed by the Sejm	23
3	Major Statutes Comprising the New Constitution	51-52
4	Passage of Bills in the Sejm	74-75
5	Straż Praw	79-81
6	The Court System	84-85
7	Laws Passed by the Sejm 1778-1786	96
8	Roll Call Results	122-144
9	Attendance Rates	145
10	Double Turni	147
11	Adjusted Attendance Rates	148
12	Measure of Consensus for the Four Years' Sejm	156
13	Degree of Consensus by Topic	157
14	Consensus Rates by Chamber and Topic	158
15	Consensus Rates by Term and by Topic	158
16	Number of Deputies by Term and by Province	164
17	Deputies' Ages in 1791	165
18	Orders of St. Stanisław and the White Eagle	169
19	Distribution of Orders Compared to Sejm Average	170
20	Wealth Profile of Deputies	172
21	Wealth Profile of Deputies' Fathers	173
22	Freemasonry and Military Careers	174
23	Previous Experience in the Sejm	175-176
24	Participation in the Confederation of Bar	177
25	The Deputies and the May Third Constitution	180
26	The Deputies and the May Third Constitution by Province and Term	181

27	Extreme Support and Opposition towards the Constitution	182
28	Extreme Support and Opposition towards the Constitution (Orders)	182
29	Parliamentary Experience and the Constitution	183
30	Orders and the Constitution	184
31	Wealth and the Constitution	184
32	Wealth and the Constitution Compared to Sejm Norms	185
33	Chi Square on Biograms	189
34	Percentage of Approval for the Constitution on the Województwo Level	191
35	Changes in Orders with Respect to the Constitution for Województwa with Extreme Support or Opposition	200
36	Wealth and the Constitution in Województwa of Extreme Support or Opposition	200
37	Ages of Deputies in 1791	201
38	Deputies Listed by Term and Age (in 1791)	202-204
39	Age by Term and Five Year Intervals	205
40	Participation Rates during the Second Term	206
41	Ranking of Age Groups According to Activism	207
42	Mean Ages (in 1791)	209
43	The Confederation of Bar and the May Third Constitution	211
44	Senate and Ministerium	219-221
45	Non-Senatorial Republic-wide Offices	221–222
46	Traditional Local Offices	222-223
47	Careers in Traditional Local Offices	226
48	First Term Clusters	233
49	Second Term Clusters	238
50	Marshals' Cluster	241

List of Figures

1	Attendance Based on Turni Results	146
2	First Term Clusters	237

PREFACE

The recent bicentennial of the Constitution of May 3, 1791 has refocussed attention on what some regard to be an old, well-worn topic. Others regard the Constitution as an obscurity, the study of which has yet to be justified. Not surprisingly the truth lies somewhere in the middle. Much that appears old at a given time may become new as ideas and perceptions are recycled in ever different combinations and as a truly novel concept is formulated or a truly new approach adopted. The May Third Constitution has a new and wider relevance today as the end of communism in East Central Europe reveals native political traditions which are now becoming political realities again.

The historiographical landscape is also changing. This study comes at the tail end of the recent fascination with quantitative methods in history, a methodology reminiscent of some nineteenth century positivist scholarship, and at the beginning of a renewed appreciation for past mentalities. The chapters of this study which do employ the nearly passé methodology of quantification will, nonetheless, hopefully begin to fill very real lacunae in the literature. Those which examine political culture—and of necessity the mentality at its base— may be positioned on the road to new historical insights and eventual methodological disillusionment. And those that take a traditional approach towards textual analysis and the historical development of institutions and ideas may bring to the fore something fresh. The hope is that whatever its location in scholarship, this study will contribute to a better understanding of constitutional reform at the end of the eighteenth century and indirectly to the changes which are now occurring.

The general approach is to make this work accessible both to individuals unfamiliar with East Central European history and to those who are. Any "Western" student of constitutionalism should take note of the long representative traditions to the east and any student of "Eastern" Europe interested in parliaments should look at newer scholarly approaches from the "West." There are, of course, dangers in courting such a broad audience: impatience from the expert, intimidation from the novice and skepticism from the "westerner." Perhaps only the interested "easterner" will be satisfied. I hope not.

The Polish-Lithuanian Commonwealth involved the lives of several nations: Polish, Lithuanian, Ukrainian, Byelorussian, Latvian and Jewish and the lives, quite obviously, of both men and women. Common heritage often causes misunderstanding and conflict as much as it does an appreciation of kinship. Since much that is discussed here is the common heritage of several nations, in all fairness, most of the place names and even proper names should be given in several translations or perhaps in the form used today. That would be fair but it would also be too awkward. It is not my intention to offend but I have decided to use spellings as they were in the eighteenth century and in the language that was common to the entire Commonwealth.

Unfortunately, this study reflects the gender bias of the old political system it studies. Women do not fit into the discussion because they did not fit into the political processes. Their position in the Commonwealth was typical of women in early modern European society. Wealthy noblewomen exercised influence behind the scenes and sometimes were crucial links in political alliances. King Stanisław August was fond of the saying "we rule the world and women rule us." But in the parliament being studied women could only be vocal spectators who quite often in approval would drop perfumed handkerchiefs over the railing onto the debate floor they could not enter. The British historian Norman Davies is, nonetheless, of the opinion that the peculiar egalitarianism of the Polish nobility encompassed women in such matters as property rights. Bogna Lorence-Kot has begun to write the history of the noble woman in the Old Polish-Lithuanian Commonwealth, a story which should be interesting once it is written.

I am pleased to be able to thank all those who have helped me in so many different ways. Financial support has come from the International Research and Exchanges Board (IREX), the United States Department of Education Doctoral Dissertation Research Abroad Fellowship, the Polish Ministry of Enlightenment and Higher Education, the Department of History at the University of Iowa and the Gordon

W. and Anne R. Prange Fellowship. I am most grateful for the assistance extended by Polish archives and their dedicated staff: Archiwum Główne Akt Dawnych, Biblioteka Narodowa Wydział Starych Druków, Biblioteka Uniwersytetu Warszawskiego Wydział Starych Druków, Biblioteka Uniwersytetu Jagiellonskiego, Biblioteka Muzeum X.X. Czartoryskich, Katolicki Uniwersytet Lubelski, Ossolineum and Biblioteka Zielińskich.

Valuable intellectual and professional support has come from Donald McCloskey, Alan Spitzer, Sarah Hanley and Michael Lewis-Beck. Chia-Hsıng Lu, George Boynton, John Kolp, Mary Strottman, Tom Lutz and Sharon Anderson have offered essential technical assistance. I am most greatful for the generous help extended in Poland by the late Andrzej Zahorski, Józef Andrzej Gierowski, Jerzy Kowecki and especially Łukasz Kądziela whose knowledge of the late eighteenth century I can only envy. Mary Sevian Love and Professor Stephen Fischer-Galati have my sincerest appreciation for making this publication possible.

Special thanks goes to Jaroslaw Pelenski. Without his help, confidence and patience this study would not have been written. His example of scholarly honesty and industry and his balanced vision of the old Commonwealth have pointed the direction.

Finally, there is the indispensible, purely human support and inspiration that comes from friends and relatives. Some of my colleagues at the University of Iowa have become real friends: Dave McCarter, Kendall Staggs, Kathy Jellison, Casey Harison and Alicia Valenzuela and especially Stephen Waring. "At large" friends include Stratos and Sharon Constantinidis, Michael Groth, Jim St. John, Marc Schelle, Tomasz Rossa, Steven Campbell S.J., Bogna and Stefan Sikora, Radosław Kwieciński, and especially Włodzimierz Kuśmierczuk, Bob Mitchell and Ed Daering. Among the relatives who have been particularly kind are Józef Kudlikowski, Jerzy Hrehoruk, Jarosław Hrehoruk, Zofia and Waldemar Duzinkiewicz, Sister Alina (Janina) Kudlikowska, Wanda Rekus, Marek Rekus and Jadwiga Duzinkiewicz. Without these dear people life would have been much more less pleasant and productive. But most important are the two individuals who constitute my entire family in the States: my Sister, Therese Baker, and, with deepest gratitude, my Mother whose love is truly unconditional and beyond adequate appreciation.

INTRODUCTION

As the eighteenth century waned, the established order of society was unexpectedly brought into question first by the idealistic war of independence in distant North America and subsequently by a much more far-reaching revolution and conflagration in the heart of European civilization, France. The last decades of the century have been called the age of democratic revolution. Few of the revolutions sought democracy and fewer achieved it even for a brief time. But the upheavals did affirm, in action, Enlightenment ideals of human rights and evidenced a pursuit of specific, individual interests that included economic considerations. Representation, *patrie* and equality—ideas that would give rise to twentieth century concepts of democracy—became integral parts of political struggles. Experiments in popular government involved controversy over the meaning of terms such as popular sovereignty and nation. Liberty became a rallying cry; and liberty meant freedom from arbitrary government. But what else did liberty entail? Clearly, the crucial state-society relationship that continues to distinguish the West reached a moment of fundamental import.

A major revolution occurred at the cusp of the 1780s-1790s on the West's eastern borders. The Polish Parliament of 1788-1792 produced the first modern European constitution and the second in the world, four years after the adoption of the American Constitution. In what would prove to be a failed attempt to "break out into [complete] independence" the *Sejm* (Parliament) reformed the governmental machinery and state-society relationships in the truncated Poland-Lithuanian Commonwealth. These events became a part of the broader European drama and of the history of modern constitutionalism.

Upon its adoption, the Polish Constitution of May 3, 1791 brought general approval and, at times, scarcely restrained praise from outside observers. In "revolutionary" America, the Philadelphian *Gazette of the United States* remarked that the May Third Constitution signified "a great and important Revolution in favor of the rights of man . . . happily begun without violence or tumult . . . a most wonderful revolution. . . ."[1] In Switzerland, the duchess of Nassau commented that "public pronouncements, private correspondence all echo the good fortune of Poland." In neighboring revolutionary France, a member of the National Assembly wondered how one man, the Polish king "could bring about a revolution more wise, more prompt and perhaps better organized than that in France."[2] In Britain, the ardent critic of the French Revolution, Edmund Burke, was perhaps the most enthusiastic admirer of the Polish Revolution in 1791. Burke praised both the means and the substance of the reforms:

> But in what manner was this chaos [Polish politics] brought into order? The means were as striking to the imagination, as satisfactory to the reason, and soothing to the moral sentiments. In contemplating that change, humanity has every thing to rejoice and to glory in; nothing to be ashamed of, nothing to suffer. So far as it has gone, it probably is the most pure and . . . [refined] public good that ever has been conferred on mankind. . . . Not one man incurred loss, or suffered degradation. All, from the king to the day-labourer, were improved in their condition. Everything was kept in its place and order; but in that place and order every thing was bettered.[3]

Finally, in Poland-Lithuania itself, after the fall of the new system, the political treatise, *O ustanowieniu i upadku konstytucyi polskiey 3go maia 1791r.* [Concerning the Adoption and Fall of the Polish Constitution of May 3, 1791] called the May Third Constitution "the last will and testament of the dying fatherland,"[4] a most positive, self-affirming demonstration of political vigor in the midst of a national tragedy.

The favorable evaluations of the event by observers outside of Poland lost their luster with the unsuccessful course of Polish history. The condemnation of silence and the judgment of irrelevance have, in a few exceptions, been mollified by mild sympathy for untimely heroism. The main exception was Marx who offered this judgment on the May Third Constitution:

Introduction 3

With all its shortcomings this Constitution appears against the background of Russian-Prussian-Austrian barbarity as the only work of freedom which Central Europe has ever produced of its own accord. Moreover, it was created by a privileged class, the gentry. The history of the world knows no other example of such generosity of the gentry.[5]

In Polish historiography and popular culture the May Third Constitution was transformed from a viable political program to a sanctified symbol of the Polish nation's vitality during the destruction of the old state. Whether the old Polish-Lithuanian state had fallen because of rapacious neighbors or because of its own fatal imperfections, the Four Years' Parliament and its constitution could not be judged except in a positive light. The polemical work by the Potocki, Dmochowski and Kołłątaj acquired an authoritative quality as enthusiasm for the Constitution grew with the diminishing chances of regaining independence. Only a minor monarchist tradition treated the Four Years' *Sejm* critically[6] and the socialist movement, emergent towards the end of the nineteenth century, refused to consider the anniversary of the Constitution as a special day. Overall, the compromise nature of the Constitution lent it wide acceptance throughout the political spectrum.

In this century, May Third became the most important national holiday in the Second Republic (1918-1939) and during the Occupation; after the Second World War it served as a defiant symbol of the "real" Poland sponsored most often by the Roman Catholic Church. For the communist authorities May First replaced May Third—the revolutionary dictatorship of the party assumed power in the name of the toiling masses thus displacing the old rule of law emanating from a bourgeois society. As a holiday, May Third was regarded as counterrevolutionary. As a historical fact, the May Third Constitution was viewed as a progressive document for its time, but its time had past in the irresistible dialectic of history.

History, nonetheless, followed directions unanticipated by Marxism-Leninism. During the first Solidarity period in 1981, the publishing house of the national organization of labor unions reprinted 50,000 copies of the *Ustawa Rządowa* [Statute of Government], the central document of the May Third Constitution. Before their collapse, the communist authorities made the anniversary of the Constitution into the holiday of the *Stronnictwo Demokratyczne*, the "democratic grouping," operating in the shadow of the Polish United Workers' (Communist) Party. In this way, the May Third Constitution was presented as a milestone in the development of the Polish intelligentsia. Thus, since 1791 the Constitution had devolved from a functioning system of reforms oriented towards a bright future to a national myth whose permanent importance was to be found in unenthusiastic, self-contradictory efforts at communist legitimization. In 1990, celebration of the May Third Constitution reemerged once again as the main national holiday.

For the historian, the significance of the May Third Constitution lies not only in its patriotic symbolism of national vitality nor in its precipitation of the Second Partition. The Constitution and the *Sejm* which produced it may be viewed as the foremost expression of centuries-long constitutional development and as a succinct reflection of wider societal realities and changes in the late eighteenth century. The Constitution of May Third figures as the central event in the last uninhibited flourishing of the Polish-Lithuanian Commonwealth. As such it brings attention to the wider question of political cultures and the opposition of "absolutism" or the absolutist ideal and native constitutionalism or representative ideals.

The Polish Parliament of 1788-92 and its most central accomplishment, the Constitution of May 3, 1791, also form an important turning point in the history of the lands of the Polish-Lithuanian Commonwealth and in the delineation of modern history in Eastern Europe. The revitalization of the old Polish state hastened that ancient entity's destruction by Russia, Prussia and Austria, creating the political constellation that would dominate the area virtually unchallenged until the twentieth century. The reemergence of a traditional ideology of mixed government, however, combined in the Polish case with a more modern conception of national sovereignty as well as the strength with which this new political force neared success and influenced almost all levels of society created powerful revolutionary legends that eventually triumphed amidst the self-destruction of the conservative order during the First World War. The tradition of controlled centralized government answerable to society was the hallmark of the Polish Constitution of 1791 and one of the main characteristics of the modern political evolution of Western civilization. This western concept of government has helped to undermine in recent decades one party systems where West and East overlap.

As the pivotal legislation of the Parliament of 1788-1792, the

Constitution of May Third culminated years of agitation for reform, both within and outside of the *Sejm*, and many months of slow, arduous restructuring of the political and administrative systems of the Polish-Lithuanian Commonwealth by the central legislative body itself. The main features of the Constitution were a redefining of the social limits for participation in political life and the revamping of the governmental apparatus to ensure a more efficient execution of laws, growth in the country's well-being and a more effective defense. Characteristic of emerging liberalism in the contemporary Enlightenment, the possession of property became the decisive qualification for participation in the representative and administrative systems. Thus, the richer stratum of townsmen was given the vote and partial representation in Parliament while landless nobles were excluded. This seemingly served to break the inordinate power of the magnates who had utilized the numeric strength of dependent or impoverished nobles to make the central state impotent. At the same time it was intended to infuse the remaining nobility with the fresh innovative spirit and wealth of the more successful bourgeoisie. The concept of nation was, moreover, gingerly extended to include even the peasants who for the first time in centuries were placed under the protection of the law and were expected to defend the Commonwealth.

These sociopolitical reforms were consistent with Polish traditions and Enlightenment ideals, yet they were also quite radical for late eighteenth century Central and Eastern Europe. National sovereignty and the rule of law were postulated over rule by an absolute monarch, be it dictated by reason or divine will. Economic utility, rather than the sanction of heredity or royal prerogative, became the basis for social distinctions. Not surprisingly the Commonwealth's "absolutist" neighbors became alarmed by this apparent Jacobin threat to their own society's base.

The second feature of the Polish Constitution of May Third ironically can be viewed as anti-revolutionary from any perspective except that of the Commonwealth. While precluding the possibility of "absolutism," the Constitution did, nonetheless, strengthen the governmental apparatus by converting the elected monarchy into a hereditary institution. No longer was the king to be the direct choice of the enfranchised but also no longer would he be the choice of foreign meddlers. The entire administration was rationalized and placed under the immediate guidance of the king but the ultimate control of Parliament. The strengthening of the monarchy was definitely antirevolutionary in the context of the French Revolution, as pointed out by the Constitution's supporters, but by making a more efficient monarchical government into a tool of popular rule (regardless of definition), it likewise appeared dangerously subversive to the conservative monarchies of the region who had, moreover, been bound more closely by their partitioning of Polish territory in 1772.

One of these neighbors, Russia, having settled its war with the Ottoman Empire, invaded the Polish-Lithuanian Commonwealth in 1792 and successfully overturned the May Third Constitution. But rather than quickly eliminating the perceived subversive threat the assault on the product of ardent, long-term reform only radicalized the Polish Revolution. The Kościuszko Uprising of 1794 followed, during the course of which the sociopolitical order of the region was even more seriously threatened with the first concrete steps taken towards the abolition of serfdom in Poland. So immediate did the danger seem that Prussia and Austria who had been attempting to militarily contain the regicidal revolution in France turned their attention eastward instead and joined Russia in the Third (and final) Partition of the Commonwealth. The Polish threat was crushed but a symbol and a revolutionary tradition had been created.

Scholarship on the May Third Constitution and the Parliament that produced it has not attained the same level of accomplishment as have Western constitutional studies. One cause for this is the very strength of the revolutionary legend in Polish culture which easily led to the enshrinement of the May Third Constitution in the sacred national pantheon. Relatively objective treatments of the subject had to await the spread of positivistic historical writing in the late nineteenth century. Foremost in this group was Waleryan Kalinka's multivolume, *Sejm Czteroletni*, [Four Years' Parliament] published in 1883. Kalinka argued that the reforms did not go far enough in strengthening the monarchy. Kalinka's work was completed in 1897 by Władysław Smoleński's study, *Ostatni rok Sejmu Czteroletniego* [The Last Year of the Four Years' Parliament]. Before the Second World War positivistic scholarship in Poland became preoccupied with monographic topics and the next synthetic study of the Constitution was Bogusław Leśnodorski's *Dzieło Sejmu Czteroletniego* [The Accomplishments of the Four Years' Parliament] which appeared in 1951, several years after the communist takeover. This mixture of positivist objectivity and Marxist structural insight has, to this day, remained one of the best works on the subject due to its scholarly merits and to the fact that the study of constitutional history was perceived as inconsistent with the building of socialism. For forty-five years, the May Third Constitution was not politically acceptable.

Substantive contributions to the study of the Four Years' *Sejm* and the May Third Constitution also came from Emanuel Rostworowski. In examining narrower issues, Rostworowski solidified scholarship on many aspects of political controversy and power balances immediately prior to the *Sejm* in his *Sprawa aukcji wojska na tle sytuacji politycznej przed Sejmem Czteroletnim* [The Military Levy Issue in the Context of the Political Situation Prior to the Four Years' *Sejm*] (1957) and settled the question of authorship of the *Ustawa Rządowa* in *Ostatni król Rzeczpospolitej. Geneza i upadek Konstytucji 3 maja* [The Last King of the Republic: The Genesis and Fall of the May Third Constitution] (1966). Rostworowski challenged the commonly held negative assessment of Stanisław August and demonstrated the monarch's crucial contributions to the reforms of 1788–1792.

The Solidarity interlude of 1980-81 briefly lifted the unspoken socialist taboo on discussions of constitutions and due process of law. Several editions of the May Third Constitution were published as well as several shorter studies. As mentioned, in order to coopt the popular myth of the Constitution, May Third had even been declared the holiday of the *Stronnictwo Demokratyczne*, the official, pseudo-party of the Polish intelligentsia. Under Jaruzelski, the danger existed that the Constitution may once again become an official object of veneration, this time in a socialist or socio-nationalist pantheon; limitations on treatment of the subject would continue because of the incompatibility of constitutionalism with Marxism-Leninism. Not surprisingly, Jerzy Łojek's (1986) *Geneza i Obalenie Konstytucji 3 Maja* [The Genesis and Overthrow of the May Third Constitution] was written from a typically external perspective, emphasizing international events over internal political contests and ideologies. The more central issues were avoided in this controversial work but new polemics were created instead amidst a vicious historian-publicist dispute over the nature of truth. A bitter discussion erupted between Łojek, who touted the traditional popular image of the traitor king, and historians who followed Rostworowski's more positive reassessment of Stanisław August. The most notable work in the uncompromising polemic against Łojek is Andrzej Zahorski's *Spór o Stanisława Augusta* [The Stanisław August Controversy] (1988) which gives a lucid picture of the last king through the eyes of historians and publicists.

West European and American scholarship has, for the most part, shown little interest in the Polish Constitution of 1791. Only R. R. Palmer's influential book, *The Age of the Democratic Revolution* (1959), treats the Constitution extensively and convincingly places it within the broad spectrum of revolutions which ushered in the modern era. This was a crucial accomplishment. Yet, Palmer did not go beyond the studies of the subject by Polish authors and other, Western European or American, historians have not followed his lead. Polish and "Western" historians continue to speak past each other.

This is especially unfortunate because of the advancement in constitutional history this century. The socioeconomic perspective has provided important insights ever since Charles Beard's *An Economic Interpretation of the Constitution of the United States* (1925). The newer approaches appear promising. Constitutions were becoming viewed as reflections of the socioeconomic realities and not simply as outcomes of detached ideological polemics or manifestations of an eternal idea working itself out in the material world—an attractive but intellectually stultifying remnant of romantic/idealistic or perhaps Whiggish thinking. The popularity of Beard's approach peaked in the 1930s and more recently it was effectively challenged by Forrest McDonald in *We the People, the Economic Origins of the Constitution* (1958). Economic determinism has proven not to be an omnipotent law of history. Yet, the role of economic interests in politics in general and constitutional reform in particular cannot be discounted even if the mechanism of cause and effect is not as simple as economic determinists, Marxian or otherwise, have assumed.

Polish studies have not totally ignored the socioeconomic context of the May Third Constitution. The venerable historian Oswald Balzer, sketched an overview in 1891 in his work, *Konstytucja 3 maja: Reformy społeczne i polityczne Ustawy Rządowej z roku 1791* [The May Third Constitution: Social and Political Reform of the Statute of Government from 1791]. Jan Dihm's unsuccessful work (1956) *Sprawa konstytucji ekonomicznej z 1791 r.* [The Issue of the Economic Constitution from 1791] addressed economic reform which might eventually have been adopted but it does not address the socioeconomic environment of the Constitution. Leśnodorski's *oeuvre* by ideological necessity touched the issue by describing class interests behind the reforms. His view seems to have concerned a popular notion that the middle nobility created the Constitution to break the power of the magnates. But was this really the case? And if it were, why did such a revolution occur and what did it seek to create?

Eighty-five years ago, Czesław Nanke in his *Szlachta wołyńska wobec Konstytucji 3go Maja* [The Attitude of the Volhynian Nobility towards the May Third Constitution] (1907) examined the sociopolitical interaction among the members of the nobility on the *województwo* or voivodeship level. While Nanke's work was methodologically not particularly innovative, it did take a fresh approach by examining relations among nobles where they counted most—at home, on the local level. More recently, in an article entitled, *"Posłowie debiutanci na Sejmie Czteroletnim"* [First Time Deputies at the Four Years' *Sejm*], Jerzy Kowecki compiled some of the characteristics of new members in the second session (1790-92) of the Four Years' Parliament. These studies have gone some distance towards answering the questions posed by standard assumptions.

The primary sources on which this work is built are quite fecund, despite losses incurred in troubled times. Any scholar would be heartbroken when tracing the efforts of nineteenth and early twentieth century archivists who gathered and organized materials, struggled to raise funds and heightened public awareness of precious remnants of the past only to have these irreplacable sources destroyed as part of the planned extermination of the Polish nation by Nazi Germany. The burning of the central Polish archives in Warsaw in September 1944 did, in fact, kill part of Poland's collective memory. The prewar inventory is still used today but most of the positions are underlined in red indicating their destruction. Foremost among the sources most relevant to the present study, but burnt in 1944, are the comprehensive records of the Treasury Commission for the Crown (Poland proper) which had included appraisals of the regular agricultural income of each nobleman under the 1790 *ofiara dziesiątego grosza* ["gift of every tenth penny"], one of the breakthrough legislations of the Four Years' *Sejm*. This source would have permitted a fairly accurate appraisal of the economic status of opponents and proponents of political change.

But valuable records remain and new ones became available years after the Second World War. Local copies of the tax records exist scattered throughout those *Xięgi Ziemskie i Grodzkie* ["Land and Town Books"] for the Crown preserved by the Germans for areas incorporated directly into the Reich. The books themselves are of immense quantity and interest. Laws that may concern the local population were haphazardly inscribed and all citizens had the right to enter any statement, agreement or complaint they saw fit. The *Xięgi* brim with often illegible Latin and Polish texts expressing the current concerns of the nobility. In addition, the tax records for the Treasury Commission of the Grand Duchy (i.e., Lithuania) were preserved by the Germans and are currently kept in Vilnius. Lithuanian, Byelorussian, and other Soviet scholars have made some use of them but Poles and this author have not gained access to them.

The post-war years have also opened private archives of magnates prominent in the Stanisławian period. Most important are the *Publiczny Archiwum Potockich* [The Public Archives of the Potockis] and the *Zbiór Popiełów* [Popiel Collection]. The latter contains the correspondence between king Stanisław August and his ambassador in Petersburg Deboli; this has been used in the present study as an essential narrative of events by one of their main protagonists.

Undoubtedly, the most significant newly available source is the so-called *Archiwum Sejmu Czteroletniego* [Archives of the Four Years' Sejm]. Returned to Poland in 1964, thirteen years after the publication of Leśnodorski's *Dzieje*, this 25 volume set includes a most varied group of documents from the *Sejm* compiled by the *Sejm* secretaries, preserved by the *Towarzystwo Naukowe* [Scientific Society] after the Partitions and subsequently carted off by the victorious Russian armies following the insurrection of 1830-31. This fate saved them from the worse fate of the Central Archives. The materials were evidently bound in the nineteenth century by an archivist whose knowledge of Polish or the Latin alphabet must have been poor. Consequently, the more than 25,000 pages of material lack a consistent order and Polish archivists have not yet produced a guide. This tremendously rich collection forms the source base for this study and its content will be discussed in more detail throughout the work.

Finally, relevant information is found in numerous local archives. Those used have been the University of Warsaw Archives, the *Biblioteka Narodowa* [National Library] Old Prints Archives, the Czartoryski Archives and the Collections at the Jagiellonian University both in Kraków, *Ossolineum* in Wrocław, archives of *Katolicki Uniwersytet Lubelski* in Lublin and the Zieliński Archives in Płock.

The recently observed bicentennial of the May Third Constitution of 1791 renewed interest in this nationally cherished but scholarly neglected subject. The issue of constitutionalism (whose discussion has been constricted in Polish scholarship for ideological reasons) and the socioeconomic causes for constitutions (developed in the West but not extensively applied to Poland) are now being reexamined. Consequently, the following study focuses on the concept of constitution in late eighteenth century Poland, the behavior of the Parliament of 1788-1792, and the socioeconomic backgrounds of parliamentary members.

Advancement in the understanding of Polish constitutionalism would contribute not only to a better knowledge of the events but it would serve to make more understandable one of the strongest traditions in Eastern Europe of a national government created by, and answerable to, a relatively broad segment of society. This tradition of constitutional government continues to exist in the cultures of most of Eastern Europe, to varying degrees; it is indicative of an essentially Western, pluralistic view of reality onto which an ideally monolithic, internally exclusive and comprehensive system and mentality had been superimposed in the last forty years. The resulting contradictions have been a fact of life that caused the essential instability of the region. The unnatural grafting of monopolistic governments has withered from a total lack of legitimacy. New freedoms are now sorting the realities and history is illuminating the present.

Eighteenth century individuals in Poland, who thought about their polity for more than immediate utilitarian purposes, almost invariably placed political issues in a broad historical context. The conceptualization of contemporary politics used a living past. Thus, this study begins with an examination of the political system from the perspective of its historical development. Next, the May Third Constitution, with its controversial relationship to historical precedent, is discussed first as an expanding body of legislation and second as a blueprint for government. The Four Years' Sejm that produced the Constitution was a nexus between this reform and the Commonwealth as a whole. Parliamentary functioning is examined in chapter three, with a focus on procedural matters and ideals, and in chapter four, on the basis of roll call information. The members of parliament formed a microcosm of the entire Commonwealth, or at least its elite, the *szlachta* [nobility]. Their characteristics and attitudes towards the new Constitution are considered in chapters five and six. Chapter seven attempts to identify political groupings in the *Sejm* and examine their socioeconomic backgrounds. Conclusions based on quantifiable information are presented in a cumulative fashion in the final pages of these three chapters; these are the most original parts of the book. Finally, the concluding chapter is a kind of synthetic postscript intended to suggest further thought. The study, taken together, describes the fateful transformation of the Polish-Lithuanian state.

The attempt at a careful handling of the primary sources creates a mechanical problem. Translations are never perfect and relationships among objects or phenomena expressed in a language for which they were never intended create inaccuracies which escalate with any discussion. On the other hand, the preservation of the original language can often alienate the reader. Striking a balance is difficult. To alleviate these problems, a glossary of foreign terms is provided at the end of the text. Hopefully, both the sensitivities and convenience of the reader and the integrity of the subject matter will be safeguarded. Eighteenth century orthography, however, has been preserved except for technical terms frequently used today; the differences are not that great and the original spellings add authenticity.

A final observation concludes this introduction. Historical development is accentuated in revolutionary times. New realities emerge and old ones are eliminated or transformed. The nature of the changes partially results from the nature of the older realities. Change is never complete nor is it ever completely absent. The older realities are living continuations of previous development and that past evolution forms an essential part of institutions and practices facing the shock of revolution. A portrayal of history as a snapshot of static reality may be useful in "freezing the action" to permit unhurried analysis but the quality of development cannot be ultimately ignored if written history is to approach lived history. Thus, the discussions that follow make frequent reference to the long-term evolution of institutions, laws and practices. This approach is further justified by the frequent preoccupation of actors in the eighteenth century drama with the heritage of the past, with past precedent. Virtue was thought to be inherited in the blood. Sometimes no clear temporal distinctions were made and, at the very least, past practices were assumed to be parents of the present.

Contemporaries and participants of the drama viewed developments in part according to the stated purpose of the 1788 *Sejm*:

> We clerical and lay councils and deputies in the presence of
> His Royal Majesty, our most loving Lord, with his greatest approbation and with the leading signature of his most

merciful hand, gathered with no other breathing spirit than the ardent demand for the most complete safeguarding and improvement of our Fatherland, we take as our only means to accomplish this goal, that is, the Union of a General Confederation under which we want all our considerations to be indivisible in the preservation of all the holiest laws which safeguard for us our holy Roman Catholic faith, the integrity of the lands of the *Rzeczpospolita* [Republic], the free republican government, the dignified person and all laws and privileges of the throne of His Royal Highness, King Stanisław August, mercifully ruling us, as well as all governmental institutions in their usual functions and limits (as well as) the integrity of civic freedom.

And since none of these most precious national honors can really be considered ours until they are all safeguarded by national strength supplied to eliminate the dangers which in so many forms may threaten our fatherland, therefore, for this end, before all others, we want not to be stingy in the offering of our property for the enlargement of the armies of the *Rzeczpospolita*, as much as we are permitted by our well-considered abilities and capabilities. We reserve the rest of the *Sejm* for those domestic improvements which we judge necessary according to (our) capabilities and equally to consider all that may be of use to the *Rzeczpospolita* without considering private matters.[7]

With this "Act of Confederation" the *Sejm* of 1788 began its customary six week meeting that would actually last nearly four years and transform the Polish-Lithuanian Commonwealth.

CHAPTER 1

THE FOUR YEARS' SEJM IN HISTORICAL PERSPECTIVE

Amidst the conviviality and pomp of thousands of *szlachta* and clergy, the *Sejm* convened on October 8, 1788 at the Senate chambers of the Royal Castle. By the end of the eighteenth century, Warsaw had grown into a substantial city no longer living from one biennial session of parliament to the next. In this bustling, festive atmosphere, King Stanisław August sought to pass through the *Sejm* military reforms and an alliance with Russia. The opposition sought, as it had in the past, mainly to oppose the king. The binding principle of majority rule and a surge of patriotism produced an unanticipated levy of a 100,000 man army, over three times its current size. But whose army was it going to be? On 10 November, the enlarged army was put under the control of a new Army Commission answerable to the *Sejm* and not the *Rada Nieustająca* [Permanent Council] that was seen as the instrument of the king and the Russian ambassador. Two months later the *Rada*, itself, was abolished and Poland stood without much of a government, living out, in effect, the old adage, "*Nie rządem Polska stoi*" [not because of a government does Poland stand].

In assaulting the executive and the perceived unremitting threat of "absolutism," the *Sejm* took on the immense burden of enlarging the army and running existing government agencies, such as the Treasury Commissions and the National Education Commission. The logic of military reform, moreover, spread to ever increasing aspects of state and society. A powerful army required an effective well-financed government based, in the Polish case, on some kind of popular sovereignty. An army that could prevent another partition also would depend on a prosperous economy and a contented population interacting according to consistent and internalized laws. In short, the military reform, passed so precipitously, intersected with political ideologies and required a complete overhaul of the Commonwealth. In the autumn of 1789, the *Sejm* decided to create a codified constitution. Thus, the *Sejm*, which by law met every two years for up to eight weeks, would stretch to four years and would have continued even longer had it not been suspended because of the Russian invasion in May 1792.

The task of the Four Years' *Sejm* became the modernization of one of the more unusual states in Europe. The *szlachta* generally cherished the Polish-Lithuanian Commonwealth as a magnificent accomplishment, the freest state in existence. But for other contemporaries and for historians this state defies easy classification. Developing from a typical estates monarchy in the Middle Ages, the old Polish state had fused with Lithuania beginning in the late fourteenth century as it concurrently acquired distinct characteristics, which would eventually separate it radically from the absolutist ideal of most extensive European states. An extraordinarily wide diffusion of political power throughout an unusually large nobility gave rise to parliamentary institutions and an estate-wide democratic ideology grounded on a system of "second," i.e., market oriented serfdom. From the casting of the parliamentary counterbalance to the monarchy, definitively by the mid-fifteenth century, until the last partition at the end of the eighteenth century, the Polish (and later the Polish-Lithuanian) state appeared to many observers as an experiment in freedom, an anomalous throwback to more primitive formations or simply a deviation from the norm. Its institutions and principles have been variously defined in statutes and understood by contemporaries and later observers.

Conceptualization of the state functioned as part of an intellectual canopy above the institutions and principles of Poland-Lithuania. The separation of public from private law marked the emergence of the modern state and this moment came to Poland during the mid-1300s when the concept *Corona Regni Poloniae* began to replace *Regnum Poloniae* with its patrimonial connotations. *Corona Regni Poloniae* continued to be used into the sixteenth century when *corpus regni*, denoting a more corporist attitude towards the state, seems to have become more popular. The term *Rzeczpospolita* became current as a Polish version of *res publica* during the Renaissance as the vernacular replaced Latin. The old concept in Polish translation was used, however, in the Union of Lublin (1569) to institutionalize and tighten the condominium between Poland and Lithuania dating from 1385/86.[1]

A similar conceptualization of the Lithuanian state seems to have occurred in the less sophisticated judicial environment of Lithuanian political thought. Beginning the conquest of most of Kievan Rus' from the Tatars, Gedymin, the Lithuanian ruler, called himself *Lethewinorum et Ruthenorum rex* in 1323.[2] Jagiełło, in the Union of Krewo (1385), united his patrimonial lands of Lithuania and Rus' with the Crown of the Kingdom of Poland: *"terras suas Litvaniae et Rusiae coronae regni Poloniae perpetuo applicare."*[3] By the sixteenth century the Lithuanian state was no longer just "our lands" but the Grand Duchy of Lithuania (Wielkie Xięstwo Litewskie).

At the Union of Lublin in 1569, *corona regni poloniae* and the *duces lituanorum* were combined into a single state most often called the *Rzeczpospolita* ("public affairs" became a commonwealth). This closer union was far from perfect with a minority of Lithuanian nobles persisting in their independent convictions that were reflected in the Lithuanian Statutes of 1588. The union was a reality colored by legal contradictions[4] until in 1791 the *Rzeczpospolita* [Commonwealth of Both Nations] became a more integrated state with three provinces: Wielkopolska, Małopolska and Lithuania (Litwa).[5] Whether this abolished the Union of Lublin—and it is possible that contemporaries understood the act differently—is an open question. But the Four Years' Parliament does appears to have stopped using the term *Rzeczpospolita*.

These official names tell a story of the changing conception of the state and its relationship to society. The *Corona Regni* expressed a separation of the state from the person of the monarch, a uniting of specified lands into an indivisible and sovereign entity and implied that, upon the death of the male line of ruler, all the state's inhabitants become its "representation."[6] The assumption that the state was, in some sense, the common possession of its society was affirmed and strengthened by the Union of Lublin. In 1569 royal and ducal possessions (both in the Jagiellonian family) became a *res publica* whose well-being was the concern of the wider public and not primarily that of the ruling dynasty. Major additional constitutional changes came in the late sixteenth century but the name and fundamental concept of the state remained unchanged until the Four Years' *Sejm*. At that time this "public concern" became a more unified unit in the common possession of the Polish and Lithuanian nations. The change from a royal state to something more broadly based and, in turn, the more thorough standardization of the system gives some indication of the changing character of the polity. Yet, the depth of the evolution was greater.

The unusual quality of the Polish-Lithuanian state largely stemmed from the growth both of representative institutions and noble privileges that were simultaneous causes and effects of the changing concept of the state. Representative institutions developed on two levels in Poland: the local *sejmik* [dietine] and the countrywide *Sejm* [diet]. The evolution of these institutions was paralleled, with some delay, in Lithuania. Regional *sejmy* arose between the appearance of the *sejmiki* and the end of the fifteenth century when they became provincial meetings held just prior to the larger *Sejm*.

The *sejmiki* were temporally the earlier emerging from the medieval *conventiones terrestras* [territorial conventions] common for the feudal decentralization during the thirteenth century. It is likely that the *conventiones* were, in turn, a continuation of the ancient *wiec* or meeting of all adult males characteristic of early Slavic societies whose most famous survivor—still in its primitive form—was the Novgorodian *veche*. A chaotic quest for unanimity was characteristic of the *veche* and had a lingering presence in Polish representative institutions.

In the fourteenth century the *conventiones* became a permanent fixture of the monarchy and acquired the name *sejmik*, a term derived from the ancient Slavic word meaning "to gather."[7] A clear distinction seems to have been made between royal officials and the mass of nobility whose estate was in the process of formation and whose exact origin is a persistent subject of debate. The authority of the *sejmiki*, as representative bodies, if not actual congregations, of the noble estate on the local level, was recognized in the 1370s as the Hungarian Angevin dynasty sought to secure its power over the patrimony of the failing senior branch of the Piast dynasty. Ludwig of Hungary issued special privileges to the Polish nobility at Koszyce (Košice) in 1374. The accruement of power to the representative bodies during changes of dynasties would become symptomatic of Polish history. The other means by which the nobility obtained new privileges was by placing demands on the king when they had assembled for war at the king's order. Thus, the need to obtain support for Prussian cities revolting against the Teutonic Knights inclined Kazimierz Jagiellończyk in 1454 to issue the Statutes of Nieszawa which officially recognized the *sejmiki*.[8]

The reunification of the Polish kingdom in the first half of the fourteenth century under Łokietek and Kazimierz Wielki brought with it the logical emergence of more centralized national representative bodies. The spread of Hussitism and intense rivalry with the clergy also encouraged increased noble interest in state affairs.[9] The first country-wide *Sejm* appeared in the second interregnum, 1382-1386. A regional *Sejm* for Wielkopolska was most active in the late fourteenth century while this institution of intermediate provincial *sejmy* became general practice in the 1420s. Monarchical governance became more convenient with, and dependent upon, the central *Sejm* which could elicit necessary military and financial support from the most powerful groups in Polish society. In 1493 the *Sejm* became a regular bicameral body[10] and shortly thereafter, in 1505, the king agreed to the *nihil novi nisi commune consensu* statute which stated that "no new" laws could be made without the consent of the nobility assembled in the *Sejm*. The *Sejm* had become indispensible. The king alone could not legally bind anything on the nobility or anyone else, except in certain ecclesiastical matter and on the royal demesne. Sovereignty, thus, accrued to the *Sejm* and became divided among its three *stany* [estates]: the king, the senate and the knights. The *Sejm* had become a permanent and powerful counterweight to royal power, more powerful than any of its contemporary counterparts including the English Parliament.[11]

In the other part of the dynastic union, Lithuania-Rus', two types of local assemblies existed until the fifteenth century. These were either assemblies of all adult males or the adult males of the *nobiles*. *Sejmiki* on the Polish model were introduced in the 1530s and 1540s. More territorial assemblies seem to have been irregular and unstructured.

With the rise of representative institutions, government had become an activity of a specific but broad stratum of people. Laws were made jointly by the king and representatives of the nobility and larger towns. Soon towns only remained as observers and the *szlachta*'s dominance in the *Sejm* was undisputed. But the growth of representative institutions was only one part of the expanding privileges of the nobility.

The Polish nobility won a wide range of immunities and privileges making it a community of free citizens and strengthening the new reality of the state based on the common action and solidarity of the citizenry. The privileges acquired by the Polish nobility were extended to Lithuanian and Ruthenian nobles as parts of Rus' and all of Lithuania were joined to the state. Later, new privileges were won by an increasingly homogeneous and numerous nobility in the sprawling commonwealth.

Table 1

Noble Privileges Bestowed by Polish Kings	
Buda (1355)	–customary level of taxes guaranteed –king to pay own expenses when travelling –nobles to be compensated for expenses in wars outside of Poland
Koszyce (1374)	–guaranteed Buda privileges and all former rights –nobles freed from all taxes except for symbolic 2 grosze on tax peasant land –guaranteed ransoming for nobles in foreign campaigns –nobles to aid in building only those castles approved by nobility –territorial integrity maintained
Piotrków (1388)	–guaranteed rights of clergy –maintained system of offices –standardized pay for nobles in foreign expeditions –nobles ransomed from domestic capture
Czerwieńsk (1422)	–*nec bona recipiantur* (due process for confiscation of private property) –separation of office of *starosta* and land judge
Jedlno (1430) Kraków (1433)	–*neminem captivabimus nisi jure victum* (inviolability of property and person)
Nieszawa (1454)	(slight variations among provinces) –no new laws or *pospolite ruszenie* (*levée en masse*) without consultation with *sejmiki* –townspeople answerable to noble courts –rights of peasants and Jews limited

Privileges issued by the Polish monarch to the nobility as a unit came only in the century between the Privileges of Buda (1355) and the Statutes of Nieszawa (1454). Earlier privileges were bestowed either on regions or on individuals; later privileges were granted by the *Sejm* with its fusion of royal and national sovereignties.[12]

The accumulation of privileges having begun with the efforts of the Hungarian Anjevin dynasty to extend its control to the failing senior Piast line, also resulted from the efforts of both the Polish magnates and nascent nobility to place safeguards against possible unaccustomed action or abuse by a foreign king. These fourteenth century privileges freed the nobility from substantive monetary obligations to the king and limited military and construction services to prescribed amounts. Restrictions on the monarch's military use of the nobility made the state potentially less aggressive or expansionist. Internally, most of Polish society was protected from the arbitrary actions of a foreigner king. Subsequently, under pressure from the middle strata of the nobility, whose economic might was rising, whose military support was essential, and whose susceptability to Hussitism had become alarming in the 1420s, royal privileges made the nobility less subjects of the monarch than partners immuned from arbitrary seizure and indispensible to decision making. The two most important privileges were *nec bona recipiantur* (1422) and *neminem captivabimus* (1433). Interestingly, the protection of property came before protection of the person; theoretically it was legal between 1422 and 1433 for a noble to be arbitrarily imprisoned by the king, yet, the seizure of his property would have been a crime. By far the more important was the *neminem captivabimus* statute that required due process of law for the arrest of a noble. Legally and effectively, the late fourteenth century and early fifteenth century privileges included the equivalent of the English Habeas Corpus Act that was to be adopted in 1679; they firmly established the principle of royal answerability before a part of society.

The basic rights of the Polish nobility were consistently extended to the social elites of neighboring states brought into closer association with Poland either through conquest or personal union. The late expert on Lithuania, Henryk Łowmiański, was of the opinion that the privileges extended to the Lithuanian boyars at Wilno (Vilnius) in 1387 were not the result of the personal union with Poland signed at Krewo the previous year but rather they were "a parallel and interdependent phenomenon . . . clearly based on the Polish model." The exact parallel was in the provision that nobles were obligated to help in the construction of only those castles which the entire land was called to build. This was a close but not an exact parallel to Polish privileges. The other rights conferred at Wilno (1387) resembled those given the Polish nobility at Buda (1355) and Koszyce (1374) only in spirit and reflected the stronger patrimonial character of the Lithuanian state: the property of nobles became independent of the *hospodar* [ruler] and nobles had more personal freedom including the right to marry a dependent female without the ruler's permission.[13]

After the Polish-Lithuanian union brought the crucial victory over the Teutonic Knights at Grünwald (Tannenberg) in 1410, the union of Krewo was renewed and the Polish and Lithuanian clans fused. At the Union of Horodło in 1413, Lithuanian nobles were symbolically adopted by Polish families and their individual concerns became mutual concerns. Cultural and linguistic differences persisted for a long time, but the privileges were the same. *Nec bona recipiantur* and *neminem captivabimus* automatically applied to both nobilities when the two privileges were granted in the next two decades. Legal parity between the Lithuanian nobility and the Polish *szlachta* was affirmed in 1447 and again at the Union of Lublin in 1569.

The extension of privileges to the common Polish and Lithuanian nobility did not originally embrace the Orthodox Ruthenian nobility in either state. The *Corona Regni Poloniae* had come to include the principality of Halicz (Halič) after the conquests of Kazimierz Wielki (1349–1360) and Lithuanian expansion into Rus', lasting most of the thirteenth and fourteenth centuries, had acquired all the territories along the Dnieper River; only wealthy Novgorod and distant Vladimir-Suzdal and Ryazan remained out of reach. In the areas of Old Rus' absorbed by Poland and Lithuania, the native Ruthenian nobility was originally denied the personal privileges and political rights of the Polish and Lithuanian elite. The 1430s brought a dramatic, decisive though incomplete resolution of this situation. The temporary dissolution of the union in 1430 led to a civil war in Lithuania-Rus' over the issue of extending public rights to the Ruthenian nobility; the Lithuanian state split into a Lithuanian and a Ruthenian part. A compromise was proposed by the Poles in 1432, offered by the Lithuanians to the Ruthenians under Swidrygiełło in 1434 and put into force only after the latter's defeat in 1439. Under the agreement, the Orthodox Ruthenian nobility obtained those privileges of Wilno and Horodło referring to fiscal matters and private law but not the right to participation in the hospodar's council. The Ruthenian gains were not substantial; old Ruthenian customary laws had apparently been satisfactorily respected by the Lithuanians. The differences in political rights were not due so much to religion as to nationality since part of the Lithuanian elite was Orthodox. Interesting, the Privileges of Buda and Koszyce were extended *in their entirety* to the Ruthenian nobility in Halicz in 1434 during the height of the internal Lithuanian conflict.[14]

The Halicz arrangement became a precedent. King Zygmunt August granted the Orthodox elite and nobility in the Grand Duchy of Lithuania full political rights at the diet of Wilno in 1563 and reaffirmed them in 1568 in anticipation of the closer association of the Poland and Lithuania at the Union of Lublin the following year.[15] In 1569 there were two Orthodox senators in the newly unified *Sejm*.[16] Shortly after the extension of political rights, religious freedom was guaranteed for Christians throughout the Polish-Lithuanian Commonwealth by the Confederation of Warsaw (1573) and confirmed by each subsequent monarch.

Nonetheless, the status of the Orthodox *szlachta* deteriorated throughout the seventeenth century and into the eighteenth. With the establishment of the Uniate (Greek Catholic) Church in 1596, those Orthodox individuals who remain "in schism" as *dyzunici* aroused suspicion and suffered discrimination.[17] But even for Uniates, political rights were not equalized. Though the Roman and Greek clergy in the Catholic Church in the Commonwealth were to be equal, the first Uniate member of the *Sejm* was Metropolitan Rostocki, admitted with great ceremony only in September 1790. Religious tolerance and political equality for the nobility remained legal norms but the popularity of non-Roman Catholics declined as a result of the Counter-Reformation and the invasions of Orthodox Russian, Lutheran Swedish, often Calvinist Transylvanian and Islamic Ottoman armies in the wake of the Khmelnytsky Uprising in the Ukraine. In 1775, the number of Orthodox deputies to the *Sejm* was limited to one per province and neither the Orthodox nor the Protestants could be senators.[18]

Privileges and political rights changed as they were extended geographically and to different ethnic groups. After 1454, a new set of immunities and rights was issued by the *Sejm*. These new rights not only further limited royal power but they also changed the social balance by limiting the rights of other groups in Polish society.

Table 2

Major Noble Rights Passed by the Sejm	
1496	–virtual noble monopoly on land ownership (exceptions: Church, Prussian towns, free peasants)
1501	–peasants tied to the land
1505	–*nihil novi*
1518	–peasant could no longer appeal to royal courts
1520	–corvée increased to one day a week
1550	–right to own municipal land; exemption from city taxes
1552	–ecclesiastical courts lose jurisdiction over nobles
1563	–nobles could "purchase" peasant local government (*sołtystwo*)
1573	–exclusive right to natural resource on noble property
1578/81	–new Tribunals as court of highest instance except for *Sejm*
1632	–lifelong tenure for highest offices

As the list of noble rights shows, constitutional development climaxed towards the end of the sixteenth century and the fading away of the "execution of the law" movement. But in addition to the new rights passed by the *Sejm*, the Henrician Articles and the *pacta conventa* gave the nobility even more significant powers that transformed the system from a limited monarchy to one that was both contractual and elected.

These new constitutional trends must be treated with care. A tendency exists when viewing the Polish monarchy to overanticipate the limited and weak nature of the institution. History is commonly read backwards with the antecedents of later realities highlighted out of proportion. Contemporaries would very well have been aghast by the projections of future historians especially since medieval and early modern people tended to think in static terms that emphasized the importance of past precedent for the present and the future. With respect to the monarchy, something of the special, unassailable and partly divine nature of the king remained in the minds of Poles as the accumulation of privileges and the growth of representative institutions changed the real power of the monarch. The election of the monarch should not be misread. The magnates of Kraków and prominent royal officials did chose Jagiełło as king in 1385 and the Polish nobility by this act saw itself empowered to chose its subsequent kings and the Lithuanians their grand dukes. And the opportunity quickly presented itself when Jagiełło had to remarry upon Jadwiga's death in 1400. After Horodło each elite did claim the right to participate in the election of each ruler. Yet, there were no real elections until after the extinction of the male line of Jagiellonians in 1572. The Jagiellonians had served like a dynasty. Moreover, the special quality of kingship or royal blood was evident even after the failed Valois election, in the election of the Hungarian, Stefan Bathory, who had married Zygmunt August's sister, Anna Jagiellonka. The growing partnership of monarch and nobility should best be seen through the lingering tincture of king as final authority. The moment of most crucial change did not come before 1572-76.

Zygmunt August bound Poland and Lithuania together at the Union of Lublin (1569) in anticipation of his childless death. Sensing its own power, the nobility sought a candidate who would best serve their interests when the last male Jagiellonian died in 1572. They chose Henri de Valois, and to ensure his pliability they demanded certain conditions; these became a proto-constitution, a permanent fixture to which all future elected monarchs would have to comply. The Henrician Articles (*Artykuły Henrykowskie*), as they were called thereafter, were the first special contract or *pacta conventa* between the nobility and a newly elected king. They stipulated that the king would be elective, that the king must renounce the right of succession, that all noble privileges would be upheld including the principle of religious freedom adopted in 1572, that matters of war and peace must be handled with the participation of the upper chamber and those concerning the *pospolite ruszenie* by the lower chamber of the *Sejm*, that the mobilized noble army could not be divided nor could it be taken abroad except with the payment of each of its members as a mercenary, that the king must maintain a small standing army, that the *Sejm* must be convened every other year, that a permanent council of senators must remain alongside the monarch and finally, perhaps most importantly, that the nobility retained the right to withdraw its oath of loyalty after due process should the king break any of the Henrician Articles. In addition, separate contracts called *pacta conventa* would be drawn up for subsequent monarchs to complement the Henrician Articles.

The sole institutional modification contained in the Henrician Articles was the council of senators which would permanently advise the king between the biennial sessions of the *Sejm*. The *senatorowie-residenci* never became a vital or influential institution partly due to the king's preponderance and the senators' lack of enthusiasm for devoting the necessary time and expense. The council consisted of sixteen or, after 1628, twenty-eight senators who would equally divide and rotate responsibilities every half year. Theoretically, this institution insured the continuous supervision of the king.[19] Their counsel, however, was not binding.

With the Henrician Articles, sovereignty in the Polish-Lithuanian state unequivocally shifted to the *szlachta* and its *sejmiki* and *Sejm*. The king continued to be considered one of the three estates alongside the "older brothers" i.e., senators (bishops, royal officials) and the "younger brothers" i.e., representatives of the nobility as a whole. But the king was an estate of one man overshadowed by the nobility which comprised 10 percent of the population. The system grounded on this principle of sovereignty was complete by the late 1500s and it remained unchanged for two centuries. Institutionally, the *Rzeczpospolita* of the Four Years' *Sejm* was the *Rzeczpospolita* during Poland's golden century as modified only after the election of Poland's last king, Stanisław August, in 1764.

The institutionalization of representation and the expansion of privilege prevented the alienation of the nobility from the state. The *szlachta* regarded the *Rzeczpospolita* as their own and as such the royal administrative system formed over the previous centuries was preserved and, contrary to trends in nascent "absolute" monarchies, the Polish nobility actually demanded the multiplication of royal offices. In the *Rzeczpospolita*, offices were opportunities, not threats.[20] Further, the lack of alienation meant that the nobles were citizens, not subjects and as such they exhibited a loyalty to the polity that was in fact the political patriotism which according to the Hans Kohn theory was the preserve of "the West."

At the same time, the *szlachta* developed a nearly neurotic fear of *absolutum dominium*. To the east, they viewed the tsars building an imperial patrimonial autocracy with the denial of a civil society and any rights to any one. To the west they watched kings claiming a divine right to absolute power, to be the state. For the *szlachta* there was no real difference between the two nor did they place the slightest relevance to any possible gap between the idea of "absolutism" and its actual power relations. Monarchs by nature sought a monopoly on lawmaking and their success could only mean the death of freedom. Vigilance must be built into the system.

Not surprisingly, contemporary observers and later historians have struggled to categorize the Polish-Lithuanian system. Historians have benefitted from the wider angle of historical distance and their interpretations have varied with changing times and changing historical approaches. Popular opinion and historiography have obviously changed with Polish history and with changing approaches in the historical profession.[21] Was the *Rzeczpospolita* a kingdom with an elected and dependent king, a republic with a life-long president, an oligarchy, a mixed system similar to Venice, blending monarchy, aristocracy and democracy or was it the most free system in Europe? In many ways, the *Rzeczpospolita* was all of these. Paradoxes and contradictions seemed to lay in its very heart.

While most historians describe the evolution of the Polish-Lithuanian state as at least a somewhat unique phenomenon (or, perhaps, even a deviation) of the estates monarchy common throughout Europe in the Middle Ages into a peculiar nobility state surrounded by more effective "absolute" monarchies, there are a few synthetic works that examine the comparative developments of socio-political systems throughout the continent and, hence, view the history of the Polish-Lithuanian system from a truly broad, comprehensive perspective.

In his article fifteen years ago, "*Dominium regale* or *dominium politicum et regale*? Monarchies and parliaments in early modern Europe," Hans Koenigsberger summarized and expounded upon the most significant literature in systemic typologies and changes centering upon the victory of estates over the monarchies in some states and the development of absolutist monarchies in others. In the first instance, Koenigsberger cites the typology for estates systems introduced sixty years earlier by Otto Hinze. According to this categorization, Poland-Lithuania is classified among countries like England, East Elbian German states, and Hungary, which having been consolidated in areas surrounding the old Carolingian Empire exemplified comparatively less advanced forms of feudalism and possessed bicameral estates assemblies; in contrast, the successors to the Frankish empire (and certain other states such as the Spanish and South Italian kingdoms) had more developed three-curial systems. The crucial difference between the two types of estates assemblies was the role of the feudal magnates. In the bicameral systems, the upper house had evolved from the king's council of lay and ecclesiastic magnates with the lower house representing the rest of the privileged class; in the three-curial system, on the other hand, "the old magnates-royal council chamber had already disintegrated before the advance of a more effective and professionalized royal administration."[22] Thus, those countries where feudalism had arisen the earliest and most fully experienced the consolidation of absolutist monarchies while those "on the fringes," such as England and Poland, the estates triumphed over the monarchs.

Dissatisfied with the lack of dynamism in Hinze's scheme, Koenigsberger sought to combine it with the three basic mechanisms of institutional change theorized by Herbert Elias in his *Über den Prozess der Zivilisation* (1939): territorial monopolization (expansion) by a state in a fashion analogous to the growth of economic monopolies in a basically free market environment, the depersonalization and institutionalization of the exercise of power concurrent with territorial consolidation and growing specialization within society and, finally, "the royal mechanism" of balancing diverse interest groups within society against each other. Koenigsberger's synthesis of Hinze's typology and Elias' dynamism is strained and incomplete partly because of his stress on particular developments and by his preoccupation with the royal mechanism. Nonetheless, his two conclusions concerning the success of the estates assembly over the monarchy in Poland-Lithuania are, at the very least, thought-provoking. In accord with Elias' schema, Koenigsberger states that "the economic development of Poland and, hence, the divisions of social functions had not developed sufficiently far to institutionalize royal authority and make it capable of effectively balancing the divergent forces in the country."[23] But according to Koenigsberger, it was only the appeal of the Reformation among the *szlachta* that brought the final eclipse of royal institutions by granting the king a victory over the nobility which he could not exploit and which placed control of the government into the hands of the magnates who had allied themselves with the king and the Catholic clergy against the Protestant nobles in 1606–07. Thus, in a broad interpretation of Koenigsberger's synthesis of Hinze's and Elias' ideas, Poland-Lithuania belonged to a category of states to which feudalism had come late and whose bicameral assemblies represented basically the same feudal class (i.e., a less specialized society) which was able to eventually neutralize the independent political power of the king. In the *Rzeczpospolita*, the most powerful segment of the nobility (i.e., the magnates) eventually achieved a political monopoly by the chance occurrence of the Reformation.

This interpretation of the evolution of the Polish-Lithuanian Commonwealth's governmental system in early modern times is simultaneously flawed and useful. Koenigsberger does not attempt a comprehensive study and, not surprisingly, his treatment of each country is superficial. The Zebrzydowski (or Sandomierz) rebellion which he viewed as a revolt of the Protestant *szlachta* against the Catholic King Sigismund Wasa, was a much more complex event whose leader, Mikołaj Zebrzydowski, has been called "a zealous Catholic and a devoted friend of the Jesuits."[24] Zebrzydowski's friends, the Society of Jesus, strongly encouraged royal absolutist aspirations and there is a consensus among historians that the magnates were the only winners to emerge from the Zebrzydowski *rokosz*. Yet, it must be pointed out that the issues involved were mainly old political conflicts such as "the execution of the law" movement, traditional competition with the king, as well as the constitutional vote of the magnates. If there was one "accidental" cause it was not Protestantism as Koenigsberger asserts, but the character and ambitions of Sigismund Wasa whose determination to regain the Swedish throne and to spread Catholicism to the Urals involved Poland in the Muscovite Time of Troubles and led to his widespread unpopularity.

Second, the central statement that in Poland "the division of social functions had not developed sufficiently far to institutionalize royal authority . . ." seems deduced *a priori* from the conclusion and begs for an explanation. It is a basic fact that public and private functions overlapped in any "feudal" system; legal distinctions were not precise. It is also true that the exceptionally powerful position of the *szlachta* in the Rzeczpospolita produced a monopoly of power by that estate and thus "social functions" tended not to be fully divided. But there was a gap between these two similar situations. The late Middle Ages and the sixteenth century were a time in which a diversified economy did develop and a fairly prosperous and influential patriciate did function to diversify the social composition of Poland-Lithuania. That the nobility had successfully reversed this trend by the seventeenth century does not deny the existence of the earlier trend towards economic and social diversification.

Moreover, the assumption that the Polish monarchy had not been institutionalized by the beginning of the seventeenth century is simply incorrect. Scholarship has long shown that the patrimonial kingships in Poland through the early part of the twelfth century were exceptionally strong and similar to Norman England. Feudal decentralization, the *rozbicie dzielnicowe* [provincial break-up] beginning in 1138, had transferred political authority from the older patrimonial, centralized state to local notables and such a transfer tended to perpetuate itself. But historians have effectively argued that the rapid reconsolidation of the state under Władysław Łokietek (1305–1333) and Kazimierz Wielki (1333–1370) was much more advanced than similar processes elsewhere in northern Europe. An especially vigorous royal administration operated on the local level through the offices of *wojewoda* [military leader] and *kasztelan* [castellan]. Moreover, as already discussed, the shaping of the concept of an abstract state only represented by the king began in Poland during the consolidation of Polish duchies under Łokietek and was accepted during the reign of Kazimierz Wielki when, under the term *Corona Regni Poloniae*, the crown came to symbolize a new state sovereignty and independence detached from the person of the monarch and was applied to all ethnically or historically Polish territories. The institutionalization of the Polish monarchy was concurrent with similar processes emergent in England and France during the Hundred Years' War.[25]

It may further be argued that, contrary to Hinze's theory, states like Poland and England, which were late recipients of feudalism, were consequently consolidated more fully than, for example, France, the heartland of true feudalism whose territorial unity, even under later "absolutism," was tempered by an overlay of unstandardized and confusing, highly varying, relationships between the king and the provinces. The unity of the not-completely-feudal kingdom spawned the more abstract conception of the state. This abstract unity was internalized at an early instance by an elite which in Poland's case had won numerous concessions from novice dynasties and as compensation for military service. The plethora of royal administrative offices became a mainstay of noble ambitions since the *szlachta* identified with the state. Thus, the late introduction of feudalism probably contributed to the early consolidation of royal authority in the "outlying" non-Carolingian lands and the simultaneous development of a generalized idea of state unity and sovereignty in the process of institutionalization of the monarchy led more directly to the notion and practice of limited monarchies in turn obviating the need for "absolutism" to forcefully break down feudal peculiarism.

The approach adopted by Koenigsbereger and the earlier synthetic works of Hinze and Elias are positive attempts to understand Polish history and systemic typology in general during the early modern period. The assumption that institutionalization of the monarchy necessarily led to an "absolute" monarchy is a schematically fixed and flawed presumption—not least because it fails to examine the meaning of absolutism—but their approach points towards a direction of study which avoids the common tendency to regard the Polish-Lithuanian system in isolation as an oddity essentially unrelated to the rest of Europe. By integrating Poland-Lithuania into their general studies they help to present to non-Polish scholars the systemic kinship of the Polish-Lithuanian state with its neighbors, a theme advocated by some Polish historians such as Oswald Balzer in his *Z zagadnień ustrojowych Polski* [Concerning the Problem of the Polish System], first published in 1917.[26] In this approach the Hungarian kingdom and, to a great extent, the Bohemian crown were quite similar to Poland-Lithuania while distant England evolved similar balances through a similarly late feudal development but with a nobility whose small numerical size was compensated by the tapping of new sources of wealth.

The focus on connections between the history of representative institutions and the social structures of their societies is important. These connections may be the key, not only for explaining the growth of royal institutions in the Commonwealth and their transformation into a state system dominated by the nobility but also for understanding the metamorphosis, without formal institutional changes, of the "nobility democracy" of the late sixteenth century into the anarchic oligarchy of the late seventeenth and early eighteenth centuries. The Four Years' *Sejm* operated in the tradition of an "estates-dominated" system and much of its positive reforms redressed the balance between king and estates—or to use more appropriately modern terms, executive and legislative branches of government—and sought to revive efficacy in the old system. The framers of the *Ustawa Rządowa*, the core document of the May Third Constitution, consciously sought in some way to return to the successful systems of the late Piasts and the Jagiellonians by confirming all noble privileges received from the reign of Kazimierz Wielki but only through that of Zygmunt August.[27] The subsequent 219 years were ignored. If this were the intent of the provision—and not merely homage to several great kings—the change could be revolutionary.

The second type of synthetic works that put the Four Year's *Sejm* into historical perspective concerns not comparisons across geography but across time within the Commonwealth. This involves the creation of viable historical periods. Periodization is an exercise in relativity and the test of a good time-scheme is the calculus of explaining the most events with as simple and meaningful conceptual constructions as possible. This exercise clearly changes with the general evolution of historical thought characterized by historical schools which in turn are affected by overall intellectual climates, tastes in selective memory, contemporary nonintellectual events and the course or accident of successful academic careers.

The first periodization of Polish history was proposed by the romantic historian, Joachim Lelewel, who lived in the early nineteenth century. Lelewel divided the history of Poland into *Polska wzrastająca, podzielona, kwitnąca, upadająca* [rising, divided, blossoming, declining Poland].[28] At the turn of the twentieth century the positivist legal historians, Oswald Balzer and Stanisław Kutrzeba, took into account the development of estates and social and economic factors to discern an early period until 1374, a second period characterized as "the period of estates" beginning with the Koszyce Privileges of that year and lasting through the first interregnum in 1575, and finally a third period lasting until the last partition and dominated by the supremacy of the gentry. Polish historians of Marxist times, including Juliusz Bardach and Bogusław Leśnodorski, adapted "scientific" materialistic interpretations of the development of human society to Polish history by extending the feudal period over the entire course of events in Poland-Lithuania up until the partitions. Some interpretations even pushed feudalism until 1864. This protracted period was divided, however, into "early feudalism," "feudal territorial disintegration," "the estates monarchy," "the gentry's democracy," "the magnates' oligarchy," and "the reforms and fall of the republic of nobles." Each interpretation yields a more precise picture of the process of change than had been offered by positivists. Moreover, Wacław Soroka argues that "the gentry's democracy" continued until the last partition.[29] The concept of a gentry democracy is provocative and isolates a distinctive element in Polish constitutional history.

Demokracja szlachecka [gentry's democracy] has been used as a largely self-explanatory term to describe the extensive self-rule exercised by the upper stratum of Polish-Lithuanian (and Ruthenian) society and enjoyed in different degrees of absoluteness and effectiveness during the early modern period. A modern equivalent of Lelewel's *gminnowładztwo szlacheckie* (literally, "noble communal rule" as opposed to *samowładztwo* ["rule by one," autocracy] and *moznowładztwo* ["rule by the strong," i.e., the magnates, oligarchy], the term *demokracja szlachecka* has been popular only since the 1950s after having been cautiously used in the interwar years.[30] An amorphous concept, in part reflecting the incomplete intellectualization of an ideal form of government and its actualization in political institutions, *demokracja szlachecka* has been most clearly defined as "a specific variety of an estates monarchy, in which only the feudal estates participated in the exercise of power and royal power underwent low limitation."[31] Numerous interpretations can be associated with a definition of such elasticity in which the nobility is designated in plural form (*stany feudalne* [feudal estates]) and a main feature of the governmental system is a trend (the slow reduction of royal power).[32]

Precise dates have been debated. For Lelewel, *gminnowładztwo szlacheckie* lasted from the Koszyce Privileges of 1374 through the reign of Stefan Batory, who died in 1586. While most historians have made the Zebrzydowski rebellion the upper time limit for *democracja szlachecka*, the earliest limit has been variously placed; for Kaczmarczyk it was the Statutes of Nieszawa in 1454 (with the system peaking between the 1550s and 1580s), for Maciszewski it was the *nihil novi* law of 1505 and for Pelenski the first interregnum in 1573 with some qualifications. Pelenski further argues that, at least for the years 1454–1573, the concept of a tripartite mixed government, used popularly and also by the foremost thinkers of the time, is more accurate and that even the purest gentry's democracy, which appeared in the last quarter of the sixteenth century, was not as complete as the magnates' victory over the monarchy and the gentry which immediately followed.

Whatever the precise dates, the *demokracja szlachecka*, definitely extant by the end of the sixteenth century, continued institutionally and ideologically to the time of the Four Years' *Sejm*: privileges of the nobility vis-à-vis the king, the lawmaking powers of the nobility and the noble estate's predominance over the rest of society were all preserved. Equality or balance within the *szlachta* is one other quality emphasized most strongly by the term. Legal equality before the law for the entire *szlachta* had been a distinguishing feature of the Polish legal system in the Middle Ages. Unlike the strictly hierarchical, pyramidic organization of lords and vassals in the most ideal feudal systems, the exceptionally numerous knights in medieval Poland had been directly subordinated to the monarch—another sign of the strength of the medieval Polish monarchy. Some poorer members of the profession did form stratified clans around magnates, but these were definitely the exception.[33] The Polish monarch continued to deal directly with magnates *and* knights after reunification in the fourteenth century. The lack of an extensive feudal hierarchy in ethnic Poland was part of the reason for the middle *szlachta*'s ascendancy after the extinction of the Jagiellonian line. This relatively democratic feature within the Polish nobility was probably a major attraction for the nobility of Lithuania and Rus' and a primary factor in the extension of Polish institutions into those areas. The magnates objected unsuccessfully.

By the late sixteenth century, and especially in the seventeenth and eighteenth, the *szlachta* developed a much cherished ideology lauding their unique equality. "*Szlachcic na zagrodzie równy wojewodzie*" (a nobleman on the enclosure [i.e., a landless noble] is equal to a *wojewoda*—the military head of a district and a senator). All shared the right of *neminem captivabimus* and all were made equal by it. All addressed each other as brothers. Each had the right to be physically present at the election of the king and to express his preference. Eventually, each had the right to halt the activities of the *Sejm* by exercising his free voice or *liberum veto* when he deemed that his interests or those of his district were being damaged. Ironically, this ideology of "golden freedoms," guaranteeing the rights of the noble nation as a whole and the rights of the individual member, was most forcefully adopted when the balance of forces within the *szlachta* had shifted in favor of the magnates and the cherished equality became more legal and theoretical than real.

Basic to the growing preponderance of the nobility was its improving economic position. *Demokracja szlachecka* had an economic side. The nobility shed its military prowess and benefitted from the revolution in commercial agriculture initially spurred by a growing internal market and in the sixteenth century augmented by the burgeoning Baltic grain trade, which in turn was a consequence of rapid economic expansion in western Europe. The *szlachta* won a monopoly of economic power through direct competition and through the institutional and legal clout conceded to them by the king. Thus, the nobility outcompeted the peasantry through economy of scale—an advantage which helped to produce the "second serfdom," the towns which were seriously hindered by the Turkish destruction of land trade routes, competition from the nobility and their own failure to cooperate among themselves and with the clergy whose bonds with Rome were loosened and which became increasingly closed to non-nobles. A momentum resulted in these changes that would accelerate with new legislation. There was no reason why the economic factors that were essential to the *szlachta*'s political importance should cease to play a differentiating role *within* the noble estate in a manner quite contrary to its fundamentally egalitarian ideology. The same economic factors that made the nobility into an estate divided the nobility according to something akin to economic classes. Ideal democracy of the *szlachta* occurred only when the central institutional role and legal equality of the nobility corresponded to, if not economic equality, then at least an approximate balance of forces among the nobles themselves. Thus, *demokracja szlachecka* was contemporaneous with the economic ascendancy of the vaguely defined middle stratum of the nobility which could counterbalance the traditional ambitions of the magnates and their influence among poor nobles. Historically this situation occurred in the sixteenth century.

The century and a half between the generally agreed upon upper limit of true gentry democracy (early 1600s) and the reforms of the Stanisławian period, which began in 1764 and culminated with the Four Years' *Sejm*, poses an interpretational problem which requires a fundamental recognition of the distinction between the governmental system (*ustrój*) and the socio-political, economic, intellectual lives of the country. In the old debate concerning the causes of the *Rzeczpospolita*'s downfall, Stanisław Estreicher criticized the view that "the form of government alone determines a state's vitality when in fact the governmental system is only an external form which does not prejudice the internal course of national life." Zakrzewski argued that studies in constitutional history ought to refrain from becoming exercises in morphology which could only minimally illuminate the "physiology" of historical development.[34] These observations are particularly applicable to Poland-Lithuania because its political institutions changed formally only until the end of the sixteenth or early seventeenth century. Afterwards, the governmental apparatus remained essentially unchanged for the following 150 years and yet, the entire character of political life and the efficacy of the system were drastically altered.

The continuity in the accepted model of government offers an example of an ideology outliving its justification. As Pelenski has pointed out, both Frycz Modrzewski in his *De republica emendenda* (1554) and Stanisław Orzechowski in *Leges seu statuta ac priviligia Regni Polonia* (1553) upheld the classical mixture of monarchy, aristocracy, and democracy—the tripartite mixed government—as an ideal achieved in the Polish-Lithuanian state of their day. The same conviction was expressed in 1632 by Szymon Starowolski. The section entitled "*Władza Polityczna*" [political authority] in his *Polska albo opisanie położenia Królestwa Polskiego* [Poland or description of the situation of the Polish kingdom] begins with the following description:

> Authority in Poland consists of three basic and simple forms of a republic, which comprise one, a few or many governments, that is, all to a certain degree based on the equality of law. We, therefore, have a king not from heredity but created through an election, who is the highest executor of laws established at the *Sejm*. We have a senate chosen from the most prominent nobility and called to the enforcement of these laws. We have the *Sejm* deputies, elected through free voting in every province and selected to pass laws at the *Sejm* who act like tribunes limiting royal power and the excessive authority of the senate.[35]

Thus, Polish political observers from the period of *demokracja szlachecka* (only a minimalist would hold that the first two do not fall into the category) and from the generally accepted period of magnate oligarchy held the same governmental model and were convinced that their contemporary Poland fit that ideal.

This mixed form of government remained relevant until the destruction of the Commonwealth. The conviction that the Polish system embodied the classical, ideal mixture of government deepened and became a tenet of Sarmatian baroque ideology as the actuality became less similar and as the system began to malfunction when faced with the internal and external challenges of the mid and late 1600s. Undoubtedly faith in an ideal replaced practical confidence in reality. A basic disparity had arisen between the ideal of equality among the *szlachta* and the actual distribution of power. *Demokracja szlachecka* remained intact as far as the limitation of monarchical authority was concerned but as the balance within the nobility was tilted, internal democracy faded.

The deciding factor for the transition of *demokracja szlachecka* to an oligarchy of magnates[36] was the decline of the position of the middle nobility. Maciszewski attributes three causes for this change: effective competition from the magnates, inheritance practices which led to the disintegration of noble estates and the absence of sufficient institutional outlets for younger members of middle *szlachta* families.[37] To these may be added: increased competition for the grain trade as a result of decreasing demand for grain in western Europe, the decline of the Baltic grain trade as a result of internal problems, the dehabilitating effects of increasingly popular Jesuitical neoscholasticism which condemned new scientific, technological innovations and the experimental mentality for improving crop yields and, finally, the greater resilience of geographically scattered magnate estates during the almost continuous warfare of the second half of the seventeenth century. A public spirited stratum of nobility declined and *demokracja szlachecka* became a magnate dominated system espousing an anachronistic Sarmatian ideology praising outmoded principles of freedom and equality.

The decay and stagnation in the century preceding the election of Stanisław August are better characterized by the Russian protectorate extended over the *Rzeczpospolita* in 1717 than the spectacular military victory over the Turks at Vienna in 1683. Indeed, the decades between these two important events are a time of greatest decline, a settling from the impoverishment of continuous war to the self-delusion of the Saxon night. The kernal of the golden freedoms which was the respect for a single dissenting voice became the blind consistency of a mind that lacks imagination and is willing to sacrifice a functioning polity for a deeply cherished principle. National politics were paralyzed along with the *Sejm* and shifted to the *sejmiki* which were dominated by magnates. Had the partitions come in the early part of the eighteenth century there would never had been the Polish Question of the nineteenth.

Impetus for reform in the eighteenth century did, however, exist and it may be divided into three chronological categories: solitary and unsuccessful attempts under the Saxon kings, limited reforms sponsored by the newly elected king Stanisław August, and finally the broad reform movement of the 1780s and 1790s. In the first category, the incessant manipulations and maneuverings of the ruling Wettins and their magnate rivals, the Potocki and Czartoryski families, were complemented by rare voices calling for more publically-spirited reform. Foremost among this minute group, as shown by Gierowski, was Stanisław Dunin Karwicki who set the tone for reform proposals throughout the eighteenth century with his advocacy of more effective parliaments. Also important was the deposed king Stanisław Leszczyński, father-in-law of Louis XV, who in 1734 issued a critical pamphlet entitled "*Głos wolny wolności ubezpieczający*" [A Free Voice Safeguarding Freedom] and Stanisław Konarski who founded the *Collegium Nobilium* in 1740 to effect political change through modernized education. In the second category, actual institutional reforms were introduced but only those survived which the Russian overlord deemed constructive for an effective administration. These included the *Rada Nieustająca* [Permanent Council] established in 1775 and modern fiscal and military measures. Stanisław August continued to sponsor educational reform and cultural growth, both of which would bear unexpectedly decisive results. Comprehensive reform came only when a growing group of political activists found a positive response among a broader and increasingly better educated base of privileged nobles and only when Russia was distracted elsewhere. This occurred in 1788.

The assumption that government should be a mixture of different agencies representing different concepts or tendencies of rule continued over the centuries. The Renaissance ideal of a mixed government easily converted in some minds into the separation of powers popular in the Enlightenment. The pragmatic system of checks and balances, that would be apparent in both the American and the Polish Constitutions, was quite prominent in the political theory of the Polish Renaissance and the empty phraseology of the Sarmatian years. Starowolski's 1632 description concentrates on such a system and praises the limiting powers of each element of government on the others. The Four Years' Parliament and the May Third Constitution of 1791 preserved this quality by constructing a balance of distinct powers for a viable government that could compete on the European field.

Talk of reform had been common during the best years of the *demokracja szlachecka* but very little was improved. Comprehensive reform came after the system had been dysfunctioning for generations and required a realistic self-criticism that could only be painful. Much was blamed on outside interference, and negative self-assessment was tempered by references to the time when the system had functioned well and virtue had been found in action not only political slogans. The main thrust of the constitutional reforms of the Four Years' *Sejm* seemed aimed against magnatorial power which had changed the reality behind the facade of *nobiliar* democracy. In 1791, the *Sejm* disenfranchised the landless nobility who had been used by their much more powerful "brothers" to dominate the *sejmiki*, the focus of legislative power and self-rule. And public spiritedness had again become more fashionable than self-interest.

The anti-magnate tone of much of the constitutional reform especially, as it would be viewed by latter generations, indicated a rising level of political culture and possible underlying changes in the social and economic positions of the nobility. The economic upturn in the mid-eighteenth century seems to have reversed the previous trend polarizing landholding into ever more minute and ever more immense estates, with the disappearance of intermediate tracts. In the second half of the century the size of landholdings changed in one direction: the smallest tended to disappear while all others grew. As a result, middle-sized holdings seemed to have reappeared and the internal economic configuration of the szlachta was altered in the direction of that which had existed in the late sixteenth century. Was the May Third Constitution the product of this change?

Summary

Viewing the May Third Constitution from the perspective of the development of European parliamentary governments and against the evolution of the Polish-Lithuanian polity, several general observations can be made. The Constitution was the product of a system that tended to grow, as Hinze observed, in areas which experienced a late and incomplete introduction of feudalism. This form of feudalism provided the concept of a contractual relationship between ruler and subjects but since the decentralized hierarchy was imperfect, the focus of political activity remained more narrowly pointed towards the centralized state which in fourteenth century Poland had become conceptually independent of the monarch's person. The legal equality of the knights *vis-à-vis* the monarchy developed into the ideological basis for a form of democracy within the noble estate that became the *demokracja szlachecka* as the nobility came to dominate society and garner privilege after privilege from the king. The most valuable concession was the sole right of representative institutions to make laws. Imbalances within the *szlachta* changed the character of the system while preserving its form and ideology until well into the eighteenth century. A changing economic climate in the eighteenth century seemed associated with the reforms that reaffirmed the principle of mixed government in a newer system of checks and balances and sought to move Poland-Lithuania to a course of evolution similar to other non-absolutist European states.

CHAPTER 2

THE SCOPE OF THE CONSTITUTION OF
MAY 3, 1791

As the pivotal legislation of the Parliament of 1788-1792, the Constitution of May Third culminated years of agitation for reform, both within and outside of the Parliament, and many months of slow, arduous and often unfocused restructuring of the entire politico-administrative system of the Polish-Lithuanian Commonwealth. The Constitution itself expressed a conception of "fundamental laws" particular to that point in the development of Polish constitutionalism. The main features of the Constitution were a redefining of the social limits for participation in political life and the restructuring of the governmental apparatus to ensure a more efficient execution of laws, growth in the country's well-being and a more effective defense.

The *Ustawa Rządowa* and the May Third Constitution

Almost axiomatically, the May Third Constitution has been identified with the *Ustawa Rządowa* [Statute of Government] of May 3, 1791.[1] In actuality, the Constitution was conceived as a much broader system of laws, without rigid limitation, structuring the government and not as the single statute passed in the revolutionary fervor of May Third. The *Ustawa Rządowa* served as a fairly comprehensive outline—but only an outline—of the new Constitution whose specific components were enumerated in some existing laws and in numerous laws subsequently passed.[2]

The *Ustawa Rządowa* is comprised of an untitled preamble and eleven articles each of which was to be further developed in more detailed laws. The articles are the: State ("Reigning") Religion, Nobility, Towns and Townspeople, Peasants, Government or the Commissioning of Public Authority, Parliament or Legislative Authority, King—Executive Authority, Judicial Authority, Regency, Education of the Royal Children, and Armed Forces.[3] Two additional documents have been associated, in scholarship, with the *Ustawa Rządowa*:

"*Deklaracyja Stanow Zgromadzonych*" [Declaration of the Gathered Estates] and the statute entitled, *Miasta Nasze Krolewskie Wolne w Państwach Rzeczypospolitej* [Our Royal Towns Free in the States of the Commonwealth]. Passed on May 5, the Declaration was an apparent afterthought, a warning against opposition to the new Constitution. The Declaration gradually became disassociated from the *Ustawa Rządowa* as the overthrow of the new system made it obsolete. The law on cities, on the other hand, is an extensive statute, almost as long as the *Ustawa Rządowa* itself, passed the previous April 16th. *Miasta nasze* was in integral part of the *Ustawa Rządowa* but it was seldom printed in its entirety.

Scholars have regarded the May Third Constitution either as the *Ustawa Rządowa* alone, or the *Ustawa Rządowa* with the Declaration (less frequently), or the *Ustawa Rządowa* with the Declaration and the Law on Towns (least frequently). This inconsistency reflects the elastic quality of the Constitution. The *Ustawa Rządowa* served only as a revolutionary framework to systematize the ongoing reforms of the Four Years' Parliament. The May Third Constitution, therefore, comprised the *Ustawa Rządowa*, the Declaration and all the other fundamental laws constructing the new system of government— contained in embryonic form in the statute of May 3, 1791.

While the concept of a constitution as a framework may be generally accepted, the actual delineation of the Constitution's limits is not apparent. A constitution may exist to which amendments are added. But that clear system did not exist in the May Third Constitution. It should be of some use to examine the evidence that would, first of all, point to the extension of the Constitution beyond the *Ustawa Rządowa* and second, indicate which statutes lay within its limits. Inconsistent thinking by framers and supporters precludes absolute clarity about the Constitution's exact limits.

The most convincing evidence to support the concept of the May Third Constitution as greater than the *Ustawa Rządowa* is found in the *Ustawa Rządowa* itself and in subsequent statutes. The law passed on May Third uses the term *konstytucya* fifteen times, mostly in reference to itself.[4] However, in at least four instances the term clearly presupposes a wider concept of constitution. An excerpt of the preamble reads:

> Acknowledging that fate has bound us solely for the strengthening and improvement of the national constitution. . . .[5]

Article VI, entitled "*Seym czyli władza prawodawcza*" [the *Sejm* or

legislative authority], states in a similar tone:
> Preventing, on the one hand, sudden and frequent changes of the national constitution and, on the other hand, acknowledging the need to improve it, after experiencing its effects on the public well-being, we set each twenty-five years as the time and period for revising and correcting the constitution.[6]

Article X, on the *"Edukacyi dzieci krolewskich"* [education of the royal children] concludes with the following passage:
> An obligation of the Education Commission will, therefore, be to present the program of instruction and education of the royal sons for the *Sejm*'s approval, and thus, in order to consistently inculcate in the formation of their laws [principles], continuously and early in the minds of future successors to the throne, religion, love of virtue, fatherland, freedom and the country's constitution.[7]

These passages show that *konstytucya* not only referred to the *Ustawa Rządowa*, in which case it is usually modified by the word *ninieysza* [this], but also to a broader national system existing in different forms at different times. The exact theoretical nature of this system is not made explicit probably because this wider meaning was in common use and needed no explanation. In several instances, *konstytucya* could at once refer both to a specific document and the broader system. Thus, a later excerpt of the preamble states:
> . . . for the general good, for the grounding of freedom, for the salvation of our fatherland and its borders, with the greatest constancy of spirit, we pass this constitution. . . .[8]

This appears in the same paragraph as the first excerpt, shown above, using *"konstytucyi narodowey"* and, yet, by intent refers specifically to the statute which follows. Consequently, the more comprehensive system includes the governmental structure outlined in the *Ustawa Rządowa* and the additional matters indicated under separate articles: religion, the nobility, the towns and townspeople, the peasantry, regency, education of royal children (actually only heirs thus excluding female offspring), and the armed forces. The articles unite social and political dimensions in the Constitution.

Konstytucya was an exceptionally broad idea that could not be exhaustedly set forth in the eleven articles of the *Ustawa Rządowa*. The abstract socio-political system declared by this statute, of necessity, extended to other laws. In this vein, the above passage continues:

... and these we declare to be holy and unchangeable in their entirety, until the nation does clearly acknowledge by its will at the time prescribed by law, the need to change its articles. All future statutes of this *Sejm* must comply in everything with this constitution.[9]

The *Ustawa Rządowa*, functioning as an outline of the wider *konstytucya*, subsumed existing laws and promised to include future ones. The statute used a variety of degrees to relate these laws. In article II, the framers of the *Ustawa Rządowa* "confirm, insure and recognize as unchanged" all noble "laws, statutes and privileges" bestowed by Polish kings and Lithuanian Grand Dukes from Kazimierz Wielki to Zygmunt August.[10] The specific laws and privileges were not mentioned either because of their sheer volume or probably because their content was generally understood. Second, the law entitled "*Miasta Nasze krolewskie wolne w państwach Rzeczypospolitey*" [Our royal cities free in the countries of the Republic] and passed two weeks earlier on 18 April is declared "*za część ninieyszey konstytucyi*" [as part of this constitution].[11] Thus, one entire law previously approved by the Four Years' *Sejm* is made an explicit part of the Constitution. Logically, from the structural point of view, other laws of a similar kind would also be included in the Constitution *once they were passed*. But in this respect, the *Ustawa Rządowa* explicitly extends constitutional validity, and probably status, to only one law:

> We solemnly safeguard as the most essential principles of civic freedom the law on *sejmiki* adopted by the *Sejm*.[12]

Unlike the Law on Towns, the Law on the *Sejmiki* was modified by the *Ustawa Rządowa* and placed within the larger description of the *Sejm*, a reversal of the traditional primacy of the local dietines. Quite possibly, this modification affected the terminology for relating the framework statute to specific laws.[13]

The *Ustawa Rządowa* is much more vague in respect to the safeguarding or even inclusion of laws about other parts of the governmental structure it sketches. A very indirect connection is made at the end of the section on the executive branch:

> For the orderly fulfilment of executive authority, we establish separate commissions having ties to the council (*Straż*) and obligated to it. Commissioners will be elected to them by the *Sejm* in order to discharge their offices over the time prescribed by law. The commissions are: (1) Education, (2) Police, (3) Army, (4) Treasury.[14]

The excerpt reads, "During the time stipulated by law," but the law or laws did not yet exist for the Police Commission nor for the unified Treasury Commission (unified, since only one was designated unlike the former separate commissions for the Crown and for the Grand Duchy). Clearly, laws detailing the institutions described in the *Ustawa Rządowa* were intended. In the same paragraph, the already existing local administrative commissions were subordinated to the *Straż Praw* but their exact position within the Constitution was not discussed explicitly. Only in one instance, a new law code, does the *Ustawa Rządowa* use special language to specifically order the creation of anything.[15] Yet, much more is ordered into existence by implication and neither in the case of the law code nor of other new institutions is there any mention of their technical relationship to the Constitution. More likely the special treatment of the unwritten law code indicates its external position with regard to the Constitution. The picture has become muddled.

The distinction between "part of this constitution" and "solemnly safeguard[ed]," and the lack of explicit inclusion within the *Ustawa Rządowa* of laws giving detailed form to the outlined apparatus, other than those regarding the towns and the *sejmiki*, could potentially be substantive and even crucial in limiting the Constitution to one document, the *Ustawa Rządowa*, if it were not for the unequivocal language of the "*Deklaracya stanów zgromadzonych*" passed after the second, "unanimous," approval of the *Ustawa Rządowa* on 5 May and often considered an appendix to the earlier statute. The "Declaration" begins:

> We abolish all former and present laws contrary to this constitution or any of its articles; *and we declare as integral parts of this constitution the specific descriptions of articles and all necessary material contained in this constitution, as a more complete designation of the obligations and form of the government.*[16] (not highlighted in the original)

In the next sentence, which orders an immediate oath of loyalty to the new system, the "Declaration" refers to the above as "*tey caley konstytucyi*" [this entire constitution]. The "whole constitution," therefore, includes the *Ustawa Rządowa*, all old laws which do not contradict it and all specific descriptions of its articles and included material as fuller specifications of the obligations and system of the government. Those taking the oath, in effect, pledged allegiance to a rudimentary formulation of the new system stated by the *Ustawa*

Rządowa and specific components still to be worked out according to these general guidelines.

The text of the Law on *Sejmy*, registered three weeks later, affirms in a separate article (XXIII), and entitled "*Ubeśpieczenie prawa o seymach*" [Safeguarding of the Law on *Sejmy*], the constitutional status of laws explicating the responsibilities and powers of the government outlined in the *Ustawa Rządowa*. Point two states:

> The only rules for parliamentary procedure from now on and forever will be the procedures and ceremonies as they are prescribed in all their detail in the present law—this entire law on parliaments we determine to be a constitutional law; we abolish all other laws previously established on parliamentary procedure.[17]

The *Ustawa Rządowa* emphasizes the central importance of the *Sejm* and, indeed, the statute reflected the *sejmocracy* of 1788–1792 but it does not mention any law by which the parliament would operate. The references to the inclusion within the *Ustawa Rządowa* of the Law on Towns, the safeguarding of the passed, but still unregistered, Law on the *Sejmiki* and the casual and very indirect mention of laws explaining the central ministries indicates that such laws were expected as they were among the backlog of bills and within the scope the task undertaken by the Four Years' *Sejm* in 1789. The "Declaration" of 5 May voices this assumption in the clearest language and the 28 May Law on *Sejmy* confirms the principle of including legislation stipulating the function of governmental institutions as part of the Constitution.

Another clue for deciphering the intended scope of the Constitution is likewise found in the law on parliaments. In describing the procedure for settling charges against the validity of individual *sejmiki*, the law uses the following phrase: "*tak iak są w rozdziale o sejmikach opisane*" [as in the section describing *sejmiki*].[18] The Law on *Sejmy* does not include a section on the *sejmiki*, rather, the reference is to the Law on *Sejmiki*. It would appear that at least to the authors of the parliament law these separate laws were *sections* of a larger work which could only be the Constitution initiated on 3 May. Such language is, however, not repeated.

Usage of the term "constitutional law" offers additional insight into the scope of the new constitution intended by the *Ustawa Rządowa*. Article VI devoted to the parliament lists three types of "*prawa ogolne*" [general laws]: constitutional, civil and criminal (and also "permanent taxes"), as well as lesser "*uchwały sejmowe*" [*Sejm* resolutions], all of which fall under the *Sejm*'s jurisdiction.[19] The Constitution would, therefore, continue to be expanded with each parliament. This could be very crucial.

Further refinement in the conceptualized scope of the Constitution appeared in two subsequent laws: "*Seym konstytucyiny extraordynaryiny*" [special constitutional *Sejm*] and "*Seymy*" both registered as laws on May 28, 1791. In the first law, an apparent hierarchy of constitutional laws was established. A principle function of the Constitutional Committee in the special constitutional parliament was the sorting of bills "*do praw politycznych konstytucyinych*" [to political constitutional laws] and "*do praw politycznych porządkowych*" [to political order laws]; the former including all bills pertaining to "laws contained in the law entitled, *Ustawa Rządowa*," and the latter "pertained to the specific descriptions and procedures of the governing authorities."[20] The provisions enumerated in the *Ustawa Rządowa* and the provisions of those laws passed to fully develop this foundation were considered distinct enough to warrant different names, yet, since both were to be considered by future constitutional parliaments both could arguably be classified as constitutional laws and hence part of the May Third Constitution. In this way, the apparent inconsistency of the Law on Towns belonging both to "*praw politycznych konstytucyinych*" and "*praw politycznych porządkowych*" is obviated. Moreover, the distinction between the two types of bills in the constitutional *Sejmy* could have been simply to expedite procedure and not a separation of constitutional laws from non-constitutional bills since "political order laws" are passable by the institution specifically designed to deal only with the Constitution.

The law, "*Seymy*," expands the definition of constitutional laws offered by the section on parliaments in the *Ustawa Rządowa*. The May Third document empowered the Chamber of Deputies to decide on all matters but added a distinction between "*prawa ogolne*" [general laws] and "*uchwały sejmowe*" [parliamentary resolutions]. "*Prawa ogolne*" were further divided among constitutional, civil and criminal laws and permanent taxes.[21] In the law on *Sejmy*, article XV makes the same distinction but alters the terminology. Bills for "*prawa ogolne*" are called "*ogolne prawodawcze*" [general legislative] and constitutional laws are simple called political laws. This is apparent in the following:

> . . . the parliamentary committee will, then, divide bills into legislative [laws] and parliamentary resolutions. (2) Among

legislative bills, the parliamentary committee will include: 1. bills for political laws, 2. [bills] for civil laws, 3. [bills] for criminal laws, [bills] for permanent taxes.

Constitutional or political laws are defined as:

> whatever concerns improvement through change or the correction of particular descriptions of the governmental system must, however, [be] without violation of the fundamental law entitled, *Ustawa Rządowa*.[22]

An apparent overlapping of categories arises when this is compared to the law on constitutional parliaments. The difference in meaning between *"prawa polityczne porządkowe"* ["political order laws"—used in the law on constitutional parliaments and considered by this discussion to be a type of constitutional laws] and *"prawa polityczne"* ["political laws"—handled by ordinary nonconstitutional parliaments) seems to hinge on the addition in the latter of *"w odmianie lub poprawie"* ["in variation or correction"]. The qualification is insubstantial because for *"prawa polityczne porządkowe"* to be introduced in the special parliament they must propose "some change or correction" in existing laws. Hence the two types of laws would seem to be one and the same and the specifications of the provisions of the *Ustawa Rządowa* in separate laws passed before and after 3 May 1791 would not be part of the Constitution because they are indistinguishable from those passable by any regular *Sejm*.

This interpretation, however, ignores crucial chronological sequence and semantic presuppositions. The *"szczególne opisy i porządek rządu"* ["specific description and order of the government" – the object of *"prawa polityczne porządkowe"*] or *"szczególne opisy formy rządowey"* ["specific descriptions of the form of government"– the object of *"prawa polityczne"*] are assumed to have a prior existence. The fact that they can be changed by both constitutional and ordinary parliaments does not necessarily negate the inclusiveness of the "Declaration." Ordinary parliaments may perfect the specific descriptions of the parts of the *Ustawa Rządowa* but clearly those specifications are to have an existence, consistent with the fundamental law, *Ustawa Rządowa*, prior to the convention of all *future* ordinary and constitutional parliaments and, according to the "Declaration" and the precedence of including the Law on Towns in this basic statute, they are component parts of the Constitution. By the usage of the term "constitutional laws" in the *Ustawa Rządowa*, the

Constitution initiated on 3 May 1791 and developed into a more complete blueprint in the subsequent legislation of the Four Years' *Sejm* could have been enlarged and altered by later parliaments; by historical necessity, however, the limit on the Constitution was permanently drawn at the end of May 1792.

Finally, it is noteworthy that in the excerpt last quoted above, the *Ustawa Rządowa* is called "the fundamental law" and not the national constitution. The May Third statute was treated as the foundation of a much larger construction.

An expanded interpretation of the May Third Constitution, in contrast to one which limits the Constitution to the *Ustawa Rządowa*, is, therefore, supported by a textual analysis of the May Third document and other legislation of the Four Years' *Sejm*. But there is also additional evidence to support this view. Such an interpretation was also shared by members of the *Sejm*. To dispel the fears of a member of the Constitutional Committee, Tomasz Nowowieyski, that the *Ustawa Rządowa* completed the *Sejm*'s work and would, therefore, necessitate its adjournment, the *Sejm*'s marshal, Stanisław Małachowski, stated that,

> in this constitution only two principle objectives have been completed in their entirety: the succession of the throne and the *Straż Praw* ["Guardians of the Laws" or council of minister]; the specification of other articles will still come before the Estates.[23]

Kossakowski, a member of the Constitutional Committee and a future leader of the counterrevolutionary Targowica Confederation, used similar reasoning to back his intention not to speak against the "importance" of the *Ustawa Rządowa* nor to subject it to any doubt. He could justify his unenthusiastic support on 5 May by the unfinished and elastic nature of the Constitution which he and the entire committee detected:

> [we] found in it the possibility of explaining in the working out of the specific articles those things which because of their compactness could cause thinking and incorrect interpretation.[24]

Two more future Targowicans, Antoni Szarmocki and Seweryn Potocki, echoed this idea. The argument was common, therefore, both to defenders of the new system and to undeclared opponents who apparently hoped that the new constitution could still be developed along their principles.

Another less well thought-out but traditional attitude identified the Constitution with all the laws passed by a particular *sejm*, regardless of whether or not they formed a logical whole. This was argued by another opponent-in-the-making, Celestyn Sokolnicki, a delegate from Poznań:

> As far as the twenty-five year period for the constitution, I can only be in favor of it since we have seen that through the frequent alteration of the constitution, the *Volumina legum* has been excessively enlarged to the point memory can encompass it only with difficulty.[25]

In this essentially old-fashion line of thinking, the *Ustawa Rządowa* did not differ from previous "constitutions" and, therefore, shared in their amorphous nature, though once completed it could not be changed until the next constitutional *Sejm*.

A final item of evidence supporting a broad interpretation of the May Third Constitution is the "*Projekt do formu rządu*"[project for the form of government], an early, incomplete draft of the constitution produced by the Constitutional Committee in August 1790.[26] The proposal lists, after an introduction, eleven very lengthy sections: "Constitutional laws and in them cardinal [laws]", *seymiki, seymy, seym* courts, council of ministers (*Straż*), police commission, army commision, treasury commission, education commission, *województwo* commissions, and "Degrees and conditions for offices in the *Rzeczpospolita*." Crucially, each section appears in similar form and length to the actual laws passed by the *Sejm*. These extensive laws were, therefore, to be considered integral parts of the Constitution and it is quite likely that the authors of the *Ustawa Rządowa* thought along similar lines, especially since its main author, Ignacy Potocki, was a member of the Constitutional Committee.[27]

The evidence supporting an interpretation of the May Third Constitution as a construct greater than the *Ustawa Rządowa*, therefore, includes, the language of the *Ustawa Rządowa*, the Declaration of May 5th and major constitutional legislation in the Four Years' *Sejm*, statements by members of the *Sejm* both supporting and opposing the Constitution, and the model of the August 1790 official draft of the Constitution. But, having shown the ambiguity in the usage of the term *konstytucya*, both in reference to a specific document and to a much wider sociopolitical system described in numerous laws, and having demonstrated the *Ustawa Rządowa* as open-ended and intended to include fuller developments of its component parts, the equally important and hazardous problem of designating those statutes comprising an integral part of the May Third Constitution still remains. The May Third Constitution is more than only the *Ustawa Rządowa* but its exact scope is still unclear.

An earlier distinction was made between elaboration on articles of the *Ustawa Rządowa* dealing with social matters and those expounding upon the responsibilities and organization of the government. The "Declaration" of 5 May 1791 defines both as parts of the Constitution but the detailed explanatory elaborations in subsequent legislation barely develop the social reforms. All privileges of the *szlachta* granted from King Kazimierz Wielki through King Zygmunt August are guaranteed and the most far-reaching 18 April law of effecting social change dealt with the bourgeoisie and was explicitly incorporated into the Constitution by the *Ustawa Rządowa*. The Law on Towns was modified by two laws adopted on 30 June: "*Urządzenie wewnętrzne miast wolnych Rzeczypospolitey w Koronie i w Wielkim Xięstwie Litewskim*" [Internal organization of the free towns in the Crown and the Grand Duchy of Lithuania] and "*Ostrzeżenie względem exekucyi prawa o miastach Naszych, dawniey Krolewskich, a teraz wolnych Rzeczypospolitey*" [Notice concerning the execution of the law on our towns, once royal and now free in the Commonwealth].[28] Matters pertaining to the social order can conceivable be included among the "*prawa polityczne konstytucyine*" ["constitutional political laws"] of the law on constitutional parliaments, despite their names, since this category of law in general terms spans all the articles of the *Ustawa Rządowa*. Social questions are also marginally treated in the numerous laws passed by the Four Years' *Sejm* delineating the functions of governmental agencies but their fuller development was limited to anticipated economic and moral constitutions that were to follow the reforms in the May Third Constitution and not to the set of approved laws. The Russian invasion intervened. As they stood the social provisions were vital, yet, the bulk of the first modern constitution in Europe was shaped by historical reality to include mainly the blueprints of the political governmental system. This is not surprising and is quite similar to the American case which preceded it.

Table 3

Major Statutes Comprising the New Constitution

CORE

Ustawa Rządowa	(3 May 1791)
"Deklaracya stanow zgromadzonych"	(5 May 1791)

SOCIAL

("all laws, statutes and privileges" accorded the *szlachta*)*

Miasta Nasze Krolewskie wolne w państwach Rzeczypospolitey
[Our royal cities free in the countries of
the Republic] (18 April 1791)

Urządzenie wewnętrzne miast wolnych Rzeczypospolitey w Koronie i w Wielkim Xięstwie Litewskim

[Internal organization of free cities in the Crown
and the Grand Duchy of Lithuania] (30 June 1791)

Ostrzeżenie względem execukyi prawa o miastach Naszych, dawniey Krolewskich, a teraz wolnych Rzeczypospolitey
[Warning concerning the execution of the law on our cities,
formerly royal, now free (in the) Republic] (30 June 1791)

GOVERNMENTAL

Legislative

Seymiki	(24 March 1791)
	(28 May 1791)**
Seymy	(28 May 1791)
Seym konstytucjiny extraordinariny	(28 May 1791)

Executive

Straż (Praw) [Guardians of the Laws]	(6 June 1791)
Kommisya edukacyi narodowej [National Education Commission]	(18 October 1773)

Kommisya skarbowa Rzeczypospolitey oboyga narodów
[Treasury Commission of the Republic of Both Nations]
(29 October 1791)

Kommisya woyskowa oboyga narodów
[Army Commission of Both Nations] (November-December 1788)***

Kommisya policyi (24 June 1791)

Kommisye woiewódzkie i powiatowe w Wielkim Xięstwie Litewskim
[Voivodeship and district commissions in the Grand
Duchy of Lithuania] (19 November 1791)

Kommisye porządkowe cywilno-woyskowe, woiewództw, ziem i powiatów w Koronie
[Civil-military administrative commissions of the voivodeships,
lands and districts of the Crown] (15 December 1791)

Judicial

Sąd ziemiański
[Noble court] (10 January 1792)

Sąd trybunalski Koronny
[Crown Tribunal] (21 January 1792)

Sąd trybunalski w Wielkim Xięstwie Litewskim
[Tribunal Court of the Grand Duchy of Lithuania]
(21 January 1792)

Urządzenie sądów mieyskich i assessoryi
[Organization of Municipal Courts and Appeals Courts]
(6 October 1791)

Sądy seymowe
[*Sejm* courts] (28 May 1791)

---

*not enumerated

**registered at the later date because of a controversy over the scheduling of the *sejmiki*[29]

***The *Kommissya Woyskowa Oboyga Narodów* replaced the Department Woyskowy on 10 November 1788 and was governed by regulations passed in ten separate laws from 26 November through 20 December 1788. A single law similar to those of the Treasury and Police Commissions finally went into effect on 31 May 1792.

The Constitution provided for a government emanating from the will of the nation, guaranteeing territorial integrity, freedom of the citizenry and "balanced social order," and consisting of three "authorities" (legislative, executive, and judicial) according to progressive ideas typical for the late eighteenth century.[30] The branches of government were distinct but not totally separate and equal. Preponderance in the system lay securely with the "temple of the national will," the *Sejm*, and true to political tradition safeguards described by forceful and redundant language restrained the newly increased powers of the executive. But all institutions falling under the categories of legislative, executive, and judicial created either before or after 3 May 1791 were integral parts of the Constitution provided they were consistent with the *Ustawa Rządowa*. This represents a tremendous amount of legislation passed by the Four Years' *Sejm*. Not surprisingly, a special committee established on 28 January 1792 to eliminate contradictions in the *Sejm*'s laws and arrange them into categories did not complete its task by the time of adjournment four months later.[31]

The articles of the *Ustawa Rządowa* were neither in the order by which they were to be developed in later legislation nor did they really comprise a strict outline. Issues of special concern, such as the education of the royal children—a concern connected with the newly hereditary throne—were given equal weight with entire branches of government. But the structure and nature of the new government were clear on the basis of textual analyses of the *Ustawa Rządowa*, other legislation of the Four Years' *Sejm*, and the model presented by the official proposal *"Projekt do formy rządu"* [project for the form of government].

The governmental institutions, comprising the ediface outlined on 3 May 1791 included in the legislative branch, the *Sejm*, the Constitutional *Sejm*, the *sejmiki*, in the executive branch, the *Straż Praw* ("Guardians of the Laws" in effect, a council of ministers) which included the king, four central ministries (Education, Police, Army and Treasury) and the local civil-military administrative commissions and in the judiciary, local noble courts, noble courts of appeal called *trybunały*, a parliamentary court and state courts for non-nobles. Specific statutes delineating these institutions numbered fifteen major pieces of organizational legislation modified by twelve minor laws.

Thus, the Constitution created by the Four Years' *Sejm* consists of the *Ustawa Rządowa*, three pieces of social legislation, and twenty-six statutes dealing with governmental organization.

The *Ustawa Rządowa* served as a linchpin for the numerous pieces of legislation instituting the new reformed government. Though the persons involved in the actual formation of these bills varied with the attendance of each session, the language within each of the adjunct laws unmistakenly connects all the laws listed above as elaborations on sections of the *Ustawa Rządowa*. Some of the legislation was passed more than eight months after May 3, 1791 and no statement was made closing the set of statutes. The Constitution was, therefore, probably intended to be a growing entity even in the years between the constitutional *Sejmy* scheduled for every twenty-five years.

The distinction between the *Ustawa Rządowa* and the abstract totality of the new system which it sketched must have been assumed but never enunciated. In a sense, there was no need. Even Sokolnicki, in his unsophisticated argument mentioned above made the separation. *Konstytcya* could refer either to the outline (the *Ustawa Rządowa*) or the outlined system. In either case, the traditional terminology was modified and room was left for permanent constitutional principles outside of the May Third statute.

Resolutions, Cardinal Laws and the May Third Constitution

The concept of a constitution had a long development in Polish parliamentary history. The May Third Constitution came at the end of several centuries of lawmaking within the *Sejm* and conceptualization about the nature of law. Its antecedents may be found in the gradual differentiation of parliamentary resolutions (*uchwały sejmowe* or *konstytucje*) during the period 1454–1606, known often as the "Democracy of the Nobility." As a legislative institution, the *Sejm* acquired special powers with the 1505 statute *nihil novi* that prohibited the creation of any law without the Parliament's approval. The *Sejm*'s powers continued to grow, and by the end of the sixteenth century the representative body and not the monarch alone was acknowledged as the actualizing organ of sovereignty. Parliamentary resolutions increasingly limited the importance of customary laws and royal decrees and themselves became the main source of law. At this time, the term, *konstytucja*, referred not to the entire political system but only to the set of laws passed by a given parliament. Thus, it was proper to speak of the "constitution of 1555" and of another from 1557, etc. With this usage the May Third Constitution could be considered the set of laws, though not all the measures, passed by the Four Years' *Sejm*.

In a sense, the departure from the traditional use of the term was not that great because the *Ustawa Rządowa* required that all laws be consistent with it and hence all the legislation of 1789-92 formed one body, one constitution, though much was irrelevant to the strict issue of governmental reform or structure. Yet, never was the term "Constitution of 1789-92" used which would have been consistent with old practice. Instead "Constitution of May Third" was employed although contemporaries preferred the core statute's name, *Ustawa Rządowa*.

The broader concept of constitution as a governmental system, and more precisely its skeleton or outline, had developed over three centuries. A distinction arose during the sixteenth century in the concept of constitution as a set of all the laws passed by a particular parliament. There were *konstytucje czasowe* [constitutiones temporales] and *konstytucje wieczyste* [constitutiones perpetuae] with the latter understood as applicable for an unspecified period of time but not necessarily for all time. Only the *artykuły henrykowskie* [Henrician Articles] of 1573 were regarded as explicit, enunciated fundamental principles to remain permanent and unchanging.[32]

In the following century, however, a new terminology was adopted. Based on *cardo-inis*, meaning a hook or hinge, the term, *prawa kardynalne* or cardinal laws, was used in 1673 by the *kapturowy* ["hooded"] *sejm* following the death of King Michał Korobut Wiśniowiecki. According to Radwański the term appeared as a result of the intense debates over the political system associated with the first interregnum (1573-76) and the Zebrzydowski revolt of 1607 that marked the political ascendance of the magnates. The concept of cardinal laws would become integrated into a traditionalist defense of the freedoms acquired by the noble class over the centuries. Not surprisingly, in reaction to the reforms sponsored by the powerful Czartoryski family beginning with the coronation of Stanisław August in 1764, the traditionalist reaction entitled a long litany of principles in 1768 as cardinal laws freezing the former oligarchic, decentralized system. Inscribed in the "constitution of 1775" as an enumeration of cherished traditionalist principles (including an elected monarch and a limited *liberum veto*) that were to act as a bulwark against "royal encroachments of corruptive modern ideas," the cardinal laws were "guaranteed" by the partitioning powers in 1775. Hence politically the term was far from neutral.[33]

The opposition of two sets of principles, as argued by Radwański, becomes symbolic of "traditionalist" and "progressive" forces, though each set (and more definitely the former) was the result of compromise among individual preferences. This part of history can be seen as a struggle of two opposing forces without either possessing an existence of its own apart from individual persons. This fits well into Kalinka's fecund insight of a "revolution in the way of thinking" ("*przewrót umysłowy*") in the last quarter of the eighteenth century.

Reality was, however, less dualistic. The concept of cardinal laws was used throughout the Four Years' *Sejm* and while it usually referred to the specific cardinal laws from 1768, and in that sense carried very reactionary connotations, its meaning as "linchpin" principles did not necessarily cast an individual's loyalty to one side or another in an ideological battle. Traditionalism and reform did indeed clash but the change in terminology—the alterring of the political arrangement—was neither as abrupt nor was the division as hermetic as might be concluded from Radwański's, or even Kalinka's, analysis.

An early step in the writing of the *Ustawa Rządowa* was the "*Zasady do formu rządy*" ["Principles for the Form of the Government"]. The last mention of a system of cardinal laws in actual legislation came on 8 January 1791 with the registration of the law entitled, *Prawa kardynalne niewzruszone* [Unchanged cardinal laws] actually passed the previous September.[34] In some of their provisions these cardinal laws contradicted the reforms that would be embodied in the May Third Constitution. Most important was the cardinal law prohibiting hereditary succession and this proved to be a very real obstacle for the acceptance of the new system. But, while the opposition was apparent in the content of this particular cardinal law, an unclear mixture of terms characterized the debates of the *Sejm* and often oblique, scholastic distinctions in legal categories continued to exist.

Among the surviving paraphernalia of the Four Year's *Sejm* there is a short essay "*Myśli o istocie praw kardynalnych*" [Thoughts on the essence of cardinal laws] accompanying a list entitled, "*Prawa kardynalne niewzruszone dawnych ustaw Rzeczpospolitey wyięte i zebrane*"

[Unchanged cardinal laws taken and collected from old statutes of the contemporaries Republic].[35] The "Thoughts" indicate the difficulties encountered when sorting out legal categories and in constructing a clear conceptual framework for the new government.

The essay begins by mentioning discussions in meetings, apparently of the Constitutional Committee, voicing the need to separate cardinal from constitutional laws and to divide the former into two classes: "unchange[able]" and "lasting." The author expresses the need to be critical and scientific about this terminology. The brevity of the essay permits lengthier quotations of its central part:

> Can those laws be unchange[able] in a nation [that] legislative authority wishes to possess? The answer to this appears to be that they can—that they should; but the meaning of terms must be agreed upon. Those laws are unchangeable not because they cannot be touched by foreign oppression or false zeal but because they cannot be touched without the fall of civic freedom and the political freedom of the entire nation, because they are so intertwined with the freedom of the citizen and the nation that should they ever be altered the citizen would become a prisoner and the nation, in part or in its entirety, would be under the oppression of a usurper. These laws are nothing else than general maxims which each free citizen feels in his heart.

The author presents a ideologically correct description of the symbolic value of cardinal laws as contrasted with the generally accepted view of foreign oppression. Next, the concepts of cardinal and unchangeable laws are separated:

> The term *kardynalne*, then, derives from the Latin *"cardo"* or *zawiasa* [hinge] according to the similarity that just as the movement of a door is dependent on hinges so the entire machine of legislative authority and executive power depends on cardinal laws. Conceptualizing unchangeable laws as cardinal means nothing else than that they are the principles of the entire legislative authority (*calego Prawodawstwa*) to the point that . . . they must be cardinal; in other words, it is proper to present them to legislative authority as a model for law-making, a boundary that even legislative authority would not dare cross.

"Unchanging cardinal laws" are conceived as models for lawmakers in determining which laws may be changed, how they can be interpreted, which new ones could be passed and what cannot even be touched because they are "blessed with truth and natural justice." The author then summarizes the document which follows by listing the specific topics of cardinal laws: those touching the conscience of all people: the holy "ruling" faith, apostacy and toleration, two laws concerning the territorial integrity of the Republic and fiefs of the Republic, one law on self-rule (*samowładność*) of the Republic, two laws concerning obedience to the law, protection of the law for everyone, the assurance of the personal freedom of each citizen[36] through laws guaranteeing free contracts, freedom of thought and speech, the security of landed property and finally, a law guaranteeing the use of real and other property. In another environment these were regarded as "basic human rights."

"Lasting cardinal laws" are next defined as those laws that can be changed only by the unanimous approval of the national will expressed in the instructions each voting district draws up for its deputies. These laws are to cover all the necessary regulations concerning "legislative authority," the dietines, the *Sejm*, membership in citizen's meetings, estates of the Republic, and executive authority.

A few observations may be made. The essay examines three topics: unchangeable laws, the concept of cardinal laws, and the specific contents of cardinal laws. Unchangeable laws were briefly treated as self-evident basic human rights. Cardinal laws were conceived as guiding principles of two kinds: those which defined the polity and its freedoms and, second, those which determined the function of the government. The former were unchangeable precepts on which the polity "hinged" to be held as the foundation of freedom in every citizen's heart and according to which the latter, the "lasting" cardinal laws were to be created. Thus, the development of constitutionalism in Poland-Lithuania was more than the simple accumulation of concessions from the monarch, rather, it included the conceptualization of universal rights.

The list of unchangeable cardinal laws was drawn from existing statutes and was, therefore, by definition traditionalist. Roman and Greek Catholicism were declared as the ruling religion and conversion from Roman Catholicism (but apparently not Greek Catholicism) was a criminal offense. People of other religions were left free to worship as they wished and religious discrimination by any authority was prohibited. A principle of national sovereignty was declared both in regards to territorial integrity and to political independence. The source of law was the clear will of the Republic and people were obligated by laws made by the nation. A unitary system of law was extended over a definite hierarchy of estates. Freely made contracts were binding on all signing parties. The old Polish *habias corpus* principle of *neminem captivabimus nisi jure victum* was affirmed as were freedom of speech, writing and printing, limited only in two cases: religion in which church censorship was maintained and potential cases of libel where the only limitation was the prohibition of anonymity. Hereditary property of all kinds was safeguarded. Finally, hereditary owners of real estate were guaranteed total discretion in using their property.

Of special importance is the absence of any mention of the elected monarchy and the *liberum veto*, the two jewels of the golden, reactionary freedom and both of which were affirmed in relatively recent statutes. Cardinal laws of the most lasting kind could, therefore, also be a matter of choice.

Despite its verbosity, due in part to an attempt at precision, the essay presents an essentially simple picture of cardinal laws. Yet, the drafted law was changed in committee since the statute, *"Prawa kardynalne niewzruszone"* is somewhat different. The primary difference between the two was the addition to the final product of what the essay's unknown author could have called "lasting cardinal laws." A very useful distinction was lost. Still worse, the concept and context of cardinal laws became further muddled and open to wide interpretation with the introduction of "constitutional laws" whose distinction from "lasting cardinal laws" was not at all clear. "Unchangeable," "lasting" and "constitutional" all blended and with them old, traditionalist concepts and newer innovations. The dichotomy collapses.

The separation of cardinal and constitutional laws did not lie in the opposition of traditionalists and progressives. In *"Projekt do formy rządu"* [Bill for the Form of Government], probably authored by Bishop Krasiński,[37] both legal terms are used and one is subordinated to the other. The first of eleven sections after the introduction is entitled, *"Prawa konstytucyine a w nich kardynalne"* [Constitutional laws among them cardinal [laws].[38] In this lengthy article devoted to constitutional laws, 61 out of 89 paragraphs are explicitly identified as cardinal laws and two others refer to laws, yet to be written, that are to fall into the same category. The essential difference between these cardinal and non-cardinal constitutional laws is the degree of generality and fundamental value to the system. Thus, the overall territorial integrity of the Commonwealth is declared cardinal (article 1) whereas the actual division into three provinces (article 5) and the relations of fiefs (Courland, Semigalia and the Piltyński district) are not (articles 2, 3, 4). General principles such as due process of law (article 61), the extension of national laws to all segments of society (article 10) and the favored position of the Catholic faith (article 6) are all considered to be cardinal laws. Classification of particular governmental institutions and their jurisdictional boundaries are treated less consistently. The goals, composition and obligations of the chief executive commissions are considered cardinal (article 61) but the relationship of these commissions with the council of ministers (*straż*) is not. The law on civil-military administrative commissions is declared cardinal (article 41) but not the law on the very crucial institutional of the *sejmiki* (article 13).

In all likelihood, the members of the Constitutional Commission did not have precise criteria to distinguish cardinal and constitutional laws. Probably no one had. Generally cardinal laws were considered absolutely unamendable; constitutional laws were permanent but amendable. The use of cardinal law did not primarily gauge traditionalism as opposed to progressivism. Statutes radically new, or perhaps revolutionarily old in the sense of returning to the practice of centuries past, could be declared cardinal laws. Article 21 of "*Projekt do formy rządu*" holds as absolutely unchangeable a permanent hereditary monarchy but this "cardinal law" could by no means be considered part of Polish traditionalist or conservative thought in the late eighteenth century. Instead, the use of cardinal laws is more indicative of an individual's rigidity and inclination to control situations or other people. Some simply believed that much more had to be defined in the polity than others. The May Third Constitution was permanent but amenable and its silence about cardinal laws made them obsolete.

Principles of Political Participation

The May Third Constitution affirmed the traditional constitutionalism of the Polish system and modified it according to the more modern principles of property and utilitarian bases for political rights and the division and balance of power within the government. The basis of power continued to be the nation, but the nation itself was redefined. Bourgeois liberal principles were being adopted by a noble elite which had for centuries prevented the emergence of *absolutum dominium*.

Polish constitutionalism dates back at least to the Statutes of Nieszawa in 1454 which established the Chamber of Deputies as a necessary part of the government. In 1505 the law *nihil novi*, as has been seen, outlawed the passage of laws without the approval of the *Sejm* and for almost a century two strong institutions coexisted and vitalized the Polish state. In an accident of history this balance was upset with the extinction of the Jagiellonian dynasty in 1572 and the voluntary abdication of the first truly elected king, Henri de Valois, two years later. At this crucial juncture, the *szlachta* made its political power unquestioned. The monarchy had practically evaporated— though no one thought of its abolition—and the economic power of the nobility based on the highly profitable international grain trade enabled the *szlachta* to render silent or passive its social rivals, the townspeople and the peasantry. The prerogatives of the *szlachta* and their real domination of society lasted even with the modification of the principles of political involvement effected by the Four Years' *Sejm*.

An essential characteristic of the domination of the *szlachta* was the theoretical equality of each nobleman.[39] Again, "the landless noble was equal with the *wojewoda*." Traditionally, the special qualities that justified the special position of the *szlachta* in society were organic—hereditary. Virtue was in the blood and hence even those noblemen who had lost all their economic advantages and materially were indistinguishable or even worse off than their peasant neighbors still possessed the virtue that had built up and preserved the republic. Ultimately the radical equality within the *szlachta* was justified by participation in the *pospolite ruszenie*, the medieval *levée en masse* of the nobility. Each (male) was equal because each risked his life for the Commonwealth. The *Ustawa Rządowa* affirms this. All the laws, statutes and privileges of the *szlachta* are guaranteed "out of respect for our ancestors as founders of the free government." Noble status in Poland was declared equal to that of foreign nobility and "all the *szlachta* should be equal among themselves."[40]

As mentioned in Chapter 1, a most curious novelty appears in the confirmation of the *szlachta*'s position: privileges are attributed to specific kings—from Kazimierz Wielki (died 1348) to Zygmunt August (died 1572). The absence of any mention of monarchs after the extinction of the Jagiellonian dynasty seems to indicated the exclusion of any privilege bestowed in the previous two hundred and nineteen years. If this were the intent of the provision—and not merely homage to several great kings—the change would be revolutionary. The young and scrupulous deputy from Wilno, Tadeusz Korsak, included this truncation of privileges along with a hereditary throne and the council of ministers as central points in his condemnatory speech in the *Sejm* and his protest against the *Ustawa Rządowa* registered at the Warsaw law court.[41] This issue, however, did not become a serious objection to the new Constitution. Korsak's point was lost behind the other two, more controversial issues he named. Most probably the limitation of privileges to those bestowed by hereditary monarchs was intended to affirm the central importance of the restored principle of succession. The precise meaning of this fundamental shift, however, is hidden in the silence of both the primary sources and the relevant literature.

Yet, the *Ustawa Rządowa* and the thrust of reforms in the Four Years' *Sejm* did modify the dominance and theoretical democracy of the *szlachta*. Undoubtedly, one of the most fundamental reforms was referred to indirectly by the *Ustawa Rządowa*—as if it was purposely being de-emphasized. Article VI subsumes into the Constitution the Law on the *Sejmiki* but the disenfranchisement of the landless and poor nobility contained in that law is never actually mentioned in the May 3rd document. (This further strengthens the necessity of viewing the Constitution as wider than simply the *Ustawa Rządowa*.) Articles IV and V of the Law on *Sejmiki* establish the new requirements for participation in the politics and administration of the Republic:

> IV. Concerning those having a place and a voice in the *sejmiki*
>
> A place and a voice in the *sejmik* of their district (shall be given to) the *szlachta* (according to the following stipulations):
>
> 1. All hereditary nobles possessing any hereditary landed property from which *in potioritate* they pay a tax to the Treasury of the Commonwealth. Also their sons *niewydzieleni* [dependents] during their parents' lifetime.
> 2. Blood brothers having hereditary property after their father (and) still childless.

3. Nobles holding mortgages but only those who pay from these holdings a sum of 100 *złoty* in the Tenth Groszy or 10 percent Tax.
4. Nobles holding lifelong landed property who pay from these a sum of 100 *złoty* to the Commonwealth's Tenth Groszy Tax.
5. Nobles in military service possessing (landed) property in their district or land in sufficient quantities (only) when furloughed in peacetime from their command.
6. All (landed) property specified in the above points should be understood as legal if duly acquired and actually held for at least a year.

V. Concerning persons without a voice in the *sejmiki*
1. Foremost the nobility, which does not actually possess the property specified in the present law on the *sejmiki*.
2. *Szlachta* on land, be it royal, church or noble land, though legally hereditary but dependent on private authority (feudal lordship) or obligated to pay rent, dues, or any other private service for the land.
3. *Szlachta* on entailed estates which, though they may be hereditary, require private service.
4. Landholding tenant nobility.
5. Those under 18 years of age.
6. Accused criminals after sentencing or decree even if not final.[42]

The *Ustawa Rządowa* paid glowing but only verbal respect for the sanctity of the centuries-old privileges of the *szlachta*; in its more detailed provisions the Constitution actually disenfranchised about 50 percent of the nobility.[43] Only those adult male nobles could participate in the Commonwealth's political life who were independent individuals unencumbered by economic servitude to other nobles (except parents) or by duty to military authority. It would seem that these restrictions applied as well to nobles who had a mixed portfolio of landed property. The change in requirements for political participation was, therefore, from right blood to right blood plus right property. Political participation became the preserve of economically independent men.

The rationale for this change was the reestablishment of a freer interplay of healthier forces in politics. The contradiction between the theoretical, customary egalitarianism of the *szlachta* and the reality of powerful blocks of improvished or minor nobles dependent on individual magnates produced, among the backers of the Law on *Sejmiki*, an aversion to such groupings in society and an emphasis on the independent individual reminiscent of Rousseau's condemnation of parties in decision-making. The general will according to Rousseau was grounded on the uninhibited judgment of each individual man. Economic dependence distorts this democratic process. In language reminiscent of "Russo" (Rousseau was so popular in the Commonwealth that his name had been Polonized), the *Ustawa Rządowa* declared that "all authority in human society has its beginning in the will of the nation."[44] The reformers in the Four Years' *Sejm* judged that the national will could be exerted only in the absence of an individual's dependence on others and to this end they were willing to sacrifice the ancient privileges that they loudly guaranteed. Interestingly, a commonwealth of independent individuals active in their own government had been typical of civic humanism.

The emphasis on property requirements for political participation was also typical of the liberalism emerging from the Enlightenment and, as with most ideologies, its roots lay deep in the past. This can be seen in the *Ustawa Rządowa*. "Freedom of the person [noble] and of landed and movable property as they served everyone for centuries" is reaffirmed among the privileges of the nobility. In fact, the Constitution recognizes "the safety of persons and of all property to whom it rightfully, legally belongs as the true social bond, the 'pupil' [kernal] of civic freedom." In typical fashion, the main danger to person and property is seen as coming from the king.[45] Thus, the constitution of the nobility yielded guiding principles similar to those of "bourgeois" liberalism.

These principles were consistently applied in reference to reform of the royal towns and existing free cities. However, the status of towns on church lands remained a controversy. While the laws *"Miasta Wolne"* explicitly excluded towns on private lands from the new rights, it remained silent on the issue of church towns. This divided the duputies along lines that were neither traditionalist nor reformist. Stanisław Sołtyk, one of the most fervent supporters of the new constitution, introduced a bill in May 1791 barring church towns from benefitting from the April law on free towns. His bill was solidly defeated (101 to 18) on 21 December 1791 but the issue remained open.[46]

The provisions were such that while half of the nobility was disenfranchized, a numerically similar group of townspeople gained control over their local politics and was restored a voice on the Commonwealth level. Analogously to the *szlachta*, the townspeople were divided according to property lines. Like all nobles, all (presumably adult males) townspeople of the formerly royal cities, except for debtors and criminals, benefitted from the *nec bona recipiantur* and *neminem captivabimus* laws which had protected person and property of the nobility since 1422-1433.[47] A prerequisite for this privilege was acceptance by the townsperson of municipal law and his registration in the "*Xięga mieszczan*" [book of townspeople] modelled on the "*Xięga ziemiańska*" [book of land-nobility]. But unlike the *szlachta*, townspeople could be registered in either of two books: one for "*possessyonatów*" [those possessing hereditary real estate] and another for "*niepossessyonatów*" [all others]. No provisions were made for registering landless nobles while all townspeople were to be registered.[48] Those entitled to be registered in the first book of townspeople, and hence those who had the right to participate in politics as a townsperson, were:

> all *dziedzice* [hereditary property owners], their adult sons, their dependent brothers, *zastawnicy* [mortgage holders] and Christian holders of lifelong property who within three months of acquiring their landholding are obligated to accept municipal law and be registered in the book of townspeople; also those immigrants bringing with them a workshop or capital. . . .

Those registered in the other book were "all residents of the town engaged in trades, crafts or whatever local profession or municipal public service."[49] Presumably the unemployed or "loose people" were not included.

Qualifications for political participation were, therefore, slightly easier for townspeople. All nobles and townspeople enjoyed personal and property security—and the nobles presumably had other unspecified privileges—and in each case those with hereditary real property were admitted to political life. Yet, employed townspeople without property were registered, landless nobles were not; the significance or intent of this is not apparent. For the propertied nobles holding mortgages or lifelong property a substantial minimum income tax requirement of 100 *złoty* was set which apparently did not apply to townspeople holding the same type of property. Moreover, in what was likely an oversight, no restrictions were placed on political participation by townspeople while in military service.

Though property requirements were slightly less stringent for townspeople, the scope of their political activity was more limited than that of the enfranchised nobility. The qualified inhabitants of the former royal, and now free towns, had the right to run their town's affairs but their influence on the Commonwealth level was more modest. For the first time since the seventeenth century, towns received active representation in the Parliament; for the first time ever, all free towns had a voice in national lawmaking. Yet, their representatives were only plenipotentiaries, not deputies, and had a voice only through their membership in the executive commissions. Each town with an appelate court could elect one plenipotentiary; from this group the provincial sessions of the *Sejm*, i.e., the *szlachta* deputies, would choose not more than two plenipotentiaries from each of the three provinces to each of two commissions (Police and Treasury) and three from each province to the *assessorya*, the highest instance of appeal for townspeople, formerly a royal court. In the commissions and the *assessorya*, the plenipitentiaries had a vote on all matters dealing with towns and trade while on all others they only had a consultative voice. As members of these executive and judicial bodies, the towns' representatives had both the right to present before the *Sejm* the towns' *desideria* (similar to the *cahiers de doléance* in France) and the right to participate in the debates—but without the right to vote. No mention was made of the rights of plenipotentiaries not chosen into the executive organs. The admittance of the townspeople into the Parliament could hardly have been more circumscribed.[50]

The fusion of the nobility and the townspeople was also incomplete. Political and legal rights were still weighed in favor of the *szlachta*. Townspeople were strongly encouraged to be ennobled ensuring the cooption of the more vital urban elements into the nobility and consequently weakening the urban estate. Vestiges of the estate system were, thus, far from insignificant.

An issue that caused particular problems was the provision in "*Wolne miasta*" prohibiting suits by townspeople regarding noble extraterritorial enclaves (*juydyki*) after April 1791. This limitation astonished municipal plenipotentiaries. These newly admitted members of the *Sejm* became unusually active in December 1791 on this very issue. Saparski tried in vain to overturn this provision. His speech showed enthusiasm for the new system as a whole—its benefits to elements in the city population were undeniable—but it also indicated an awareness that the new system had actually been created in the interests of the *szlachta*.[51]

Despite the survival of the estate system, a process of uniting the wealthier elements of both the *szlachta* and the townspeople into a common citizenry was initiated. Restrictions on the type of property each estates was permitted to own were lessened. Nobles acquired the right to hold property in the free cities—whereas previously private noble property formed only extraterritorial enclaves within towns—and even to be inscribed into the book of the townspeople and to participate in the internal affairs of their respective towns; townspeople, on the other hand, could for the first time in centuries own agricultural estates but access to the *sejmiki* remained closed.[52]

A second factor favoring the increased bonding of the estates and transcendence above the estates system was the idea of patriotism and specifically the emphasis on utility to the Commonwealth. The *Ustawa Rządowa* declared the desire to strengthen the state as the main rationale for enfranchising the townspeople of free and royal cites and for giving them self-government.[53] The traditional acknowledgement of heroic military service to the Commonwealth being rewarded with ennoblement was now augmented by recognition of economic service. A concerted effort was made to attract foreign skilled labor and capital and to reward outstanding economic achievements.

The principle of public utility brought political rights to townspeople but not to the peasantry. In a potentially revolutionary move, however, the Constitution extended the protection of the law to the peasantry. The wording of the measure was purposely vague making contemporaries unsure as to its exact meaning, except for the stipulation that all new agreements between the peasant village or individuals and a property holder (noble or bourgeois) were guaranteed by the state with the peasant having the right to appeal injustices to the Commonwealth's (and not the landowner's) courts. The rule of law was therefore, theoretically, greatly expanded. The justification for this was expressed in some of the most eloquent and honest language in the *Ustawa Rządowa*:

> The agricultural people, from whose hands flow the most abundant wealth of the country, who comprise the largest

population in the country and equally the country's most potent strength, so through justice, humanity and Christian obligation as through our own well-understood interest, are accepted under the protection of the law and the government.[54]

New peasant immigration was encouraged by granting personal freedom to all new arrivals and to all returning former residents of the Commonwealth. These could then conclude contracts with landowners which would be backed by the power of the state and sanction of the law. No provision was made to enable peasants and new immigrants to acquire full rights to plots of land but neither were any obstacles placed in their way; this was especially true in the case of new arrivals. The Constitution, therefore, encouraged population growth and the enlargement of the surviving free peasant element.[55] This sufficed to greatly alarm Catherine II who declared "that the greater part of our Byelorussian peasantry would leave for Poland and the remainder would cause me unrest."[56]

The reforms of the Four Years' *Sejm* sought to bind the inhabitants to the Commonwealth not by force but by common interests. Religion had been a divisive factor since the Counter-Reformation and hence religious groups were courted. Roman Catholicism maintained its position as the "ruling religion" and conversion from the Roman Church was prohibited but the practice of other religions was to be unencumbered.[57] Efforts were made to increase the loyalty of the Uniates by granting the Metropolitan of Rus', Archbishop Teodozy Rostocki of Kijów (Kyyiv), a permanent, full seat in the Senate. Among the final legislation of 1792, considered during the war with Russia, was a comprehensive law reforming the Uniate Church.[58] This work, however, was not completed before the "temporary" adjournment at the end of May. Interestingly, the Orthodoxy of about 15 percent of the population concentrated in the eastern Byelorussian and Ukrainian borderlands was viewed as a sign of disloyalty, vigorously encouraged by Russia, and was strongly discouraged.[59]

Patriotism and social utility also manifested themselves with reference to military service. The *Ustawa Rządowa* declared the army as the levy (*wyciąg*) of the nation's strength. This terminology reveals either careless use of language or an essential transformation in the definition of nation (*naród*). Scholars, including Kaczmarek and Kowecki, believe the latter was the case. All social groups were to serve in the Commonwealth's army: nobles, townspeople, peasants, Roman Catholics, Uniates (Greek Catholics), the Orthodox, Protestants, Jews, Polish speakers, Ruthenian speakers, Lithuanian speakers, German speakers, Yiddish speakers, and combinations of these. Military service had been the basis of *szlachta* equality. Could it be that the reformers sought to include all the diverse groups living in the Commonwealth in their definition of "the nation"?[60]

To summarize several observations can be made. First, as was characteristic of emerging liberalism in the contemporary Enlightenment, the possession of property became one of the most important qualifications for participation in the representative and administrative systems. Thus, the richer stratum of townsmen was given the vote and partial representation in Parliament while the poor nobility was excluded. The theoretical equality of the *szlachta* gave way to the inequality typical of classical liberalism. Social utility determined political rights. This served to break the inordinate power of the magnates who had utilized the numeric strength of impoverished members of their estate but at the same time it infused the remaining nobility with the fresh innovative spirit and wealth of the more successful bourgeoisie.

Second, the concept of nation was expanded past the traditional (at least since the sixteenth century) confines of the *szlachta*. It was gingerly extended to include all the inhabitants of the Commonwealth, even serfs on private estates who for the first time in centuries were placed under the kind of legal protection extant for church and royal peasants. The sense of loyalty and membership now became more modern because of its greater inclusiveness and this national identity remained, on the whole, political and was neither of the ethnic nor the integral variety that would have limited the Polish nation to Polish speakers.

But this nationalism was not democratic. The reforms created three categories of men. The first was a combination of nobles and bourgeoisie who qualified to take part in the political processes. The second was the un- or disenfranchised nobility and bourgeoisie both of whom had certain rights but no political voice. These two categories would be analogous to the active and passive citizens in the French constitution from later in 1791. Finally, the rest of the population would form an unprivileged majority who, however, were acknowledged by the *Ustawa Rządowa* as having a stake in society. All groups had the ethical responsibility to defend the country.

These sociopolitical reforms were at once quite radical and quite moderate. In the broader context of Eastern Europe they were nearly revolutionary, surpassing in the political sphere those of Joseph II. National sovereignty was postulated over rule by an "absolute" monarch whether justified by reason or by divine right. Economic utility, rather than the sanction of simple heredity or royal prerogative, became the basis for social distinctions. Self-government was given to the royal towns and the peasants were placed under the protection of the law. The Commonwealth's neighbors became alarmed by this seemingly Jacobin threat to their own society's base.

In the more narrow confines of domestic constitutional development, the principles of political involvement and nation expressed in the reforming laws of the Four Years' *Sejm* were progressive with features approximating a Western bourgeois ideology. The reforms modified the estate system—and their implications or logical development (viewed in hindsight) could have led to the transformation of this essentially feudal political system into a capitalist one—but a revolutionary reshuffling of society and the total elimination of legal inequality was not a part of the compromise behind the May Third Constitution. The idea of sovereignty in the nation—the nation as the source of all secular authority—was at once modern ("enlightened" and "bourgeois") and ancient ("aristocratic" and even "sarmatian"). Crucially, the shift in the definition of nation (*naród*) and of political rights preserved the dominance of the nobility minus those elements who, by a more modern definition of social utility (economic rather than immaterial – "virtue"), were undesirable. No doubt townspeople benefitted. No doubt even peasants found something beneficial. No doubt the reforms were a real act of collective political generosity by the *szlachta* which was redefining itself. The prime objective, nonetheless, remained to preserve "the well-understood interests" of the *szlachta*.[61]

Structure of Government

The redefined political rights were only a part of the great reforms. The stated purpose of the Four Years' *Sejm* was to ensure the safety of the Commonwealth. In addition to changing the social base of support, the major effort of the assembly was to construct an effective governmental system tapping the vital strengths of the country—ultimately for an effective military defense. Even a new hybrid enfranchised body of citizens could not defend their republic against foreign pressures and ensure internal well-being without an efficient administration. Shunning the powerful governments of Poland's absolutist neighbors, the reformers sought to build a modern system grounded on traditional constitutionalism.

National sovereignty was postulated as superior to rule by an absolute monarch, whether justified by divine right or human reason. This old and fundamental principle in Polish political thought emerged as exceptionally modern in the context of ideological changes in eighteenth century Europe. The *Ustawa Rządowa* further stated that law and authority in human society come from the nation and that authority is divided into three kinds: legislative, "the highest executive" and judicial.[62]

Three secondary principles bolstered this central, cherished basis of the polity. The thrust of the new system was towards centralization. The formulation "highest executive" is rather odd since reference was made not only to central executive organs but also to local ones. The terminology served to emphasize, however, the shift from administration at the *sejmiki* level during the decentralization of the Saxon period to the construction of a revitalized central government. Similarly, legislative authority was identified with the *Sejm*, though the scope of activity alotted the *sejmiki* was far from insignificant.

In addition to focusing on the national level, the Constitution weighed the system in favor of the legislature. The three types of authority were conceptually distinct but the three branches of government were neither entirely separate nor entirely equal.

Third, the old ideal of unanimity was jettisoned in favor of majority rule, i.e., majority rule within the enfranchised minority. The *Ustawa Rządowa* declared "everything everywhere should be decided by majority vote." This overstated principle reflected a modern respect for qualified equality and, in the specific setting of Polish politics, majority rule was also an efficiency measure. Collegiality appeared as an extension of majority rule. Decisions in the executive and judiciary organs, as in the legislative, were all to be made by votes and not through the discretion of one individual. Hence, the *liberum veto* and all confederations were completely and permanently abolished.

The basic institutional features affected by the Constitution are a topic of continued debate among scholars.[63] The old *Rzeczpospolita* was transformed in the rational spirit of the Enlightenment accommodated to indigenous constitutional traditions.

The Constitution abolished the dual system of government created by the Union of Lublin in 1569 but it did not end the union as such. A more integrated state was created with only vestigial institutional distinctions between the Crown and the Grand Duchy and divided into three equal provinces: Wielkopolska [Great Poland], Małopolska [Little Poland] and Litwa [Lithuania]. The final legislation came on 2 October 1791 with the passage of "Mutual Assurance for Both Nations" and the administrative standardization of 2 November 1791.[64] The "Mutual Assurance" ended the trend towards complete integration with a compromise. Lithuanians received a special numeric advantage in the unified institutions. Also the uniform division of the Republic into three provinces each with 10 *województwa* and 68 deputies to the *Sejm* had another significance. This reapportionment was needed to harmonize representation with demographic realities.[65]

The mathematically elegant system only partially produced this equity. Reapportionment benefitted Małopolska and Lithuania but Lithuania was more than just one of three equal provinces. In the legislative process, Lithuania held a third of the votes after its incorporation of Polish Livonia. But in at least two executive commissions it was treated as an equal of the entire Crown. Thus, half of the commissioners of the Treasury and the Army were to be Lithuanians and the presidency of the commissions was to alternate between Lithuanians and persons from the other two provinces. (The Police Commission seems to have been a different case.) In a sense then, the legislative disproportion which had favored Wielkopolska-Mazowsze was replaced by a executive disproportion in favor of Lithuania. The Grand Duchy became an equal, but special, province.

The centralized government was reconstructed according to the principle of a greater separation and balance of powers. In language reflective of progressive eighteenth century political thought and the pressing circumstances of the Polish revolution-in-the-making, the *Ustawa Rządowa* declared in order that:

> the integrity [or entirety] of the state, civic freedom and social order may be permanently preserved in balance, the government of the Polish nation should consist of three authorities and by the will of the present law these should

forever consist of *legislative authority* in the assembled estates, the highest *executive authority* in the king and the *straż*, and *judicial authority* in jurisdictions established for this purpose or about to be established[66].

A permanent balance of national integrity, civic freedom, and social order ensured by the neat compartmentization of authority—this succinctly summarizes the spirit of the May Third Constitution.

Despite the eloquence of the *Ustawa Rządowa*, the reformers were inconsistent in their designation of the three authorities. The three branches referred to were limited only to the central government, yet, the actual reforms extended to the very lowest levels of the political system. This inconsistency could be eliminated by interpreting "*rząd*" [government] as always referring to just the central organs. But in each article devoted to each particular authority all the institutions from the highest to the lowest were described, though the point of emphasis is on the central level. Maintaining this emphasis the three branches may be summarized as follows:

Legislative Authority

The *Sejm* remained the focus of popular sovereignty and exercised a monopoly over lawmaking, the budget and taxation. The upper chamber, the *senat*, lost most of its influence and after the death of the present king, Stanisław August, was to become partly elected. The lower chamber, the *izba poselska* [Chamber of Deputies], held the real power and its 204 members were elected biennially at the local *sejmiki* [dietines] by landowning nobles; significantly, as mentioned earlier, the cities were once again represented, this time 24 plenipotentiaries who exercised limited voting rights. In the words of the *Ustawa Rządowa*, the Chamber of Deputies formed "the temple of lawmaking."

Parliamentary procedure was rationalized. All bills, whether proposed by the king but brought to the *Sejm* in the form of *instrukcje* drafted by the local dietines or new projects proposed by representatives (only members of the Chamber of Deputies could introduce new legislation) were first screened by a committee of five (with each province represented) and were debated by the two chambers according to the order, categories and voting requirements outlined in Table 4.

Each bill had to first be passed by the Chamber of Deputies before it could be introduced in the Senate. This insured the preponderance of the two hundred and four representatives of the *sejmiki* who, under the leadership of the marshal, constituted the national organ for creating law, i.e., the organ of national sovereignty. Though the Senate was not abolished, as some reformers during the Four Years' *Sejm* had wished, this 132 member assembly of *wojewodowie* [palatines], *kasztelanowie* [castellans], bishops and ministers under the presidency of the king could do little more than use a suspensory veto to delay the enactment of legislation by two years; if passed again by the Chamber of Deputies in the next Parliament that bill would become law.

Table 4

Passage of Bills in the Sejm

TYPE OF BILL	DESCRIPTION	% NEEDED FOR PASSAGE IN EACH HOUSE
I. *Prawodawcze* ["Legislative"]		
A. Political Law	"Whatever pertains to the perfecting and correcting of specific statutes concerning the form of government without altering the fundamental law entitled, *Ustawa Rządowa*"	two-thirds
B. Civil Law	"Those laws which establish standards by which citizens should behave among themselves with regard to property, relations and agreements"	simple majority
C. Criminal	"Those laws that describe which acttions by citizens are crimes and what their punishment should be"	two-thirds
D. Taxes	"Permanent offerings and taxes for the enlargment of the public treasury"	three-fourths

II. *Uchwały Sejmowe*
["Resolutions"]

First category	"Whatever pertains to the conclusion of federal and offensive treaties with foreign powers, dispensation of the army, contraction of public debts permanent organization of the army and the levying of military taxes"	two-thirds
Second category	"Those bills which include trade treaties and related material, proclamations of peace, allocation of treasury funds, temporary wartime levies, coinage and those that may affect national education without alterring basic principles"	simple majority of both houses

III. *Dezyderje*

Individual requests from the provinces, and palatinates, lands, districts, and whatever concerns internal order the army's internal administration, improved organization of the treasury ennoblement of foreigners and Poles.	simple majority of both houses

The *Sejm* was effectively restructured from an institution comprising three estates ("knightly estate," "senatorial estate" and "royal estate") into a unitary representative body of the enfranchised. The independent status of the senators was slated for gradual elimination by the stipulation that replacements for lay senators were to be nominated by the king and confirmed by the *Sejm* during the remainder of Stanisław August's reign while in the future the king would only be able to nominate one of two candidates chosen by the *Sejm*. The ministers in the supreme executive council, the *Straż Praw* [Guardian of the Laws], were excluded from the Senate. The status of bishops did not change.

The king no longer constituted a separate estate but became the president of the Senate with the power to break tie votes. The royal prerogative of formally calling the *Sejm* was made obsolete with biennial ordinary *Sejmy* scheduled for a seventy day session beginning on 1 October not counting Sundays or holidays and with a possible prolongation of thirty days.

The position of the *Sejm* was further enhanced by the creation of the *Sejm gotowy* or "ready *Sejm*." The law on parliaments stipulated that the *Sejm* must always be ready to convene during the entire two year period between elections to the "*ordinaryjny*" *Sejm* in times of crises such as war, "internal disorders threatening revolution, the collision of governmental agencies," threats of famine, the king's death or serious illness and in the event of the king's insistence on a measure rejected unanimously by the *Straż Praw*.[67] Representatives and senators were obligated to assemble at the place and time stipulated by letters issued four weeks prior to the emergency *Sejm* and sent to the local civil-military administrative commissions for distribution to each of them. Very importantly, should the king refuse to convene the special *Sejm*, the *marszałek sejmowy* (*Sejm* marshal, an official elected first as a representative of a local district of citizens and then by the Chamber of Deputies as its leader) had the power to do so.

In essence, the Chamber of Deputies made up of representatives of the nation became a self-directed institution for the first time in Polish history. The "lower" chamber subsumed the other two estates and together they constituted an always "ready" parliament whose members were elected by district but were representatives of the entire nation. The always ready *Sejm* was intended to ensure continuity of lawmaking. To adjust broader constitutional questions, special constitutional parliaments were planned for twenty-five-year intervals to update the Constitution and the first of such assemblies was scheduled for 2 October 1816. In this way the vital process of expressing the national will in legislation and adjusting the political system to changing realities were to be safeguarded.

On the *województwo* and *ziemia* [land] level, the basic legislative organ was the *sejmik* ["little Sejm"] of which there were three types in each jurisdiction: the *sejmik elekcyjny*, the *sejmik relacyjny* and the *sejmik gospodarczy*. The first of these, the electional *sejmik*, chose all the elected offices on the local level of noble government: the members of the civil-military administrative commissions, the judges to the *sądy ziemiańskie* or noble courts of first instance and also the representatives to the *Sejm*. In addition, the electorial dietine drafted "instructions" for the representatives who under the new system were not bound by them. The *sejmik elekcyjny* was a combination of the old *sejmik elekcyjny* which had elected the local judges and the *sej-*

mik poselski whose sole purpose had been to elect deputies to the *Sejm* and write their instructions. The second type of dietine, the *sejmik relacyjny* was the continuation of the ingenious old system by which representatives of the local district reported back to their constituents after the adjournment of the *Sejm*. This served both to inform the local citizens of national events and to control the actions of the representatives whose mandate could be revoked and who could be faced with public sanction and the disapproval of their peers at home. Finally, the *sejmik gospodarczy* or economic dietine combined the old *sejmik deputacki* and *sejmik gospodarczy* by electing members of the provincial Tribunal courts and attending to general local needs without, however, possessing the right to tax.

The statute on *sejmiki* (28 May 1791) strictly delineated their functions and composition and specified their terms, permanent meeting sites and district boundaries (redrawn to a nation-wide standardized plan in November 1791). In their biennial meetings, the *sejmiki* were headed by a marshal with the assistance of an "administrative circle" consisting of senators and other dignitaries among the local nobility, or in the case of the *sejmik elekcyjny*, of a six member "electorial commission." Issues were decided by majority votes of all the present eligible voters and approved resolutions were gathered into *lauda*. A move to introduce secret ballots to the local assemblies was voted down after heated debate. A prominent feature of the *sejmiki* under the May Third Constitution was the voters' registry called the *księga ziemiańska* [book of the landed nobility] which was a significant rationalization of the political system.

Article VI of the *Ustawa Rządowa* affirmed the law on the *sejmiki* as "the most relevant and basic principle of civil freedom" since it was on this level, specifically through the *sejmik*, that each enfranchised person entered into the legislative process. The Four Years' *Sejm* brought to fruition the arrested trend to recentralize legislative powers back onto the national level by restricting the authority of the *sejmiki* over matters such as taxation and military recruitment. The *sejmik gospodarczy* still administered to some needs of the *województwo* or land but the actual, important lawmaking occurred in the *Sejm* while the *sejmik elekcyjny* was limited to debating bills proposed by the king, preparing *instrukcje* reflecting the views of the local nobility and drafting *dezyderja* concerning local needs to be handled by the *Sejm*. The only effect that a citizen could have on the formation of national laws if he were not elected to the *Sejm* was through the choice of representatives and the drafting of the *instrukcje* and *dezyderja* at the election *sejmik* and the taking to task of returning representatives. The centralization tendency was most pronounced considering that the deputy had become a representative of the entire nation.

Executive Authority

The executive branch was also strengthened and expanded. Employing what would become a standard definition of the executive, the *Ustawa Rządowa* stated that "the executive authority is strictly responsible to keep watch over the laws and their fulfillment."[68] For this end a rather intricate three tier system was constructed—a system perhaps too cumbersome to work very efficiently. At the top, the king functioned as the president of the council called the *Straż Praw*.[69] This combined authority was the somewhat curious result of the attempt to solidify the brittle institution of the monarchy while preserving the principle of sovereignty originating with the nation. The Constitution declared the king as "the father and head of the nation" entrusting him, under specific conditions and controls, with the nation's administration. In an endeavor to provide a stable and continuous government, the monarchy became hereditary in the Saxon house of Wettin with subsequent dynasties being elected by the nation, the king's person remained inviolable and the king was bound to the new political order and to specific *pacta conventa*.

The reintroduction of a hereditary monarchy ironically was antirevolutionary in nature from any perspective except the Polish. While barring any possibility of growth towards "absolutism," the Constitution did, nonetheless, strengthen the governmental apparatus by converting the monarchy from an elected to a hereditary one. No longer was the king to be the direct choice of the enfranchised but also no longer would he be the choice of foreign meddlers. The strengthening of the monarchy would be anti-revolutionary in the context of the French Revolution, as pointed out by the Constitution's supporters, but by making this more "normal" monarchy into a tool for popular rule (understood with qualifications) it likewise appeared dangerously subversive to the conservative monarchies of the region.

In the context of Polish constitutional development this was perceived by many as finally the long-dreaded introduction of absolutism. Whereas before every noble could help elect the king and then renounce his allegiance should the monarch break the Henrician Articles and his particular *pacta conventa* or should the king become incapacitated, in the new Constitution the king could not be controlled. The king could not be elected nor was he accountable to society even though he was king "by the grace of God and the will of the nation." Kings by their nature sought *absolutum dominium* and as in the Roman Republic, sovereignty would pass from the citizens to the *princeps* and finally to an *imperator*.

Yet the powers of the hereditary king in the May Third Constitution really were quite limited. As before the king nominated the bishops, senators and ministers within the stipulations of the law, exercised authority over the army in wartime, held the power of clemency and headed the administration. Though immuned, the king was no longer an independent force; he could only act as head of the administration and then only through his council, the *Straż Praw*, where he was only one of many and each royal act had to be countersigned by at least one minister. Apart from this function his authority was neglible except in time of war.

Instituted as the highest executive organ, the *Straż Praw* formed a constitutionally regulated body in which the king's power combined with the nation's in a central control agency over the Great Commissions and ultimately over the local administrative bodies. A redundancy existed in the fact that "all decisions given by the *Straż* can only be issued through the intermediacy of the government commissions." Thus the council of ministers did not include the heads of the commissions of police, treasury, or army although it did include the head of the Roman Catholic Church in the Republic as president of the National Education Commission. The *Straż Praw* served as a kind of clearinghouse for matters concerning the separate major commissions. What may appear as a redundant institution towards the top of the system seems more logical when it is viewed as a trans-

Table 5

Straż Praw

MEMBER	OBLIGATIONS
(voting)	
King	
Primate (president of Na-	communicate all relevant laws and recommendations from the *Sejm* to the governmental commissions.

tional Education Commission) Ministers of Police War Treasury	receive reports from these commissions and present them to the king and council at the appointed time. convey properly authorized royal decisions in the council to the commissions for execution. report every violation or negligence of the law by the Commissions.
Minister of the Seal (Interior)	communicate all relevent laws and recommendations from the *Sejm* to the courts. receive reports from the courts concerning court registries and the attendance records of judges. report any transgressions of the law by the courts. convey censures and reminders from the king in council to the courts. report to the king all *sigillaty* issued from his chancellery. apply the council seal to every royal decision properly countersigned by one of the ministers. maintain the council's chancellery for internal affairs.
Minister for Foreign Affairs	contact with the Commonwealth's foreign representatives. conferences with foreign ministers temporary foreign negotiations and protection of the state's foreign interests; these to be reported immediately to the council. enforcement of foreign treaties; in war-threatening situations: summon the *Sejm* and protect all the Commonwealth's foreign interests and citizens abroad. maintain funds allocated by the *Sejm* for foreign affairs. inform the council of all foreign negotiations. supervise diplomatic personnel; enforce the oath. report to each regular *Sejm* on the progress of foreign policy, negotiations and the disposal of funds.
(non-voting) *Marszałek sejmowy*	ensure that the *Sejm*'s directives and laws are properly carried out. ensure that the *Sejm gotowy* is convened when

	prescribed by law; convene it himself if need be. examine all the council's records. ensure the absolute secrecy of matters related to foreign affairs.
Royal heir	membership upon reaching adulthood and swearing allegiance to the Constitution; no duties or vote.

formation of the monarch. The king and the council were to be essentially one entity. "The king in council" fused the hereditary king with top elected officials into a kind of collective monarch.

Subordinated to the *Straż Praw*, the second tier of the central administration was, nonetheless, directly responsible for the realization of domestic policy and the execution of political and administrative laws. The Great Commissions were charged with administering four services deemed essential for the *Rzeczpospolita*'s prosperity: education, the armed forces, treasury and internal order (police).

In many respects, the most important for the long term well-being of the Republic was the Commission of National Education established in 1773 as the first institution of its kind anywhere and incorporated with few modifications into the new Constitution. The Commission consisted of four representatives and four senators elected every six years by the *Sejm* and presided over by the primate. The *Sejm* Committee for the Rectification of the Form of Government, the official constitution-framing body, expressed the Commission's function in modern patriotic or nationalistic terms. The Commission was charged with insuring that "the citizenry's youth will be conditioned through standardized education and instructions into citizens who love the nation's freedoms (and) care for their integrity and are competent to fulfill their duties so that freedom and love of the fatherland may in this same spirit be bequeathed to future generations."[70] The Commission supervised a unitary system of secular schools including two universities (at Kraków and Wilno), district schools in the larger towns and elementary schools planned for every Catholic parish in the Commonwealth. Among these were newly founded teachers' institutes and schools for women and Jews.[71] The formation of a comprehensive national academic policy and curriculum affecting everyone from peasant to royal heir was withdrawn from the *Sejm*'s jurisdiction and entrusted to the Commission of National Education. This would seem to indicate an increased awareness that not only was national education vital but that it required centralized direction that was, at least, partly professionalized and detached from shifting parliamentary processes.[72]

Unlike the semi-autonomous Commission of National Education, the other Great Commissions were designed as variations of a particular administrative model applied to specific fields of activity. The Great Commissions' presidents were drawn from the appropriate royal ministers—titular vestiges of the old system—while the commissioners were elected at the biennial meetings of the *Sejm*: fifteen for the Police Commission (three senators, six "from the knightly estate" and six municipal plenipotentiaries); fourteen for the Army Commission (two senators, six military men and six civilians); sixteen for the Treasury Commission (two senators, eight members of the *szlachta* and six municipal plenipotentiaries). Parliamentary representatives were prohibited from serving on the Great Commissions. These salaried commissioners, along with their archives and staff, performed the primary administrative functions in the Republic.

In many respects, the Army Commission's scope of activity was the most circumscribed though it encompassed the most urgent tasks. The Commission was limited to administering the army's finances and supplies; purely military considerations, such as army regulations, were beyond its jurisdiction. Funds covering soldiers' pay, uniforms, ammunition, and equipment were drawn from the Treasury Commission while forage and food came from the local populations and were administered with the aid of local civil-military administrative commissions. In addition, the Army Commission maintained the "invalid fund" and reported quarterly to the king and biennially to the *Sejm*.

The Treasury and Police Commissions, on the other hand, extended their responsibilities beyond primary services such as tax collection and public tranquility. Administration of and the desire to expand public finances prompted the Treasury Commission into an active policy of improving conditions for internal trade and manufacture.[73] The safeguarding of public order and the supervision of the free towns also included the promotion of "general comfort" (*wygoda*) of the nation which included "the abundance and cheapness of basic materials, facility in production, exchange and transportation, the freedom to sell all goods by eliminating all monopolies . . .," followed by the general administration of the postal service, "supervision over public properties serving the population's comfort, health and entertainment," that is, everything from bathhouses to saloons and public theatres and finally "universal care and charitable assistance for every form of poverty, destitution and infirmity due to old age and invalidism" and the employment of beggars and prisoners in public works.[74] Each Commission was given complete freedom to develop concrete methods for fulfilling these objectives but, as a consequence, they were obligated to give an accounting of their activities in biennial reports to the *Sejm* and the commissioners were answerable before the Sejm's courts.[75] Frequently the actual implementation of specific projects created by the Treasury and Policy Commissions was performed by the administrative commissions at the lowest level of the national executive system.

As with the Great Commissions, the local civil-military administrative commissions came under the supervision of the *Straż Praw*. In actuality, this supervision was indirect and most of the interaction was between the local commissions and the Great Commissions respective to their powers and obligations: with the Commission of National Education over the running of parish schools,[76] with the Army Commission concerning the recruitment and quartering of soldiers, the stockpiling of military supplies and the protection of the civilian population from the army itself, with the Treasury Commission concerning all fiscal and economic matters and finally with the Police Commission over the administration of the free towns.

The civil-military administrative commissions were apportioned to districts according to population and service in them was a kind of apprenticeship made mandatory for promotion in the government. These commissions, moreover, became tools for the local execution of the national laws and programs as well as the more circumscribed directives of the local economic dietines.[77]

Judicial Authority

The May Third Constitution reorganized the Commonwealth's courts into a dual system: in civil and criminal cases courts based on social classification were retained; in cases between civilians and the military or between individuals and public institutions, newer courts attached to governmental agency were created.

Contrary to the theoretical separation of legislative, executive and judicial powers, legislative and administrative bodies possessed their own courts which could prosecute their own officials, subordinate agencies and even punish private individuals for transgressions against the institutions' integrity or for failure to execute orders or directives. The entire administration had the power to impose, at times substantial, fines without trial. The judicial function of settling all disputes between civilians and the military was the most "relevant" primary duty of the civil-military administrative commissions but to prevent them from overextending their jurisdiction, the members of these commissions were answerable to the provincial Tribunal courts for trying improper cases.

Table 6

The Court System

Court System I: Civil and Criminal Cases

Social Classification	Court
Nobles	1st instance: *sądy ziemiańskie*: ten member local courts elected by the dietines 2d instance: *trybunały*: 25 member (34 in Lithuania) provincial courts elected by dietines *sądy graniczne*: two instances elected by dietine to delineate town and village boundaries
Peasants a) private b) royal c) church	*sądy dominalne* [lord's court] *sądy referendarskie* [royal courts] church courts –all had the right to appeal to the royal courts
Townspeople	1st instance: *sądy miejskie*: municipal courts with mayor and four elected judges 2nd instance: *sądy wydziałowe*: district courts with six elected members 3rd instance: *sądy asesorskie*: one in Warsaw, one in Wilno consisting of one chancellor not in *Straż*, 4 nobles and 4 townspeople elected in provincial sessions of *Sejm*

Court System II: Civil-Military and Private-Public Cases

Governmental Agency	Jurisdiction
Sejm	crimes against the nation or the government
Marshal's court	criminal cases involving security of king or Sejm
Treasury Commission	violations of the public treasury, forging of treasury notes, appeals of inheritance cases and trade matters involving breached contracts between citizens and foreigners extensive accountability of municipal officials
Army Commission	second instance for all cases between civilians and the military
Police Commission	cases concerning the finances of free cities, auctions, weights and measures
Civil-Military Administrative Commissions	first instance for all cases between civilians and the military
Special appelate court for Courland	all cases

The governmental system as a whole was not designed to follow an absolute separation of legislative, executive and judicial powers despite its professed intentions. Only the judiciary, strictly speaking, did not assume lawmaking or executive functions; in all other institutions there was overlapping. Not only did the central governmental commissions have their own courts but they also indirectly affected the legislative process by having their members regularly attend sessions of the *Sejm*, though without the right to vote. The king was the head of the executive branch, yet, he also was president of the Senate and had some residual authority in the courts.

The broad powers of the *Sejm* (and specifically the Chamber of Deputies), however, were of another magnitude altogether. This "temple of lawmaking" not only chose but held accountable the members of the Great Commissions. Even the *Straż Praw* had to explain its actions to the *Sejm*. The executive apparatus was clearly distinct but not independent. Moreover, the *Sejm* had its own court which, if given a loose interpretation, could try most any case it regarded to be of national importance. Apparently, the *Sejm* court had the power of judicial review on the constitutionality of laws. The system had a clearly stated ideal of three separate and presumably equal branches but a reality in which each overlapped in certain instances on the others and the legislature predominated.

This domination of the *Sejm* is neither surprising nor inconsistent with the concept of sovereignty of the nation. Law has only one source, the nation. Therefore, it is the nation's prerogative, if not its duty, to ensure enforcement of its laws through its representatives. There were three conceptually distinct stages in the actualization of the nation's will but there was only one source of law, and one final judge of its efficacy.

Summary

In general, the May Third Constitution was an elastic and growing set of statutes centered on the *Ustawa Rządowa*, distinct but not necessarily contradictory to cardinal law, which redefined the rules for participation in the polity according to a mixture of noble interests, traditional civic humanism and modern liberal-bourgeois elements and which restructured the governmental apparatus along republican lines and eighteenth century principles of efficiency. The newly defined nation reflected a transformation of patriotism and nationalism among the *szlachta*. The long established consciousness of unity based on the political rights of the *szlachta* was being broadened to, in some way, embrace all the residents of the country, though active citizenship was dependent on property qualifications. The new governmental structure was designed to securely ground lawmaking powers in the nation while effectively channelling them through collegiate bodies, strengthened by a hereditary, but safely harnessed, monarchy. This reorganization of the governmental apparatus, according to the revived principle of comprehensive and stable administration and the expansion of the political systems social base, synthesized a generation of reform efforts.

Perhaps most crucial to the Constitution was the reform of the executive which counteracted the old assumption that weakness was the best guarantor of freedom. From time immemorial, with some exceptions, that part of the state which manifested itself in real actions had lay securely in the king's hands. The basic failure of the Polish-Lithuanian system from the mid-seventeenth and throughout the eighteenth century had been the limitation of royal power without the creation of an effective state apparatus controlled by the *Sejm*. The problems had collectively been only half solved: "absolute" monarchial rule had been unequivocally stifled but the administration continued to be thought of as the preserve of the king. In practice, the Four Years' *Sejm* departed from this tradition and it actively governed the country. In its Constitution, the *Sejm* returned this function to the king as part of the neat triad division of government, yet, it also made sure that the king would be dominated by the nation represented in the legislative branch.

The tragic flaws of the old Commonwealth's political system seemed at last to have been solved. The change was part of the conservative approach to reform adopted in the Four Years' *Sejm*. The language sounded like Montesquieu's but the separation of powers did not depart from Polish political tradition. In fact, it had a striking similarity to the mixed form of government expressed in the sixteenth and seventeenth centuries by Andrzej Frycz Modrzewski and Szymon Starowolski. The succinct 1632 characterization of *demokracja szlachecka*, given in chapter one, can be read in reference to the reformed system presented in the May Third Constitution:

> Authority in Poland consists of three basic and simple forms of a republic, which comprise one, a few or many governments, that are all to a certain degree based on the equality of law. We, therefore, have a king not from heredity but created through an election, who is the highest executor of laws established at the *Sejm*. We have a senate chosen from the most prominent nobility and called to the enforcement of these laws. We have the *Sejm* deputies, elected through free voting in every province and selected to pass laws at the *Sejm* who act like tribunes limiting royal power and the excessive authority of the senate.[78]

The division of power and its functions are similar. The king in 1632 and 1791 was seen as not only "the executor of laws" but of "laws established at the *Sejm*." The separation of powers was in both cases tempered by the predominance of the parliament. A distinct judicial authority for "the enforcement of these laws" existed but in contrast to the earlier conception, the new system provided for a separate set of courts different from the Senate which, as the seat of "the most prominent nobility," in reality the magnates, was overshadowed by the Chamber of Deputies. Finally, the legislative power remained concentrated in the *Sejm* and specifically the lower chamber of "freely elected" deputies who would also be charged with overseeing other parts of the government.

The spirits of the two forms of government were similar. But some changes appeared after 150 years. As mentioned, the function of the Senate was altered and its theoretical classical role transferred to the courts. The second difference, and one that brought much controversy, was the source of royal power. In *demokracja szlachecka* after 1572, each king was elected; in the May Third system each dynasty was elected but within the royal family the succession of power became hereditary. This was a substantial change that looked back to the state of affairs under the Jagiellonians. Third, the emphasis on a balance of the "one, few, or many" was reformulated as a balance of different powers in the government rather than in society.

More striking is the association of the division, separation and balance of powers with the rule of law in society and equality before the law for a significant portion of society. In centuries past, the *szlachta* had acquired privileges and political power, now those benefits were being reapportioned even as far as to include the peasants in the provision that lord/serf agreements would be guaranteed by the government. A major rallying cry of eighteenth century reformers imbued with Enlightenment ideals seems to have been taken for granted by Starowolski as part of *demokracja szlachecka* even during the time of magnate predominance. This continuity is clear and the latent modernity intriguing.

Though Edmund Burke probably never heard of Szymon Starowolski, the two seem to have agreed on the ideal form of government. According to Burke, the British state possessed an ancient constitution expressing the "original contract." This constitution was fixed in "King, Lords and Commons," the British equivalent of "*król, senat and sejm.*" Interestingly, Burke connected the "ancient constitution" with the concept of contract so popular in eighteenth century political thought. The contractual nature of government was a fundamental assumption in Poland, institutionalized in the Henrician Articles and the *pacta conventa*. Burke justified revolutions only to reestablish the balance in the mixed government of the ancient constitution. The May Third Constitution likewise sought to correct an imbalance by first, reintroducing hereditary kingship which had existed until the extinction of the Jagiellonians and second by reducing the power of the senate i.e., the magnates. Burke's analysis seems valid. "Everything was kept in its place and order; but in that place and order every thing was bettered."[79]

Yet, the consequences of this proved disastrous. Shortly after the Russian invasion in 1792, the Four Years' *Sejm* "temporarily" adjourned itself handing over the administration and total control over the prosecution of the war to the king, Stanisław August. The war was not rigorously pursued, surrender came all too easily and the grand edifice of constitutional reform was abandoned.

The reformers had intended that the *Ustawa Rządowa* provide a unitary schema for a growing political constitution that would be supplemented by, and serve as a foundation for, two projected constitutions, one "moral" the other "economic."[80] Events decided otherwise. The May Third Constitution, instead served as a point of departure for the more radical, democratic, reforms of the 1794 Kościuszko Uprising.

In the aftermath of the Russian-Targowica victory in 1792 and in the universal shock of the Second Partition, the leaders of the reform movement issued an extensive two-volume defense of the May Third Constitution, entitled, *O ustanowieniu i upadku konstytucyi polskiey 3go maia 1791* [Concerning the establishment and fall of the Polish constitution of May 3, 1791] in which the recently defeated work was repeatedly declared as "the last will of the perishing fatherland."[81] Potocki's and Dmochowski's judgment was partisan, propagandistic and hauntingly correct. Though the 1788–1792 reforms were superceded in radicalism by those of the Kościuszko Uprising, they were not surpassed in scope and precision. In the following century of occupation, the May Third Constitution possessed an aura of sanctity to patriotic Poles as an unequivocal statement indicating a healthy revival in the old Commonwealth on the verge of its destruction. The modernized constitutionalism of May Third remained as relevant as the idea of independence. Yet, neither the Duchy of Warsaw nor the Congress Kingdom nor the Second Republic self-emergent at the end of World War I was the Poland of the May Third Constitution. The former two states mirrored their sponsors (France and Russia) and the intervening century had brought sweeping changes throughout the continent making all previous reforms obsolete. From the historical perspective, the progressive 1791 Constitution is, therefore, necessarily inverted back towards the annals of the old Commonwealth mirroring parliamentary traditions and changes at the beginning of a national awakening and disaster.

CHAPTER 3

PARLIAMENTARY PROCEDURES AND THE FOUR
YEAR' SEJM IN LIGHT OF STANISŁAWIAN
ANTECENDENTS

The May Third Constitution was truly a turning point in Polish history. The seemingly endless labor of the Four Years' *Sejm* had, quite suddenly, produced the foundations of a new order. But the lasting significance of the Constitution was not what its framers had intended. The promise of an effective government based on the rule of law produced by a relatively broad section of society prompted neighboring states to destroy the Commonwealth. Consequently, the Constitution became a legend—the last will and testament of a dying fatherland. The May Third Constitution as a legend served to preserve the idea of a vigorous state guaranteeing cherished freedoms. Each generation through 1918 would be willing to risk life and property to recreate that ideal.

But another legacy has attracted less attention. The activities of the Four Years' *Sejm* have left behind a rich picture of political culture. The formulation and enactment of legislation expressed in concrete form the representative will of the Polish-Lithuanian nobility. The passage of laws expanding the military and the treasury constituted the primary function of the Four Years' *Sejm* which in the specific historical conditions of intensified domestic political awareness and a favorable international climate produced continuously expanding reform culminating with a comprehensive restructuring of the governmental system. The processes of forming and passing laws was crucial to the final product and expressive of current political culture.

The legislative process and its theoretical justification grew out of past practices and significantly influenced the character of the reforms. Methods of handling political proposals, conceptual categories determining the manner in which they were decided, and traditions of political representation had an importance at least equal to the individual imput of *Sejm* members each of whom had the right to propose bills. Since debates in the parliament were frequently punctuated by confrontations of actual procedure with norms prescribed by law or by the adaptation of spontaneous behavior to structured methods and previously enunciated principles, attention can arguably be placed initially on the legal framework of the legislative process. These parliamentary procedures used in the Four Years' *Sejm* had been shaped over the centuries by practices of varying efficacy. Most recently, old customs had been modernized in the early parliaments under Stanisław August and consolidated through repeated use in the *Sejmy* of the 1770s and 1780s.

Majority Rule, the Principle of Unanimity and the Institution of the Confederation

Legally, majority rule was the guiding principle for the passage of laws during the Four Years' *Sejm*; the confederated state of the 1788–1792 parliament suspended the customary requirement for unanimity. The two norms, however, continued to coexist uncomfortably during the Four Years' *Sejm* and in actual practice unanimity, though not required, was still preferred.

The central importance of the majority principle is evident in the oaths taken by the two leaders of the Chamber of Deputies, Stanisław Małachowski, the marshal for the Crown, and Count Kazimierz Sapieha, the marshal for the Grand Duchy of Lithuania:

> I will not issue any sanctions or private acts under any title, or assignats, but only those matters will I place among the *Sejm*'s acts which were decided *per pluralitatem* by the confederated estates; in the counting of ballots and the announcement of *pluralitate* I will behave with integrity. If in any matter a senator, minister or deputy should order a secret ballot then, in the order stipulated by law, I will proceed, one after the other, accurately and justly count these votes and announce the majority decision. Only in tax matters will I not accept secret ballots but will receive votes orally and announce them to the convened estates; and that all activity may be known to the estates and the country I swear to behave in this way upon danger of their becoming invalid. So help me God.[1]

Such was the legal norm not only for the leaders but, in a general sense, for all members of the *Sejm*.

Centuries old parliamentary practices exercised a strong influence, however. One of these was the majority principle itself. Prior to the restriction of the *liberum veto* in 1768 and its complete abolition in 1791,[2] majority rule was practiced in the *Sejm* for the election of the marshal and committee members and also during parliaments which had been confederated. Actual procedure in the Four Years' *Sejm* blended legal norms with public habits from old traditions. Two equally old principles competed: the unanimity norm of regular parliaments and the majority rule of a confederation. Both sprung from the early popular institutions of the medieval Polish state and both were backed by the very potent force of ancient tradition.

The unanimity principle is most commonly identified as the fatal flaw of the Polish parliament. Rightly so, but the use of the unanimity principle, in the form of the *liberum veto* to adjourn parliaments, had been a relatively recent development. Traditionally, the *Sejm* (whose origins date to the 1400s) operated successfully with the norm of unanimous decisions. Unanimity was reached through compromise and, in the end, each law received the approval of all members. Each deputy (but none of the senators) had the right to initiate negotiations through his free voice (*liberum veto*). This was considered a most consistent and logical practice to protect the rights of individuals and of local areas represented by the delegates. Oppression by the majority was, thus, theoretically eliminated. While never praising the pre-May Third system, Burke observed that "the very faults in the constitution of Poland made it last; the veto which destroyed all its energy preserved its life."[3]

In 1651, the *liberum veto* was used for the first time not to initiate compromise but to end a parliament. The delegate exercising his free voice fled, which prevented any possibility of compromise. Those left behind felt obligated to respect his objection.[4] Twenty-one years after this first use of the *liberum veto* to insist on an extreme adherence of the unanimity principle by actually breaking up the *Sejm*, the ancient institution of the confederation was first applied to an ordinary *Sejm*. Traditionally applied to parliaments only during interregna, the confederation was used as a means of overcoming the danger of dissolution because of the absence of a complete consensus. Thus, less than a generation after the practical (but not legal) establishment of mandatory unanimity as a fundamental part of the "golden freedom" of the Polish parliamentary system, a counterweight was adopted for some emergency situations.

The confederated *Sejm* originated from the separate institution of the confederation, an emergency union of forces based on a distinctly medieval binding by personal oaths with the aim of executing a particular policy, a phenomenon which, according to Gierowski, had been common to medieval Europe and survived at least until the seventeenth century in the Holy Roman Empire and in Scotland where it was known as "covenant."[5] Commonly viewed as a violent symptom of the *Rzeczpospolita*'s political chaos, the confederation actually was perceived by Polish contemporaries as perfectly legal. And even foreigners were not unanimous in their condemnation. The French General Dumouriez, who participated in the Confederation of Bar (1768–1771), saw nothing more legal than the act creating this revolutionary institution.

Confederations had a firm foundation in traditional law made evident through a series of proclamations and in patterns of behaviors.[6] In a confederated *Sejm*, all three estates (the king, the senators, and the knights) held their meetings jointly and all decisions were made according to the majority will as was the practice in all confederations.[7] Eleven *Sejmy* were confederated between 1672 and 1788–92 inclusive. Each was, therefore, theoretically devoted to one purpose and its members took a personal oath to remain bonded together until that purpose had been achieved.

In the 118 years between the first confederated *Sejm* and the abolition of confederations by the Constitution of 1791, there persisted a reluctance—exaggerated by the imposed confederation of the Partition *Sejm* in 1773–1775,[8]— to permanently apply this form of personal allegiance to ordinary sessions of the Parliament. A perfect consensus remained the ideal even after the application of the majority principle to certain *sejmiki* in several the palatinates of the Crown in 1764 and 1766[9] and the limitation of parliamentary *liberum veto* in 1768.

In the late seventeenth century, modifications in ordinary parliamentary procedure had been tried as a means other than a confederation to limit the abuse of the essential freedom to demand unanimity,[10] but to little avail. Somewhat more effective, and less unpopular, was the use of *prorogata* or extensions of parliaments for additional time to work out compromises. The beginning of Stanisław August's reign in 1764 brought the first institutionalized limitation of the *liberum veto*.

The 1768 law entitled, "Parliamentary Order," sought to establish procedure in the *Sejm* for all time by making it more explicit and by amending statutes passed four years earlier, which experience had shown to be too ambiguous and incomplete.[11] The restricted principle of unanimity and the codes of parliamentary procedure passed in 1768 remained in force until the Four Years' *Sejm* despite the retraction of other reform measures which had been pushed through the 1768 parliament by the king and the Czartoryski family with the intent of significantly strengthening the monarchy. Recent publications have described in general terms the changes in parliamentary procedure.[12] Concerning majority rule, the 1768 law confirmed the established practice that both the selection of the marshal and the verification of deputies' credentials (the so-called *rugi* or expulsions) should be decided *in turno*, that is, by a roll call vote with a simple majority deciding the issue. As a significant innovation the statute incorporated the changes in rules governing the passage of laws as stipulated in the "Second Separate Act" of the 1768 Eternal Treaty between the Commonwealth and the Empress of All the Russias. This act was subtitled ". . . including the cardinal laws of the Polish Commonwealth for eternity maintained and never subject to change and the *materiae status* which only by unanimity should be decided in a free parliament." Thus, article seventeen reads:

> The *liberum veto* in free parliaments in *materiae status* should always be maintained in full force and these matters of state are always to be decided by unanimous votes. (The treaty) maintains for all time the power of each member of the *Sejm* to destroy the activities of the *Sejm* in *materiae status* through one specific contrary free vote given either orally or through a manifesto.[13]

The clause at once seemed to expand the scope of the *liberum veto* and to preserve the old counterbalance of the confederation. The destruction of a *Sejm* through a manifesto against a particular proposal among the *materiae status* seemed to imply that the member of the *Sejm* perpetrating the veto need not actually be present at the given session. On the other hand, the clause refers only to *Sejmy wolne* [free *Sejmy*] and not to *Sejmy skonfederowane* [confederated Sejmy][14] and to *materiae status* or state matters and not to all issues considered in debates.

Thirteen clauses in the "Second Separate Act" list the *materiae status* and repeatedly emphasize the requirement for a complete consensus if any one of them were to be changed. The matters of state consist of the following:

(1) taxes
(2) the size of the army
(3) alliances, "connections," unions, friendships or trade agreements with foreign powers
(4) declarations of war and peace treaties
(5) full rights for the newly ennobled and for accepted foreign nobles are extended only after three generations; holders of public offices or *juryzdykcje* should be well *possessionitatis* in the Commonwealth[15]
(6) the type and value of all domestic money and all foreign currency accepted for use by the Treasury Commission
(7) changes in the power and prerogatives of the Ministry of War and Peace in the Crown and in the Grand Duchy as well as court positions in the country; the creation of new offices in both parts of the Commonwealth and at all levels
(8) rules for the *Sejm* and the *sejmiki* passed by the present parliament
(9) obedience owed every public office, the value of decrees and the prerogative of the *Trybunał* and those of the Grand Duchy
(10) the power of the *senatus consilia* established by the 1717 *Sejm* (confirmation of the budget of this body will however belong to the economic matters)
(11) acquisition of hereditary landed property in the Commonwealth by the king
(12) calling of general mobilization
(13) property rights.[16]

These areas covered the more important functions of government and, therefore, the 1768 Treaty and Statute permitted only a limited circumscribed variety of legislation to be free from the constraints of mandatory unanimity. This attested to the persistent mortification of the government and the limited sovereignty of the country in the mid-eighteenth century, even after a generation of peace. Those matters not subject to the *liberum veto* were, however, greater than in the 1651–1768 period and permitted steady growth in basic legislation.

Beginning in 1768, the majority rule applied to *materiae aeconomica* defined as matters covered neither by cardinal (unchangeable) laws nor by *materiae status* (changeable but only by a unanimous vote). The nature of this material can be seen in the issues passed during regular *Sejmy* in the following two decades. Of the nine regularly scheduled parliaments between 1768 and 1788 only five were actually held and not confederated: 1778, 1780, 1782, 1784, and 1786; two, 1770 and 1772, were not held because of the wars of the Bar Confederation, an extraordinary parliament functioned under Russian supervision from 1773 until 1775, and the 1776 *Sejm* was confederated. In general categories, laws passed by these ordinary *Sejmy* were as follows:

Table 7

Laws Passed by the Sejm 1778–1786

	MATERIAE STATUS	MATERIAE AECONOMICA			
		Executive Regulation			Other
		Election*	Censure	Directive	
1778		10	13	2	16
1780		14	2	1	15
1782**	4	6	0	0	10
1784	2	10	5	7	22
1786	2	12	5	2	10

*Election and review executive commissions
**The 1782 *Sejm* was interrupted.

The ordinary non-confederated *Sejmy* between the passage of the 1768 procedural laws and the Four Years' *Sejm* did produce a reasonable amount of *materiae status* and *materiae aeconomica* legislation. Formal unanimity was met on eight trade and diplomatic measures (*materiae status*). Half of the *materiae aeconomica* reviewed, corrected, directed and elected the central administrative organs, in particular, the *Rada Nieustająca* (Permanent Council), the central governing council between *Sejmy* created by the confederated *Sejm* of 1776 in violation of the cardinal laws.[17] The other half constituted lawmaking in the strictest sense. Of this legislation, measures directed at specific individuals occupied a significant portion:[18]

1778	6 out of 16	(37.5%)
1780	6 out of 15	(40.0%)
1784	3 out of 22	(13.6%)
1786	3 out of 10	(30.0%)

With the apparent exception of the 1778 Walewski-Herburtowski decision,[19] these "private cases" all had public aspects and were either ennoblement legislation or cases involving individuals connected with the *Sejm* or in dispute with a foreign power or private persons but only in public capacities. Particularly plentiful were matters related to the tenure or administration of lands belonging to the king or the state.

Legislation in the "other" *materiae aeconomica* category, exclusive of these "private cases," formed the strictly legislative body of measures that, along with some of the regulation of the executive organs, altered or supplemented established elements in the conduct of public life. This diversified legislation included measures guaranteeing a monopoly of the nobility in the Department of Foreign Affairs (1778) and in the officer corps of the *Szkoła Rycerska* [Knightly Academy] (1780), various new guidelines for the administration of government lands (mainly in 1778 and 1780 but also in 1786), order for post-parliamentary *sejmiki* (1778), quotas for Lithuanians in the *Szkoła Rycerska* (1778), regulation of notes of credit (1778) and the lifting of their prohibition for nobles (1780), national debt management (1778, 1780 and 1784), rewards for outstanding military service by individuals and groups (the Tatars) (1778 and 1786) and official gratitude for private donations of men and arms to the armed forces (1784), recruitment restrictions (1780), a consumption law (1780), prohibition of the veniality of military offices (1784) and fiscal reform for the Tarnów diocese (1786). Much of this legislation possessed a tone of noble or conservative reintrenchment but this did not prevent the extension of cultural and welfare services. The 1780 *Sejm* made mandatory the gratis deposition of one copy of each work published in the Commonwealth both at the Załuski State Public Library in Warsaw and at the Wilno Library. The same parliament passed a bill expanding local administrative authority and concern over hospitals.

Army reform and codification of the legal system were special concerns of these regular, unconfederated *Sejmy*. Interestingly, the 1778 parliament directed that army legislation be postponed until 1780, at which time it would be considered *per pluraritatem*. The constraints of the 1768 "eternal treaty" persisted in the shadow of the recent partition and with the very evident Russian presence limiting the resulting law (actually a cluster of seven laws) to improved administration of existing military resources. Codification of the legal system was, however, not under similar restriction and became a central topic of the *materiae aeconomica*, though, the 1780 parliament emphatically defeated the long-awaited law code of Stanisław August compiled by Andrzej Zamoyski and forbade for all time its reconsideration. Nevertheless, in 1784 no fewer than fifteen laws were passed codifying trial procedure throughout the Commonwealth and these were further refined by the following parliament.

The enacted *materiae aeconomica* legislation indicates the productivity of the parliament under the 1768 provisions showing the concrete issues on which members could agree free of the *liberum veto*. Because of the limited sovereignty of the Polish-Lithuanian Commonwealth at this time, the framers of the legislation eschewed radical reform and could not address vital issues such as actual expansion of the military forces; improvements were made in the existing structures. Expansion of the central administration continued in this relatively stable and creative period through the combined actions of the *Sejm*'s monitoring of the executive offices, the rationalizing efforts of the central organs themselves and the benevolent supervision of the king. Moreover, participants in the political system on the Commonwealth level grew more accustomed to mundane, productive activity at the center of which was the reformulated principle of majority rule.

By the convening of the Four Year's *Sejm* in the fall of 1788, therefore, majority rule in the central legislature was used to select officials and committee members of the parliament and the executive commissions, to control the activities of the executive, to attend to national matters of varying importance and to litigate public cases of private individuals. Additionally, on the national level the majority principle was used in clearly defined emergencies, that is, in the confederations, in the National Education Commission and in the Treasury and Army Commissions expanded in 1775.

On the local level, however, the majority principle was the accepted norm for political life after 1764. The kernel of the "golden freedom" was legally prohibited in many *sejmiki* while others used it much more sparingly than at the national level. This is a most interesting fact. The persistence of the majority principle in the *sejmiki* accounts, in part, for their acquisition of national governmental functions during the period of parliamentary paralysis stemming from the abuse of the *liberum veto*. The difference in the principle of decision-making arose from a distinct perception of the nature of the local bodies. The close-knit association of nobles on the *województwo* level assumed bonds, a commonality of life, which did not require the safeguard of the "free voice" to protect the minority or individuals from the tyranny of the majority. The force of neighborhood life assumed a convergence of interests, and perhaps even of blood, which simply obviated the need for such a mechanism.

The reverence for, and the growing reliance on, the "free voice" in the *Sejm* had reflected a concern that regional or neighborhood interests, not necessarily individual concerns, might suffer as a result of wider political life.[20] Interestingly, the rationale of *liberum veto* proponents paralleled the concept of general will offered by Rousseau. Majorities of any kind did not equal the accord that must be at the heart of a true community. Until the mid-seventeenth century, political culture had been high enough to accommodate unanimity. But just as the military prowess of the Commonwealth began to be undermined with a half century of rebellion and invasions, individuals seemed to have taken for granted the polity's strength even with the paralysis of the *Sejm*. In situations where individuals refused to compromise, the extension of the explicit practice of majority rule on the republic level through the confederation of *Sejmy* beginning in 1673 indicated the continued cohesiveness, however imperfect, of the Commonwealth. Acceptance of the majority principle presupposed a permanence of the consensus for the existence of the body politic. This often subconscious awareness of national bonds among the nobility was expressed in literature and speeches, usually of questionable value, but it was also made more explicit in a second political move. The distinction between the *materiae status* and the *materiae aeconomica*, almost a century later, attested not only to the Commonwealth's limited sovereignty but it also reflected a growing sense of national ties among individual neighborhoods and the nobility as a whole. Explicit majority rule in clearly defined cases processed in normal national life enunciated these bonds of Republic-wide unity. The final enthroning of the majority principle by the *Ustawa Rządowa* in 1791 "everywhere and for everything"[21] proved a victory for this national consciousness and cohesiveness in a modern form that actually resurrected the *de facto* state of affairs prior to the mid-seventeenth century.

An uncomfortable coexistence of the rational, practical principle of majority rule and the conservative, radically democratic and usually highly idealistic, espousal of unanimity characterized the Four Years' *Sejm* throughout its lengthy sessions. A day prior to the adoption of the confederation on 7 October 1788, Franciszek Kwilecki, substituting the old marshal,[22] pleaded in his keynote address:

> After fulfilling the law concerning the first activities of the *Sejm* and justifying myself before our worthy colleagues, I am confident that I need not encourage our Brothers to unanimity and concord, to the rejection of private interests, to unity of thoughts for the good of and the help of our beloved Fatherland because with this purpose we have been sent to this place by our Brothers remaining in the country.[23]

Much time was spent in the 1788–1792 *Sejm* by a given majority in attempts to persuade the minority to abandon its opposition. The most extreme example of this were the lengthy debates on 22 December 1789 concerning an article of the bill entitled "Principles for the Form of Government." The crucial point to disenfranchise landless nobles from participation in the local *sejmiki* was blocked effectively for a long time by the young and scrupulous Sapieha, the Lithuanian marshal, and by Józef Mierzejewski, a deputy from the Podole *województwo* and long-time client of Hetman Branicki. A roll call would have succeeded but it was never called. Sapieha conceded first and in the end, hours of stubborn opposition by Mierzejewski against the exclusion of "his brothers" evoked repeated pleas from the king that the deputy "withdraw from creating hardships in this point" and, as the editor of the *Dziennik czynności Sejmu* [Diary of *Sejm* Activity] recorded, that "out of shear humanity he permit the conclusion of this material." Mierzejewski complied but the respect for dissenting opinions and the desire to achieve, at least tacit, unanimity on the essential issues caused the loss in the king's own words "of truly salvific time."[24]

The pursuit of unanimity was explicitly intended to save time (although such efforts themselves could be time-consuming) and as a way of maintaining general political consensus. The last argument was used most often by the king. The most important issues concerning the basic interests of the nation were, in practice, to be approved only through a complete consensus even when the agreement of the

Sejm members was unenthusiastic and only in appearance.

This was especially true of the May Third Constitution. Soon a myth was created to encourage support for the new system. The events of 5 May 1791 were interpreted as a manifestation of unanimous support for the *Ustawa Rządowa*. Numerous speeches employed this theme. On the following 22 September, the king, attempting to build a consensus for a new note to be sent to the Saxon court,[25] referred to the "consensus" four months earlier:

> the memorable days of May 3rd and 5th when the doubled gathering of deputies, through unanimous agreement, gave us the work of happiness and prosperity for the nation.[26]

The note was sent but the political strategy of a mythical, perfect accord may not have been wise. The artificial unanimity from 5 May 1791, enforced rigorously by "The Declaration of the Gathered Estates" of the same date and by "The Declaration Concerning Manifestations" from 9 December 1791[27] resulted in frustration among of the opposition, secret or repressed doubts and the dangerous example of establishing a rule of law by breaking existing law. "The Declaration of the Gathered Estates," dated May 5th, and often taken as part of the *Ustawa Rządowa*, in effect, forbade opposition. The "*Deklaracja względem manifestów*" from December reacted briskly to opposition.

> Whoever would decide to enter manifestos or protests against the *Sejm* now in session or against the *Ustawa Rządowa* or whoever in the Republic would decide to accept such manifestos into the public record, that person will be regarded under power of this law as a disturber of the peace and he should be taken to the *Sejm*'s courts and punished for undermining public tranquility.

All such manifestos and protests already recorded were declared nonexistent. This law, however, did solemnly safeguard the right to criticize the Constitution in public debates. Such a provision was adopted "to end cynical or angry interpretations" of the Constitution. And, of course, the "*Deklaracja względem osób woyskowych nieprzysiąłych*" from 22 January 1792 did strip the future Targowica confederates Adam Rzewuski and Szczęsny Potocki of their army positions. The myth of unanimity and the restrictions on signs of disatisfaction would have worked only if the concurrent cooption of opponents had produced truly loyal supporters. This seems to have been the case, yet the gamble yielded an outcome contrary to the intentions and interests of the reformers. The principle of majority rule, though more familiar because of recently acquired parliamentary habits, was still regarded as inappropriate for matters of fundamental importance.

Procedures and Proceedings

Despite attempts at inspiring or forcing unanimity the opposition proved to be too significant or stubborn in 120 cases during the more than 500 sessions of the Four Years' *Sejm*. In these cases, roll call votes called *turni* were taken. The procedure for *turni* was simple. All members of the *Sejm* could propose a roll call vote at anytime which, however, did not ensure that one would be conducted. The *Sejm* leadership often tried to steer the united chambers away from a *turnus*, debates on the wording of propositions would sometimes last up to three days and, on occasion, there were *turni* among proposals for *turni*. Once agreed upon, the roll call would proceed first among the senators and ministers and then the deputies, all in an established order of districts and importance (the latter only for the ministerium). Since each vote could be accompanied by a speech, *turni* would last up to four hours; new *legitis curiatae* [house rules] eliminated the confusion caused by speeches and votes given out of turn. A secret ballot could be ordered either before the *turnus* or with a member's vote. The oral roll call proceeded regardless of the request for a secret ballot; such requests, however, could not be denied except for tax bills which were restricted by the Act of Confederation to oral votes. In practice, requests for secret ballots were often withdrawn especially when the margin in the *turnus* was large. The results of the secret ballot were final.

Under specific circumstances, then, the *turni* were the focal points in the enactment of legislation in the *Sejm*. As such they constituted critical moments in the activity governed by the parliamentary procedure codified in the 1768 statute and modified by three laws passed during the Four Years' *Sejm*: "Solemn Conferral of Order in the Present *Sejm*" (5 January 1791), "Abolition of the 1768 Constitution entitled 'Parliamentary Order' in Respect to the Point Describing the Decision of Bills According to Categories" (6 February 1791), and the fundamental law "*Sejmy*" (28 May 1791).[28] These statutes were complemented by laws accelerating the processing of specific matters and details in the outlined procedure were determined by tradition.

For its first two years, the Four Years' *Sejm* operated according to the provisions of the 1768 statute modified by the adoption of a confederation. The statute regulated three types of parliaments: ordinary, extraordinary and convocational, with the most attention accorded the first mentioned and most common. Activities of the ordinary (or regularly scheduled biannual) parliaments were divided into four periods although the statute did not stipulate them as such. Though confederated the Four Years' *Sejm* was considered "ordinary." A summary of the regulations governing ordinary parliaments provides a view of the norms governing, in part, the *Sejm* of 1788-1792.

The description of the first period concentrated on the proceedings of the House of Deputies prior to its first joint meeting with the Senate. Beginning two days before the formal opening of the *Sejm*, written complaints against the deputies could be brought to the marshal of the previous parliament. Charges would include irregularities in electoral procedures or personal complaints against new deputies; in either case, the accusing party or its plenipotentiary had to file a copy of the charges for which they would receive a receipt. These complaints were considered behind closed doors after the opening of the new *Sejm*. All decisions in these ejections (*rugi*) were made by majority votes. Deputies-elect against whom complaints had been filed but who were absent during the consideration of their cases would not be confirmed in their posts and would suffer legal "infamy."

In the continued absence of spectators, the election of the new marshal of the Chamber of Deputies was conducted after the completion of the *rugi* and the departure of those deputies-elect who had been "butted." No interruptions between these two functions were allowed although in the Four Years' *Sejm* Wojciech Suchodolski from the Chełm *województwo*, one of the fervent "*gaduły*" or chatterboxes of the parliament, attempted to raise a separate issue and justified this breach of rules by his right to free speech.[29] The nomination and voting for the new marshal began with the first *ex ordine* deputy of the *województwo* heading the order of districts in the province whose turn had come up for holding the marshal's staff with the three provinces, Wielkopolska, Małopolska and Lithuania, alternating. The new marshal, of necessity, had to come from one of the leading districts and his election, *ad turnum* i.e., by roll call and majority vote, had to be completed by the end of the third session. In the Four Years' *Sejm*, Stanisław Małachowski from the Sandomierz district was elected by acclamation. The swearing in of the new marshal and his assumption of the *laska* or staff, the symbol of his authority, from his predecessor had to occur in the presence of the deputies and the newly admitted spectators.

The selection of other officials and committees followed. The new marshal chose his secretary from among native born noblemen. Two representatives (either deputies or senators) of each province were likewise chosen by the marshal to the Constitutional Committee empowered to verify the proper processing of each submitted bill. Next, members of the *Sejm*'s court (six individuals per province) were chosen as were delegates for each of two committees, one to audit the books of the Treasury Commissions and another to review the actions of the Army Commissions. In *Sejmy* after 1768 these were multiplied to include commissions examining the *Rada Nieustająca* and the Commission of National Education.

After exchanging delegations, the two chambers finally united to greet the king.[30] According to custom, each member of the *Sejm* kissed the king's hand. This show of respect initiated the second period in the activities of the *Sejm* which consisted of the following: the reading of the *pacta conventa* between the king and the nation accompanied with a free discussion of these terms,[31] a reading of royal propositions to the parliament, material remaining from the previous *Sejm*, until 1775 the resolution of the *senatus consilium*, royal nominations of senators to the Constitutional Committee and to committees designated to evaluate the work of executive commissions, the oaths and signatures of these nominees, the presentation of reports by ambassadors to other countries and of the examining committees, the election of new members of the executive commissions, and the free expression of views on public needs by the senate and the ministerium. The last mentioned was to occur *non ex turno*.

The most crucial legislative activity was scheduled for the third period during which the two chambers were once again separated with the Chamber of Deputies returning to its usual meeting place. Economic matters were treated first. Each member of parliament had the right to submit bills to the marshal who under no circumstances could refuse to accept them. The bills, however, were screened for ambiguities by the Constitutional Committee though the authors had the final say on the bill's wording and the committee and marshal could only present their objections and corrections when the bill was initially read before each chamber. The marshal and the Constitutional Committee also categorized each bill as either *materia status* or *materia aeconomica*. During each daily session appropriate bills were read aloud by the parliamentary secretary and printed copies were distributed to the senators and deputies by permanent ministers, the Great Marshals or in their absence the Court Marshal of either the Crown or Lithuania depending on the venue of the *Sejm*. A deliberation time of at least one day was stipulated for each bill after printed copies had been distributed. In the event that unanimity was not reached on a particular bill after this period of deliberation, each chamber still meeting separately was to concurrently conduct a roll call vote or *turnus* under the direction of either of the Great or the Court Marshals in the Senate and the *Sejm* Marshal in the Chamber of Deputies. Each *turnus* could be repeated (a provision which seemed never to have been used in the Four Years' *Sejm*) and a secret ballot conducted upon the wishes of any of the parliamentary members. The method of conducting a secret ballot was identical to that practiced in the law courts called the *Trybunały* and will be described later. The final result of each vote was communicated to the other chamber by a special delegation and the combined majority determined the acceptance or rejection of the bill; voting, therefore, was not strictly speaking by order. Ties were resolved by the king's vote communicated to the chambers by the Crown or Lithuanian Marshal. The marshals were responsible for announcing the final decision and, along with the Constitutional Committee, for signing the approved bills.

The coordination of activity between the two chambers appears to have been complicated and problematical. Moreover, the clear attempt at orderliness evident in the 1768 statute produced a curious stipulation that was to cause much delay and frustration in succeeding parliaments. Each project could be divided into subcategories (not just *materiae status* or *materiae aeconomica*) and each part of the bill so distinguished could be subject to a roll call.

The period of separated chambers concluded with the consideration of matters of state. As indicated these bills could pass only by unanimous votes. The use of the *liberum veto*, the *nie pozwalam* or "I do not allow" declaration of a member of parliament not only rejected the presented bill under consideration but nullified all previously approved *materiae status* and forbade the discussion of additional measures. The safety of the person using the *liberum veto* was guaranteed by the 1768 statute even after his departure from the *Sejm*, a condition reminiscent of the first *nie pozwalam* in 1651 by Sociński who exercising it immediately left Warsaw, to the frustration of fellow *Sejm* members eager to dissuade him. In this provision the constraints on ordinary, unconfederated, *Sejmy* are most evident.

In the final phase of the *Sejm*, the two chambers were rejoined to promulgate the newly approved laws. All bills passed in the current parliament and, in case of an envoked *liberum veto* only approved economic measures, were read aloud and compared to original copies. The final legislative activity of the *Sejm* was the signing by the *Sejm* marshal and the Constitutional Committee of the constitution, i.e., the compilation of new laws and the registration of these laws by the same marshal in the *gród*.[32] The *Sejm* ended with a second kissing of the king's hand.

The 1768 statute, "Parliamentary Order" also specified the substitution of the *Sejm* marshal by the first dignitary of the province from which the excused marshal came,[33] and the chronology of the parliament. The opening of the *Sejm* was moved from the Monday after St. Michael's to the first Monday after St. Bartholomew's (August 24th). Accordingly, the *sejmiki poselskie*, held six weeks prior to each *Sejm* to elect the deputies and to formulate their written instuctions and particular wishes (*dezyderia*) of the districts, were moved till after St. Margaret's. Denoted were also the periods segregating the parliament's activities. The election of the marshal had to occur by the third day of the *Sejm* and the first joining of the chambers by the second day thereafter. The second period was to last until the end of the second week, the third from the beginning of the third week till the end of the fifth and the last period was apparently limited to the concluding week.[34] The statute further stipulated that each session must end by 8:00 p.m. unless a roll call had been begun.[35]

The 1768 statute proved satisfactory for over twenty years although it did not ensure smooth running or productive parliaments. The enumerated procedure was complemented by customs of lesser importance developed over the long history of the *Sejm*. The kissing of the king's hands, already mentioned, was a custom of great symbolic importance. Seating arrangements were never officially established though the order was fixed. The selection by lot of special committee members employed a young child picking out colored balls from a vase as the names of parliamentary members were read one by one; a black ball indicated selection, a white one rejection. This was innocence in the realm of politics.

Parliamentary procedure in the Four Years' *Sejm* modified the 1768 statute to suit the needs of a confederation and ultimately the perceived national emergency. The Act of Confederation suspended the *liberum veto* and technically limited the debates solely to military and fiscal matters. The Declaration of 6 December 1788 stated that there would be no time limit for the parliament while in the end the final adjournment date was set at 30 June 1792.[36] The two chambers were permanently united with leadership of the parliament passing to the *Sejm* Marshal (Małachowski) who was concurrently marshal of the Confederation in the Crown and to a lesser extent to the Lithuanian Marshal of the Confederation (Sapieha) chosen from among the Lithuanian delegates. The filling of committees and commissions was not completed as usual in a solid block at the beginning of parliament but rather it was interspersed among legislative debates: the Constitutional Committee was selected prior to other business but the Army Commission was filled on 27 December 1788 and the *Sejm* courts only on 19 June 1789. Finally, the state of confederation dictated majority rule in all questions and possible secret ballots on all matters brought to a vote other than taxes. Formal procedure for confederated *Sejmy* had never been compiled but the debates of the Four Years' *Sejm* indicated that all other house rules were followed.

The "Act of Confederation" stated that the solemn goal of the present *Sejm* was

> to eliminate dangers which in so many forms may threaten our Fatherland . . . by not chinsing on offering from our property for the increase of the Commonwealth's [strength] to the extent that our well considered abilities permit.

Later proceedings of the *Sejm* expanded the scope of business to more comprehensive domestic reforms and to the consideration of all matters of importance to the Commonwealth, in particular to what contemporaries called "*forma rządu*" [form of government]. Private interests were prohibited.[37] The original and eventual goals were clearly, logically interrelated. Expansion of the army required taxation, greater revenues required economic growth to avoid draining the country's resources, economic growth necessitated an almost endless array of measures from the regulation of rivers, roads and transportation to accurate statistics and rewards for increased production or for greater immigration and finally the significantly larger army, increased revenues and active stimulation of the economy required a much more developed central administration. Implicit behind the reforms was the creation of an expanded, efficient government. Thus, as the prolonged sessions of the *Sejm* showed, the task undertaken by the "Act of Confederation" was actually the repair of the entire Commonwealth. This task had been the subject of discussion for generations as neglect had worsened the situation and as conditions changed on the continent during the eighteenth century.

The "*Prorogacja*" [Prolongation] of 6 December 1789 declared the term of the *Sejm* open-ended. Debates consumed far more time than anyone had anticipated and it became apparent that the 1788 *Sejm* would not finish its task before the scheduled elections for the 1790 *Sejm*. Initially delaying the elections until February 1791, the *Sejm* reversed its stance and rescheduled the *poselskie sejmiki* for 16 November with the provision that both sets of deputies would serve in the new *Sejm* beginning on 16 December 1790 and that the newly elected members would be asked to join the confederation. During its second half, the Four Years' *Sejm* possessed a Chamber of Deputies twice its normal size reducing the political power of the Senate in conditions of majority rule. The presence of up to 155 senators and 359 deputies plus the king did not facilitate a speedier formulation of legislation to comprehensively reform the Commonwealth. Moreover, to a far greater extent than before, the *Sejm* actually behaved as an executive authority running much of the government in the period between the dismantling of the old offices and their replacement with permanent new structures.

The generally recognized slowness of the *Sejm* was not, however, solely due to the ambitious, exhaustive scope of the intended reforms and the added responsibility of closely monitoring the entire government. Abundant contemporary criticism focused on the apparent ineffectiveness of the proceedings and the eternal longwindedness of most of the parliamentary members. Traditional styles of rhetoric favored wordiness for its own sake; empty complicated phraseology devoid of meaning after years of mechanical repetition and obfuse expressions of politeness inevitably added much time to the inately complicated task of repairing the Commonwealth. Moreover, some individuals used the traditional baroque style of speech-making as a sometimes mistaken means of improving their public images or as a means of forestalling reform.

Not surprisingly, towards the end of the first term of the *Sejm* a committee was created to draft a modified set of *legis curiatae* or house rules. The move was prompted by the impending doubling of the Chamber of Deputies and it was unclear whether these were intended to be permanent or simply temporary until the more comprehensive reform had been passed. The work of the committee was initially discussed in the second week of December 1790 but final debates were delayed until after the arrival of the new deputies on the 16th. The result was the 5 January 1791 statute, passed 30 December 1790 and entitled, *Uroczyste zaręczenie porządku Izby na teraźnieyszym Sejmie* ["Solemn Conferral of Order in the Present *Sejm*"].

This, the first of the laws modifying parliamentary procedure during the Four Years' *Sejm*, contained thirteen clauses. The law addressed very fundamental issues and provided solutions reflecting a general agreement in the *Sejm*.[38] All senators and deputies should remain in their places. This basic item of order was repeated in article 11—apparently it remained a problem. Basic etiquette was to be imposed by article 5 forbidding speaking out of turn or *interlocutorie* (i.e., among those assembled).[39] On each bill or point under consideration a member was allowed to speak only twice: once before and once during the *turnus* (articles 4 and 6).

The remaining articles described modified rules for the passage of laws and for voting. It was required that each session should pass at least one project or clause daily (article 4) which led, contrary to earlier practice, to numerous late night sessions with some lasting as late as 4:00 a.m. Projects relevant to the given topic at hand were to be selected by the confederation marshals and the Constitutional Committee (article 3) which was expanded (article 2) to include five members, the two marshals and one person from each province (article 13). The old requirement that each bill be reread after revision and compared to the original by the Constitutional Committee was maintained but new terms for deliberation were set. Each new regular bill had a mandatory three day deliberation period between its distribution in printed form to each member of Parliament and the debate over the bill in plenary session, a measure curiously similar to the practice proposed by Thomas More in his *Utopia*.[40] Bills drawn up during the daily provincial meetings of the *Sejm* required only one day (article 7). The term "deliberation" specifically referred to the discussion between the Constitutional Committee and all interested members of the *Sejm*. During this mandatory deliberation period the Constitutional Committee would accept proposals from members of Parliament amending the bill and, to save time, the Committee would either incorporate these propositions into the bill before it was debated in plenum or draw up a statement explaining its opposition to a particular change.[41] It was common practice for the original bill to be fused with various other projects and suggestions before emerging from deliberation. Some seriously doubted the value of such amorphous legislative creations.[42] Noncompliance with this reform by backers of the Constitution of May Third was later to pose an obstacle for its wider acceptance; the *Ustawa Rządowa* would be introduced and passed by acclamation on the same day. The consideration of bills by the Constitutional Committee and the registration of newly adopted laws were expedited. New laws were to be signed immediately by the marshals while the Constitutional Committee was to endorse them in a separate conference room (article 8) whose location has not yet been determined by historians.

Finally, voting practices were standardized. Presence at the *turni* was made mandatory except for health related absences, no one could refuse to participate in a roll call (an apparent prohibition of absentions), those who took part in the roll call were required to also cast a secret ballot if one was approved and, reminiscent of earlier rules, everyone was to remain in his place (article 11). Secret ballots employed balls (article 10).[43] The new regulations went on to require that every opinion expressed during a *turnus* be recorded in the *gród*: those of the senate and ministerium by the crown marshal or his replacement and those of the deputied by the confederated *Sejm* marshals (article 12).[44]

For some, these adjustments were intended only to accelerate proceedings prior to the passage of a comprehensive law reforming the entire *Sejmy*; for others, they were to be permanent. In a letter to Deboli, Stanisław August called the 5 January law a good set of *legitis curiatae*—with one exception: the requirement that at least one measure be passed each day. He pointed out that the very next day after this law was passed this very clause was broken.[45]

The influence of the 1768 statute proved to be quite stubborn, however. After a month long recess, the *Sejm* on 8 February 1791 began debate on a measure offered by Michał Zaleski, deputy from Troki in Lithuania, and supported by Marshal Małachowski, intended to present bills to the *Sejm* not according to the order they had been deposited with the *Sejm* Committee but rather according to subject matter. Immediate opposition came from the castellan of Biecz and a deputy from Inowrocław, Dezyderyusz Leszczyński who defended the 1768 regulations. Marshal Małachowski backed down but insisted on accepting the bill as an oral directive (*zlecenie ustne*).[46]

Whether intended as permanent or not, these adjustments proved to be inadequate. On 17 February debate stalled with two procedural *turni*. The debates had admittedly been complex, involving ideological conflicts of the most fundamental kind over whether to proceed with the restructuring of the political system by first reforming the *sejmiki*—the most basic level of the legislative process—or with a continued consideration of cardinal laws. Political deadlock was magnified by procedure. The deputy from Orsza, Ludwik Gutakowski, claimed that there has never been a case in history that a free nation should proceed so slowly. "The Fatherland is perishing," he declared, "and we must perish with it. The 1768 law was imposed to maintain anarchy in Poland; it is the true offspring of the *liberum veto*."[47]

A brief and far more significant measure, passed on 21 February 1791, overturned as "imperfect and harmful to the order and speed of the debates that portion of the 1768 parliamentary order law describing the method and custom hitherto practiced deciding bills according to categories, points, '*periody*' (?) and words."[48] Previously each section within a bill could be considered separately. The adoption of the new bill leads to the conclusion, supported by accounts of the debates, that the 1768 law had encouraged the imposition of more specific categories than the two major ones, state and economic, and the scrupulous consideration of texts had made each word potentially subject to a roll call vote. In a speech on 17 October 1791, Ignacy Potocki described the old state of affairs in the following manner: "precious time flowed for small things and most often on eternal disputes simply concerning the distinction of categories. The 1768 law has been the cause of this."[49]

The new regulations did quicken proceedings.[50] With the exception of the Civil-Military Administrative Commissions, the new form of local government passed in November 1789, the reformed governmental edifice was erected in roughly the year following the passage of the new parliamentary procedure laws. Other factors, however, were also influential. The newly elected deputies have traditionally been viewed as contributing fresh ideas and energy. Undoubtedly, this factor played an important role. Perhaps equally as significant was the combination of the impetus and logic of the reforms reaching a stage of fruition expedited by the new regulations on parliamentary procedure.

A month following the adoption of the *Ustawa Rządowa* the *Sejm* passed comprehensive regulations expounding article 6 of the new constitution and defining the nature, function and order of the central legislative body in the new governmental structure. More than four to five times the length of the 1768 statute, the fundamental law, "*Sejmy,*" expressed the crystallizing ideology of the reform movement making the *Sejm*, and more specifically, the Chamber of Deputies not only the "temple of the legislative process" (a traditional formulation) but also the "manifestation and embodiment of national sovereignty" and the permanent center of government. As such, the *Sejm* became a *sejm gotowy* ["ever-ready *sejm*"] meeting biennially but always prepared to be convened by the king or by the marshal. The king, ceasing to be considered a separate estate, was reduced to president of the Senate and head of the *Straż Praw* [Council of Ministers] in which he exercised an extra tie-breaking vote but otherwise had an equal vote to all other members of the two institutions, even in regards to the Senate's suspensory veto that would delay the passage of a bill until the following parliament. The role of the Senate suffered even more drastic reduction with senators and ministers exercising a voice in the parliament only in matters concerning their offices. In a similar capacity plenipotentiaries from the towns were introduced into the *Sejm* possessing a voice in matters affecting their own interests; the towns, though technically only through their membership in the executive commissions, did become part of the parliament.

A new ceremony introduced into the first joint session of the two chambers symbolized the expanded role of the *Sejm*. The law stipulated that:

> . . . as a reminder that all executive power begins and has its source in the nation, that offices execute the laws according to the dictates of the nation, the chancellor will declare from the throne: "From the power of the law, the estates in parliament of the Commonwealth suspend all authority and activities of the executive office."[51]

This suspension of executive offices and the assumption of administrative functions by the parliament reflected a *de facto* prerogative of the *Sejm* empowered by the "Act of Confederation" of 1788. All matters handled by the administration itself undergoing reform could touch the safety of the nation; as a result they could be, and often were, reviewed and decided by the representative will of the nation. To a great extent, the *Sejm* in session subsumed the functions and burdens of the entire government. The slowness of the Four Years' *Sejm* whose practice was the basis for the new *Sejmy* law should, therefore, not be surprising.

By the law of 20 June 1791, the central role of the *Sejm* remained the formulation and passage of legislation. The traditional chronology was maintained: separate preliminary meetings of the lower chamber, initial joint sessions, separate legislative sessions and the second confirmatory and concluding joint meetings. The strictly legislative process was limited to the third period and was treated in articles 15-17 of the "*Sejmy*" law. With the full acceptance of the majority principle, the former distinction between *materiae status* and *materiae aeconomica* lost all meaning. Bills were, however, sorted into new categories: first as "legislation," proclamations of the *Sejm* or as *dezyderya* and second, within each group according to their importance. Legislation was subdivided into political bills requiring a two-thirds government within the context of the *Ustawa Rządowa*: civil laws requiring a simple majority and concerning those norms by which citizens interact in private agreements, considerations, and property; criminal bills passable by a two-thirds majority and including offerings and regular levies to the public treasury. The second category was subdivided into, first, projects requiring a two-thirds majority (political treaties, declarations of war, public debt, army appropriations and taxes for military purposes) and, second, projects needing only a simple majority (trade agreements and similar matters, peace treaties, administration of the treasury's income, conscription during wartime, coinage regulation, and education). *Dezyderja* referred to specific wishes of the *województwa, powiaty,* lands and towns but apparently excluding private petitions and required only simple majorities for passage.[52]

Article 15 defined the activities of the *Deputacja Sejmowa* which replaced the former Constitutional Committee.[53] The foremost function of this *Deputacja* in an ordinary *Sejm* (as opposed to the Constitutional *Sejmy* newly established and scheduled for every twenty-five years) was as before to appraise the constitutionality of bills and to sort them according to category. The precise order for considering bills in the *Sejm* was determined by the *Deputacja* though the general order outlined above was followed and priority was given to projects offered by the king or changes made by executive bodies between parliaments. Preserved were both the old right of the reviewing board to present its comments and the prerogative of a bill's author to have his project read unchanged in parliament. The internal functioning of the *Deputacja* followed the general scheme for other commissions: majority rule, the presence of at least one member from each province, etc.[54] To aid in operations, the board received the cooperation of the *Sejm* secretary and chancellor plus one *subalternat* [assistant] from the *Straż Praw* and from each executive commission. Decisions were to be printed at government expense according to the stipulated categories and distributed to the *Sejm* three days prior to the separation of the chambers. The additional three day mandatory deliberation period between the publication and distribution of entire bills and their discussion in the chambers was preserved. Departing from the prerogatives of the old Constitutional Commission, the *Deputacja Sejmowa* was to prepare bills for the ennoblement of at least thirty persons per *Sejm* taken from the municipal plenipotentaries and all those who so requested and had bought an entire village or town.

As described in articles 16 and 17, the actual consideration, alteration and passages of legislation would occur during the separate meetings of each chamber following the joint opening ceremonies and review of the central executive organs.[55] Procedures were standardized. The *Sejm* secretary would read bills and comments uninterrupted according to the order determined by the *Deputacja*. Passage of a measure depended on a combination of majority proportions described earlier and the proportional strength of the two chambers varying with each type of law. Political, civil and criminal bills were subject to a suspensory veto by the Senate. Thus, if such a bill were passed by the lower chamber it went immediately to the Senate which would decide by *turnus* the question, "should the proposed law be suspended for further national deliberation or should it be implemented immediately." The veto must be approved by the same margin required for the bill's passage in the Chamber of Deputies. If approved, the veto would delay the bill till the following *Sejm* where it would immediately become law if passed again by the Chamber of Deputies. A separate procedure was stipulated for tax bills and *uchwały sejmowe* (*Sejm* resolutions or proclamations)—no mention being made of *dezyderja* which, however, were probably included in this group.

Bills in this category had to be passed by the prescribed majorities of the two chambers combined. This arrangement reflected both the declining strength of the Senate and a fuller perception of the relative importance of different kinds of legislation.

The bulk of article 17 described voting procedures. After a bill's reading the *Sejm* marshal in the Chamber of Deputies would ask if there was unanimous approval—a practical measure reminiscent of the former preeminence of the unanimity principle. The objection of, at least, a single member would necessitate the following *ad turnum* proposition: "should the bill be accepted in its entirety or should it be revised?" In the event that a deputy should object to the entire bill he should voice the counter proposition: "should the bill be rejected or revised?" and a roll call vote should take place between these two propositions. Once rejected a bill could not be reconsidered in the same parliament. If the marshal's proposition were accepted, voting in each chamber would begin immediately and the results announced by the respective marshals. Only if the bills failed would the marshal initiate a plenary discussion after which members opposed to the measure should meet in a separate room with the *Deputacja*. Business on the chamber floors would continue during this deliberation but the return of the corrected bill would interrupt proceedings. Should the bill fail again it could not be resurrected in the same parliament. All *turni* had to be followed by a secret ballot except for measures pertaining to permanent taxation and the organization of the armed forces. The inclusion of certain military matters was an interesting addition to the original stipulation that only taxes would not be subject to a secret ballot in a confederated *Sejm*. Each approved bill was to be signed by the *Sejm* marshal and the *Deputacje* in the *Sejm* conference room and the *Sejm* secretary was to register the new law in the acts of the city where parliament was held.[56] The final clause of the article stipulated that persons to be ennobled must be recommended by a *Sejm* member and approval both of their applications and waivers of the *scartabellat*[57] required three-fourth majorities.

The first three paragraphs of article 21 outline the time allocated for each session. The *Sejm* was to begin at 10:00 a.m. and last five hours until 3:00 p.m. The deputy *primus ex ordine* would substitute the marshal in his absence. Only holidays could interrupt the sequence of daily sessions and the plenary meetings of each chamber were to be extended past 3:00 p.m. only if a *turnus* were in progress. Provincial sessions could be scheduled outside these meetings.

Most of article 21 was devoted to voting practices. Discussion of proposed legislation was to be interrrrupted at 1:00 p.m. at which time the marshal asked if anyone wished a roll call vote. Such a vote could be called earlier and must be conducted immediately upon such a request. The rules stated earlier that each member must participate in both the roll call and secret ballot votes were repeated as was the stipulation that each must vote only in his turn. Absence during the roll call forfeited the right to take part in the secret ballot. The *Sejm* Marshal in the Chamber of Deputies and the National Marshal in the Senate were responsible for supervising the voting in their respective chambers; power was shared in joint sessions. Informal discussions of up to one hour could be called by any deputy; the striking of the marshal's staff would bring the chamber back to order. Free discussions were prohibited. Should several deputies ask for the floor simultaneously, the dispute would be settled by the traditional order of members. Secret ballots were to be conducted as follows:

> . . . on the table there will be a container which should be divided by an internal partition into two halves one of which should be painted white and with the sign *affirmative* and the other black with the sign *negative*—these signs will represent the votes for a particular proposition. The front of the container should be open so that a hand could be placed inside hidden to deposit the balls. The inside of the container should be lined with cloth. Balls for voting are all to be of the same size, shape and color and their number should equal [those voting]. . . . [Depending on debate arrangements the person voting will be called by the appropriate official, handed a ball and in public deposit his vote.] In the event that there should be found in the container more balls than distributed the whole process would need to be repeated.[58]

This procedure for secret ballots appeared to be traditional and was used throughout the Four Years' *Sejm*.

Finally, article 21 of the "*Sejmy*" law regulated participation in the voting process. In addition to one vote in the regular ballot the king possessed an additional tie-breaking vote. The king's vote could be submitted either orally or in writing and as such would be counted in the secret ballot. Importantly, the statute permitted the conduct of regular business in the king's absence, a measure consistent with the provision that the *Sejm* for the first time in Polish history could be called by someone other than the king or marshal during the king's lifetime.

Generally, the law, "*Sejmy*," regulated the functions of this central legislative body in the new or reanimated political principles of representation and efficiency. Consistent with traditional thinking, the *Sejm* was acknowledged as the "temple of legislation" but, reflecting a new mentality, a new concept of representation was utilized. Deputies ceased to be politically bound to the explicit demands and wishes of their constituencies, rather, they became representatives of the entire nation. This was another sign that the commonality of local life was, once again, reaching the Republic level. The reaffirmed and reconstituted principle of representation justified an increased curtailment of the importance and independence of the Senate, making the Chamber of Deputies the actual producer of legislation. As was so common in the moderate reforms of the Polish Revolution much of the old was preserved and some powers were, therefore, retained by the ancient institution of elder statesmen. The Senate participated in the passage of legislation and possessed, together with the king, the power of a partial suspensory veto. But the predominance of the former lower chamber meant that the prescribed rules of parliamentary order in the *izba poselska* became the rules governing the mechanism for law-making.

Efficiency was crucial as the second principle animating procedural reform. The Revolution sought to take advantage of what appeared to many as the last opportunity to safeguard national independence and territorial integrity. Efficient government was generally acknowledged to be as vital as the military reforms which initiated the confederation in 1788. Efficient, yet not entirely untraditional, government was the goal of both the reforming party and other members who later opposed the Constitution. Basic procedural schemes were maintained as the majority principle was applied "everywhere for everything" and meetings were expedited by the severe limitation of discussion. The old respect for parliamentary minorities was preserved in the provision for deliberation outside the chambers between the *Sejm* officials and the opposition to a given bill. Discussion in the chambers was limited by restricting each member's speaking freedom to two speeches, one prior to the roll call vote and one during the *turnus* itself. A separate article was dedicated to detailed regulation of *Sejm* sessions and to precise voting practices.

The three afore discussed laws reforming procedure during the Four Years' *Sejm* embodied new ideologies and political compromises and were practical solutions for procedural difficulties and manifestations of traditional mentalities apparent in actual debates. Contemporary criticism often dwelt on the *Sejm*'s low productivity, numerous extensions, inordinate concern with detail, especially the classification and division of bills in accord with the 1768 requirements and, finally, chaotic and longwinded debates. Such a climate undoubtedly encouraged the serious absenteeism of the first term and continuation of this line of thought surfaced after the adoption of the *Ustawa Rządowa* in the often voiced claims of the adherents of the new political order contrasting the new rapid synthesizing of laws with the former slowness in proceedings. The new *legitis curiatae* were a response to these problems and a factor in their apparent reversal.

The procedures used in the first two and a half years of the 1788–1792 *Sejm* continued practices codified in 1768 as adapted to a state of confederation. The laws from 5 January 1791 and 6 February 1791 modified these *legitis curiatae* and their final form for future parliaments was delineated as a part of the fundamental law, "*Sejmy*" passed the following June. The applicability of the new June 1791 procedure to the current *Sejm*, however, was a matter of opinion. Some deputies believed that it did indeed apply while others persisted in believing that the *Sejm* continued to operate according to the procedures of a confederation, an institution expressly prohibited by the *Ustawa Rządowa*.[59]

Summary

From normative, legal and practical perspectives, the conduct of business in the Four Years' *Sejm* was both an outgrowth of earlier practices and a perceived and partial model for future parliaments confidently planned for in the comprehensive reforms. As a confederated *Sejm*, the Four Years' *Sejm* expanded the majority principle to all legislation. The repeated handling of *materiae aeconomica* by the parliaments of 1778–1786 accustomed the lifelong senators and the elected deputies, many of whom served several terms, to reach workable compromises on a set of issues and to officially acknowledge the existence of an unpersuaded minority. In effect, political culture was undergoing fundamental changes. The extension of this mentality to *materiae status* and even to cardinal laws in the confederated *Sejm* of 1788-1792 no longer seemed a radical departure from past practices but rather a natural move in the context of weakening outside pressure. Facilitated too was the permanent adoption of the majority principle in the Constitution of May 3, 1791 as a kind of perpetual confederation throughout the Commonwealth when individual confederations were officially banned. Future parliaments were also bequeathed the near monopoly on power enjoyed by the Chamber of Deputies in the 1788-1792 *Sejm* adapted to the reconstituted periodization of procedures.

Proceedings in the Four Years' *Sejm* were slowed by numerous factors: the sheer scope and interrelatedness of the task, the variety of opinions on each issue, a great concern for detail, obstruction against specific changes and a tradition of elaborate speech-giving. But as in any truly parliamentary system the climax of the legislative and reform processes in the Four Years' *Sejm* officially lay in the conversion of projects of all kinds into laws. Voting, therefore, was one of the most crucial and interesting aspects. Extension of *pluralitatis* decision-making from *materiae aeconomica* to all matters in the confederated *Sejm* developed habits of debates and voting that became the legal norm in the new system but which encountered the resistance of the entrenched ideal of unanimity. The habit of striving for perfect consensus is evident throughout the debates. It is indicative both of a profound respect for the concerns of each individual and the essential fragility of the political bonds. In the latter case, the tradition of confederations and re- (or anti-) confederations meant that each decision in the *Sejm* could potentially escalate into a nationwide split. Less dramatically, unbending, uncompromising factionalism could also undermine any parliamentary system. These dangers and the justified fear which accompanied them persisted. The May Third Constitution outlawed all confederations and applied majority decisions to everything. The striving for a unanimous decision "crowned by a threefold outburst of acclaim" remained for many a beautiful but suicidal ideal inherited from better times when the external security of the Commonwealth had permitted such a luxury. Yet, the political culture was changing from the hesitant, highly polite interaction of individuals whose bonds over the geographical expanse of the *Rzeczpospolita* still did not assume the allegiance solemnly declared, on occasion, in confederations to an interacting community sufficiently bonded together to acknowledge disagreements and political minorities.

CHAPTER 4

SOME GLIMPSES AT PARLIAMENTARY BEHAVIOR

Contradictory characteristics compete for the overall picture of the Four Years' *Sejm*. On the one hand, the lengthy parliament produced a comprehensive system of reforms earning the name of revolution among its contemporaries. At the same time, the Four Years' *Sejm* did not save the *Rzeczpospolita* and much of the parliament's long duration seemed a precious but lost opportunity. In recent decades, the term "*Sejm Wielki*" has gone out of fashion. Whereas previously the Parliament of 1788–1792 could be referred to, popularly and in scholarly treatises, either as "*Sejm Wielki*" [the Great *Sejm*] or as "*Sejm Czteroletni*" [the Four Years' *Sejm*], currently the former is almost never used.[1] The change in terminology could be due to fickled or trivial fashion, but a real difference in perception does exists between "the Great *Sejm*" and "the Four Years' *Sejm*." Was the Parliament of 1788–1792 great or merely large and lengthy?

Previous chapters have shown that proceedings at the Four Years' *Sejm* were slowed by established procedure and practice that exhibited a lingering compulsion for unanimity, frequent use of florid, time-consuming speech-making, efforts of a large diverse body of individuals grappling with the immense task of comprehensive reform, an impractical reflex of the *Sejm* to engage in the everyday operations of the government, and finally, possible obstructionism by elements opposed to any change. A variety of minutes and other contemporary accounts convey similar impressions which subsequently were incorporated into historical literature.

The general behavior of the Four Years' *Sejm* as an institution can also be described quantitatively through the use of *turni* records. Roll call votes punctuated the parliament at moments of political conflict. A *turnus* would be held on controversial issues usually of great, but not the greatest, importance (in which some kind of unanimity was still preferred), though there were numerous exceptions and roll calls became more acceptable with the practice becoming permanently incorporated into parliamentary procedure for future *Sejmy*. One hundred twenty of these *turni*, also called *kreskowania* or "dash-makings," were held during the Four Years' *Sejm*. These not only expressed the tradition of lawmaking with a movement towards an established comprehensive majority principle but they also united the central legislative function with quantifiable characteristics of the deputies and senators and indirecting of their constituencies. Working from the microcosmic level of roll call votes a macrocosmic understanding can be developed. The approach here is to logically analyze the records and, only when that task is accomplished, to confront the findings with interpretations in the most important literature.

The available sources permit a reconstruction of the results for all 120 *turni* though several specific results for individual chambers and secret ballots are missing. The handwritten minutes in the *Archiwum Sejmu Czteroletniego* (ASW) appear to be the most reliable source despite several missing months and these have been used as the backbone of this compilation.[2] The minutes written simultaneously to the *Sejm* debates have then been confronted with and supplemented by printed minutes: *Dyaryusz Sejmu Ordynaryinego pod związkiem Konfederacji Generalney Oboyga Narodow Warszawie Rozpoczętego Roku Pańskiego 1788* [Minutes of the Regular *Sejm* under the Union of the General Confederation of Both Nations begun in the year of Our Lord 1788], *Dyariusz Sejmu Ordynaryinego pod związkiem Konfederacji Generalney Oboyga Narodow Warszawie Rozpoczętego Roku Pańskiego 1790* [Minutes of the Regular *Sejm* under the Union of the General Confederation of Both Nations begun in the year of Our Lord 1790], *Dziennik Czynności Sejmu Głównego Ordynaryinego Warszawskiego pod związkiem Konfederacji Oboyga Narodow agituiącego się 1789* [Diary of the Main Regular *Sejm* of Warsaw under the Union of the Confederation of Both Nations debating in 1789], *Dyaryusz Krótko Zebrany* [Briefly Compiled Minutes]. More importantly, many of the tally forms used by the *Sejm* secretary and possibly others for roll call votes have survived. Four different printed forms were used: one for the Senate and a separate one for the House of Deputies each in a 1788 and a 1790 version. There were several printings of these tally sheets for each term with corrected spellings. Printed tally sheets have been located in the *Archiwum Sejmu Czteroletniego* (ASW) at AGAD, the *Stare Druki* [Old Prints] collections of the University of Warsaw and the Fryderyk Moszyński files of the *Katolicki Uniwersytet Lubelski*. In addition, ASW contains several handwritten lists and rough, separate, tallies of subtotals and roll call propositions.[3] All results have been compared to inconsistently accurate press accounts in the *Gazeta Warszawska* and the *Kalendarzyk Narodowego i Obcego (1791-92)* [Little National and Foreign Calendar 1791-92]. The propositions and results for the *turni* and secret ballots are presented below:

Table 8

Roll Call Results

Date	Proposition
101788	Should the members of the retiring Army Department take an oath according to the first read bill with the condition of free revision? Or should the army of both nations take an oath through its commanders designated by the *Sejm*?
1	senators deputies abstaining total secret ballot
	+063-012 +087-087 +150-099 +128-121
110388	Should there be an Army Department with (specific) regulations? Or should there be an Army Commission with (specific) regulations?
2	senators deputies abstaining total secret ballot
	+070-019 +079-095 +149-114 +122-140
111288	Should the Army Commission always meet in the Grand Duchy of Lithuania every third biennium beginning with the next *Sejm* or not?
3	senators deputies abstaining total secret ballot
	+059-009 +125-028 2 +184-037 +138-084
111588	Should commanding generals be eligible for the Army Commission or not?
4	senators deputies abstaining total secret ballot

Some Glimpses at Parliamentary Behavior 123

		+069-002	+122-022	1	+189-024	
112288	Should the Army Commission in the next *Sejm* be selected immediately after the joining of the Chambers or after the election of the Treasury Commission?						
5	senators	deputies	abstaining	total	secret ballot
	023-052	+098-068		+121-120	+126-111
112488	Should army writers (*pisarze wojskowi*) be excluded from all future *sejmiki*? Should be found (at *sejmiki*), *affirmative*; should not be found (at *sejmiki*), *negative*.				
6	senators	deputies	abstaining	total	secret ballot
	+039-022	+066-078	1	+105-100	+085-117
121388	Should the proposition from the speaker be accepted or that from the deputy from Chełm?				
7	senators	deputies	abstaining	total	secret ballot
	+069-008	+115-037		+184-045	

(Speaker: Should the Army Commission meet in the place designated for the Regular *Sejm* in the Crown or not? Chełm: Should the Army Commission meet during the duration of the *Sejm* in the place designated for the *Sejm* or in another place without the *Sejm*?)

121388	Should the Army Commission meet in the place designated for the regular *Sejm* in the Crown or not?				
8	senators	deputies	abstaining	total	secret ballot
	+072-003	+120-032		+192-035	+170-055
121688	Should the Keepers of the Seals (*Pieczętarze*) along with the others deputated take the oath or not?				
9	senators	deputies	abstaining	total	secret ballot
	+017-037	+053-077		+070-114	+092-086
011989	Should the Permanent Council with all its provision from 1775–1776 be abolished or not?				
10	senators	deputies	abstaining	total	secret ballot

	+021-007	+099-004	62	+120-011

020589 Should the Dragoon Regiments be converted to Companies (*Pułki*) of Forward Guard or not?

11   senators   deputies   abstaining   total   secret ballot

+039-002   +113-001   +152-003

020689 Should a squadron (*chorągiew*) of the Crown National Cavalry consist of 150 heads or 100 heads?

12   senators   deputies   abstaining   total   secret ballot

+024-021   +095-030   +120-051(sic)

022089 Should the bill be adopted with the amendment of the Brześć Litewski deputy or without it?

13   senators   deputies   abstaining   total   secret ballot

+001-033   +038-065   +039-098   +057-080

(concerning "*Zaleczenie ostrożności possessyonatow*" [Recommendation for caution among landowners])

022789 Should royal estates enprivileged with a lifelong tenure (*dzierżawa*) which pay the *kwarta* in addition to the two *kwarta* according to the new assessment also pay land tax on the second half?

14   senators   deputies   abstaining   total   secret ballot

+012-043   +074-073   +086-116

040489 Should the corrected and amended bill from the Podlaski deputy be accepted or the corrected bill from the Lublin deputy?

15   senators   deputies   abstaining   total   secret ballot

+021-023   +081-071   +102-094

042389 Should the commissioners for accessing taxes on land and church property be designated by the *Sejm* or should they be chosen by the *województwa*, lands and districts?

16   senators   deputies   abstaining   total   secret ballot

+032-002   +056-035   +088-037

Some Glimpses at Parliamentary Behavior 125

050489	Should the legally stipulated *grosz* from the labor used in factories evaluated according to place and custom be designated for the public treasury? (Or) should it be voluntarily offered by the factory owner? Should be from the designated labor, *affirmative*; should be offered according to the will of the owner, *negative*.
17	senators deputies abstaining total secret ballot
	017-019 +057-026 +074-045
051289	Should the "Offering of the Tenth *Grosz*" be paid in half by the *possessor* for the *stawny* without a return to the hereditary owner or in its entirety without a return to the hereditary owner?
18	senators deputies abstaining total secret ballot
	+006-035 +036-062 +042-097
051489	Should the amendment from the Kalisz deputy be accepted or not?
19	senators deputies abstaining total secret ballot
	+022-010 +044-034 +066-044
	(Mikorski: "Should the hereditary owner fail make a mortgage payment, from that moment he would pay the additional income tax to the Republic's Treasury.")
051589	Should the amendment by the castellan of Sącz be accepted with the Bracław's deputy's change or without it? Should be accepted with the change, *affirmative*; should be accepted without changes, *negative*.
20	senators deputies abstaining total secret ballot
	+000-033 +004-079 +004-112
	(Chołoniewski [Bracław]: exemptions for mortgage holders from the 10 percent tax)
052289	Should Clause 11 about the *Wyderkasse* be accepted or not?

21	senators	deputies	abstaining	total	secret ballot
	+009-018	+053-032		+062-050	

052989 Should the percent from the post-Jesuit sum be paid in the Crown as in the Grand Duchy i.e., seven from each hundred or five from each hundred? Should be paid at seven (percent), *affirmative*; should be paid at five (percent), *negative*.

22	senators	deputies	abstaining	total	secret ballot
	+007-022	+045-037		+052-059	

061289 Should real and mobile property received under the 1778 law be subject to payment? Or only (that received) after the registration of this law? After the 1778 law, *affirmative*; after the present law, *negative*.

23	senators	deputies	abstaining	total	secret ballot
	+002-028	+014-049		+016-077	

061589 Should the given amendment (by Potocki [Lublin]) be accepted or not?

24	senators	deputies	abstaining	total	secret ballot
	+027-000	+076-004		+103-004	

(bill concerning *kaduty*)

061889 Should the *intraty* from Royal Domains be the same as from landed property i.e., from regular income or from the total (income)? Should be drawn from regular income only *affirmative*; should be taken from total income, *negative*.

25	senators	deputies	abstaining	total	secret ballot
	+022-003	+047-036		+069-039	

071789 Should the Bishops of Kraków, Princes of Siewierz, receive a net annual income of 100,000 or according to the old income? Should receive 100,000 *affirmative*, remain according to old incomes, *negative*.

26	senators	deputies	abstaining	total	secret ballot
	+006-011	+056-009		+062-020	+056-023

072889 Should the salary of the hetmans be decreased or not? Should be decreased, *affirmative*; should not be decreased, *negative*.

27	senators	deputies	abstaining	total	secret ballot
	+000-018	+018-060	1	+018-078	

080389 Should the salary for future guards and field camp officers be maintained or not? Should be maintained, *affirmative*; should not be maintained, *negative*.

28	senators	deputies	abstaining	total	secret ballot
	+015-004	+043-024		+058-028	+045-039

080689 Should the 6,000 zł. salary from the Lithuanian Treasury for the general-by-the-king from the approved 1778 constitution be tied to rank or not? Should be tied, *affirmative*; should not be tied, *negative*.

29	senators	deputies	abstaining	total	secret ballot
	+020-001	+056-006		+076-007	

080789 Should transport carts of citizens obligated by contract to bring them to Kiszynów and other warehouses in Wołoszczyzna (Bessarabia) be permitted across the boundary or not? Should be let across the boundary, *affirmative*; should not be permitted abroad, *negative*.

30	senators	deputies	abstaining	total	secret ballot
	+013-002	+028-024		+041-026	+036-030

081189 Should export across the Dniestr be closed from the registration of the universal in the local town (court) or from the regular day, 1 September?

31	senators	deputies	abstaining	total	secret ballot
	+002-015	+016-058		+018-073	

081189 Should point 4 in the Universal be accepted with the amendment from the Kalisz deputy or without the amendment? With the amendment, *affirmative*; without the amendment, *negative*.

32	senators	deputies	abstaining	total	secret ballot
	+004-008	+030-025		+034-033	+039-028

(Suchorzewski: limit passage across the Dniestr to 100 wagons at a time)

081889 Should the salary for "the Great Lithuanian Guard" be maintained *ad ascensum vel decessum* of the current day or should it immediately cease? Should be maintained, *affirmative*; should not be maintained, *negative*.

33	senators	deputies	abstaining	total	secret ballot
	+016-002	+050-020		+066-022	+047-040

090489 Should the actual *gaze* for the regiment and company *szeffs* be maintained *ad ascensum vel decessum*? Or with an allotment of only 10,000 Polish *złoty*? The *gaze* existing up to now should be maintained, *affirmative*; should be allotted 10,000 Polish złoty, *negative*.

34	senators	deputies	abstaining	total	secret ballot
	+026-004	+050-030		+076-034	+045-060

100689 Should the *rotmistrz* be placed now among the order of appointing brigadiers, vice-brigadiers and majors or not?

35	senators	deputies	abstaining	total	secret ballot
	+018-002	+060-018		+078-020	+057-040

101689 Should hides from butchers be turned over to the Treasury *in natura* or money (be sent) from the butchers? Hides should be handed over *in natura*, *affirmative*; should be (given) money from butchers, *negative*.

36	senators	deputies	abstaining	total	secret ballot
	+010-013	+034-023		+044-036	

102389 Should the hides of bulls and cows slaughtered for private use at noble manors and among the peasants in the villages be brought to the public treasury without payment or not?

Some Glimpses at Parliamentary Behavior

37	senators	deputies	abstaining	total	secret ballot
	+001-017	+037-040		+038-057	

102789 Should any further exemptions other than those included in the above law be allowed or not?

38	senators	deputies	abstaining	total	secret ballot
	+003-025	+016-069		+019-094	

111689 Should the giving of temporary recruits be permitted in the Crown or not? Should be permitted, *affirmative;* should not be permitted, *negative.*

39	senators	deputies	abstaining	total	secret ballot
	+011-009	+037-038		+048-047	+043-049

111989 Should recruits be taken on the basis of the *dym* (homestead)? Or according to population of the male sex? From homesteads, *affirmative;* according to population, *negative.*

40	senators	deputies	abstaining	total	secret ballot
	+013-013	+045-041		+058-054	+061-040

022390 Should citizens be obligated to present a voluntary assessment of their real property? Should be obligated, *affirmative;* should not be obligated, *negative.*

41	senators	deputies	abstaining	total	secret ballot
	+025-008	+039-060		+064-068	

030290 Should the amount of offering and tax increased by the "*Koekwacyjna*" [Adjustment] Committee in the future be paid to the Treasury by hereditary landlords or not? Should be paid *affirmative;* should not be paid, *negative.*

42	senators	deputies	abstaining	total	secret ballot
	+001-016	+019-060		+020-076	

030890 Should a *Kommissoryat* be established or not?

43	senators	deputies	abstaining	total	secret ballot
	+005-000	+089-002		+094-002	

030990	Should cloth for "the great army uniform" belong to the *Kommissoryat* or to the commanders (*szeffowie*)? To the *Kommissoryat*, *affirmative*; to the commanders *negative*.				
44	senators	deputies	abstaining	total	secret ballot
	+010-008	+044-035		+054-043	+053-044
033090	Should the recommendation of the Committee for Foreign Affairs permitting *provisore* the title of Great Deputy to the Port be accepted or not? Should be accepted, *affirmative*; should not be accepted, *negative*.				
45	senators	deputies	abstaining	total	secret ballot
	+016-006	+049-014		+065-020	+051-034
041290	Should Prince Wirtemberg be accepted into the service of the *Rzeczpospolita* according to the bill or not? Should be accepted, *affirmative*; should not be accepted, *negative*.				
46	senators	deputies	abstaining	total	secret ballot
	+036-000	+061-002		+097-002	+075-019
041590	Should the bill from the deputy from Smoleńsk be decided upon or that of the Army Commission? Smoleński's bill, *affrimative*; the Army Commission's bill, *negative*.				
47	senators	deputies	abstaining	total	secret ballot
	+012-005	+057-004		+069-009	
	(concerning the correction of property assessments)				
042690	Should the Kowel *starostwo* made hereditary in 1775 remain taxed as a noble property according to the bill or should it be taxed at 30 percent?				
48	senators	deputies	abstaining	total	secret ballot
	+016-005	+045-018	1	+061-023	
043090	Should the clause from the printed bill be accepted, *affirmative*; or the amendment of the deputy from Kalisz, *negative*?				

49	senators	deputies	abstaining	total	secret ballot
				+024-077	+064-037

(taxation of former royal *demesne*)

051190   Should the amendment by Suchorzewski from Kalisz be accepted or the amendment by Mikorski from Kalisz? Suchorzewski's amendment should be accepted, *affirmative*; Mikorski's amendment, *negative*.

50	senators	deputies	abstaining	total	secret ballot
	+005-021	+047-041		+052-062	+062-050

(Suchorzewski: "*Prawo Donatyw i Zamian*"
Mikorski: tax adjustments should be based on original property values)

061190   Should the proposition from the Troki deputy receive a roll call or that of the Poznań deputy? Troki's proposition should be voted upon, *affirmative*; Poznań's proposition should be voted upon, *negative*.

	senators	deputies	abstaining	total	secret ballot
	+038-000	+070-034		+108-034	+103-039

51   (Brzostowski [Troki]: Should the pre-*Sejm sejmiki* take place at the time stipulated by law or should these *sejmiki* be postponed this one time until 9 February 1791 because of the Republic's needs?

Zakrzewski [Poznań]: Should the extension of the confederation until 1 March 1791 be under the current deputies or with additional, new deputies?)

061490   Should the pre-*Sejm sejmiki* (occur) at the time stipulated by law or should they be delayed until 9 February 1791 because of the Republic's needs? Should be delayed until 9 February 1791, *affirmative*; should (occur) at the time prescribed by law, *negative*.

52	senators	deputies	abstaining	total	secret ballot
	+033-001	+082-015		+115-016	+111-020

071390	\multicolumn{5}{l}{Should a collection for the completion of the fund to maintain the army be established or not?}
53	senators	deputies	abstaining	total	secret ballot
	+017-000	+044-010		+061-010	
071690	\multicolumn{5}{l}{Should the bill with the amendment in these words "proportionally to the method of taxation or appraisal of homesteads" be accepted or without the amendment? Should be accepted with the amendment, *affirmative*; or should be accepted without the amendment, *negative*.}
54	senators	deputies	abstaining	total	secret ballot
	+005-013	+027-026		+032-039	
083190	\multicolumn{5}{l}{Should the correction of "the Form of Government" begin with the writing *rather than the decision* (sic) of the Cardinal Laws or from the description of the *sejmiki*?}
55	senators	deputies	abstaining	total	secret ballot
	+023-002	+076-019	1	+099-021	
091490	\multicolumn{5}{l}{Should the number of ministers be decreased or not?}
56	senators	deputies	abstaining	total	secret ballot
	+004-027	+042-056	1	+046-083	+061-067
093090	\multicolumn{5}{l}{Should (members) of (Royal) families from neighboring powers be chosen to be our kings or should they be excluded from candidacy?}
57	senators	deputies	abstaining	total	secret ballot
	+014-004	+056-030		+070-034	+061-043
093090	\multicolumn{5}{l}{Should any exceptions be considered now?}
58	senators	deputies	abstaining	total	secret ballot
	+005-011	+030-051		+035-062	+043-054
100790	\multicolumn{5}{l}{Should the bill from the Kalisz deputy be decided upon or that of the Wołyń deputy?}

59	senators	deputies	abstaining	total	secret ballot
	+023-000	+078-006		+101-006	

(Mikorski [Kalisz]: should the confederation be extended or not?
Świętosławski [Wołyń]: should the *Sejm* be suspended for four months?)

100890 Should the first point of the bill extending this union of the confederation be adopted or not? Should be adopted, *affirmative*; should not be adopted, *negative*.

60	senators	deputies	abstaining	total	secret ballot
	+020-000	+070-003	5	+090-003	

101290 Should the present deputies making up the current union be kept in the *Sejm* Confederation of new deputies elected by *województwa*, lands and districts in the upcoming *sejmiki*?

61	senators	deputies	abstaining	total	secret ballot
	+016-007	+048-028	4	+064-035	+067-026

101490 Should the election of deputies occur at the *sejmiki* on 16 November of the current year or not? Should, *affirmative*; should not, *negative*.

62	senators	deputies	abstaining	total	secret ballot
	+019-008	+058-015	001	+077-023	-024

101590 Should the Wołyń deputy's amendment be accepted or not?

63	senators	deputies	abstaining	total	secret ballot
	+004-010	+014-052	3	+018-062	

(Świętosławski: "still and for those former places which the *województwa* were to recess for new meetings.")

101890 Should the Poznań deputy's bill be decided now or delayed until the "Form of Government"?

64	senators	deputies	abstaining	total	secret ballot
	+001-018	+010-051		+011-069	

	(Zakrzewski: instructions and deputies to be approved by secret ballot)
102190	Should the proposal from the Brasław deputy be decided or that of the Chełm deputy? The Brasław deputy's should be taken (for decision), *affirmative*; the Chełm deputy's, *negative*.

senators	deputies	abstaining	total	secret ballot
+003-013	+023-028		+026-041	+037-029

65	(Wawrzecki: "Should we now decide about the Bełz *województwo* or delay it till the "Form of Government?" Suchodolski: the Chełm Land should represent Bełz.)
102290	Should the bills permitting the election of deputies from "fallen-away" *województwa* demanding them be decided now or delayed until the description of the "Form of Government"?

66	senators	deputies	abstaining	total	secret ballot
	+010-009	+031-036		+041-045	+032-052

102290	Should *"suspensy"* [waivers] for senators, ministers, and deputies be abolished or should they be abolished with exceptions? Should be abolished, *affirmative*; with exceptions, *negative*.

67	senators	deputies	abstaining	total	secret ballot
	+011-004	+039-008		+050-012	+034-023

102590	Should the contributions from church, (Order of) Malta and royal (*stołowe*) estates be given in equal amounts to (those from) hereditary (noble) estates or should they be higher according to the bill?

68	senators	deputies	abstaining	total	secret ballot
	+014-002	+033-027		+047-029	

102690	Should a share of the grain contribution, according to Army Regulations, be for officers or not?

| 69 | senators | deputies | abstaining | total | secret ballot |

	+016-000	+042-013		+058-013	+045-024

102990 Should the Oszmiański deputy's bill be accepted with the Wołyń deputy's amendment or without the amendment? Should be accepted with the amendment, *affirmative*; should be accepted without the amendment, *negative*.

70 senators deputies abstaining total secret ballot

016-007 +036-023   +052-030 +043-034

(bill: "Moving of the Post-*Sejm Sejmiki*"
Świętosławski: dates must be established)

121690 Should Ośniałowski and Działyński elected under the marshaldom of the *stolnik* of Chełm be maintained or Rutkowski and Paprocki elected under the marshaldom of the Skarnikiewicz of Chełm?

71 senators deputies abstaining total secret ballot

            +193-047 +128-109

122390 Should there be an oath?

72 senators deputies abstaining total secret balllot

            +139-130 +109-138

122890 Should there be the point from the Livonian deputy or from the Wołyń deputy?

73 senators deputies abstaining total secret ballot

+004-018 +066-117   +070-135 +073-128

(Trembicki [Livonia]: "Should a *turnus* ordered by any member of the *Sejm* be given by the marshals or should it be delayed?"

Stroynowski [Wołyń]: "On each topic every member of the *Sejm* may speak twice, once before a vote once during the vote and no session will be adjourned without the approval of one bill or one part of a bill.")

010491 Should the proposition from the speaker be given a roll call vote or that of the Gniezno deputy?

74 senators deputies abstaining total secret ballot

+011-012 +090-116   +101-128   +058-128

(Marshal: "Should the bill from the Podole deputy be accepted with or without the amendment?")

Rożnowski [Gniezno]: "Should we begin with the *sejmiki* or the cardinal laws?")

010791	Should the decision on the "Form of Government" with the *sejmiki* or with cardinal laws?
75	senators deputies abstaining total secret ballot
+022-016   +152-073   +174-089   +174-080
012091	Should the following bill be accepted with the Warsaw deputy's amendment or not?
76	senators deputies abstaining total secret ballot
+007-016   +049-082   +056-098   +064-089

("Not the entire province but each *województwo*, land and district will chose the venue of its *sejmiki*.")

012591	Should only those *zastawnicy* [mortgage holders] who pay 100 *złoty* in taxes from the sum put on estates be active participants in the *sejmiki*? Or should also those who pay any sum whatsoever in the 10 *groszy* tax (10 percent tax) to the Treasury?
77	senators deputies abstaining total secret ballot
+018-004   +086-103   +104-107
012791	Should point 5 presented by the Committee be accepted or should (the point) from the Nur deputy be accepted? That given by the Committee, *affirmative*; that presented by the Nur Deputy, *negative*.
78	senators deputies abstaining total secret ballot
+088-092   +078-100

(Zieliński [Nur]: nobility *possessorowie* of land estates paying a tax of at least 100 [złoty])

| 012891 | Should the *dzierżawcy Arędorowi szlachta*, according to the Kalisz deputy's bill, belong to the *sejmiki* or |

should they not belong at all? Should belong, *affirmative*; not at all, *negative*.

79	senators	deputies	abstaining	total	secret ballot
				+087-095	+068-112

020791 Should the persons involved in the purchase of the palace (for the Russian ambassador) be freed from accountability or not?

80	senators	deputies	abstaining	total	secret ballot
				+185-020	+157-044

021091 Should the proposal from of the Kasztelan of Smoleńsk or that from Kraków receive a roll call vote?

81	senators	deputies	abstaining	total	secret ballot
				+185-020	+157-044

(Kasztelan of Smoleńsk: Should the above law giving [exclusive] active roles in the *sejmiki* to *dziedzicy* [hereditary landowners] be abolish or notd?
Jordan, deputy from Kraków: Should the hereditary *szlachta* having *possessye* [but] being in whoever's service have an active voice [*activita*] in the *sejmiki* or not?)

021091 (Jordan's proposal)

82	senators	deputies	abstaining	total	secret ballot
	+018-005	+098-054		+116-059	+094-075

021191 Should only those nobles with hereditary property be eligible for all elected offices who pay 100 *złoty* in taxes or all those who have an *vocem activica* at the *sejmiki*?

83	senators	deputies	abstaining	total	secret ballot
	+006-008	+029-109		+035-117	

021491 Should army personnel excluded from all civilian offices be admitted to the function of deputy or not?

84	senators	deputies	abstaining	total	secret ballot
	+026-001	+139-014		+165-015	+108-043

021591	\multicolumn{5}{l}{Should a role call vote be taken on the proposition from the Żmudź deputy or (on that) from the Livonian deputy?}
85	senators	deputies	abstaining	total	secret ballot
	+001-024	+040-123		+041-147	+064-116

(Should each person in active military service leave his *gaze* in the army *kasa* for the needs of invalids?)

021591	\multicolumn{5}{l}{Should the Żmudź deputy's bill be decided now or left for military matters?}
86	senators	deputies	abstaining	total	secret ballot
	+002-021	+035-109		+037-130	+051-109
021891	\multicolumn{5}{l}{Should the proposal from the speaker be accepted or (the one from) the Gniezno deputy? Speaker's proposition, *affirmative*; Gniezno deputy's proposition, *negative*.}
87	senators	deputies	abstaining	total	secret ballot
	+025-008	+065-085		+090-093	+100-084

(Speaker: "Should the bill presented by the Kraków deputy concerning the completion of the *sejmiki* be decided? Or should the bill presented by the Constitutional Committee be decided?

Gniezno: "Should the bill from the Kraków deputy be decided or not?)

021891	\multicolumn{5}{l}{Should the bill from the Kraków deputy be decided or not?}
88	senators	deputies	abstaining	total	secret ballot
	+035-000	+159-013		+194-013	

(for committee to examine bill on *sejmiki*)

031491	\multicolumn{5}{l}{Should the bill on *sejmiki* compiled by the committee delegated by the Estates be accepted in its entirety? Or set aside for corrections? Should be accepted in its entirety, *affirmative*; should be set aside for corrections, *negative*.}
89	senators	deputies	abstaining	total	secret ballot

Some Glimpses at Parliamentary Behavior 139

	+016-022	+025-133		+041-155	

032491 Should the bill on *sejmiki* corrected by the Committee designated by law be accepted in its entirety or should it be set aside once again for corrections? Should be accepted in its entirety, *affirmative*; should be sent for corrections, *negative*.

90	senators	deputies	abstaining	total	secret ballot
	+027-002	+110-038		+137-040	+107-064

040591 Should the bill on Towns be decided first or the bill on *Sejmy* be considered first?

91	senators	deputies	abstaining	total	secret ballot
	+010-016	+111-045		+121-061	

040891 Should the bill changing the tax on hides be decided (in the version) by Wawrzecki, deputy from Brasław, or (in the version) by Sołtyk, deputy from Kraków?

92	senators	deputies	abstaining	total	secret ballot
	+021-001	+116-022		+137-023	

041291 Should the bill presented by the *marszałek* be accepted or Sokolnicki's, deputy from Poznań?

93	senators	deputies	abstaining	total	secret ballot
	+025-001	+107-013		+132-014	+108-031

(Marshal: Przedbendski to pay 300,000 *złoty* to the Treasury for the Solec *starostwo*,
Sokolnicki: the sum should be conditionally reduced to 240,000 *złoty*)

050291 Should the sum of 100,000 Polish *złoty* alloted on the Niechworów *starostwo* by the 1775 constitution be maintained or abolished? Should be maintained, *affirmative*; should be abolished, *negative*.

94	senators	deputies	abstaining	total	secret ballot
	016-007	+043-049		+059-056	+045-054

051291 Should the bill on *Sejmy* read and corrected in its first part be accepted? Or should it be sent again for corrections?

95	senators	deputies	abstaining	total	secret ballot
	+021-000	+092-008		+113-008	+090-024

051991 Should the temporary sum of 175,000 Polish *złoty* on the Lublin *starostwo* alloted by the 1775 constitution be abolished or not? Should be abolished, *affirmative*; should not be abolished, *negative*.

96	senators	deputies	abstaining	total	secret ballot
	+000-025	+029-070		+029-095	+046-076

052091 Should 30,000 *złoty* be confirmed on Gołęcin?

97	senators	deputies	abstaining	total	secret ballot
	+006-002	+049-009		+055-011	

052091 Should the equivalent provision of 18,122 *złoty* be granted to the deputy from Łęczyca or not?

98	senators	deputies	abstaining	total	secret ballot
				+040-028	+040-028

(concerns income form the Sobotka estate made hereditary by a previous *Sejm*)

052391 Should the opinion of the Treasury Commission concerning the 154,367 *złoty* on the Kolski *starostwo* be upheld, *affirmative*; or not, *negative*?

99	senators	deputies	abstaining	total	secret ballot
	+008-000	+067-005		+075-005	

052391 Should the bill concerning Szawolicki presented by the Marszałek of the Grand Duchy of Lithuania be accepted, *affirmative*; or that of (the deputy) from Poznań, *negative*?

100	senators	deputies	abstaining	total	secret ballot
	+012-001	+039-026		+051-027	+039-035

052691 Should the amendment by Siemiański from Sieradz

concerning "*sejmiki deputackie*" for the provinces of the Crown be accepted or not?

101   senators   deputies   abstaining   total   secret ballot

+004-018   +021-067   +025-085   +032-079

060691   Should the corrected bill from the bills by Woyczyński, deputy from Rawa, and Potocki, deputy from Bracław, be accepted? (Or) should the bill from Czerniechów be accepted? Should the corrected (bill) be accepted, *affirmative*; should Czerniechów's bill be accepted, *negative*.

102   senators   deputies   abstaining   total   secret ballot

+029-000   +097-004   +126-004   +102-012

061091   Should the sum of 100,000 Polish *złoty* assigned to the Krasnosiel *starostwo* be accepted, *affirmative*? Or not accepted, *negative*?

103   senators   deputies   abstaining   total   secret ballot

+007-001   +038-026   +045-027   +041-028

061491   Should the opinion of the Committee be accepted or the project from the Nur deputy?

104   senators   deputies   abstaining   total   secret ballot

+001-002   +046-013   2   +047-015   +044-015

(Committee examining Treasury Commission rules on Ożarowski-Ossoliński property dispute)

061791   Should the bill for a Police Commission from the Constitutional Committee, twice corrected, be accepted or should it be sent for further corrections?

105   senators   deputies   abstaining   total   secret ballot

+018-001   +082-010   +100-011

092791   Should the bill from the Constitutional Committee be accepted? Should the bill from the Committee Examining the Treasury Commission of the Two Nations be accepted? Should be accepted from the Constitutional Committee, *affirmative*; should be accepted from the Committee for

Examining the Treasury Commission of the Two Nations, *negative*.

106	senators	deputies	abstaining	total	secret ballot
	+018-002	+102-023		+120-025	+108-036

100391 Should the bill on the *Assessorya* in two parts and with corrections from the Constitutional Committee and others read here in the Chamber be accepted? Or should it be sent for further correction to the Constitutional Commission? Should be accepted, *affirmative*; should be sent for further correction, *negative*.

107	senators	deputies	abstaining	total	secret ballot
	+012-005	+080-033		+092-038	+073-056

102191 Should the bill concerning ecclesiastic towns just read be adopted? Or should it be sent for further corrections to the Constitutional Committee?

108	senators	deputies	abstaining	total	secret ballot
				+008-101	

103191 Should the proposition for a roll call be sent to the Constitutional Committee? Should the proposition between two bills, i.e., the deputy from Czerniechów's for the Constitutional Committee's, be given a roll call vote?

109	senators	deputies	abstaining	total	secret ballot
	+014-013	+088-056		+102-069	

110391 Should the bill for a Declaration by the *Sejm* Marshal and the Marshal of the Lithuanian Confederation and just read be adopted?

110	senators	deputies	abstaining	total	secret ballot
	+042-002	+158-008		+200-010	

110791 Should the bill, several times corrected by the Constitutional Committee and just read, concerning candidates be accepted or should it be sent for further corrections?

| 111 | senators | deputies | abstaining | total | secret ballot |

Some Glimpses at Parliamentary Behavior 143

    +012-002 +080-041   +092-043 +060-056

120691 Should the bill for a declaration presented by Zboiński, deputy from Dobrzyń, corrected now and just read be accepted or not?

112 senators deputies abstaining total secret ballot

    +022-001 +114-019   +136-020 +125-024

121991 Should the proposition from the Speaker be given a roll call vote? Or should the proposition for a roll call vote from Świętosławski, deputy from Wołyń, be adopted?

113 senators deputies abstaining total secret ballot

    +013-034 +139-028   +152-062

    (concerning royal demesne)

011792 Should the bill just read and concerning the Tribunal Court in the Crown be adopted or should it be sent for further corrections?

114 senators deputies abstaining total secret ballot

    +009-007 +053-021   +062-028 +043-045

012692 Should the bill designating the sum of 540,000 *złoty* for the Police Commission, which the *Sejm* will audit (later) be adopted or not?

115 senators deputies abstaining total secret ballot

    +006-001 +065-005   +071-006

012792 Should the bill from Niemcewicz, deputy from Livonia, be adopted or that of Sołtyk, deputy from Kraków?

116 senators deputies abstaining total secret ballot

    +003-013 +036-045   +039-058 +051-043

    (censure of Szczęsny Potocki and Adam Rzewuski)

051892 Should the just read amended bill on the Army Commission be adopted? Or sent for further corrections?

117 senators deputies abstaining total secret ballot

	+008-001 +057-029	+065-030	+055-040
052192	Should the bill just read be adopted or should it be sent for further modification to the Constitutional Committee?		
118	senators deputies abstaining total secret ballot		
	+016-008 +107-007	+123-013	
	("Regulation of Disuniates and Dissidents in Poland")		
052292	Should the bill from the Committee for *Etat* eliminating *Fortrayi* be adopted? Or should it be sent for further corrections?		
119	senators deputies abstaining total secret ballot		
	+010-004 +082-016	+092-020	+082-027
052692	Should the entire bill presented by the Committee on Courland be adopted or sent for corrections?		
120	senators deputies abstaining total secret ballot		
	+007-008 +046-050	+053-058	+056-055

Observations based on this raw information supplement the narrative of minutes and the impressionistic reconstructions of historians. Attendance, the frequency and character of political controversies and conflicts, the direction of legislation and tendencies for agreement on specific issues, are aspects central to the history of this crucial parliament and can be extrapolated from these 120 roll call votes.

Attendance

By law, ordinary *Sejmy* met biennially for six weeks with a possible extension of two weeks and, by custom, confederated parliaments remained in session until the special goal of the confederation had been achieved. Spanning 188 weeks, punctuated with holidays and recesses, the Four Years' *Sejm* was unusually lengthy but it was not unprecedented. The extraordinary confederated *Sejm* of 1773 lasted into 1775 and was infamous for widespread corruption culminating in the distribution of numerous *starostwa* [rented royal lands] among its leadership and more crucially for its ratification of the First Partition.[4] This *Sejm* had created a bad reputation for inordinately protracted parliaments and a reluctance to confederate *Sejmy* by which Stanisław August had hoped to improve the Parliament's effectiveness. Contemporaries and historians, however, have neglected the constructive measures taken by the 1773–1775 *Sejm* towards expanding the central administration.[5]

Attendance during the nearly four years of debates varied but over most of the period it was low as indicated by the voting results, Table 9 and Figure 1.[6]

Table 9

Attendance Rates

Attendance	Highest	Lowest	Mean	s.d.
Sejm	79.2 (11.03.88)	12.4 (6.14.91)	33.7	13.6
Senate & Ministerium	57.4 (11.03.88)	1.9 (6.14.91)	17.8	10.5
Chamber of Deputies	98.3 (11.03.88)	16.3 (5.20.91)	44.6	17.9

	First Term Mean s.d.	Second Term Mean s.d.
Sejm	36.3 15.0	30.0 10.5.
Senate & Ministerium	19.9 11.9	17.8 10.5
Chamber of Deputies	50.7 18.6	34.9 11.7

The roll call votes indicate cycles in attendance. The Four Years' *Sejm* had two prolonged recesses: January 1790 and July-August 1791. Member participation declined, as would be expected, during the two major religious holidays, Christmas and Easter and also for the St. John's summer solstice fairs and at harvest time in July and August. Attendance tended to peak in early December of each year. A drastic, permanent decline in attendance came in the second half of April 1789. The percent participating in the opening term of the second term in December 1790 was only two-thirds that of the opening session in October 1788 but when comparing the two sessions this two-thirds ratio applies only to the Chamber of Deputies.

Figure 1. Attendance Based on Turni Results

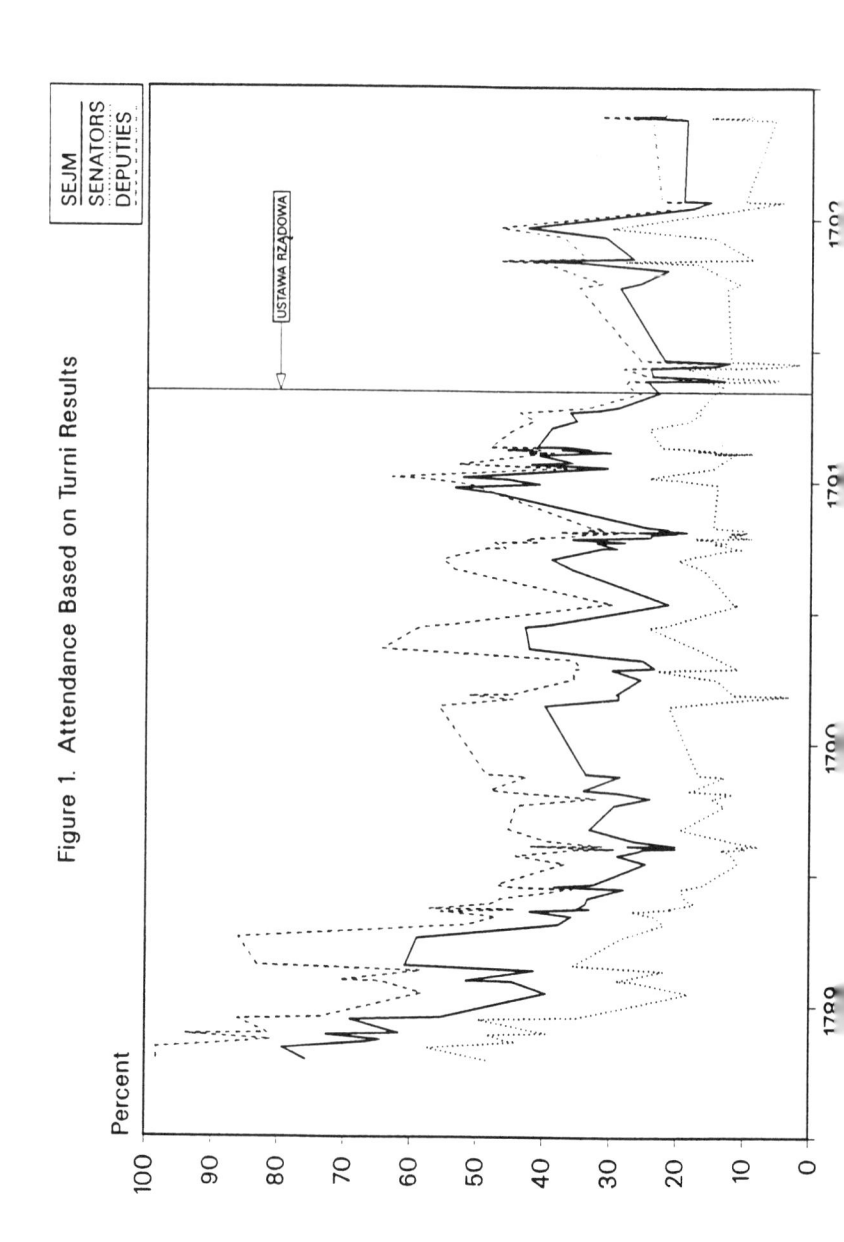

Apparently, a significant number of first term deputies left in 1789 and never returned. The data does indicate that in October 1790 and June 1791 the attendance rates of the two chambers converged. In the former case deputies left Warsaw to attend the local election dietines which seemed not to have concerned those senators who remained consistently active in the *Sejm*.

On occasion attendance declined to such low levels that questions were raised regarding a quorum. Members of the *Sejm* objected to the handling of important business with only sparse attendance. On 25 October 1790, the energetic deputy from Kraków, Jan Jordan, opposed, precisely on such grounds, a *turnum* vote on his resolution that would have increased taxes on royal estates and those of the Order of Malta over the level set for regular noble estates. In the absence, however, of rules concerning a quorum, the continuation of the session and voting on significant issues depended on the disposition of the members and most importantly on the two *marszałkowie*.[7]

The attendance data, while consonant with historians' interpretations, definitely underestimates actual attendance. Significant numbers of deputies and senators attended only part of the daily sessions and it seems that *województwo* delegations rotated attendance to make sure that the *województwo* would always have some input in

Table 10

Double Turni

Date	Combined	Separate	Separate as % of Combined
10.22.90	77	67	87.01%
		47	61.04%
02.15.91	183	143	78.14%
		144	78.68%
05.23.91	92	72	78.26%
		65	70.65%
06.12.91	159	93	58.49%
		133	83.65%
		mean:	74.49%

the *Sejm* debates but at the same time their members would have time to conduct business in the capital or perhaps to rest. This is discernable in cases when two roll call votes were taken on the same day. By counting the total number of members present at either of the two *turni* during the day a more accurate assessment of participation emerges. Calculations can be made on four such instances in the *Stan Rycerski* [Knightly Estate] or Chamber of Deputies (see Table 10).

In the event that generalizations could be made on this narrow information limited to the Chamber of Deputies, it would mean that attendance calculations based on roll call votes estimate only 74.49 percent of the actual attendance rates. Extension of this estimate to the Senate would probably *overestimate* participation since attendance in the Senate varied less than in the Chamber of Deputies. Adjusted attendance figures area as follows:

Table 11

Adjusted Attendance Rates

	Mean	First Term	Second Term
Sejm	45.2	48.7	40.3
Senate	23.9	26.7	23.9
Ministerium			
Chamber of Deputies	59.9	68.1	46.9

Throughout the Four Years' *Sejm*, therefore, somewhat over half (59.9 percent) of the deputies and somewhat less than a fourth (23.9 percent) of the senators attended regularly. Regular attendance at the Senate increased in the second term while that of the deputies declined significantly by 14.5 percent of normal attendance. Thus, the chamber containing the most successful and, indeed, those who may be considered the most magnatorial individuals was marginally more involved after 16 December 1790 when the major reforms were passed; deputy participation declined partly because of the more limited means of the Knightly Estate (deputies could not afford an indefinite stay in Warsaw) but also the decline could have reflected a disenchantment with the widening reform movement and, later, with the May Third Constitution.

In general, the Senate was less involved in the debates with an unadjusted rate of 17.8 percent or between a third and a half of that of the Chamber of Deputies. This consistantly low rate reflected both the advanced age of most of the senators and the declining influence of their institution even prior to the Four Years' *Sejm*. Participation by the bishops was greater than that of the Senate's lay members. Deputies in the majority did attend. Overall, attendance in the *Sejm* was not as dismal as presented in the historical literature.

Attendance also explains part of the political atmosphere after the adoption of the *Ustawa Rządowa*. It is not a valid assumption that most of the deputies who were not present in Parliament were opponents. Many deputies, especially from the first term, had left Warsaw not as a political statement but out of financial or personal necessity or perhaps out of weariness. But crucially, attendance did improve at times after the May Third Revolution and it did generally follow preestablished long term patterns. Based on roll call votes, attendance on 19 December 1791 was 214 (167 deputies and 47 senators). This can be compared to 263 members (225 deputies and 38 senators) present almost a year earlier on 7 January 1791. The Christmas season traditionally brought nobles to Warsaw, and while overall attendance was off by a fifth, the number of senators present actually increased by almost a third. Thus, if attendance indicated support (which it need not have), some of those who by definition belonged to the elite among the enfranchised showed support for the Constitution. The overall decline of about a fifth was smaller than in the analogous period from January to December of 1789. Did these members legitimatize the Constitution by their presence?

Political Controversy

Confederated to accomplish a set of national goals, the Four Years' *Sejm* was the forum for a variety of political controversies. The stated purpose of the 1788 Parliament was to safeguard the liberties and the political, social and governmental system by first of all developing the armed forces and, second, by attending to whatever improvements in the *Rzeczpospolita* may be deemed useful. The military was substantially increased and eventually a new codified constitution was produced.

The character of debates and disputes over army reform and others that emerged initially as extensions of military issues describes the political culture of the times, the perceived problems facing the *Rzeczpospolita*, the interests of the members and their constituencies, and parliamentary dynamics. The roll call votes in turn provide raw information concerning these debates.

The character of political controversy is partly illustrated by the frequency of roll call votes. The frequency of *turni* did not correspond to fluctuations in attendance. Nor did roll call votes seem to become more frequent with the passage of time. There were 70 *turni* or 2.69 per month during the first term and 50 *turni* or 2.77 per month in the second half of the *Sejm*. The doubling of the Chamber of Deputies had no apparent effect on the frequency of roll call votes but it did seem to have increased the number of secret ballots: 32 secret ballots or 1.23 per month in the first term but 33 secret ballots or 1.83 per month in the second, an increase of 40.7 percent. Thus, roughly 46 percent of the *turni* in the first term were followed by secret ballots while after the doubling of the Chamber of Deputies the rate was 66 percent. No single individual or group of individuals was responsible for the increase in secret ballots. The most likely explanations for the increase in secrecy were an enhanced awareness of pressures operative in public roll calls, an increase in those pressures or an escalation of political controversy.

A period of enlivened activity lasted from September until November 1790, with debates intensifying *prior* to the departure of many delegates for the November election *sejmiki* and, more significantly, prior to the arrival of second-term delegates. The intensity of activity resumed after the convening of the expanded parliament through the adoption of the new constitution and into June 1791 when members departed for the annual summer peak in agricultural activity. Judging from the frequency of the roll call votes, issues were most contested in October 1790 both for this period of enlivened debates and for the *Sejm* as a whole. Twelve *turni*—10 percent of the total number of roll call votes—occurred during this month. This skewed the distribution of first term *turni*; roll calls did in fact become more frequent during the second term.

Two developments may have contributed to this flurry of activity and controversy. First, procedural *turni* were initially used in June 1790 and with increased frequency and regularity beginning with the following September. Second, constitutional issues began to be considered in earnest after the debate planning the 1790 term. The second factor is the more significant and its appearance even prior to the arrival of the new delegates, commonly seen as the most important cause of the increased ferment, is explained by two factors: the logic of fulfilling the objectives stated in the "Act of Confederation" i.e., military and fiscal reforms necessitated structural, constitutional changes and second, the approaching deadline for elections to a new *Sejm* forced a consideration of the purpose and nature of the long, confederated parliament.

Reversals of roll call votes were indicative of particularly sensitive issues and illustrative of *Sejm* dynamics. Controversy was substantially higher in secret than in oral roll call votes. Thirteen of the 120 roll call votes were reversed under conditions of secrecy. This inconsistency points to pressures on the *Sejm* floor from colleagues, other delegations and spectators. These reversals are indicative of some of the most controversial matters treated by the Four Years' *Sejm*:

1. On 3 November 1788, shortly after the *Sejm* was first convened, the Army Department was replaced by the Army Commission. The initial voice vote of 149 (56.7 percent) positive (i.e., in favor of the existing Army Department) and 114 (43.3 percent) negative was reversed with the secret ballot vote of 122 (46.6 percent) positive and 140 (53.4 percent) negative. The support of 27 members for the measure eroded, though there is the possibility that some members who voted negative changed their minds but an even greater number voting positive switched sides. The issue was, indeed, of great importance. The Department, as part of the Permanent Council (*Rada Nieustająca*), was viewed as an instrument of Stanisław August and ultimately of Catherine. In the debate concerning authority over the armed forces, the creation of the Army Commission was truly radical. The creation of the Army Commission meant that the armed forces would now be answerable directly and solely to the *Sejm*—a situation that had not even existed prior to the 1776 *Sejm*. Previously the two alternatives were royal authority or the leadership of the lifelong hetmans who invariably were magnates. Thus, the creation of an Army Commission answerable to the *Sejm* potentially struck not only at royal authority but also at the influence of the magnates.

2. A month and a half later, on 16 December 788, the *Sejm* voted to require that Keepers of the Seal (*pieczętarze*) take an oath to the *Sejm*. The initial vote of 70 (38 percent) positive and 114 (62 percent) negative was overturned; in the secret ballot 92 (51.7 percent) voted positive and 86 (48.3 percent) negative. Had all the members who apparently missed the secret ballot voted against the measure a tie would have ensued. This vote is indicative of the growing sejmocracy of the Four Years' *Sejm*.

3. In its regulation of the armed forces, to which most of the first two years were devoted, the *Sejm* decided on 4 September 1789 not to reduce the pay for either regiments or their commanding officers (which stood at 10,000 Polish *złoty*). The initial vote of 76 (69.1 percent) positive against 34 (30.9 percent) negative was overturned in secret ballot by a vote of 45 (42.9 percent) positive against 60 (57.1 percent) negative. More than a third of the initial support had eroded. The issue was particularly sensitive since the armed forces were one of the avenues by which impoverished nobles could make a living. A cutback in allocations, while making the armed forces more cost effective, would severely hurt the lower nobility.
4. One of the earliest, most popular, resolutions of the Four Years' *Sejm* was the creation of a 100,000 man army to guarantee the Commonwealth's independence. The difficulty in raising such an army occupied most of the *Sejm*'s time and led to more comprehensive economic and later constitutional questions. In an effort to quickly bolster the army, even before passage of the long delayed comprehensive army bill, a bill was introduced for the levy of temporary recruits from among peasants on noble estates. This measure narrowly passed on 16 November 1789 48 (50.5 percent) to 47 (49.5 percent) only to be overturned in secret ballot with a vote of 43 (46.7 percent) in favor to 49 (53.3 percent) against. Apparently, public patriotism gave way to private interest in the anonymity of the secret ballot. Each recruit would have meant a loss of income for the noble landowner, a tax not in species or kind but in work power.
5. On 30 April 1790, an amendment to a bill regulating taxation of royal estates was passed by secret ballot despite the prohibition of secret ballots on matters of taxation. Apparently the understanding of taxation was limited to taxation of the nobility. The initial vote was 24 (23.8 percent) positive and 77 (76.2 percent) negative; the final vote was 64 (63.4 percent) positive and only 37 (36.6 percent) negative.
6. On 11 May 1790 two rival representatives from the Wielkopolska region of Kalisz proposed two methods for the assessment of taxes on estates which had been exchanged: Mikorski wanted the Treasury Commission to make its own estimates while Suchorzewski argued that taxes should be based on sales contracts. Mikorski's bill initially won by a margin of 62 (54.4 percent) to 52

(45.6 percent); ultimately Suchorzewski's bill prevailed 62 (55.4 percent) to 50 (44.6 percent).
7. On 21 October 1790, when attendance was low in anticipation of the deputy *sejmiki*, the *Sejm* initially favored giving the Chełm land power to represent the remnant of the Bełz *województwo* that had not been taken by Austria. The vote was 41 (61.2 percent) to 26 (38.8 percent). In the secret ballot, however, the members accepted 37 (56.1 percent) to 29 (43.9 percent) the proposal that they decide about the Bełz issue now or delay it until the Form of Government would be decided. In effect, the members had second thoughts and in a subsequent voice vote they decided to put off the issue completely. The question of representation for areas totally or in part lost in the Partition was quite sensitive. Lay senatorial seats from ceded areas such as the Smoleńsk area were kept but not ecclesiatical offices. As a rule, if even a small scrap to territory remained in the *Rzeczpospolita*, that district usually retained some representation.
8. The second *turnus* in the expanded *Sejm* voted down a proposal for a binding oath on new members. The initial vote on 23 December 1790 was 139 (51.7 percent) in favor versus 130 (48.3 percent) against. The secret ballot vote was 109 (44.1 percent) positive and 138 (55.9 percent) negative.
9. One of the fundamental reforms of the Four Year's *Sejm* was the law on *sejmiki* [local dietines]—"the fount of democracy." In a vote on 18 February 1791, a bill by the Constitutional Committee was defeated in favor of a vote on the bill from the Kraków deputy, Jordan, which itself was put to a roll call vote later the same day and defeated. The vote to decide the Kraków deputy's bill was approved in open roll call 93 (50.8 percent) to 90 (49.2 percent) but the secret ballot favored a decision between the two bills, 100 (54.3 percent) to 84 (45.6 percent). This illustrates the tangle of procedure and political controversy.
10. In the lull before the historic May Third session and prior to the return of most of the members from Easter holiday, the *Sejm* voted to abolish the 100,000 *złoty* income on the royal estate of Niechworów that had been allotted by the 1776 Constitution to a private individual. The initial vote to maintain the allocation was 59 (51.3 percent) positive to 56 (48.7 percent) negative; the final secret vote favored abolition, 54 (54.5 percent) to 45 (45.4 percent). The *Sejm* regularly channelled into military purposes

income from royal estates (*starostwa*) which had been allocated to private individuals. This type of secondary fiscal issues was apparently raised when larger constitutional issues were being avoided for one reason or another.

11. On 17 January 1792 the *Sejm* rejected a bill regulating the Tribunał Courts for the Crown. The initial vote was 62 (68.9 percent) positive to 28 (31.1 percent) negative; the final secret vote was 43 (48.9 percent) positive to 45 (51.1 percent) negative.
12. A major crisis climaxed on 27 January 1792. The *Sejm* adopted a bill from the Livonian, Niemcewicz, to strip Adam Rzewuski and Szczęsny Potocki of their army posts since they had refused to take an oath to the May Third Constitution. A more moderate measure from Sołtyk, deputy from Kraków was initially adopted 58 (59.8 percent) to 39 (40.2 percent) but overturned 51 (54.3 percent) to 43 (45.7 percent) in secret ballot. Szczęsny Potocki subsequently became a leader of the Targowica Confederation that backed the Russian invasion four months later.
13. On 26 May 1792, just prior to the suspension of the *Sejm* because of the Russian invasion, the governance of Courland, a fief, was finally settled. The initial vote was 53 (47.7 percent) in favor to 58 (52.3 percent) against; the final, secret ballot was 56 (50.4 percent) positive and 55 (49.5 percent) negative.

The topics under consideration were complex and interrelated as manifested by meandering and often disorganized debates. But the instances of vote reversals seemed to center, most often, on two issues: taxes and sovereignty. In three of these instances the secret ballot changed a decision on finances: taxation of royal estates, the levy of temporary recruits from among serfs and taxes on a specific mortgaged royal domain. By the rules of the confederation, bills concerning permanent taxes could not be subject to a secret vote, therefore, these tax issues fall into the margin of fiscal questions.

More important were questions connected with the idea of sovereignty. These were of two kinds: territorial issues (representation for Bełz and status of Courland) and loyalty to the *Sejm* (Army Department, oath for Keepers of the Seal, oath for new deputies and Rzewuski's and Szczęsny Potocki's refusal to take an oath to the *Ustawa Rządowa*). Akin to these was the question of the composition and functioning of the *sejmiki* as the source of law, hence the crucial initial instrument through which the national will was expressed.

Arguably, the nature of sovereignty and the power of mechanisms to enforce the will of the nation were subjects of particular controversy. The reversal by secret ballot would seem to indicate that these questions either prompted the most peer pressure in the *Sejm* or evoked the greatest doubt in the mind of its members.

Another indication of the character of political controversy is the type of issues deemed appropriate for roll call votes. As mentioned earlier, some *turni* were conducted between propositions for *turni* and these can be included in a general category of procedural roll call votes that did not directly yield legislation. The second category of *turni* (those directing producing legslation) can be further broken down according to the topic of legislation: constitutional (33.3 percent), military (10.8 percent), taxes (19.2 percent), fiscal (10.8 percent) and political (23.3 percent).

But while frequency of *turni*, reversal of *turni* by secret ballots, and type of issues subject to *turni* all cast some light on the nature of political controversy, a much more useful indicator is the tendency towards unanimity in the *Sejm*. Here too, the results of roll call votes permit the measurement of the degree of controversy on the various issues considered. A very simple calculation produces a measurement of consensus: the absolute value of the difference between positive and negative votes divided by the total votes indicates the degree of agreement.

$$c = \frac{|\text{total positive} - \text{total negative}|}{\text{total votes}}$$

Thus, as the measure "c" approaches the limit of 1 the greater the consensus, as "c" approaches the limit of 0 the greater the disagreement. For instance, if the ratio of positive to negative votes were 10 to 2, "c" would equal .66 ($[10-2]/12$) but if the ratio were 6 to 6 ($[6-6]/12$), "c" would be 0. It is irrelevant whether raw votes or percentages are used. This measure can be used to indicate the tendency for consensus on propositions ending in votes and the cohesiveness of the two chambers and the parliament as a whole.

The numerical preponderance of the Chamber of Deputies accounts for the similarity of figures between it and the *Sejm* as a whole. Overall, for the 111 divisions for which there is specific information, the Senate and Chamber of Deputies were, on average, divided three to one (c = .455) on issues that came to a roll call vote. The Senate and Ministerium exhibited greater concensus, roughly four to one

Table 12
Measure of Consensus for the Four Years' Sejm

	Mean	Stan. Dev.	Minimum	Maximum
Senators	.617	.304	.00	1.00
Deputies	.440	.291	.00	.98
Combined	.455	.292	.00	.96
Secret ballot	.240	.194	.01	.79

(c = .617); the difference of opinion was less in the smaller chamber which included the more elite magnaterial elements of the *szlachta*. In the broader, more representative Chamber of Deputies consensus was somewhat less frequent with issues, on average, being decided by a margin of 72.5 percent to 27.5 percent (c = .440).

The tendency towards consensus also varied according to the issue being decided and according to term as indicated in Table 13.

Categorization of the divisions is, by definition, arbitrary and risky. Most proposals concerned complex issues with overlapping categories. Since the divisions were not categorized in the Four Years' Parliament, the categorization of the primary topic of debate is a decision taken at historical distance.[8] In at least one instance, the historical perspective and contemporary thinking contrasts; the confederated *Sejm* could not hold secret ballots on taxation, yet, in three cases (11 and 16 November 1789 and 30 April 1790) that does seem to have been the case. Nonetheless, such categorization can be carefully attempted to produce an interesting hierarchy of consensus.

The greatest consensus, therefore, was among senators on political issues and the greatest disagreement was among deputies about taxes. Interestingly, the lowest degree of consensus among the senators was still higher than the highest degree of consensus among the deputies. The senators were most unanimous on short-term political issues and the least in agreement on long-term, constitutional matters. For the deputies, military reform brought the most agreement while the taxes, that would ultimately pay for them, caused by far the greatest controversy. Constitutional matters evoked an "average" degree of controversy among the deputies.

Table 13
Degree of Consensus by Topic

Constitutional

	Mean	Stan. Dev.	Minimum	Maximum
Senators	.576	.206	.04	1.00
Deputies	.469	.278	.04	.92
Combined	.465	.295	.01	.93
Secret ballot	.250	.206	.01	.79

Military

	Mean	Stan. Dev.	Minimum	Maximum
Senators	.643	.353	.07	1.00
Deputies	.539	.272	.01	.98
Combined	.525	.316	.00	.96
Secret ballot	.257	.155	.06	.50

Taxes

	Mean	Stan. Dev.	Minimum	Maximum
Senators	.616	.327	.00	1.00
Deputies	.343	.312	.00	.98
Combined	.389	.302	.00	.96
Secret ballot	.180	.104	.01	.79

Fiscal

	Mean	Stan. Dev.	Minimum	Maximum
Senators	.663	.246	.29	1.00
Deputies	.517	.251	.07	.86
Combined	.497	.238	.03	.88
Secret ballot	.213	.151	.07	.49

Political

	Mean	Stan. Dev.	Minimum	Maximum
Senators	.664	.279	.05	1.00
Deputies	.438	.308	.00	.94
Combined	.479	.302	.01	.96
Secret ballot	.259	.230	.03	.69

Table 14
Consensus Rates by Chamber and Topic

Senators		Deputies	
political	.664	military	.539
fiscal	.663	fiscal	.517
military	.643	constitutional	.469
taxes	.619	political	.438
constitutional	.576	taxes	.343

In a sense, therefore, the political elite, if it can be identified with the Senate, was quite cohesive except possibly on fundamental

Table 15
Consensus Rates by Term and by Topic

First Term

Issues

	All	Secret Ballot	Senators	Deputies
constitutional	.424	.186	.606	.385
military	.504	.161	.616	.530
taxes	.374	.180	.602	.327
fiscal	.522	.180	.688	.494
political	.474	.265	.631	.437
all	.438	.208	.621	.407

Second Term

Issues

	All	Secret Ballot	Senators	Deputies
constitutional	.484	.284	.559	.515
military	.588	.385	.725	.566
taxes	.712	—	.926	.681
fiscal	.479	.239	.642	.537
political	.489	.248	.786	.442
all	.485	.275	.617	.505

constitutional issues. Deputies, perhaps because of their more precarious economic status or perhaps because of their accountability to local constituencies, were most divided on taxes but, at the same time, they had a more uniform view of the military that would defend their state and, incidentally, often provide them with a living.

Several observations come readily. The overall degree of controversy or consensus did not greatly differ from one term to the other but there was a noticeable increase in "c" for the doubled set of deputies. The increased consensus among the deputies was marginal across the board except for two instances: taxes, for which there was only one vote and "c" was doubled and on constitutional matters where "c" rose from .385 (69 to 31 percent) to .515 (75 to 25 percent). At the same time, consensus on constitutional issues among the senators declined slightly. The senators, on the other hand, found more agreement in the second term on military and political matters. From among those issues which brought the greatest controversy, that is, those subjected to a secret ballot, for the *Sejm* as a whole, there was more agreement in the second term on constitutional, military and fiscal matters. The most important observation is the increased consensus among deputies during the second term on constitutional issues. This may explain the much higher productivity of the Four Years' *Sejm* in the first half of 1791 or it may reflect a parliament increasingly limited to reform minded deputies. Evidence in the minutes and overall attendance figures indicate that the former was the case.

Summary

Based on the hundred twenty roll call votes taken during the Four Years' *Sejm*, the estimates of attendance and characterizations of political controversy reveal an assembly whose ranks thinned significantly in 1789 and who tended to divide roughly two to one on issues thought appropriate for a vote. Overall attendance for the four years and two terms was about 33.7 percent, with a rate of 45.2 percent after adjustment for daily rotation of members. Attendance tended to be cyclical on a yearly basis and the overall decline for the second term was smaller than for the first. The smaller and less active Senate had a higher degree of consensus. With attendance ranging from an unadjusted total of 57.5 percent down to 2 percent and a mean of 18 percent, the Senate seemed almost marginal and its highest level of controversy, on constitutional matters, was still milder than that of the Chamber of Deputies on any category of issues. The relative strength of the deputies—at least in numbers, which counted on matters brought to a roll call vote—was seen in their 44.6 percent average attendance rate adjusted to 59.9 percent. Nonetheless, the range was great for the deputies. The highest rate of attendance was 98 percent, the lowest was only 16 percent—just below the mean for the Senate. Controversy was most heated among the deputies on the taxes needed to pay, in part, for the military reform on which they agreed most. Debates were sometimes conducted with less than a hundred of the five hundred members present. But the passage of the *Ustawa Rządowa* did not seem to counteract the attrition due to the unusual length of the Parliament.

CHAPTER 5

SEJM AND COUNTRY

By law, and in practice, the Sejm was closely tied to the political nation, the *szlachta*. The principle of representation—part of the "golden freedom" essential to the *szlachta*'s traditional ideology—was guaranteed, on the Republic level, primarily through institutional devices: the electional *sejmiki* which chose the deputies, instructions which bound the deputies to the wishes of their constituencies and the post-parliamentary "report" (*relacyjny*) *sejmiki* which brought real accountability. These structures were supplemented by communication between the *Sejm* and local constituents through official universals, regularly public sessions, published *Sejm* proceedings and newspaper coverage. Most obviously and perhaps most importantly, parliamentary members were themselves the point of essential connection between the *Sejm* and the country.

During the Four Years' *Sejm*, 536 individuals (359 serving as deputies, 158 as senators and 19 as ministers) represented about 850,000 *szlachta* in a post-partition population of 8.8 million.[1] As stated in chapter 4, attendance rates reduced this level of representation. On average, 216 were present. Numerically representation in the Four Years' *Sejm* compares with up to 1,200 from a population of 26 million for the 1789 National Assembly in France and 50 out of 2 million for the Constitutional Congress in the United States. These numerical relations may not mean much and as samples of the population the *Sejm*'s members were made atypical by their political ambitions or sense of duty and their popularity or political skills. Nonetheless, they constituted a point of contact between the reforms of the Four Year's *Sejm* and the political nation. Their characteristics should shed light on this crucial parliament, on the composition of the political nation and on the *szlachta*'s relation to the new constitution.

Despite the importance of the Four Years' *Sejm*, biographical information about its members is fairly incomplete. Some quantifiable characteristics can be gathered for all members of the Chamber of Deputies from *Sejm* records.[2] These include term, province, district, accession to the confederation of 1788, title or non-senatorial office held during the parliament. Beyond this, the task of compiling biographical sketches for all the *Sejm* members would be a monumental endeavor were it not for the *Polski słownik biograficzny* [Polish Biographical Dictionary] and, to a much lesser extent, the *Wielka encyklopedia* [Great Encyclopedia] of the Polish Academy of Science. To date the dictionary is complete only through "R" but not all deputies whose names start with letters from "A" to "R" are included and for some only sketchy information is given. Thus, 169 out of the 359 deputies are listed in the *Słownik*. Though the information is surprising incomplete, there is a regularity in the compiled facts that permits comparison.

While the biographical information in the *Polski słownik biograficzny* and the *Wielka encyklopedia* gives a good (or the best possible) indication of the backgrounds and life experiences of *Sejm* members, the data does not constitute a truly random sample. At least two factors were at work dispelling pure chance: the physical survival of primary sources concerning the background and life experiences of the deputies and the numerous choices by numerous editors and writers of the secondary sources whether or not to include specific individuals. Auxiliary factors influencing the nature of the sources included geography and wealth that could have effected the survivability of records and politicized historical views of biographers may have increased the remembrance of perceived "patriots" and relegated to oblivion the opponents of the historically popular Constitution except for those of exceptional fame or notoriety.

The operating assumption in this study is that though the data is incomplete and these two factors may have played a role in preventing pure randomness, these distortions are unavoidable and minimal. In a sense the entire universe of existing information has been utilized. Moreover, it is unlikely that individuals whose names came after the letter "R" were more prone to support either side of the constitutional issue. Keeping in mind these imperfections, the best possible, though perhaps somewhat impressionistic, picture of the individual and collective characteristics of the 359 deputies does emerge. The relevant characteristics given include educational background, religion, travel abroad, relations to officeholders, orders bestowed, previous service in parliament, relation to the Confederation of Bar, relation to the new constitution, membership in the *Zgromadzenie Przyjaciół Konstytucyi Rzadowey* [Society of Friends of the Governmental Constitution], wealth, non-agricultural income, relation to wealth, membership in the Masonry, military service, connections to France, Austria, Prussia and Russia, and diplomatic experience. Other characteristics of interest were future careers: membership in the counterrevolutionary Targowica Confederation (1792), participation in the Kościuszko Uprising (1794) and offices held in the Grand Duchy of Warsaw (1806–1815) and the Congress Kingdom (1815–1831).

Characteristics of the Four Years' Sejm

The picture of the Four Years' *Sejm* unfolds along two dimensions: geographical administrative divisions and the grouping of deputies according to term. The historical development of the *Sejm* divided the deputies into three provinces plus Livonia whose status was an anomaly and whose importance will be discussed later. This division had an important parliamentary function. Separate provincial sessions at the *Sejm* were intended to smooth the work of plenary meetings. In the years 1788–1792, Great Poland (Wielkopolska), Little Poland (Małopolska), Lithuania (Wielkie Xięstwo or Grand Duchy) and Livonia were represented by 359 individuals and a set of corresponding senatorial offices. Theoretically equal, the representation of each province did vary roughly according to population. Wielkopolska, geographically the smallest but economically the most advanced, had 133 deputies or 37 percent of the total. Małopolska, the largest, but with uneven development, had 117 or 32.6 percent while the Grand Duchy of Lithuania, which once had been independent, possessed 97 deputies or only 27 percent of the total. The fragments of Livonia which remained in the *Rzeczpospolita* were represented by 12 men, 3.3 percent of the *Sejm*. Since Livonia had been a joint holding of the Crown (i.e., Wielkopolska and Małopolska) and the Grand Duchy (Lithuania), four Livonians were considered representatives of the Crown, four of Lithuania and four of Livonia alone.

Further, each province was a historical composite. Wielkopolska included the once independent duchy of Mazowsze (Mazovia) but lacked northern Wielkopolska proper and Royal Prussia which had been lost in the first partition.[3] Małopolska included the ethnically Polish territories of Małopolska proper (Kraków, Sandomierz and Lublin) and Podlasie plus much of Rus' which itself could be divided into the western territories of Chełm, Wołyń and Podole and the eastern *województwa* of the Bracław, Kijów (Kyyiv) and Czernichów (Chernihiv). Moreover, southern Małopolska and most of Red Rus' had been lost in 1772 (1775).[4] Lithuania spanned ethnic Lithuania, all of Black Rus' and most of White Rus' (Belarus), some of which had been ceded in 1772. The trend during the Four Years' *Sejm* was to convert the parliamentary practice of three provinces into a more standardized system replacing the Lublin duality of Crown and Grand Duchy. Laws in the autumn of 1791 standardized the three provinces thus culminating centuries of slow administrative development.[5]

The division of the *Sejm* into provinces was complemented in the Four Years' *Sejm* by a division according to term. After prolonged discussion it was decided in September 1790 to continue the Confederation of 1788 but also to uphold the law requiring parliamentary elections every two years. This resulted in a unique doubling of the number of deputies and much controversy. With deaths, promotions and replacements there were 179 first term deputies and an additional 180 in the second term. The deputies were grouped according to both criteria as follows:

Table 16
Number of Deputies by Term and by Province

Term	Wielkopolska	Małopolska	Lithuania	Livonia
1788	66	58	49	6
1790	67	59	48	6
	133	117	97	12 = 359
	37.0%	32.6%	27.0%	3.3%

These two dimensions, geography and term, facilitate the analysis of the deputies' individual characteristics.

Age and Education

Collectively, the deputies were in the prime of their lives and most had been educated in church schools. In 1791, ages ranged from the twenty-year-old Józef Dominik Kossakowski of the Wilkomierz district in Lithuania to the seventy-eight-year-old Tomasz Dłuski of Lublin in Małopolska; both had been elected only the previous November. The mean age for the entire *Sejm* in 1791 was 41.2 years. The variations from this norm were great only for Lithuania and Livonia:

Table 17

Deputies' Ages in 1791

Term	Wielko-polska	Mało-polska	Lithuania	Livonia	All
1788	44.14	41.75	40.50	33.66	41.8
1790	43.70	41.09	36.27	30.00	40.4
mean	43.95	41.5	38.9	31.8	41.2

Born at mid-century the majority of deputies for whom information has been found were taught in church schools: 24.6 percent solely by the Piarists, 32.8 percent solely by the Society of Jesus and another 3.3 percent by both. An additional 6.5 percent had complemented their Jesuit education with studies abroad or other, non-church, schools. Together 27.9 percent had been under the direct influence of the reform minded Piarists and 42.6 percent under the more conservative Jesuits. Overall there was a shift in the character of education between the two terms. Both Piarist and Jesuit education fell (25.7 percent to 23.1 percent and 37.1 percent to 26.9 percent) while education abroad and "other" increased (5.7 percent to 19.2 percent and 8.6 percent to 15.4 percent).

Though, the variations by term were not significant, the character of education did vary greatly geographically. Jesuit influence was by far strongest in Wielkopolska where it was complemented by a relatively high rate of education abroad. 57.9 percent of the Wielkopolanian deputies for whom there is information received a Jesuit-only education while less than a tenth of that number (5.3 percent) were trained by their more innovative rivals, the Piarists. This powerful, conservative, counterreformation education for the majority was followed by a high instance of "other" mainly private tutoring (21.1 percent) and by schooling abroad (10.1 percent). The combination of conservative Jesuit education, private tutoring and foreign schooling was unique to the Wielkopolska delegation.

Educational background was much more varied and progressive in Małopolska. Piarist education was much more common than in Wielkopolska. 26.9 percent of Małopolska deputies for whom there is information received schooling solely in Piarists schools, 7.7 percent combined Piarist and Jesuits educations and another 7.7 percent combined these two types of schooling with both private schooling and sojourns at foreign schools; 42.3 percent of the Małopolanians, therefore, were at least in part educated by Piarists. This was roughly equivalent to the Jesuit influence: 19.2 percent had a Jesuit-only education, 11.5 percent Jesuit and foreign, 7.7 percent Jesuit and Piarist and 3.8 percent Jesuit and other for a grand total of 42.2 percent educated at least in part by the Society of Jesus. In addition, 11.5 percent were educated privately, another 11.5 percent received an education abroad and 3.8 percent by the new schools of the National Educational Commission.

The progressive influence of the Piarists was even stronger among the Lithuanian and Livonian deputies. Exactly half of the Lithuanians, for whom there is information, were educated by the Piarists, a third by the Jesuits and the rest were evenly divided between a foreign education and National Education Commission schools. Among the Livonian delegation this profile was more pronounced: half were educated abroad, and the rest were evenly divided between Piarist and National Education Commission schools. In contrast to the other delegations, especially the Wielkopolanians, none of the Livonians were Jesuit educated.

Commonly, therefore, deputies were educated either by Jesuits or Piarists while the other educational institutions played a minor role. National Education Commission schools were, on the whole, secularized Jesuit schools after the Society was banned by the Pope in 1773. Though the Jesuit staff often stayed on, these schools did receive direction from Warsaw and the universities at Kraków and Wilno. Two more schools had been created to impart a modern education on the nobility: the Collegium Nobilium founded by Stanisław Konarski in 1742 and a military academy, the Szkoła Rycerska [Knights' School] created by the king in 1765. Only very small minorities of the deputies about whom there is information attended these innovative institutions: 7 percent and 6.3 percent respectively. In both cases, most of these graduates were elected to the first term and the largest group came from Małopolska. Geographical doubling occurred only in Brześć Litewski (2 graduates of the Szkoła

Rycerska, Julian Ursyn Niemcewicz and Kazimierz Nestor Sapieha), Kraków (Kwasery Puszet - Szkoła Rycerska; Ignacy Dembiński - National Education Commission) and Lublin (Morski - Szkoła Rycerska; Stanisław Kostka Potocki - Collegium Nobilium). Significantly, this small group of deputies included some of the most active in the *Sejm*: the Lithuanian Marshal Sapieha, the publicist Julian Ursyn Niemcewicz, Tadeusz Kościałkowski (Lithuania, Wiłkomierz district) and the Ossoliński brothers from Podlasie. Interestingly, these particularly active deputies all came from ethnic borderlands between the Crown and the Grand Duchy.

Travel

The majority of deputies had not travelled abroad before being elected. First term deputies were more travelled than their later colleagues with 22.7 percent having travelled extensively, and 6.8 percent in a more limited manner compared to 9.6 percent and 5.5 percent respectively for the second term. The rates varied greatly among the provinces. Half of the Livonian deputies had travelled abroad, 30.5 percent of the Małopolanians, 18.7 percent of the Wielkopolanians and only 13.9 percent of the Lithuanians. Apparently, as will be seen later, the inclination for reform along the lines of the new Constitution was strongest in some of the areas where travel abroad had been more limited.

Religion

The deputies were religiously homogeneous, at least with respect to church membership. The Calvinist Paweł Grabowski from Wołkowysk (Lithuania) was joined in 1790 by the fellow reformed church members Zygmunt Grabowski also from Wołkowysk and Adam Bronikowski from Gniezno in Wielkopolska. But these were the only "dissidents"; the *Sejm*, apparently, had neither Lutheran nor Orthodox members. The absence of Lutherans is explained by the territorial losses from the first partition since Lutherans had lived mainly in Pomorze or in the cities which were not represented.[6] Orthodox nobles were not welcomed in the *szlachta* after the mid-seventeenth century.

A separate and not well understood issue is the position of Uniates—Catholics of the Slavonic (Greek) rite. Theoretically both rites of the Catholic Church were equal in the *Rzeczpospolita* yet, little evidence exists of Uniates at the sejmiki or as deputies. It was not until the summer of 1790 that a single Uniate bishop—Teodozy Rostocki, the metropolitan of all of Rus'—entered the Senate though the two church hierarchies had been declared equal at the creation of the Uniate Church in 1596. It would appear that the *szlachta* which participated in the political processes was thoroughly Polonized, even with respect to the Roman rite, or anti-Uniate pressure was strong down to the local level. An alternative explanation would be that being Uniate may not have been an issue.

It is difficult to measure anticlericism—both enlightened and traditional—among the deputies but it was undoubtedly widespread. The *szlachta* eyed church property as a resource to finance the enlarged armed forces and many resented the apparent uselessness of the clergy. The most vocal critic of the clergy was Jacek Jezierski, castellan of Łuków, would also point out that the Church had given its blessing to the partition in 1772. Members of the *Sejm* accepted Catholicism as a vital part of *szlachta* culture but at the same time many held very critical views of the clergy.

Offices and Vanities

The theoretical equality of the *szlachta* did not prevent most of the deputies from actively seeking distinctive titles in a widely accepted hierarchy of merit. These titles referred either to traditional local offices, to a variety of other military and civil offices, or to minor national titles. In some cases, when personal accomplishments were lacking, deputies used the "wic" or "son of" title, such as *wojewodowic* [the son of a *wojewoda*]. *Sejm* records give a complete listing of these titles for each deputy during his parliamentary tenure. In both terms and throughout the *Rzeczpospolita*, with the usual exception of Livonia, the most common titles were the two highest local offices (*podkomorzy and chorąży* [standard-bearer]), *starostowie* [administers of certain royal estates] and chamberlains.

In addition to offices, a nobleman could be awarded two national marks of distinction: the Order of the White Eagle established by the Wettins in 1705 and the Order of St. Stanisław created upon the accession of King Stanisław August Poniatowski in 1764. The older of the two was the more prestigeous with the St. Stanisław medal most often serving as a prerequisite.

Figures tracing these awards are quite interesting:

Table 18
Orders of St. Stanisław and the White Eagle

Entire Sejm	1788	1791	1792
no medals	67.7%	54.9%	26.8%
St. Stanisław	24.4%	28.7%	47.6%
White Eagle	.6%	2.4%	4.3%
both	7.3%	14.0%	21.3%

	1788		1791		1792	
Term	1st	2nd	1st	2nd	1st	2nd
no medals	56.8%	80.3%	42.0%	69.7%	34.1%	63.2%
St. Stanisław	30.7%	17.1%	33.0%	23.7%	29.5%	23.7%
White Eagle	1.1%	0.0%	3.4%	1.3%	5.7%	2.6%
both	11.4%	2.6%	21.6%	5.3%	30.7%	10.5%

The figures show both the advantages of serving in the *Sejm* and of being among the more experienced or valued first term deputies. The 1788 figures would seem to indicate a disparity between the political importance of the two sets of deputies. The substantially lower instance of orders among second term deputies was probably symptomatic not only of youth but also of lesser skill in the political arena. A less likely alternative explanation is that second term deputies valued the medals less than their colleagues. Whatever the reason, this disparity in orders persisted somewhat during the parliamentary tenures of second term deputies. At the end of the Four Years' *Sejm* the political standing of second term deputies, as measured by the awarding of orders, was still slightly behind that of first term deputies *at the opening of the Sejm in 1788*.

Variations were also significant among the provinces:

Table 19
Distribution of Orders Compared to Sejm Average

	1788			1791			1792		
	W	M	L	W	M	L	W	M	L
no medal	-10.8	-3.3	+12.7	-7.8	-4.1	+10.3	-8.4	-1.8	+ 8.9
St. Stanisław	-14.8	-5.8	- 4.8	+10.5	-6.7	- 0.4	+8.5	-6.5	+ 1.5
White Eagle	- 0.6	+0.9	- 0.6	+ 1.5	-0.7	- 0.2	+1.6	-0.9	0.0
both	- 3.4	+8.0	- 7.3	- 4.2	+11.4	- 9.2	-1.7	+9.2	-10.4

W = Wielkopolska   M = Małopolska   L = Lithuania

Thus, while the overall rate was highest for Wielkopolska, the difference was in the relatively low honor of St. Stanisław. Małopolska also had a higher than normal rate but the difference was in those who had both orders. In Lithuania, while the number of St. Stanisław awards approached the *Sejm* norms, there was a general lack of the more prestigeous White Eagle.

Wealth

The measurement of wealth poses several problems. Records for the 10 percent (*"dziesiątego grosza"*) tax on agricultural income, passed by the *Sejm* in 1789, would provide a basis for comparison among the deputies even if the information was consistently distorted. Unfortunately the tax information for the Crown was lost with the burning of the Crown Treasury Commission archives by the Germans in 1944 and the records of the Grand Duchy Treasury Commission, while they are intact in Vilnius, have not been available to this author. Some information on the tax in the Crown has been preserved in local records but these would only indicate a lower limit to fortunes since the *szlachta* commonly attempted to avoid disasters by scattered its holdings. The tax information for the Kraków *województwo* has also been preserved, in alterred form, in materials compiled before the Second World War for a planned historical-geographic dictionary.[7]

The terminology used in the eighteenth century to distinguish groups among the *szlachta* would seem to be an alternative to the unavailable tax information. This, however, is complicated by the tension between an ideology that postulated the absolute equality of the nobility and customary classifications based only in part on material criteria. In the old *Rzeczpospolita* all adult male nobles were considered equal but some were *panowie* [lords] juxtaposed to the *szlachta*, a distinction reflected in the division of the *Sejm* into the Senate and the *stan rycerski* [estate of the knights]. Another category was *szaraczkowie* or *szaraki*, "the gray ones" who were poor but owned land. These were also known as *szlachta zagrodowa* [backyard], *ciąstkowa* [fragment], or most often *drobna* [small]. Other common eighteenth century distinctions in the estate that officially was perfectly equal were *possessionaci*—those who held land—and those who did not and *dziedziczowie*—who had hereditary possession of land - and those who did not. *Szlachta gołota* [naked] also referred to the landless nobility. *Ziemianie* was yet another term to classify nobles; it referred to those who worked the land (*ziemia*)—not necessarily with their own hands—though the same word occasionally would refer to peasants as late as the nineteenth century.[8]

Historians have tried to create order in this chaos by imposing categories based solely on wealth. The often used divisions have been the small *szlachta*, the middle *szlachta* and the magnates or the poor, middle, wealthy (*szlachta*) and the magnates. The latter set has been used consistently by contributors to the *Polski słownik biograficzny* on which the biogram information is largely based. The distinction between middle and very rich sometimes is made by implication with special references to wealth that distinguished an individual from the middle *szlachta*. The division is imprecise but quite real in the wider view. It is also consistent with information found outside of the *Słownik* but the distinction between middle and wealthy will require further investigation. In the absence of other, more ideally suited, information these categories have been accepted, not without some misgivings.

The major variation from the norm occurred in Wielkopolska where among the *Sejm* delegation there was a much smaller group of magnates than in either of the other two provinces. The very rich were strongest in Wielkopolska where the next lower category, that of the middle *szlachta*, was as strongly represented as it was in Lithuania. The concentration of wealth was definitely at its highest level in Małopolska and lowest in Wielkopolska. The difference between the Lithuanian and Małopolanian delegations was not so much the 2 percent variation in magnate representation as the concentration in Lithuania of wealth below the "very rich" level in the middle nobility

Table 20
Wealth Profile of Deputies

	Entire Sejm	First Term	Second Term
poor	5.5%	4.3%	7.4%
middle	11.9%	10.1%	15.0%
very rich	66.1%	66.7%	65.0%
magnate	16.5%	18.8%	12.5%

	Wielkopolska	Małopolska	Lithuania	Livonia
poor	5.9%	4.7%	0.0%	50%
middle	14.7%	7.0%	14.3%	25%
very rich	73.5%	65.1%	64.3%	25%
magnate	5.9%	23.3%	21.4%	0%

and the absence of poor nobles. It is likely that the poor members of the Małopolska delegation were dependent on the magnates. The Livonian delegation, as always, was quite distinct with the lowest level of wealth.

An individual's wealth by itself may not be significant without reference to family fortunes. Comparisons among the wealth of delegations for specific provinces with analogous figures for delegates' fathers seem to indicate crucial shifts. The differences seem to have been largest in Wielkopolska. In contrast to their fathers, the Wielkopolanians had an 8 percent increase in those who were very rich and there was also the appearance of a group of poor deputies. The other two categories (magnates and middle nobility) declined almost by half from father to son. This would seem to indicate an advancing group of very rich nobles, a decline in the representation of magnates and some general impoverishment. These shifts would seem to confirm the thesis that the power of the magnates was being replaced by an independent upper middle class of nobles.

Table 21
Wealth Profile of Deputies' Fathers

	Entire Sejm	First Term	Second Term
poor	5.7%	4.8%	7.1%
middle	21.9%	15.9%	21.4%
very rich	54.3%	55.6%	37.1%
magnate	18.1%	23.8%	14.3%

	Wielkopolska	Małopolska	Lithuania	Livonia
poor	0.0%	7.3%	0.0%	75%
middle	24.1%	17.1%	29.0%	0%
very rich	65.5%	51.2%	54.8%	0%
magnate	10.3%	24.4%	16.1%	25%

Such a conclusion seems logical but it must be tempered by the realization that generational shifts occurred only on the provincial delegation level and that the discrepancy is a function of the incompleteness of the data. There are but a few instances where the wealth classification of a delegate was different from his father. In Wielkopolska, Jan Potocki was classified as very rich while his father was a magnate. In Małopolska, the same applied to another Potocki, Jerzy. A substantive distinction between "very rich" and "magnate" is very doubtful in such cases.

A very real difference did exist in the case of Tomasz Dłuski from Lublin who built a modest fortune out of his father's poverty. In Lithuania, Mateusz Butrymowicz came from a middle noble family and climbed into the very rich category while his colleague Wojciech Pusłowski climbed onto the magnate level. Among the Livonians the same illusion of an "impoverished son" applied to another Potocki, Piotr, Stanisław Kublicki, however, did come from a very poor family but by 1788 could be classified as middle nobility. Overall, the phenomenon of a younger generation less prosperous than their fathers is an illusion.

Additional, Minimal Factors

Freemasonry, military careers and foreign connections were distinguishing features of eighteenth century nobles, yet, seldom were they found among deputies of the Four Years' *Sejm*. Freemasonry seemed only to be a factor among the unique Livonian delegation. The Livonian deputies were also different with respect to military careers but the information is very limited. Another word of caution is necessary. Many members of the *szlachta* had military titles without any real military experience.

Connections with Russia, Prussia, Austria, and France as well as diplomatic experience were even weaker. Seldom did the percentages exceed 10 percent. Contacts were highest in Wielkopolska and diplomatic experience was most common among the Małopolanians. None of the Lithuanians seems to have had official diplomatic experience.

Table 22
Freemasonry and Military Careers

Freemasonry

	Sejm	First Term	Second Term
member	12.9%	11.9%	14.3%
nonmember	87.1%	88.1%	85.7%

	Wielkopolska	Małopolska	Lithuania	Livonia
member	14.9%	8.8%	11.6%	37.5%
nonmember	85.1%	91.2%	88.4%	62.5%

Military Careers

	Sejm	First Term	Second Term
none	74.2%	74.1%	85.7%
some	16.4%	17.6%	9.5%
professional	9.4%	8.2%	4.8%

	Wielkopolska	Małopolska	Lithuania	Livonia
none	77.1%	71.7%	79.1%	50.0%
some	8.3%	18.3%	16.3%	50.0%
professional	14.6%	10.0%	4.7%	0.0%

Previous Political Experience

Regular meetings of the *Sejm* every two years built up a reservoir of experienced part-time parliamentarians. Slightly less than half of the deputies had served previous to the Four Years' *Sejm*. First term deputies and the delegation from Wielkopolska were the most experienced. 56.3 percent of the deputies elected in 1788, for whom there is information, had previous service in the *Sejm* compared to 39 percent of their second term colleagues. An even higher percentage of Wielkopolanians of both terms (62 percent) had been to earlier *Sejmy*. The rate among the Małopolanians approached the overall average (50.8 percent compared to 49.2 percent) while the Lithuanians and Livonians were substantially less experienced with rates of only 35.6 percent and 12.5 percent respectively. The highest level of experience for any single delegation was 65.6 percent for first term Małopolanians. The depth of experience was greater for the set of first term deputies which included many more individuals with previous service in three or more parliaments.

On the individual level the most experienced deputy was Prince Adam Czartoryski of Lublin who had attended eight *Sejmy* prior to his election in 1788. He was followed by Stanisław Małachowski (Sandomierz *województwo*, Małopolska), Józef Mikorski (Gostyniń land, Rawa *województwo*, Wielkopolska) and Jan Ośniałowski (Dobrzyń land, Inowrocław *województwo*, Wielkopolska) each with seven previous *Sejmy*. The most experienced Lithuanian was Kazimierz Nestor

Table 23
Previous Experience in the Sejm

Previous Terms	Sejm	First Term	Second Term
0	51.8%	43.7%	61.0%
1	16.5%	19.5%	13.0%
2	14.6%	13.8%	15.6%
3	6.7%	10.3%	2.6%
4	4.9%	5.7%	3.9%
5	.6%	1.1%	2.6%
6	2.4%	2.3%	1.8%
7	1.8%	1.1%	
8	.6%		

	Wielkopolska	Małopolska	Lithuania	Livonia
0	38.0%	49.2%	64.4%	87.5%
1	16.0%	18.2%	15.6%	12.5%
2	20.0%	14.8%	11.1%	
3	8.0%	8.2%	4.4%	
4	8.0%	4.9%	2.2%	
5			2.2%	
6	6.0%	1.6%		
7	4.0%	1.6%		
8		1.6%		

Sapieha (Brześć Litewski). The leadership of the parliament came, not surprisingly, from these experienced deputies: Małachowski was marshal of the Crown deputies and Sapieha marshal of the Lithuanians. Interestingly there was a geographic concentration of several experienced individuals. Of those with six previous Sejmy, two came from metropolitan areas (Antoni Michałowski - Kraków and Adam Moszczeński - Poznań) and two from the Mazowsze region of Wielkopolska (Michał Karski - Rożan land and Józef Radzicki - Zakroczym land). The said Mikorski also represented a formerly Mazowsze area and Ośniałowski came from an adjacent region.

The Confederation of Bar

In the unreformed system, the institution of the confederation was just as equal as the *Sejm*, though it was used less frequently. As mentioned in chapter 2, *Sejmy* could be confederated but the classic confederation was an armed insurrection against perceived abuses of the political system. The contractual relationship between the king and the *szlachta* as formulated in the Henrycian Articles, released nobles from their oath to the king should he abuse his power. Large segments of the *szlachta* perceived just such a situation when, with partial backing from Catherine of Russia, Stanisław August had sought to strengthen royal authority in the years immediately following his election in 1764. Under the banner "Faith and Freedom" the *szlachta*, whose manifesto was proclaimed in the Podolian town of Bar, spent five years battling royal and Russian troops. A year after the confederation was crushed in 1771, a third of the Republic's territory was seized in the first partition as a means of lowering tensions among Prussia, Russia and Austria.

A small number of deputies to the Four Years' *Sejm* had participated in this unrest twenty years earlier. Of those about whom there is information, 13.9 percent had actively participated in the Confederation of Bar, an additional 1.3 percent had been among the revolt's leaders and 1.3 percent had actively opposed it. This varied according to term and province:

Table 24

Participation in the Confederation of Bar

	first term	second term	
participants	17.9%	9.5%	
leaders	1.2%	1.4%	
opponents	1.2%	1.4%	
	Wielkopolska	Małopolska	Lithuania	Livonia
participants	18.8%	15.8%	4.7%	25%
leaders		1.7%		
opponents	1.5%			

Though the figures are quite limited they do give some impression of differences in this form of political activity. As in the case of parliamentary service, first term deputies were the more experienced. The level of participation among the Crown delegations was essentially the same, though the Małopolanians may have played a more important role. The Lithuanian delegations of both terms were much less seasoned in either type of political experience.

Summary by Province and Term

The 359 deputies of the Four Years' *Sejm* exhibited significant variations in their personal characteristics and life experiences. Having examined different factors according to province and term, composite portraits of each province and each term emerge.

The delegation from Wielkopolska was, on average, the oldest and most experienced in the Four Years' *Sejm*. With a mean age of 43.95 years, the Wielkopolanians had the most experience in *Sejmy* and a relatively high participation rate in the Confederation of Bar. The delegation fit into the general pattern of local officeholding but had a higher rate of St. Stanisław medals. Almost a quarter had military experience, four fifths of whom seemed to have been career officers. As throughout the *Rzeczpospolita*, freemasonry and strong connections with foreign powers seemed to have been very rare. Economically the very wealthy were definitely the strongest element both among the Wielkopolanian deputies themselves (73.9 percent) and their fathers (65.5 percent). Finally, Wielkopolanian education seemed singularly influenced by the Society of Jesus (57.9 percent) with a significant amount of foreign schooling (10.5 percent). This seems to have given the delegation both a conservative and a comparatively sophisticated character.

The delegation from Małopolska was, on the other hand, concurrently the most diverse and the most typical in the Republic. Its mean age of 41.46 years approached the *Sejm* average of 41.2. Politically the deputies' past parliamentary experience was typical as was their participation in the Confederation of Bar. Though local officeholding was also average, the instance of orders was higher especially with respect to the more coveted Order of the White Eagle. This would seem to indicate success in the traditional prestige system. Military titles were also higher. The magnate element was definitely very strong among the Małopolanians and their fathers but it was never the majority. The education of the delegation was, however, the most diversified with an equal division between Piarist and Jesuit schools. The Małopolanians had the highest rate among the three provinces of study and travel abroad.

Of the three provincial delegations, the Lithuanians were the youngest and the least experienced. With the mean age of 38.9 years in 1791 the delegation also had the highest rate of parliamentary novices (64.4 percent) This inexperience was evident in the lower participation rate in the Confederation of Bar and the rarity of orders. The general pattern of officeholding was, however, typical. In wealth, the percentage of magnates and the very rich was equivalent to those of Małopolska while the level of middle nobility was roughly the same as in the Wielkopolanian delegation. The difference lay in the complete absence of poor nobles. In marginal characteristics the Lithuanians displayed even lower rates. The Lithuanian did include among their number two religious dissenters. But the distinquishing characteristic of the Lithuanian delegation was its educational profile: Piarist influence was particularly strong.

Livonia was, of course, a real exception in most categories. The extremely young Livonian delegation (31.8 years) was the least politically experienced, the least travelled and the least influenced by the Jesuits. In fact, none of the Livonians seems to have been educated by the Society of Jesus. The deputies appeared to be a group of political outsiders who found a rare career opportunity in representing the fragments of Livonia left in the *Rzeczpospolita*.

Variations also occurred between the two terms in the doubled *Sejm*. Collectively, the deputies elected in 1790 were younger than their colleagues elected in 1788, though their age was slight higher than that of 1788 deputies at the time of their election. The age differences between terms on the province level varied from the insignificant in Wielkopolska (-.44 years) and Małopolska (-.66) to the substantial in Lithuania (-3.23) and Livonia (-3.66). As a result there was a difference of fourteen years between first term Wielkopolanians and second term Livonians.

Several other characteristics were common to second term deputies. The new deputies had less previous parlimentary experience, a lower participation rate in the Confederation of Bar, less travel abroad, fewer offices, fewer and lower orders. Economically, the mix of strata remained basically the same: the percentage of magnate deputies declined slightly (from 14.8 percent to 12.4 percent) while that of the very rich also decreased (from 66.7 percent to 65.0 percent), the middle and lower nobility increased by marginal amounts. The very rich predominated in both terms. Religious influence in education seems to have declined especially with respect to Jesuit schooling. With these differences, historians have aptly observed that the 1790 deputies brought new life to the prolonged parliament.

Attitudes towards the May Third Constitution

From the available biogram information about two thirds of the deputies (67.1 percent) supported or came to support the new Constitution while a third (32.9 percent) were in opposition. The Constitution was a somewhat more divisive issue than other constitutional matters. The measure of consensus, "c," for the Constitution was .342 while the mean value of "c" for the entire *Sejm* was .465 and .485 for the term in which the May Third Constitution was passed. The Constitution accentuated general ideological differences.

Table 25
The Deputies and the May Third Constitution

	All Deputies	First Term	Second Term
opponents	32.9%	30.0%	35.9%
supporters	63.4%	68.6%	57.8%
	} 67.1%	} 70%	} 64.1%
converts	3.7%	1.4%	6.3%

	Wielkopolska	Małopolska	Lithuania	Livonia
opponents	32.6%	44.2%	21.2%	0.0%
supporters	65.1%	53.8%	69.7%	100.0%
	} 67.4%	} 55.7%	}78.8%	
converts	2.3%	1.9%	9.1%	

Variations did follow provincial and term divisions. Support for the *Ustawa Rządowa* was softer among the less experienced, younger, less travelled, less religiously educated, less magnate influenced second term deputies. The ratio of support/opposition varied in a spectrum across the *Rzeczpospolita*. Wielkopolska fit the norm, support was significantly lower in Małopolska, significantly higher in Lithuania and unanimous in Livonia. Support, therefore, was strongest in the province with a high level of magnate influence and an absence of poor nobles and in Livonia where the magnate element was weakest. Of the three provinces, support was strongest where wealth was concentrated most, education was most strongly influenced by the Piarists, education and travel abroad was rare and political experience weakest. Support was weakest in the province with the strongest magnate and Jesuit influences.

Differences increase when the term dimension is overlayed onto the provinces. Leaving the exceptional case of the Livonian delegation aside, the more experienced first term Wielkopolanians and first term Lithuanians showed particularly strong support for the May Third Constitution (71 percent and 85 percent respectively). The greatest uncertainty was among second term Lithuanians and the strongest opposition was among first term Małopolanians. The strongest support came from the Lithuanians elected in 1788 and the strong opposition from Małopolanians chosen the same year. The characteristics of these two groups yield interesting comparisons. In some respects

Table 26

The Deputies and the May Third Constitution by Province and Term

	Wielkopolska		Małopolska	
term	I	II	I	II
opponents	28.6%	36.4%	46.2%	42.3%
supporters	71.4%	59.1%	53.8%	53.8%
		} 63.6%		} 57.6%
converts		4.5%		3.8%

	Lithuania	
term	I	II
opponents	15.0%	30.8%
supporters	80.0%	53.8%
	} 85.0%	} 69.2%
converts	5.0%	15.4%

they were similar. The difference in mean age was only two years and in each case the averages, 40.7 years and 38.5 respectively, were slightly below the norms for the province and term. Neither was there much difference in previous parliamentary experience with a 40 percent and 42.9 percent novice rate. This does indicate, however, that these Lithuanian supporters of the new system were more experienced than their fellow deputies from the Grand Duchy.

There were greater differences in education, travels, wealth and orders. Half of the first term Małopolanian delegation which exhibited such great opposition to the new Constitution was Jesuit educated with the rest evenly split between a Piarist and a foreign education. First term Lithuanians, among whom there was such a high percentage of support, were 80 percent Piarist educated and 20 percent Jesuit educated. Sixty percent of these Małopolanians had travelled abroad while 73.3 percent of the Lithuanian apparently had not.

The wealth structure was also different for first term Małopolanians and first term Lithuanians:

Table 27

Extreme Support and Opposition towards the Constitution

	First term Małoplanians (opponents)	First term Lithuanians (supporters)
wealth		
poor	14.3%	0.0%
middle	0.0%	0.0%
very rich	57.1%	87.5%
magnate	28.6%	12.5%
family's wealth		
poor	20.0%	0.0%
middle	0.0%	29.4%
very rich	40.0%	58.8%
magnate	40.0%	11.4%

In a sense the conflict over the *Ustawa Rządowa* pitted very wealthy Lithuanians against magnates in Małopolska. Though this group of Małopolanians was the wealthier they did not see a rise in their political fortunes as measured by the possession of orders. Advancement, however, was great for first term Lithuanians:

Table 28

Extreme Support and Opposition towards the Constitution (Orders)

	First term Malopałanians		First term Lithuanians	
orders	1788	1791	1788	1791
no medal	30.0%	30.0%	78.6%	57.1%
St. Stanisław	20.0%	20.0%	21.4%	21.4%
White Eagle				7.1%
both	50.0%	50.0%		14.3%

The first term Lithuanians who showed such great support for the *Ustawa Rządowa* experienced rapid advancement just prior to May 1791, albeit they started from a much lower base. The first term Małopolanians who showed the highest opposition experienced no change. Perhaps, this attests to satisfaction or dissatisfaction about the functioning of the system with the Małopolanians being quite discouraged. Or perhaps this is indicative of royal patronage.

Opponents and Supporters

Having examined the characteristics of the deputies to the Four Years' *Sejm*, the attitudes of the provinces and the deputies grouped by term, a final perspective on the biographical data comes in the examination of two groups collectively: the supporters and opponents of the new system. Here the characteristics are directly connected to the political issue but information continues to cleave on the two dimensions of term and geography.

Table 29

Parliamentary Experience and the Constitution

Number of previous terms at election	Opponents	Supporters
0	52.6%	46.9%
1	18.6%	19.8%
2	15.8%	13.6%
3	5.3%	3.9%
4	2.6%	7.4%
5		1.2%
6	2.3%	1.2%
7		3.7%
8		1.2%

Support for the new Constitution was somewhat stronger among first term deputies (70.0 percent opposed to 64.1 percent) who collectively were the more seasoned parliamentarians. This experience is evident in individual factors associated with political activity. Table 29 summarizes previous parliamentary experience for the two groups. The profiles are quite similar except in regard to those deputies with no previous parliamentary experience and with those having the greatest experience. A majority of opponents was new to the *Sejm*; a majority of supporters had previous experience. On average the opponents had attended one *Sejm* before being elected to the Four Years' *Sejm* while on average supporters had attended one and a half parliaments. On the other hand, opponents of the new Constitution were twice as likely to have participated in the Confederation of Bar, but here the figures are extremely small.

Table 30
Orders and the Constitution

	Opponents			Supporters		
orders	1788	1791	1792	1788	1791	1792
no medals	63.8%	55.3%	55.3%	66.2%	51.2%	41.2%
St. Stanisław	21.1%	28.9%	18.4%	27.5%	27.5%	26.2%
White Eagle			2.6%		5.0%	6.3%
both	15.8%	15.8%	23.7%	6.3%	16.2%	26.2%

The two national orders of St. Stanisław and the White Eagle were indicative of political success or personal vanity. For whatever reason, opponents of the new Constitution who did not have a medal never received one, though perhaps in an attempt at cooption some with the St. Stanisław medal were awarded the more prestigious White Eagle. Supporters continued their rapid acquisition of honors.

Table 31
Wealth and the Constitution

	Opponents		Supporters	
wealth	self	family	self	family
poor	11.5%	15.8%	3.8%	3.8%
middle	7.7%	10.5%	11.5%	23.1%
very rich	53.8%	36.8%	71.2%	55.8%
magnate	26.9%	36.8%	13.5%	17.3%

Economic standing and background followed a similar pattern as political experience among the provincial delegations. Variations in wealth do seem to have been a factor in a deputy's attitude towards the *Ustawa Rządowa*. There seems to have been a greater concentration of considerable wealth, but not magnate status, associated with the Constitution while the impoverished nobles and the magnates were more associated with the opposition. Supporters fit the *Sejm* norm much more closely than did opponents:

Table 32

Wealth and the Constitution Compared to Sejm Norms

	Opponents	Sejm Norm	Supporters	Difference Opponent/ Supporter
Wealth				
poor	+6.0%	5.5%	-1.7%	7.7%
middle	-4.2%	11.9%	-0.5%	3.8%
very rich	-12.3%	66.1%	+5.1%	17.4%
magnate	+10.4%	16.5%	-3.0%	13.4%

This seems to confirm the old observation that magnates and poor nobles were the more conservative and others were more progressive with the qualification that a distinction existed between middle and very wealth nobles.

Educational background also yields a less than completely clear picture. Two conclusions are certain. None of the opponents of the new system had an education abroad, either alone or in combination with another type of schooling, while supporters did have a slightly higher than average instance of foreign education (17.9 percent versus 11.5 percent). None of the opponents received schooling at a National Education Commission institution while supporters fit the *Sejm* average but this factor was probably insignificant because of the very low instance of deputies having attended the recently created facilities.

A contradiction arises in the more crucial question of domestic ideological influences. Piarists spearheaded educational reform in eighteenth century Poland-Lithuania, yet, opponents of the new, and apparently progressive, constitution, had an 11.8 percent higher rate of attendance at Piarist schools than the *Sejm* norm. Supporters predictably were less likely to have been educated by the conservative Jesuits, the rate was 9.7 percent lower than the *Sejm* norm, but their attendance rate at Piarists schools was only 3.8 percent higher than the norm. A possible explanation is that the progressive influence of Piarist education in Małopolska was cancelled out by other factors. In Wielkopolska the Piarists were rare while in Lithuania their influence did seem to coincide with the province's strong support for the May Third Constitution.

The convictions of the deputies in regard to the May Third Constitution remained generally constant in subsequent events. 85.5 percent of the supporters joined the Society of Friends of the Constitution; 94.6 percent of the opponents did not. 78.3 percent of the supporters of the new Constitution did not back the Targowica Confederation while 74.3 percent of the opponents did. But the disillusionment with Targowica and the harsh realities of the Second Partition, which even the most reactionary of the Targowicanians had not expected, eroded the oppositionist position. While, as could be expected, a large majority (79.1 percent) of the supporters of the May Third Constitution, for whom there is information, backed the Kościuszko Uprising, 41.7 percent of the opponents did as well. Political divisions over the *Ustawa Rządowa* remained durable in the continuing political struggles under relatively normal circumstances, but when the very existence of the state—not solely its form—came into question, the divisions became less distinct.

Summary

Deputies to the Four Years' *Sejm* represented the *szlachta* or, more specifically, the politically active segments of the "political nation." The double representation gave a heightened representational quality to this group, bringing onto the public arena individuals who would otherwise not have become deputies at that time or perhaps ever. Atypical because of their political roles, the deputies may also have had other qualities which set them off from their noble "brothers." Presumably, voters did not intentionally choose mediocre individuals. But even when deputies were disappointing, they must have offered at some point an image of the type of person in whom others had confidence or towards whose position others aspired. Arguably, the deputies could have been a kind of model for the *szlachta* who chose them.

With its imperfect sampling and occasionally thin data, biogram information reveals a *Sejm* dominated by the wealthier elements of the *szlachta*, though not necessarily the magnates. Religiously homogeneous, the deputies came to the historic *Sejm* with some previous parliamentary experience, some travel abroad and some military connections but few if any ties with the Masonry or with foreign governments. In the crucial area of ideological and intellectual formation, most of the deputies were educated in domestic church schools.

Variations appeared along provincial lines and according to term. The very wealthy nobleman were most typical of Wielkopolska, the magnates were more evident in Małopolska and Lithuania although in these two provinces they were never in the majority. The oldest, politically most experienced, deputies were concentrated in Wielkopolska; youth and lack of experience was most characteristic of Lithuania. Jesuit influence was strongest in Wielkopolska, Piarist influence in Lithuania. Second term deputies brought more youthful energy, a stronger Piarist-molded outlook and greater political inexperience. Livonia in most respects was unique.

Attitudes towards the new Constitution also varied according to province and term. Particularly strong support came from Lithuania and Livonia; particularly strong opposition came from Małopolska. Regionally specific factors seem to have tied Piarist influence to reform in Lithuania but not in Małopolska. Variations from *Sejm* norms associated the very wealthy with the new system and magnates with the opposition. The rate of support was higher among first term deputies.

In summation, the biogram information modifies commonly accepted generalizations about the Four Years' *Sejm* in at least four respects. The strongest progressive element was in Lithuania, not in more developed Wielkopolska. A reformist attitude cannot be *unconditionally* tied to education but in Lithuania the Piarists did seem to have had an effect. Nor is the information on the reaction of magnates and the reform of the "middle" *szlachta* unequivocal. Biogram information tends to associate eagerness for reform with an intermediate group of very wealthy nobles. Finally, though the influx of new deputies in 1790 seems to have accelerated parliamentary processes, those new members were less experienced and some would eventually be more inclined to oppose the changes that those processes ultimately did produce.

CHAPTER 6

CONSTITUTION AND COUNTRY: COMPLICATIONS, ELABORATIONS, AND EXPLANATIONS

If the arguments of the previous chapter are sound, support for the May Third Constitution was associated with greater political experience, Piarist education in Lithuania, the Livonian at large delegation for the entire *Rzeczpospolita* and a group of very wealthy nobles throughout the country while opposition was linked most intensely to Małopolska. Two common measurements of statistical significance raise questions concerning the validity of these rather limited generalizations and the strength of the evidence. At the same time, they raise the possibility of more specific theses. The arguments of the last chapter can be complemented with newer observations on geography, age, social stratification and office holding.

The first measure of statistical significance used is Pearson's R. Even after absenteeism had been filtered out of the calculations, only one statistically significant correlation using this measurement exists between attitudes towards the new Constitution and other singular factors: supporters of the Constitution tended to be members of the *Zgromadzenie Przyjaciół Konstytucji Rządowej* [Society of Friends of the Constitution]. This association is not surprising since members of the Society should by definition have supported the Constitution but it also indicates that the supporters were well organized and that, perhaps, the whole reform had a conspiratorial quality. Yet, the lack of other correlations would in itself be a very interest phenomenon. If Pearson's R is a valid measure, neither wealth, education, travels abroad, geographical base nor religion etc., would have played a significant factor in predisposing a deputy to favor or to oppose the May Third Revolution. Crucially, the absence of a correlation between wealth or non-agricultural wealth and the Constitutional factor would seem to indicate that the notion of the reforms as a consciously devised instrument of the middle or very wealth nobility against the magnates does not have a basis in solid fact or at the least that it should be extensively modified. This would be an important finding.

With one obvious, and therefore essentially useless, positive thesis and a host of negative theses (no connection to wealth, to geography etc.), the analysis of the members of the *Sejm* seems of little value. But while individual factors might not correlate, broad, isolated characteristics seldom exist in the real world, especially in society. Combinations of factors or adjustments of the factors themselves and sets of deputies yield information on who supported or opposed the Constitution and why.

Moreover, Pearson's R does not seem to be the best measure of statistical significance. A cursory look, aided by intuition and common sense, at the relationship of the May Third Constitution and the Targowica Confederation shows an inverse relationship yet Pearson's R is only .3, well below the .7 threshold commonly held as indicative of a significant relationship. The chi square coefficient works more satisfactorily with the type of data on which this study is based.

Using an arbitrary cut off at 5.0 for chi square, the following factors had a significant relationship to support or opposition to the May Third Constitution:

Table 33

Chi Square on Biograms

District	120.69	Kościuszko	14.54
Office '91	116.45	Province	11.08
Office '92	110.00	Nonagricultural	10.87
Office '88	92.12	Relative's wealth	9.84
Relative's office '88	90.00	Order '92	8.16
Relative's office '91	90.00	No. of *Sejmy*	8.05
Relative's office '92	88.50	Duchy of Warsaw	6.91
Age	87.15	Education	6.87
Zgromadzenie	68.99	Szkoła Rycerska	6.78
Targowica	56.85	Order '91	6.44
		Order '88	5.70
		Confederation of Bar	5.58

The only significant factor by virtue of Pearson's R, membership in the Zgromadzenie, does not carry the highest chi square value. Part of the reason for this is that chi square seems to be sensitive to factors with numerous components each of which is compared to the other issue, support/opposition to the *Ustawa Rządowa*. While this indicates a consistency in ranking internal to the factor it also does show an overall relationship. Thus, *województwo* and district representation, offices held, offices held by fathers and age were characteristics that somehow influenced deputies in their attitudes towards the new system, perhaps in a tighter relationship than that between the Constitution and membership in the Society of Friends of the Constitution. Leaving aside variables which connect deputies with post-constitutional events, and factors already discussed in the previous chapter, factors with high chi square values can be grouped into the following topics: geography, age, and social stratification as related to offices and honors. In addition, measures of statistical significance may not apply to this set of information. Arguably, the biogram information may be considered to be the entire universe of available information. Since either evaluation of the data is plausible, the statistical significance measures have been left in this study.

Geography

The previous chapter examined attitudes towards the May Third Constitution on the level of province. The Małopolanians were shown to have played a central role in the opposition and the Lithuanian delegation was evidently the most solidly in favor of the *Ustawa Rządowa*. The unique Livonian delegation was unanimous in its support for the Constitution, yet, Livonia were not a true geographic region. Its representation was more symbolic and its representatives were chosen from interested individuals from throughout the country. Additionally, the provinces were themselves composites which hid inner variations. As mentioned each province contained a region incorporated over the centuries: Wielkopolska had Mazowsze, Małopolska had Podlasie and vast areas of Rus' and Lithuania had Black Rus' and much of White Rus'. These and other differences were reflected in the divisions along sub-provincial lines (*województwo* and *ziemia*) in respect to the new Constitution.

Table 34

Percentage of Approval for the Constitution on the Województwo Level

Sejm average: 67.1%

Below the Average	(province)		Above the Average	(province)	
0.00%	Łęczyca	W	66.66%	Mińsk	L
14.29%	Wołyń	M	71.40%	Bracław	M
25.00%	Czernichów	M	75.00%	Żmudź	L
42.86%	Podole	M	85.70%	Sandomierz	M
50.00%	Chełm	M	90.00%	Wilno (Vilnius)	L
50.00%	Lublin	M	100.00%	Brześć Litewski	L
50.00%	Nowogródek	L	100.00%	Inowrocław	W
50.00%	Sieradz	W	100.00%	Gniezno	W
60.00%	Kalisz	M	100.00%	Płock	W
60.00%	Mazowsze	W	100.00%	Podlasie	M
60.00%	Troki	L	100.00%	Rawa	W
62.50%	Kraków	M	100.00%	Smoleńsk	L
63.63%	Poznań	W	100.00%	Livonia	
66.66%	Kijów (Kyyiv)	M			

No information is available for two *województwa*: Brześć Kujawski and Połock.

Numerous districts fell very close to the *Sejm*'s norm of a 67.1 percent approval rate for the Constitution, thus obscuring the distribution and depth of opposition and support. It is safe to say that support was commonly around two-thirds of the deputies in each województwo. Those that diverge significantly from this norm are of special importance. If 10 percent plus to 10 percent minus were taken as an arbitrary exclusionary range of essentially similar approval rates then Żmudź, Bracław, Kijów (Kyyiv), Kraków, Mińsk, and Poznań would be eliminated. Those *województwa* that remain on the list arguably show particularly strong support or opposition.

No immediately evident, comprehensive, pattern emerges for the geographic distribution of strong support or opposition to the Constitution. A single explanation for the distribution is unlikely. Much of the strongest support came from areas tied to the grain trade (Dobrzyń, Podlasie and Rawa) and strong opposition did come from

Wołyń and Podole which were cut off from extensive international trade, at least via the Vistula. But the strongest opposition came from Łęczyca, a centrally located, grain producing region in Wielkopolska. It can be observed, however, that many of the *województwa* with the strongest support were located either in eastern Wielkopolska or in regions of ethnic frontiers, Podlasie and Brześć Litewski.[1]

The highest rate of opposition came from the central Wielkopolanian *województwo* of Łęczyca, although the unanimous opposition was based on a minority of deputies. Of Łęczyca's eight deputies, there is information on only three (Konstanty Janikowski, Felix Kretkowski and Cyprian Nakwaski) all of whom are known to have opposed the *Ustawa Rządowa*. In some respects these individuals differed from their colleagues of the same *województwo* and from the *Sejm* as a whole. With a mean age in 1791 of 41 years (Janikowski and Nakwaski) they were somewhat younger than other Łęczycans (45.3), and Wielkopolanians (44) but the same as the Chamber of Deputies (41.2) as a whole. Unfortunately, information about educational background is unavailable but it does seem that none of the Łęczycans had travelled abroad extensively. Only Nakwaski received a medal (St. Stanisław) before 1791; his colleague, Franciszek Jerzmanowski received one after 1791, perhaps in an attempt to persuade him to support the reforms. Jerzmanowski seems to have come to favor the Constitution because he eventually joined the Zgromadzenie. The Łęczycan opponents were somewhat experienced politically since two had each attended two previous *Sejmy* and one had been a participant in the Confederation of Bar. Information about wealth is very limited. From the entire Łęczycan delegation an estimate of wealth can only be made for two of the Constitution's opponents, Janikowski was poor and Nakwaski was very rich but not a magnate. None of the three seems to have had any professional military service or connections to foreign governments. The depth of their opposition was not great since one of the three actively fought the Confederation of Targowica (Kretkowski) and two fought in the Kościuszko Uprising (Kretkowski and Jerzmanowski).

Though not unanimous, the opposition of the Wołyń *województwo* was more definite. All seven Wołynians, whose positions are known, were initially opponents though one, Ignacy Krzucki, later came to support the Constitution, at least officially, before joining the Targowica Confederation. The six diehard opponents were Kajetan Aksak, Józef Klemens Czartoryski, Benedykt Hulewicz, Stanisław Kostka Hulewicz, Józef Olizar and Józef Piniński.[2] These opponents fit the province and *Sejm* averages for age. The educational background of only three opponents is known; B. Hulewicz and Olizar were taught by Piarists and Czartoryski was educated by Jesuits and abroad. Czartoryski as a magnate travelled abroad extensively and had connections with Austria and Prussia. Czartoryski had been awarded both medals before 1788 and Olizar the St. Stanisław medal; during the course of the Four Years' *Sejm* Stanisław August did grant S. Hulewicz the St. Stanisław and Olizar the White Eagle Order. Economically, Aksak and B. Hulewicz were poor and possibly dependent on magnates, Olizar and Piniński were very rich and Czartoryski was a magnate. These Wołynians were very inexperienced politically. Having attended five previous Sejmy Czartoryski was the only Wołynian with parliamentary experience; most had been elected only in 1790. Their opposition was apparently genuine and solid; at least four backed Targowica (Aksak, both Hulewiczes, Piniński) and only two Kościuszko. Krzucki differed from his diehard colleagues in being a military officer (a *towarzysz* [noble comrade] in the national cavalry) and in attending one *Sejm* prior to 1788. He also attended the Szkoła Rycerska and was very wealthy. His wavering continued since he eventually supported Targowica. Overall, the Wołynian delegation was led by its senior and most experienced member, J. K. Czartoryski.

The third most solidly oppositional delegation came from Czernichów (Chernihiv) also in the Ruthenian lands of Małopolska. As with Livonia and Smoleńsk this group held a symbolic representation of a lost land and the deputies functioned as a kind of at large delegation from the ethnically Ruthenian lands in the east. From the eight deputies, four were definitely opponents (Michał Czacki, Kajetan Kurdwanowski, Kajetan Miączyński and Michał Ignacy Radzimiński) and only one was a supporter (Antoni Ledóchowski). Biographical information is very thin. Both the opponents and the supporter were about the same age (39 to 36 years old). Educational information exists only for Czacki who studied with the Jesuits and abroad. As a whole, the opponents were more widely travelled. Czacki and Miączyński had both medals and the supporter, Ledóchowski, received the St. Stanisław in 1791. Three had participated in the Confederation of Bar and their experience in the *Sejm* was slightly higher (2.25 compared to two previous *Sejmy*) than Ledóchowski's. Two opponents, Kurdwanowski and Miączyński, participated in the Confederation of Targowica and none in the Kościuszko Uprising. Ledóchowski, on the other hand, was consistent in his support for the new system. He belonged to the Zgromadzenie, shunned Targowica and supported Kościuszko. Only Miączyński was a mason. Information on wealth is available for only two members: Czacki seems to have been a magnate (he was also the only member with known connections to Austria and France) and the supporter, Ledóchowski, was very wealthy. Interestingly Ledóchowski was the son of a *wojewoda* and by virtue of this status he could be considered a member of the *magnateria*. Ledóchowski also seems to have differed by being a military man. Generally, the Czernichów (Chernihiv) delegation represented the conservative-minded *szlachta*, if not the *magnetaria*, in the Ruthenian lands of the *Rzeczpospolita*.

Another *województwo* with a possible concentration of opposition lay adjacent to Wołyń. Podole had an opposition rate of 43 percent among its deputies based on the two secondary sources used in this study.[3] Information is available on half of the delegation; there were four opponents (Stanisław Kosecki, Józef Mierzejewski, Jan Onufry Orłowski and Antoni Złotnicki) and three supporters (Pius Franciszek Boreyko, Onufry Morski, Józef Zajączek). The biographical information is also sketchy for this geographically remote region. The wealth on both sides was substantial. In education, there is no information on the opponents but the supporters received a variety of schooling: Morski was educated by the Jesuits and abroad while Boreyko received a private education. The ages were essentially the same. Politically, the Constitution's supporters were the more experienced: Boreyko had been to four previous *Sejmy* and Morski to one for a rate of 2.5 *Sejmy*. The opponents on the other hand had a rating of 1.5. None had participated in the Confederation of Bar. The opponents had more orders than did the supporters: Mierzejewski and Orłowski had St. Stanisław medals and Jerzy Potocki both by 1792 while the first medal to be held by a Podolian deputy supporter was the St. Stanisław medal received in 1792. In their political behavior subsequent to May Third, the opponents were not entirely consistent. None, of course, were members of the Zgromadzenie, only one was a participant of the counterrevolution and one supported the Kościuszko Uprising. From among the Podolian supporters, one joined the Zgromadzenie, none Targowica and two the Kościuszko Uprising.

To the other extreme from Łęczyca, Wołyń, Czernichów (Chernihiv) and Podole were *województwa* with unanimous or nearly unanimous approval rates among their deputies whose views are known. Of those listed in the chart above, several areas only had one or two deputies remembered by posterity. Others had a more significant number of deputies whose attitudes towards the May Third Constitution are known. Thus Brześć Litewski, Smoleńsk and Podlasie are of greatest interest since all had a fair number of deputies whose unanimous support is known while Wilno and Sandomierz, though their delegations were not unanimous, showed strong support on the basis of fairly complete information.

Out of a delegation of eight, Brześć Litewski had three immediate supporters (Kazimierz Sapieha, Mateusz Butrymowicz, Tadeusz Matuszewic [sic]) and one convert, Stanisław Niemcewicz. The average age for this group was 36.75 years. They were educated by Piarists and Jesuits and Sapieha attended the Szkoła Rycerska. Only Butrymowicz had a medal (received in 1791), none had participated in the Confederation of Bar and the average experience in the *Sejm* was 1.5. The supporters were steadfast in their convictions. Two joined the Zgromadzenie, none Targowica and all four fought with Kościuszko. The supporters were very wealthy but not magnates. The three had some military experience.

Very little is known about the Smoleńsk deputies except that Dominik Eydziatowicz, Konstanty Jelski, Michał Radziszewski supported the Constitution. Antoni Chrapowicki was a member of the Zgromadzenie but it is difficult to know when he came to support the Constitution. Politically they seemed to have been inexperienced and they were surprisingly old with an average of 54.3 years, a full ten years above the average for the entire Chamber of Deputies.

The Podlasian delegation was different. Out of the eleven deputies from Podlasie, at least three were supporters of the May Third Constitution; there is no information about the existence of any opponents. The two Ossolińskis, Jan and Józef, were educated by Piarists and Franciszek Piotr Potocki received his schooling privately and abroad. None had served in the *Sejm* prior to their elections to the Four Years' *Sejm*. Potocki had participated in the Confederation of Bar. Both Ossolińskis joined the Zgromadzenie and fought on the side of Kościuszko but Potocki ascribed to Targowica after the king's surrender and did not participate in the 1794 revolt. (Interestingly, five from the delegation supported the Kościuszko Uprising.) The delegation was a mixture of magnates and very wealthy nobles. Potocki belonged to the former and the Ossolińskis to the latter group. The mean age of the supporters from Podlasie was 44.6 years in 1791. Though the Wilno delegation did not show unanimous support for the May Third Constitution, this *województwo* was not only large, with twenty deputies it had the largest representation in the *Rzeczpospolita*, but its adherence to the new order was quite extraordinary. The deputies represented five *powiaty* (Wilno, Oszmiana, Brasław, Wilkomierz and Lidz), all in the Lithuanian, Polish and Byelorussian borderland. The attitudes of ten are known: seven were supporters (Józef Kociełł, Tadeusz Kościalkowski, Bogusław Mirski, Stanisław Mirski, Dominik Narbutt, Wojciech Narbutt, Tomasz Wawrzecki), one was a convert (Tadeusz Korsak) and two were opponents (Józef Dominik Kossakowski and Franciszek Romanowicz). Of the supporters, one (W. Narbutt) was Piarist educated, two (Kościałkowski and W. Narbutt) had attended the Collegium Nobilium and none seemed to have travelled abroad. Politically, none had participated in the Confederation of Bar (age was a factor), three (D. Narbutt, both Mirskis) had served in previous *Sejmy*, each twice, with a total *Sejm* rating of 1.17 for all seven supporters from Wilno. The number of individuals with a medal rose from 2 in 1788 to 4 in 1791 and 5 in 1792. The depth of their conviction in favor of the new system is striking. All seven supporters were members of the Zgromadzenie, none joined Targowica and six fought to defend the Republic in the Kościuszko Uprising. They all came from the very wealthy szlachta, one (Kociełł) was a military man but none were masons or had connections to foreign governments. They were also considerably younger than the *Sejm* norm with an mean age of 32.8, about average for the Lithuanian delegation.

The one convert from Wilno *województwo*, Tadeusz Korsak, had been Jesuit trained and was a political novice on the national level with no previous Sejm experience, confederations or orders. Much esteemed by his colleagues, Korsak initially opposed the May Third Constitution because it had been adopted in violation of the *legitis curiatae* but later he came to the conclusion that its benefits to the Commonwealth outweighed any of its faults. Ultimately, his support for the reforms included not only membership in the Zgromadzenie but Korsak gave his life defending the Praga suburb of Warsaw against the Russians during the Kościuszko Uprising. As a true middle *szlachcic*, Korsak was poorer than were the immediate supporters. He also was not a mason nor did he have connections with foreign governments. Korsak was a newcomer on the national scene at the age of 51 in 1791.

There is biographical information for only one of the Wilnoan opponents. Kossakowski was atypical because of his youth. At twenty in 1791, he was the youngest member of the *Sejm* and by definition inexperienced. He joined the rest of his very wealthy, though not of magnate status, family in their support of Targowica.

The other *województwo* with strong support for the new system was Sandomierz. Covering extensive territory along the Vistula between Warsaw and Kraków, Sandomierz had fourteen deputies in double set. Of these, six are known to have been supporters (Antoni Karski, Kazimierz Karski, Jan Nepomucin Dunin Karwicki, Michał Korwin Kochanowski, Jan and Stanisław Małachowski, [Crown marshal of the *Sejm*]) and one opponent, Józef Mężeński. The supporters contrast strongly with the single known opponent among the Sandomierzians. From among the six supporters, one (Jan Małachowski) was Piarist educated, and another (Stanisław Małachowski) was privately educated. Only the Małachowskis seem to have travelled abroad. Four of the six supporters were elected in 1788 with two having served previously for a rate of 1.5 *Sejmy*. The Four Years' *Sejm* was Stanisław Małachowski's eighth parliament. None had participated in the Confederation of Bar. The support for the new Constitution was not as solid as that from Wilno. Only one (Kochanowski) was a member of the Zgromadzenie but two (Kochanowski and Jan Małachowski) did join Targowica albeit after the surrender. As Marshal and true to his reputation for impartiality, Stanisław Małachowski was not a member of the nascent political party, the Zgromadzenie. Three (J. Karwicki, Kochanowski and J. Małachowski), however, did defend the state in the Kościuszko Uprising. Economically the two Małachowskis were magnates while the rest were very wealthy nobles. One (Małachowski) had diplomatic experience, two (Karwicki and Kochanowski) had military experience and one (Kochanowski) is known to have been a mason. The mean age of the supporters was 40.7 years. The opponent Mężeński, on the other hand, was a member of the middle *szlachta* educated by Jesuits, private instructors and abroad but with no previous political experience and had been elected only in 1790. Mężeński became a member of the Targowica Confederation.

In summary, geographically the strongest support for the Constitution was among the delegates who came from *województwa* along the transitional zone from Polish to Lithuanian and Byelorussian areas (Podlasie, Brześć Litewski and Wilno) as well as an old ethnically Polish *województwo* in Małopolska (Sandomierz). Opposition was strongest in the heart of Wielkopolska (Łęczyca *województwo*) and most especially in the Ruthenian *województwa* (Wołyń and Podole) of Małopolska, as distinguished from what at the time was considered the Ukraine proper (Kijów [Kyyiv] and Bracław), and in the at large Ruthenian delegation of Czernichów (Chernihiv). But while further study of this phenomenon would be appropriate it is not possible at present. Instead composite portraits of deputies from these special areas do offer some interesting patterns.

Factors with either a strongly positive or a strongly negative relationship to the Constitution are amplified by a focus on *województwa* with the highest support or opposition among their deputies. Examination of these characteristics is hampered by the imperfection of the limited biographical information. Yet, the limitation, the selectivity of time, may offer a more or less accurate sampling. The distinctiveness of the twenty-six supporters, twenty opponents and three converts from the *województwa* considered above lies in their age, education, military service, political experience, orders and wealth.

While the mean ages of these supporters and opponents did not differ greatly (38.3 and 37.1 respectively), they did vary more from the overall mean for the Four Years' *Sejm* (41.2). The ardor of relative youthfulness may have been a factor though the differences were quite small. The converts, on the other hand, were somewhat older than the *Sejm* norm (43.0) and, thus considerably older than the immediate proponents (by 4.7 years) and opponents (by 5.9 years).

Education also seems to have been a factor. Fully 60 percent of the opponents, for whom there is information, received some kind of training by the Jesuits while the comparable figure for supporters was 20 percent. Fifty percent of the supporters, in contrast, were educated, at least in part by Piarists while 40 percent of the opponents were. Since twice as many opponents as supporters received some training abroad (40 percent as opposed to 20 percent) but both groups seem to have travelled abroad to the same degree (25 percent did travel), it would seem that the deciding factor with respect to education in this small select group could very well have been the Jesuit influence. Additionally, while attendance rates at the Szkoła Rycerska were the same, none of the opponents had attended the Collegium Nobilium but 18 percent of the supporters had. The Society of Jesus and the secular Collegium Nobilium may have had opposite but unequal influences in the formation of character and world views that in some way were reflected in the acceptability of the Constitution.

The question of character may also have been in part related to military experience. Only 12.5 percent of the opponents, but 30.4 percent of the proponents in this special group, had military experience prior to 1791. Though admittedly a very small subgroup, two of the proponents about whom there is information, but none of the opponents, had made the military their primary career. The military mentality, perhaps in particular discipline or loyalty to higher authority, may have predisposed some to immediately support the restored hereditary (but still constitutional) monarchy of the May Third Constitution.

Another kind of discipline may have also played a role. Supporters of the new system from the *województwa* with the highest support and opposition rates were much more politically experienced on the national level than the opposition. Sixty-seven percent of the supporters had been to at least one previous *Sejm* with an overall rating of 1.7 previous *Sejmy* for the entire group. Only 47.1 percent of the opponents had had previous experience and the group rating was 1.0. Moreover 65 percent of the supporters had been in the Four Years' *Sejm* two and a half years before the revolution while 55 percent of the opponents had come to the Sejm only six months earlier. The opponents in this special sample were less experienced and new to the Four Years' *Sejm*. Perhaps not surprisingly, they did have more experience in the equally legal but innately unparliamentary Confederation of Bar. Close to a third (29.4 percent) of those opponents for whom there is information had been participants in this revolt "for faith and fatherland" while the comparable figure for supporters was only 4.5 percent.

The arguably more experienced parliamentarians who were the Constitution's supporters were recipients of the king's favor in the form of medals as shown in Table 35. Supporters began with fewer medals but received them steadily throughout the Four Years' *Sejm*; medal distribution to the opponents virtually stopped. It is not clear whether support was rewarded with favor or its result but it does appear to be fairly certain that Stanisław August did not see any point in patronage of deputies from the *województwa* with the strongest opposition among their delegations. This, of course, does not mean that the king did not target other citizens in those recalcitrant regions for persuasive favors.[4]

Table 35

Changes in Orders with Respect to the Constitution for Województwa with Extreme Support or Opposition

Order	1788		1791		1792	
	pro	con	pro	con	pro	con
no medals	78.3%	64.7%	56.5%	52.9%	47.8%	52.9%
St. Stanisław	17.4%	17.6%	26.1%	29.4%	34.8%	17.6%
White Eagle	0.0%	0.0%	4.3%	0.0%	4.3%	0.0%
both	4.3%	17.6%	13.0%	17.6%	13.0%	29.4%

Finally, income distribution was quite different for the two groups:

Table 36

Wealth and the Constitution in Województwa of Extreme Support or Opposition

	Supporters	Opponents	Sejm
poor	0.0%	23.1%	5.5%
middle	0.0%	15.4%	11.9%
wealthy	81.3%	38.5%	66.1%
magnate	18.8%	23.1%	16.5%

The distribution is striking. Once again, and this time in the *województwa* with the highest support among their deputies, the very rich and the magnates in particular backed the new Constitution.

The deputies from *województwa* with extreme approval and disapproval rates were also consistent in their subsequent political behavior. None of these twenty opponents ever joined the Zgromadzenia; 82.4 percent of the supporters did; 71.4 percent of the opponents joined Targowica; 76.5 percent of the supporters never did, even after the king's accession. Only 50 percent of the opponents supported

Kościuszko as opposed to 85 percent of the supporters. This figure, however, means that half of these fervent opponents of the May Third Constitution were willing to join their political antagonists when the question of continued independence became the pressing, or desperate, issue. Disagreement over the May Third system in the most extreme *województwa*, therefore, broke along lines of education, wealth and political experience but it was not equivalent to a question of patriotism.

The Age Factor

As shown earlier, the age of every member of the Four Years' *Sejm* cannot be determined. The *Polski słownik biograficzny* and the *Wielka encyklopedia* of the Polish Academy of Science do, however, yield the birthdates or approximate ages of 125 out of the 359 deputies. This information gives a good (or the best possible) indication of the overall age complexion at the *Sejm*, though the data may not constitute a truly random sample. Keeping in mind the imperfection of the data, even as a sample, a realistic, perhaps somewhat impressionistic, picture of age in the Four Years' *Sejm* is shown in Table 37.

An argument may be made that there is not a statistically significant difference between the average ages of each of the terms. Using the Student's t test neither the mean of the first term nor the mean of the second varies significantly from the mean of the entire *Sejm*:

Table 37

Ages of Deputies in 1791

	Total	First Term	Second Term
mean	41.2	41.8	40.45
number	125	70	55[5]
s.d.	12.16	10.73	13.83

1.16 and 1.18 are each well within the acceptable range for .10 significance. It is assumed that the variation from the mean of the entire *Sejm* can be used to compare the age composition of each term. Moreover, at election time the mean age of first term deputies was less (38.8 years) than that of second term deputies (39.4 years). This reverses the situation on May 3, 1791. From these two perspectives, no significant variation in the t test and the actual reversal of average youthfulness at election time with that in 1791, would seem to indicate that the age composition of the two groups of deputies was essentially identical and youthfulness did not have an effect on participation during the crucial months leading up to the adoption of the new Constitution. Yet, this interpretation is far from perfect.

Table 38

Deputies Listed by Term and Age (in 1791)

First Term	Second Term
20–24 years	
Ożarowski (1769)	Chreptowicz (1768
Sobolewski ('70)	Kossakowski J. D. ('71)
	Kossakowski M. ('69)
25–29 years	
Borch ('64)	Aksak ('63)
Brzostowski, M. ('62)	Dąmbski ('66)
Jabłonowski ('62)	Gieysztor ('62)
Kociełł ('64)	Gliszczyński ('66)
Małachowski Ja. ('64)	Iliński J.A. ('66)
Matuszewicz ('65)	Iliński J.S. ('65)
Narbutt ('62)	Komorowski ('65)
Potocki ('62)	Luszczewski ('64)
	Mostowski ('63)
	Pusłowski ('62)
30–34 years	
Grabowski ('59)	Batowski ('60)
Karwicki D. ('57)	Bronikowski ('58)
Kochanowski ('57)	Kaczanowski ('60)
Lubieński ('58)	Linowski ('59)
Mączyński ('57)	Mielżyński F. ('61)
Mokronoski ('61)	Olędzki ('60)
Niemcewicz J. ('58)	Ossoliński Ja. ('60)
Ossoliński Jo. ('58)	
Plater ('58)	
Potocki Ja. ('61)	
Wawrzecki ('59)	

35–39 years

Czacki ('53)
Działyński K. ('56)
Glinka ('54)
Kiciński ('52)
Kicki A. ('54)
Mierzejewski ('56)
Mirski S. ('56)
Morski O. ('52)
Potocki Je. ('53)
Potocki S. K. ('55)
Potocki S.S. ('52)
Sapieha ('54)

Breza ('52)
Dembiński ('53)
Działyński ('54)
Jezierski ('53)
Karwicki J. ('55)
Kretkowski ('52)
Ledóchowski A. ('55)
Niemcewicz S. ('53)
Nozarzewski J.D. ('55)
Piniński ('55)
Sołtyk ('53)
Zajączek ('52)

40–44 years

Czyż ('47)
Hulewicz B. ('50)
Karski A. ('47)
Kościałkowski ('50)
Kublicki ('50)
Ledóchowski ('47)
Małachowski Jo. ('51)
Miączyński ('51)
Nakwaski ('48)

Choiecki ('48)
Karp M. ('49)
Kicki O. ('50)
Kiełczewski ('50)
Krzucki ('50)
Otwinowski ('50)

45–49 years

Butrymowicz ('45)
Czetwertyński ('44)
Łempicki ('45)
Morawski ('43)
Moszczeński ('42)
Oborski ('43)
Potocki F.P. ('45)
Radziszewski ('43)
Zakrzewski I.W. ('45)

Jaroszyński ('42)
Karski K. ('43)
Pruski ('42)
Puszet ('46)
Rogowski ('43)
Rzewuski ('43)

50–54 years

Bniński ('40)
Chołoniewski ('40)
Czartoryski J. ('40)
Gutakowski ('38)

Jelski ('38)
Korsak ('41)
Miełżyńdki M. ('38)

Jarzmanowski ('37)
Kuczyński I. ('38)
Lasocki ('41)
Lipski ('39)
Madaliński ('39)
Moszyński ('38)

55-59 years

Czartoryski A. ('34)   Jasieński ('32)
Karp B. ('34)   Ośniałowski ('35)
Kossakowski ('35)
Małachowski S. ('36)
Oskierko J. ('35)

60-64 years

Grocholski ('30)   Psarski ('30)
Kuczyński ('31)   Puzyna ('29)
   Rakowski ('30)

65-69 years

Damski S. ('24)
Kwilecki F. ('25)

70-74 years

75-79 years

   Dłuski T. ('13)
   Karski M. ('14)
   Radzicki ('15)

A wide range in ages creates large standard deviations and negates the usefulness of comparing means. On 3 May 1791 the oldest deputy was seventy-eight years old and the youngest twenty. Both of these extremes were second-term deputies and the wide range in ages seems to have obscured the actual differences between the mainstreams of each term. An arguably significant difference in the age composition of each term does emerge when deputies are grouped into five-year intervals and the members in each group are taken as a percentage of the total available ages for the relevant term.

Though there was a large increase in the number of very old members (ages 75 to 79) for the second term, on the whole, there does seem to have been a general shift downward in age. From the first term to the second, the decline in percentages among the 40 to 59-year-olds (16.6 percent out of a total negative change of 21.9 percent) was nearly made up by the increase in percentages among the 35 to 39 and 20 to 29-year-olds (14.1 percent out of a positive change of 19.7 percent). With respect to percentages, the role played by 50 to 59-year-olds was replaced by 25 to 29 and 35 to 39-year-olds.

Table 39

Age by Term and Five Year Intervals

Age	Entire Sejm N	%	First Term N	%	Second Term %	N	Change in Percentages
75-79	3	2.4	0	0	5.5	3	+ 5.5
70-74	0	0	0	0	0	0	-
65-69	2	1.6	2	2.9	0	0	- 2.9
60-64	5	4.0	2	2.9	5.5	3	- .1
55-59	7	5.6	5	7.1	3.6	2	- 3.5
50-54	13	10.4	10	14.2	5.5	3	- 8.7
45-49	15	12.0	9	12.9	11.0	6	- 1.9
40-44	15	12.0	9	12.9	11.0	6	- 1.9
35-39	24	19.2	12	17.1	21.8	12	+ 4.7
30-34	18	14.4	11	15.7	12.7	7	- 3.0
25-29	18	14.4	8	11.4	18.2	10	+ 6.8
20-24	5	4.4	2	2.9	5.5	3	+ 2.6
	125	100.0	70	100.0	100.3	55	- 2.2

Moreover, the concentration in age narrowed from the first term to the second: whereas in the first 84.2 percent were spread relatively evenly throughout the 25-54 year range, in the second 74.7 percent were more highly concentrated in 25-49 year range; 44.2 percent of the first term deputies were between 25 and 39 years old while 52.8 percent from the second term fell into this group.

The given age distribution does not necessarily reflect the effect specific age groups had in the *Sejm*. In fact, participation in roll calls, which can to some degree indicate that input, shows greater activity among the 30 to 35-year-olds of the second term than among their 20 to 29-year-old colleagues of either term.

The more youthful deputies remained active throughout the second term with the second term 30 to 34-year-olds having the highest roll call rate followed by identical showings of all 20 to 24-year-old deputies and 35 to 39-year-olds from the second term. The sustained rate of over 50 percent participation in second term roll calls would indicate not only physical endurance and material ability to maintain a second household in Warsaw but also, at the very least, a passive acceptance of the major reforms passed in the first half of 1791.

Simple participation percentages do not, however, in themselves indicate the influence of an age group. The younger members could have been overshadowed by individual senior deputies. This is difficult to measure. Participation rates have more meaning when the number of deputies is taken into account. This is shown by the variable vr(n).

Table 40

Participation Rates during the Second Term

Age	First Term		Second Term	
	voting rate	vr(n)	voting rate	vr(n)
20-24	54.3	108.6	54.3	162.9
25-29	23.6 (26.9)	188.8	37.9 (53.8)	379.0
30-34	39.2 (46.7)	431.2	61.6 (67.6)	431.2
35-39	30.7 (43.6)	368.4	54.3 (54.3)	651.6
40-44	28.3 (40.5)	254.7	46.6	279.6
45-49	35.1 (52.7)	315.9	21.4 (36.2)	128.4
50-54	26.3 (35.9)	263.0	48.6	145.8
55-59	20.6 (25.0)	103.0	42.1	84.2
60-64	21.4	42.8	25.7	77.1
65-69	25.7	51.4	--	---
70-74	--	---	--	---
75-79	--	---	30.5 (41.4)	91.5
		2127.6		2431 ?

The voting rate in parentheses excludes participants with less than 10 percent.

vr(n) = voting rate x number of deputies

Overall, the voting rates for each five year group magnified by the group's size confirms the earlier observation that a concentration of youth in the second term replaced a more even age distribution among first term deputies although the most active age group in the first term was younger slightly (30-34) than in the second (35-39).

The ranking according to activity and number of the age groups is given in Table 41. The participation rates are even higher for the most active groups early in the second term when they reached to over 80 percent. Remembering the nature and limitations of the data, it can be said that by far the most active group in 1790–92 were second term 35 to 39-year-olds though the smaller number of second term 30 to 34-year-olds had a higher simple roll call participation rate.

Table 41

Ranking of Age Groups According to Activism

	vr(n)
second term 35-39	
	- - - - 600
	- - - - 500
both terms 30-34	
	- - - - 400
second term 25-29	
first term 35-39	
first term 45-49	
	- - - - 300
second term 40-44	
first term 50-54	
first term 40-44	
	- - - - 200
first term 25-29	
second term 20-24	
second term 55-59	
second term 45-49	
first term 20-24	
first term 55-59	
	- - - - 100
second term 75-79	
second term 55-59	
second term 60-64	
first term 65-69	
first term 60-64	
	- - - - 0

The deputies blocked off in five-year intervals who had the greatest participation/impact formed an interesting group—however much their grouping might be artificial. Two groups seemed most influential: the 35 to 39-year-olds from the second term who far exceeded the other groups in their number and participation rate and second, this group plus 30 to 34-year-olds from both terms.

Thirty-five to thirty-nine-year-olds elected in 1790 comprised an interesting group. Most were from the Crown (six from Małopolska, five from Wielkopolska and only one from Lithuania). The stances of ten of the twelve with regard to the Constitution are known: 2 (20 percent) were opponents, 6 (60 percent) were supports and another 2 (20 percent) were converts; the high percentage of converts versus opponents distinguished this group from the *Sejm* norm.[6] Interestingly there were only three other deputies in the entire *Sejm* regardless of age, who initially opposed the Constitution and then came to support it.[7] A very large percentage (77.8 percent) of this group belonged to the Zgromadzenie. One of the two opponents supported the counter-revolutionary Targowica Confederation and opposed the Kościuszko Uprising; the other opponent was not a diehard dissident since he did not support the overthrow of the new system but did fight in the Kościuszko Uprising and went on to hold governmental offices in both the Duchy of Warsaw and the Congress Kingdom.[8] Overall, 90 percent of this group for whom there is information supported the Kościuszko Uprising. Very little is known about their education: one was educated by Jesuits, one abroad, and one in a National Education Commission school. Two, however, did attend the Collegium Nobilium. Of the nine for whom there is information, five (55.6 percent) were new to service in the *Sejm* and two each (22.2 percent) had attended one and two previous *Sejmy*. Thus, the group appeared rather inexperienced but not much more than the *Sejm* as a whole where 52.2 percent had been novices. Of the eight for whom an estimate of wealth is known, six (75 percent) were considered "very wealthy" and the other two (25 percent) were middle nobility.[9] Strikingly, 20 percent had military experience and another 30 percent were professional military officers. A third were masons. This particularly active group would indicate that at least an important segment of the reformers were young and wealthy nobles with a strong military influence.

The larger group of second term 35 to 39-year-olds and all 30 to 34-year old deputies of both terms presents an even more vivid picture. Among this group of thirty deputies 76.9 percent were supporters, 7.7 percent converts (84.6 percent combined supporters) and only 15.4 percent opponents; 82.6 percent became members of the Zgromadzenie. Two-thirds (66.7 percent) would never join Targowica while 95.7 percent, for whom there is information, would fight in the Kościuszko Uprising. This group, therefore, was decisively "progressive." Their breakdown by province was: 36.7 percent Wielkopolska, 36.7 percent Małopolska, 16.7 percent Lithuania and 10 percent Livonia. A third were educated by the Piarists, a fourth by Jesuits, another fourth went to school abroad, 8.3 percent received private tutoring exclusively and another 8.3 percent went to a National Education Commission school. Overall 16 percent attended the Collegium Nobilium and 15.4 percent the Szkoła Rycerska. Over a third (38.5 percent) were known to have travelled abroad. This group had less parliamentary experience than the *Sejm*'s norm, in part, no doubt, due to their age: 61.5 percent were attending their first *Sejm* and the most experienced (15.4 percent) had only been to two previous parliaments. The medal rate among this group rose from 15.4 percent in 1788 to 38.5 percent in 1792. The overwhelming part of the group appears to have belonged to the very wealthy *szlachta* (70.6 percent), 17.6 percent to the middle nobility and 11.8 percent were poor. Though none were magnates, 31.6 percent had fathers in the *Senat* (10.5 percent were sons of *wojewódowie* and 21.1 percent sons of *kasztelanowie*). Since this group was highly visible, the impression must have been that in the months up to May 3, 1791 there was a strong presence of young wealthy nobles or sons of senators advocating change.

Table 42

Mean Ages (in 1791)

	Entirety	Term 1	Term 2
Sejm	41.2	41.8	40.4
supporters	39.5	40.2	38.6
opponents	42.8	42.3	43.5
converts	41.3	—	41.3

Age as a factor predisposing a particular attitude towards the Constitution is evident not only in this special group but it emerges as a significant influence when the deputies are divided by term.

While the younger second term delegates showed the greatest activity in the months preceding the May Third Constitution and though the means of the two terms did not vary significantly, the disparity in age between supporters and opponents of the revolution was in fact rather clear-cut. On the whole, advocates of change embodied in the Constitution were 3.3 years younger than opponents with a still greater difference for second term deputies (4.9 years). Almost predictably, the mean age of the handful (five) of delegates who over time came to support the Constitution fell neatly between the means of the other two groups. This would seem to confirm the observation that age was indeed a factor in a deputy's inclination or disinclination towards these particular reforms.

The reason for the apparent correlation between age and support for the the new constitution is a matter of speculation. In the case of the greatest disparity, the second term supporters of constitutional change were, on average, born in late 1752 while the opponents in late 1747. This would mean that at the outbreak of the last and unsuccessful anti-Russian but politically conservative national uprising, the Confederation of Bar, the supporters were still minors (15 years of age) while the future opponents of the May Third Constitution had already reached maturity (20 years of age) and could have taken part in regular military and guerrilla operations. The suppression of the Confederation of Bar was followed by the First Partition. Possibly the futility and dangers of breaking the foreign grip and the resulting constitutional guarantees of the partitioning powers had made a greater impression on the consciousness of older members who then would oppose drastic changes during the Four Year's *Sejm*.

An alternative, or perhaps complementatary, influence could have been the impact of the intellectual, and especially the ideological, ferment after the First Partition. Intellectual revival and political polemics charged the 1780s in the Commonwealth with an intensity unknown for generations. Political struggles and factional maneuvering were nothing new as attested to by the series of confederations during the early years of Poniatowski's reign leading to the First Partition. But the debates conducted with quills and presses in the years immediately preceding and during the Four Years' *Sejm* were no longer clashes among similar factions or the protests of isolated, original visionaries. The Confederation of Bar (1768–1772) fought under the slogan "Faith and Freedom," understood in a reactionary manner, radicalized the *szlachta* and, to a lesser extent, society as a whole.

In the decade before the Four Years' *Sejm*, literate individuals initiated a societal self-examination in the context of improving chances for regaining full national sovereignty. The public debates and quietly dramatic circumstances of the 1770s and 1780s fostered a process of crystalization in which different worldviews, different mentalities, were made more precise, where ideologies began to emerge from old Sarmatianism, old reform traditions, the Enlightenment which blew with the predominantly western winds and new attitudes formed by new socioeconomic circumstances. In the Four Years' *Sejm* these were, with difficulty, transformed into successful or failed legislation. The actual legislation seemed often like half measures, pale reflections of more forceful, provocative ideologies evident in the parliamentary and extraparliamentary debates. Compromise was at the core of parliamentarianism. Moreover, upon examination the clash between modern and traditional mentalities devolves into a convection of innumerable ideological shadings.

While the age factor did not statistically correlate with the Constitution factor, the occurrence of the Confederation of Bar precisely at the period of maturation of many of the deputies may have exerted a profound effect. The age at which future opponents and supporters of the May Third Constitution encountered the Confederation of Bar and future supporters experienced the intellectualized struggle for people's minds amidst intensifying national consciousness may have predisposed them differently towards reform. Of equal likelihood, however, was the submersion of the age factor in other unrecognized circumstances and considerations.

The attitudes of deputies who actually participated in the Bar Confederation further complicate the picture. The approval rates towards the Constitution for the earlier rebels does appear to differ greatly from non-participants:[10]

Table 43

The Confederation of Bar and the May Third Constitution

	Bar Confederates	Non-participants
supporters	53.3%	70.4%
opponents	46.6%	29.4%

Age was probably a factor.

The most noteworthy irregularities among the Bar Confederates was the absence of Lithuanians, which cannot readily be explained, and the high number of deputies from Livonia. The latter were loose individuals with political ambitions but who often lacked a territorial political base. It is striking not only that so many of these individuals participated in the Confederation of Bar but that all four also supported the May Third Constitution. This may be a sign of their discontent in the 1760s and in 1791. More established former Confederates in delegations of either strong support or hostility for the Constitution tended to reject the reforms.

Socioeconomic Stratification, Service and Prestige

A more telling relationship existed between attitudes towards the Constitution and a deputy's socioeconomic position. As indicated, supporters in *województwa* with strong support or opposition tended to come from a stratum of very wealthy nobles appearing between the middle *szlachta* and the magnates. But while wealth may have played a role, an individual's standing in the *szlachta* did not depend exclusively on material factors. A person's socioeconomic position was social and not only economic. Civic service also lent a prestige of equal, if not greater, importance.

Social esteem and concepts of society underwent fundamental changes during the late Stanisławian period. Reform in the Four Years' *Sejm* meant a change from one image of the political system to another—even if the differences were more that of efficiency than of fundamental change. A new compromise of political images replaced an old collage of expectations and norms. Motives for change reflected wider motivations which pique a historian's interest. Biographical information can hint at changing mentalities. After the district represented, the next top six biographical factors connected by chi-square with support for the new Constitution were the offices held by the deputies themselves and by their fathers. The role of careers is connected to the intraclass and class interests favored by historians as an explanation for the revolution of 1791.

History as class struggle is the most extreme approach. For Marxists this struggle is the dialectic generating antagonistic classes based on economic factors. Relations of production and social consciousness define a class. The standard, most modern interpretation of the Four Years' *Sejm* and the May Third Constitution was formed by the late historian, Bogusław Leśnodorski.[11]

Leśnodorski regarded the May Third Constitution as a product of a new ideology emerging amidst the still unfinished process of class formation at the cusp of the feudal and capitalist epochs. The reformers, as did many other members of the Polish elite, blended ideas of the Enlightenment with indigenous political traditions but only, according to the lastest synthesis on the subject, to bolster the medieval estate nature of the political system. The new ideas of laws of nature were interpreted and applied in such ways as to safeguard the interests of the *szlachta*. *Prawa niewzruszone*, the traditional category which approximated natural laws or, in less modern minds, divine laws superceded the constitution but were in fact the noble privileges issued from the times of Kazimierz Wielki to Zygmunt August (1333–1572) guaranteeing *szlachta* domination. The notion of social contract served to affirm the status quo.[12]

Leśnodorski further argued that, in contrast to Western Europe, the collective took precedence over the individual in the Polish understanding of human rights. The noble estate rather than each individual was endowed with natural rights and only the collective could forgo any of its specific prerogatives.[13] The logical development for this line of reasoning became law, in a rather surprising manner, when the *Ustawa Rządowa* and other reforms of the Four Years' *Sejm* disenfranchised the poor nobility, partially enfranchised the wealthier bourgeoisie and extended the protection of the law over the peasantry. This was completely consistent with the declared purpose of the Constitution to save the fatherland and with it to further "our rightly understood interests."

But Leśnodorski's interpretation can be extended. The first two reforms (disenfranchisement of landless nobles and enfranchisement of the rich bourgeoisie) did more than simply protect the interests of the *szlachta*. They redefined the *szlachta* according to a revived and revised ancient value of service to a polity which, in a real sense, belongs to the nation and is neither the patrimonial property of a dominant family nor the hereditary prerogative of a "legitimate" dynasty or an abstract state nor even the hereditary right of an estate. Land and wealth were becoming the crucial test of service that cut across the old *szlachta*/non-*szlachta* divide. The peasants were not included although outstanding individual service was on occasion rewarded by a noble patent and more radical reformers, such as Kołłątaj, sought more rights for the "village folk." The new "political nation" was a stratum of individuals with proven or reputed service to the polity. Social divisions were not eliminated; the hierarchy was simply refined. The *Ustawa Rządowa* further postulated a broader notion of nation extending it beyond the *szlachta* to all inhabitants of the *Rzeczpospolita* regardless of social and political standing. Even a vague statement embraced the peasantry in the nation.[14]

The reforms created three categories of people. The first was a combination of nobles and bourgeoisie who qualified to take part in the political processes. The second were the dis- or unenfranchised nobility and bourgeoisie both of whom had certain rights but no political voice. These two categories were analogous to the active and passive citizens stipulated in the French constitution from later in 1791. Finally the rest of the population formed an unprivileged majority who, however, were acknowledged by the *Ustawa Rządowa* as having a stake in society; representation was apportioned according to total population figures and all groups had the ethical responsibility to defend the country.

Grounding their views on the old opposition of *szlachta* and *magnateria* still current in the eighteenth century, other historians have emphasized different aspects of class and intra-noble stratification. In the seminal work *Uwarstwienie społeczne*, Andrzej Wyczański used classifications for tax purposes to distinguish strata within the *szlachta* and society as a whole in sixteenth century Poland-Lithuania. Among the *szlachta*, Wyczański distinguished four groups: the magnates whose taxes exceeded 60 *złoty*, the very rich who paid between 30 and 60 *złoty*, the middle nobility (2–30 *złoty*) and the poor (below 2 *złoty*).[15] For society as a whole, Wyczański argued for eight strata based on tax rates and social prestige: wealthiest, wealthy, upper middle, middle, lower middle, lower, poor and excluded.[16] But crucial to Wyczański's approach is the assumption that tax assessments of offices in the sixteenth century reflected their generally accepted value in society. Economic worth was not the sole determinant of class and in the *Rzeczpospolita* the corporate consciousness of the nobility was based on the noneconomic criteria of service in the Republic's offices.

Wyczański's study invites an analogous analysis for the eighteenth century. The likely problem here is the perennial approximation of historical categories to historical realities. A fundamental distinction exists between the social stratification based on the *szlachta*'s own value system and the materialistic concept of social divisions according to wealth used as a tool of analysis by historians or even logical divisions such as Wyczański's. Moreover, Wyczański's groupings are arbitrary divisions *ex post facto*. A category such as the "lower middle strata" in sixteenth century or even eighteenth century Poland-Lithuania would have been considered an affront to the most cherished value of noble equality. The crucial factor seems not to have been wealth but a perception of social utility based on service to the Commonwealth—a non-material criterion.

The noble mentality harmoniously united seemingly incompatible principles into its self-image. The *szlachta* were all equal, yet, appropriate gestures in interpersonal relations varied according to the individuals' economic power. An example was the customary greeting kiss which ranged from a kiss on the cheek for equals to a kiss on the arm or elbow and finally to prostration on the ground for the most economically disparate nobles.[17]

Nobles also valued each other depending on their official civic service. Equality was unquestioned, yet, the assumption that an eternal and essentially static order in reality existed permeated people's minds. The nobility of the eighteenth century *Rzeczpospolita* habitually and consciously accepted a system of social stratification theoretically based on public service and heredity. First of all, this distinguished the *szlachta* from the rest of society. A characteristic part of this system was the strong tendency to regard this virtue (in this context, public service) as hereditary. Each nobleman was seen to contain within himself the service performed by all his ancestors; by his very nature he was supposed to be inclined towards similar actions. All other social groups were thought to be disinclined towards public service. The *szlachta* usually thought that only they were *szlachetni*, that is, virtuous.

Within the social hierarchy the szlachta occupied a privileged place but stratification theoretically stopped at the boundaries of nobility. This essential characteristic of theoretical equality, had attracted Lithuanian and Ruthenian elites to the Polish system and resulted in their Polonization. Wealth served only to bend the system and open opportunities but never did it act as an official source of prestige.

Equality within the *szlachta* was, however, the norm but not the reality. In a lengthy oft-quoted statement a deputy from Liw, Pius

Kiciński, described the split between the *"panowie"* [lords] and the rest of the *szlachta*:

> Not from law but from proud usurpation are there differences among the nobility in Poland. Some call themselves *panowie* [lords] not because they were always rich or because from birth they had some special authority over others, but because they come from those generations who have arranged among themselves a quiet agreement to be the first class, to oppress their brothers who in their lordly language we know as the small or simple *szlachta*, of which there are among us here at the Sejm more than a third. Who does not know that these families can easily be recognized by the following characteristics: that, as mentioned, they are born as *jaśnie Oświeconi* ("brightly enlightened") or *jaśnie wielmożni* ("brightly capable"), that only they are capable at birth of everything which in the Rzeczpospolita is excellent or profitable; that only they are not covered by law or justice because it is not proper to think that any of these impressive statesmen could sin against anyone. It is they that speak most of equality but hunger least for it. Were any of them ever a district *cześnik* [cupbearer] or *skarbnik* [treasurer]? Have any of them undertaken a land or urban judgeship? Do they not marry only among themselves, [and] live among themselves? Do we not see that they aspire to their aristocratic intention to perpetuate by law what they possess through usurpation so that . . . they would forever govern in Poland? And is it not unjust of the king to dare once in a while to set a petty nobleman on [one of] the senatorial or ministerial chairs which have been the undisputable property of lords to the extent that they seldom left one house? Now the ministerium [is] debased and the senate [is] debased. Because who is sitting in them? It is a disgrace to say—not those from the first families but almost solely the simple *szlachta*![18]

These observations by this staunch supporter of the king hold a wealth of information. First, clearly the formation of an aristocracy in Poland was seen by some as unjust and extralegal. Second, the power of the magnates was not necessarily always based on wealth; members of the aristocracy formed an exclusive group and tried to perpetuate their dominant positions while being the most vocal exponents of equality. Third, these lords used particular forms of address to distinguish themselves from the rest of the nobility. Finally, the aristocracy shunned local offices but aspired to monopolize senate and ministerial seats. At the time of the Four Years' *Sejm*, King Stanisław August had only partially broken the monopoly of the aristocracy in the senate and ministerium.

The appearance of an aristocracy contradicted the centuries old, cherished principle of absolute equality among the nobility: "*szlachcic na zagrodzie równy wojewódzic*" [a backyard noble (is) equal to the *wojewoda*]. New titles had been outlawed at the Union of Lublin (1569) but this was circumvented by special forms of address and by the usage of office titles which in the eighteenth century had become a virtual titlemania. The criterion which had distinquished the *szlachta* from the rest of society unofficially reached into the estate itself. Stratification according to service extended to intersect with an unspoken stratification according to wealth expressed in the nonverbal gestures of kissing and prostrations.

The split between "*panowie*" and *szlachta* within the *szlachta* had manifested itself in open hostility during the Confederation of Bar, less than a generation before the Four Years' *Sejm*. With utter disgust, Repnin, the powerful Russian ambassador noticed in 1768 what Konopczyński would later call "the liberation of the middle and small *szlachta* from the authority of the powerful lords." In direct opposition to the aristocracy, the middling *szlachta* devoted "body and soul" to the defense of "faith and freedom" in this mass revolt of the *szlachta* against Russian influence.[19] Theoretically, distinctions within the *szlachta* resulted from service to the *Rzeczpospolita* as indeed Starowolski in 1632 had written that the Senate was chosen from the most prominent nobles to render a service as enforcers of the law.[20] This old value, a fundamental norm even in Sarmatian obscurantism, came to parallel Enlightenment values expressed contemporaneously to the Four Years' *Sejm* in article one of the French Declaration of the Rights of Man and the Citizen: "Men are born and remain equal in rights. Social distinction may be based only on common utility." This analogy, however, must be understood in the context of a society which still practiced serfdom and another that maintained colonial slavery.

In summation, traditional *szlachta* ideology distinguished the nobility from the rest of society not on the basis of wealth but of virtue.

Virtue was perceived to be hereditary and expressed in public service. Social hierarchy was a moral order and the theoretical equality of the *szlachta* was tempered by graduations of virtue expressed in titles of offices held as forms of service to the community. The existence of an aristocracy drew its source from the idea of inherited virtue but was never in total harmony with the value of public service. Significantly, titles of offices acquired a hereditary quality although the offices usually were not: sons of a particular officeholder received the title "son of . . . " e.g., *cześnik - cześnikowicz* [cupbearer - cupbearers' son]. The status of a nobleman ideally depended on his public service—common utility—and the past services of his family to the Commonwealth.

A fundamental transformation was made by the Four Years' *Sejm*. Its advocates consciously sought the restoration of an old norm, as they saw it, dangerously perverted by time. The reform had a conservative quality. Revolution, after all, originally meant a restoration, often back to a mythical system that approximated a divinely willed immutable order; the philosophical implications of reform are never immediately drawn. The proponents of reform did not necessarily overtly accept the concept of continuous change or dynamism. Such was probably the case with the principle of social utility that appeared in the statutes of the Four Years' *Sejm*. Reformers sought to revive the old value of social prestige based on civic service by eliminating the abuses of magnates. The method used was to link civic service or social utility with something quite akinned to wealth—hereditary landownership *or* wealth sufficient to pay a specified amount of taxes—and to make this the criterion for political participation.

The deputies of the Four Years' *Sejm* faced conflicting values: the theoretical equality of all nobles, the traditional distinctions according to service in old offices and the new distinctions according to service as measured in wealth. It is likely that all three coexisted to various degrees in each individual deputy's value system. The traditional distinctions, however, probably indicate the stratification most familiar to the noble consciousness. These warrant attention.

Hierarchies of offices permeated the *szlachta* and the Commonwealth.[21] Apart from the ecclesiatical hierarchy with its international character and the military organization with its chain of command, there was a system of national and local offices, as well as hierarchies of positions in royal and magnate households. National and local offices hold the greatest relevance to the status of *Sejm* members.

National offices fell into two categories: senators and ministers (joined in 1768) and a smaller group of national nonsenatorial offices. The elevation of the ministerium seems indicative of a growing, expanding state. Each senator and minister possessed life-long tenure and fit into a strict hierarchy as listed in the turnus tally sheets. These are listed in Table 44. As observed by a member of the Four Years' *Sejm*, Pius Kiciński, and confirmed by the historian, Teresa Zielińska, the Senate was almost the exclusive preserve of the magnateria or aristocracy.[22]

Table 44

Senate and Ministerium		
SENATORS		
(Collegium Ecclisiastum)	Archbishop of Gniezno	
	Bishops of Kraków	Żmudź
	Kujawy	Chełm-Lublin
	Poznań	Kijów
	Wilno	Kamieniec
	Płock	Livonia
	Łuck	Smoleńsk
(Wojewodowie)	Kasztelan of Kraków	Wojewoda of Lublin
	Wojewoda of Kraków	Połock
	Poznán	Bełz
	Wilno	Nowogrodek
	Sandomierz	Płock
	Kasztelan of Wilno	Witebsk
	Wojewoda of Kalisz	Mazowsze
	Troki	Podlasie
	Sieradz	Rawa
	Kasztelan of Troki	Brześć-
	Wojewoda of Łęczyca	Litewski
	Starosta of Żmudź	Chełmno
	Wojewoda of Brześć Kujawski	Mścisław
	Kijów	Malbork
	Inowrocław	Bracław
	Ruś	Pomorze
	Podole	Livonia

		Smoleńsk	Czernichów
			Gniezno

(Kasztelanowie)

Kasztelan of	Poznań	Mińsk	Kruszwic
	Sandomierz	Livonia	Oświęcim
	Kalisz	Czernichów	Kamień
	Wojno	Mazowsze	Spicimirz
	Gniezno	Sącz	Inowłodz
	Sieradz	Międzyrzec	Kowal
	Łęczyca	Wislic	Santok
	Żmudź	Biec	Suchorzew
	Brześć-Kujawski	Rogozin	Warsaw
	Kijów	Radom	Gostyniń
	Inowrocław	Zawichost	Wiz
	Lwów	Lędz	Racięż
	Wołyń	Srzem	Sieprc
	Kamieniec	Zarnów	Wyszogrodek
	Smoleńsk	Małogoszcz	Rypin
	Lublin	Wieluń	Zakroczym
	Połock	Przemyśl	Ciechanów
	Bełz	Halicz	Liw
	Nowogródek	Sanok	Sron
	Płock	Chełm	Lubaczew
	Witebsk	Dobrzyń	Konary Sieradzkie
	Czersk	Połaniec	Konary Łęczyckie
	Podlasie	Przemet	Konary Kuiawskie
	Rawa	Krzywińsk	Busk
	Brześć Litewski	Czechów	Żytomierz
	Chełmno	Nakielsk	Owruck
	Mścisław	Rospirsk	Łuck
	Elbląg	Biechów	
	Bracław	Bydgoszcz	
	Gdańsk	Brzeg	

MINISTERIUM

Marszałek Wielki Koronny (Great Marshal of the Crown)
Marszałek Wielki Litewski (Great Marshal of Lithuania)

Hetman Wielki Koronny	(Great Hetman of the Crown)
Hetman Wielki Litewski	(Great Hetman of Lithuania)
Kanclerz Wielki Koronny	(Great Chancellor of the Crown)
Kanclerz Wielki Litewski	(Great Chancellor of Lithuania)
Podkanclerz Koronny	(Crown Vice-chancellor)
Podkanclerz Litewski	(Lithuanian Vice-chancellor)
Podskarbi Wielki Koronny	(Great Crown Vice-treasurer)
Podskarbi Wielki Litewski	(Great Lithuanian Vice-treasurer)
Marszałek Nadworny Koronny	(Crown Court Marshal)
Marszałek Nadworny Litewski	(Lithuanian Court Marshal)
Hetman Polny Koronny	(Crown Field Hetman)
Hetman Polny Litewski	(Lithuanian Field Hetman)
Podskarbi Nadworny Koronny	(Crown Court Vice-treasurer)
Podskarbi Nadworny Litewski	(Lithuanian Court Vice-treasurer)

Significantly, a disproportionate number of the very active second term supporters of the Constitution in their late thirties—the group discussed earlier—were sons of senators, i.e., magnates. For the 359 men who served as deputies, the backgrounds of the fathers of 145 (40.4 percent) are known and of these 44 (30.3 percent) were senators or ministers. For the specified particularly active group of 12, the backgrounds of the fathers of 8 (66.6 percent) are known and of these 4 (50 percent) were senators. All were *wojewódowie* or *kasztelanie*; none were ministers raised only recently to the Senate. All four sons of magnates were advocates of the Constitution.[23]

The bulk of the *szlachta*, however, could only aspire to the pinnacle of national service and honor in the Senate and ministerium but it did spend tremendous amounts of energy in the more realistic task of rising through a hierarchy of largely ceremonial remnants of medieval ducal and local offices. The intermediary ranks between the local and senatorial offices were the national positions listed in Table 45.

Table 45

Non-Senatorial Republic-wide Office	
obożny	(camp-keeper)
sekretarz	(secretary)
referendarz duchowny	(clerical referent)
referendarz świecki	(lay referent)

podczasy (cupbearer)
krajczy (carver)
miecznik (swordkeeper)
podskarbi nadworny (court vice-treasury)
asesor sadu nadwornego (court judicial assessor)
pisarz wielki (great clerk)
instygator (prosecutor)

These, however, were comparatively few. The offices for which most did vie were on the *województwo* and *powiat* levels. Though they

Table 46

Traditional Local Offices

Crown (Wielkopolska and Małopolska)

1. *podkomorzy*	*	(chamberlain)
2. *starosta grodowy*	*	(elder of royal city)
3. *chorąży*	*	(standard-bearer)
4. *sędzia ziemski*		(land court judge)
5. *stolnik*		(esquire carver)
6. *podczasy*		(cupbearer)
7. *podsądek*		(vice-judge)
8. *podstoli*	*	(steward)
9. *cześnik*		(cupbearer)
10. *łowczy*		(master of the royal hunt)
11. *wojski większy*	*	(great security officer)
12. *pisarz ziemski*	*	(land clerk)
13. *miecznik*		(swordkeeper)
14. *wojski mniejszy*	*	(lesser security office)
15. *skarbnik*		(treasurer)

Grand Duchy (Lithuania)

1. *ciwuń*		(bailiff)
2. *marszałek*	*	(marshal)
3. *podkomorzy*	*	(chamberlain)
4. *starosta grodowy*	*	(elder of royal city)
5. *chorąży*	*	(standard-bearer)
6. *sędzia ziemski*	*	(land court judge)
7. *wojski*		(security officer)

8.	stolnik		(esquire carver)
9.	podstoli		(steward)
10.	pisarz ziemski	*	(land clerk)
11.	podwojewodzi	*	(vice-wojewoda)
	podstarości	*	(vice-starosta)
12.	sędzia grodzki	*	(city judge)
13.	pisarz grodzki	*	(city clerk)
14.	podczasy		(cupbearer)
15.	cześnik		(cupbearer)
16.	horodniczy	*	(city official)
17.	skarbnik		(treasurer)
18.	łowczy		(master of the royal hunt)
19.	miecznik		(swordkeeper)
20.	koniuszy	*	(equerry)
21.	obożny		(camp leader)
22.	straznik		(guard)
23.	krajczy		(carver)

varied regionally they had been largely standardized and ranked within each of the two main parts of the *Rzeczpospolita* (see Table 46).[24] During Stanisław August's reign these appointments were a royal prerogative enabling a construction of a royal grouping or party. While only those indicated with an asterisk performed more than purely symbolic functions, appointments and promotions were theoretically reflective of the individual's value to society and, in some cases, actual monetary power. Though the absurdity of climbing a ladder of functioning offices interspersed with outmoded, fictional positions must have created an element of fantasy in the average nobleman's mind and in the political system as a whole, aspiration for these offices indicates, to a certain extent, a person's acceptance of the political system and the actual position occupied by an individual may be taken as indicative of his social position, modernity, or practicality. Movement up the ladder was a measure of success within a highly hierarchical society but theoretically egalitarian estate.

Traditional local offices were not the only positions of service and prestige available to the lay nobility nor were they universally sought. Flanking them on the one side were senatorial seats and national non-senatorial offices while on the other there were such new titles as *szambelan* [chamberlain] or titles connected with the armed forces and the civil-military administrative commissions. Sons of magnates did not seem to vie for the traditional offices. Titles such as *cześnik* were not held by any of the seven Potockis elected as deputies to the Four Years' *Sejm*; the local titles may have seemed irrelevant for a family with either ministerial and senatorial titles or simply with real economic power. Kiciński's observation was accurate. The one exception was the title of *starosta* which seems to have been eagerly sought by everyone. This ancient title may have had an elite, senatorial quality to it since one *starosta*, that of Żmudź (Samigitia), was, in fact, a member of the Senate. Complicating matters, *starosta* actually referred to at least two functionally different offices. One, the *starosta grodowy*, was technically in the king's employ, a member of the hierarchy of offices and the person responsible for specific unalienated royal estates. The *starosta niegrodowy*, was the hereditary owner of estates that had formerly belonged to the royal *demesne*. These distinctions were not evident in the titles themselves.

The nobles who used new non-traditional titles may have done so either as the only viable alternative to local offices that in some areas may have been prerogatives of local notable families—as was the case in the Mozyr district where the Oskierko family traditionally held the post of *podkomorzy* [older term for chamberlain]—or simply because, in one form or another, these nobles were alienated from the ideology or practice of the political system. Since, however, the individuals under study were elected to the parliament, politics were important to them; therefore, those without local offices either were blocked by others' prerogatives, by age or by chance or a few may have found the old hierarchy irrelevant or perhaps even repugnant. These individuals were either the young, the disillusioned or the "progressive." It is likely that those who did hold traditional local offices were, therefore, members of the middle or very wealthy *szlachta*, most probably either well established in their district or with a rather traditional approach to politics.

Of the 359 deputies at the Four Years' *Sejm*, 225 (63.2 percent) held traditional local offices and 10 (2.8 percent) non-senatorial positions in 1788–1792. The hierarchy of traditional offices, therefore, exerted some importance on at least two-thirds of the deputies. Officeholding was not distributed evenly according to term. A significant majority was concentrated in the first term: 56.5 percent of the traditional local offices and 70 percent of the smaller number of non-senatorial national positions were held by first term deputies. Second term deputies were either young and had not had time to obtain offices, or they were less successful in their efforts or simply less interested.

A slightly different picture emerges with the distinction between the two types of *starostowie*. Only an estimated 13 out of the total 44 *starostwa* were, in fact, *grodowe*.[25] *Starostwa* that were not *grodowe* were not considered offices. In this case 52.2 percent, rather than 63.2 percent, of the total number of deputies held traditional local offices and 54.7 percent, rather than 66 percent, held all the traditional and non-senatorial positions. The ratio between the two terms does not change.

Officeholding must have had some connection with a deputy's attitude towards the reform movement of the Four Years' *Sejm*. Based on the limited available sources, 65.9 percent of the opponents of the new constitution held traditional local offices while 51.7 percent of the supporters held such positions or titles. There is a danger of overemphasizing an association between the holding of traditional offices and political conservatism but such a marginal relationship seems to have existed.

Careers were not static phenomena. Each deputy who held a traditional office held it as part of a process of improving his position or as a voluntary or involuntary political terminus. For some, the climb up the ladder of functioning and purely titular offices was a matter of importance and perhaps a matter frequently compared with expectations and future career hopes. Arguably, career progress, as estimated by movement up this traditional hierarchy, could be connected to acceptance or rejection of the May Third Constitution.

As with other sources on the Four Years' *Sejm*, the data base for careers is incomplete. While the local titles for all the deputies are known as part of the *Sejm* records this information does not extend beyond the temperal limits of the parliament. Title information is also listed in the *Kalendarz Polityczny* and the *Series* (lists of deputies for each *Sejm*), but both of these sources apply only to deputies who had served in *Sejmy* previous to 1788. The full course of careers over a lifetime, taking into account age and office, has been established for only 45 of the 359 elected deputies: 25 supporters of the Constitution from the Crown, 11 opponents from the Crown, 6 and 3 respectively from the Grand Duchy.[26] The progress of individual careers can be represented by slopes with the y values from the above listing of offices and the x values as years. On this basis, the means have been compiled in Table 47.

Several precautionary observations should be made. A larger number of offices has resulted in higher slopes for the Grand Duchy than for the Crown. Unfortunately, the information about Lithuanian

Table 47
Careers in Traditional Local Offices

	Crown		Grand Duchy	
	pro	con	pro	con
slopes				
until 1791	.298	.220	.392	.354
until last promotion	.361	.272	.437	.411
career	.287	.115	.315	1.000
other				
age at 1st office	31.8	35.1	31.6	20.3
years in last office	7.0	9.5	4.0	11.3
promotions	2.3	1.8	1.8	1.6

opponents is useless since it exists for only three deputies, all from the antiroyalist pro-Russian Kossakowski family. Comparison on the constitutional issue with respect to age and careers is impossible for the Lithuanian deputies. The information on Lithuanian supporters, however, has intrinsic value in itself as well as in comparison with the Crown.

The most interesting contrasts, and perhaps the most significant observations, are with the Crown deputies. Clear differences exist. Though the final career level reached is not vastly different for supporters and opponents (lifelong slope .298 versus .220) the other career characteristics are. Supporters began their careers in the traditional offices at age 31.5, 3.5 years *earlier* than those on the other side of the constitutional issue. They had more promotions at shorter intervals. The career slope for those who supported the Constitution was .287 in contrast to .115 for opponents; in other words opponents had experienced a promotion rate only 40 percent as high as those who backed the reforms.

At least two interpretations are possible. First, the quicker pace of promotion for those who came to support the May Third Constitution might indicate relative satisfaction with royal actions since it was the king's chancellery that determined officeholding; this might be equivalent to a more general contentment with the political atmosphere. Since these deputies must have valued local offices, however traditional, and since there was nothing in the reforms per se that threatened these honors, they could have been content with the direction political life was taking. The general support for the Constitution by the local *sejmiki* in February 1792 affirms this broad consensus among the *szlachta* on the direction of the reforms.

On the other hand, it is equally likely that the contrasts in career histories indicate the presence of a specially cultivated royal party. Stanisław August promoted those he could trust or perhaps control. A closer look at other biographical information of each group seems in order for a future study.

Summary

Observations about representation on the sub-provincial level, age and intra-*szlachta* standing augment earlier conclusions about support and opposition for the May Third Constitution. In addition to the theses that the Four Years' *Sejm* consisted of mainly landed nobles (who comprised about 44 percent of the *szlachta*) and that support for the new constitution was associated with greater political experience, Piarist education in Lithuania, the Livonian at large delegation for the entire *Rzeczpospolita* and a group of very wealthy nobles throughout the country while opposition was linked most intensely to Małopolska, the following conclusions seem feasible on the basis of the analyses in this chapter:

1. Geographically, the strongest support seems to have been along the northern ethnic borderland regions of Podlasie, Brześć Litewski and Wilno, in the Smoleńsk, at large, delegation from Lithuania and in the Małopolanian area of Sandomierz.
2. Geographically the strongest opposition was in the southern Ruthenia *województwa* of Wołyń and Podole, the at large Ruthenian delegation of Czernichów (Chernihiv) and the Wielkopolanian area of Łęczyca.
3. A composite portrait of deputies from these extreme *województwa* indicates that at least in these areas:
    a. delegations with greater unanimity for or against the Constitution tended to be younger than the *Sejm*'s norms,
    b. the amount of travel abroad by deputies was irrelevant,
    c. Jesuit education tended to disincline deputies from the Constitution,

d. greater parliamentary experience was associated with support for the reforms,
   e. participation in the Confederation of Bar was associated with opposition to the new system,
   f. supporters acquired more of the prestigeous medals during the Four Years' *Sejm*,
   g. deputies with more regular military experience tended to support the new Constitution,
   h. supporters were limited to very wealthy nobles and some magnates while opponents came more evenly from all strata of nobles.
4. The most active deputies in the months leading up to the May Third Constitution were by far second term deputies between the ages of 35 and 39, inclusive. These, however, were not unanimously inclined to support the revolution.
5. The second and third most active groups of deputies by age in this period consisted of 30 to 34-year-olds from each terms. Taken as a whole, this group showed extraordinary zeal for the May Third Constitution. They and the second term 35 to 39-year-olds were highly visible, creating the impression that in the months up to May 3, 1791 there was a strong presence of young wealthy nobles or sons of senators advocating change.
6. Overall, supporters of the new system were slightly younger than were opponents. While there may be no statistically significant difference between their ages, the average difference of five years between second term supporters and second term opponents may have been enough to separate those who had matured before or during the Confederation of Bar and those whose maturation came later. The latter group seemed more inclined to support the May Third Constitution.
7. The Constitution's supporters in the Chamber of Deputies had fewer traditional local offices than did the Constitution's opponents. Those supporters from the Crown who did, however, hold traditional offices tended to have received them at a younger age and their careers had been more rapid and hence probably more satisfying. Opponents with traditional offices, on the other hand, received them later and then tended to stagnate in a particular office.

Words of cautions should be repeated. The data, as stated, is not complete and the working assumption has been that this incompleteness is essentially random. It is possible that the results reflect an unconscious selection based on wealth, geography and politics over the past two centuries. Moreover, the use of different measurements of significance continues to have a problematic quality. Nonetheless, the conclusions do not show logical inconsistency either in their construction or in their relation to each other.

Analysis of the biograms does not yield one overriding explanation for disagreement over the May Third Constitution. Instead, smaller vortices of particular factors seem to have operated. The new constitution seems largely to have been received by individuals individually. The limited, highly specific patterns that seemed to have been discerned attest to the complexity of consciousness. Hesitation from a failed revolt, training by religious groups, confidence due to youth or successful careers, parliamentary experience, military discipline, material independence were all characteristics that contributed in some way to a deputy's attitude toward the Constitution.

CHAPTER 7

POLITICAL GROUPINGS

Parliaments and political groupings have a nonsufficient cause and effect relationship. Representative systems generate political groupings within or outside a parliament. Non-representative systems produce either political groupings which tend to be very small, as in oligarchies, or monopolies, as in authoritarian or totalitarian systems; illegal groupings also remain small as long as the nonrepresentative system is functioning well. Political groupings are associations of people bound together consciously or unconsciously by a specific political issue or by ideology, by economic interests or in longer standing associations, by family, territory or patronage. The irrationality of human interactions also binds or disrupts political groupings as personalities draw together or repulse. Discussion and bargaining, which are the *raison d'être* of parliaments, assume disagreement and groupings. In the Four Years' *Sejm* groupings were of three kinds: persistent prepolitical divisions, pre-existing political groups, and newer alignments resulting both from the tempo and nature of the emerging reform program, from other parliamentary events, and from changes among the electorate.

Even after the truncation of territories in 1667 and 1772, the Polish-Lithuanian state comprised some 522,300 sq. km. and encompassed a population of 8,800,000.[1] One of the two prepolitical divisions in the Chamber of Deputies was territorial. While the state united two political units, the Crown (Korona) and the Grand Duchy of Lithuania (Wielkie Xięstwo Litewskie), by 1788 the concept of three provinces had become generally accepted. Throughout the Four Years' *Sejm* deputies on occasion grouped according to province: Wielkopolska, Małopolska and Wielkie Xięstwo. This separation appeared in the institution of provincial meetings of the *Sejm*,[2] the principle of provincial rotation and major legislation[3] but surprisingly not in the 22 October 1791 law bringing still closer together the Republics' two components. Another non-political division, used in the previous chapters, was the accident of election either in 1788 or in 1790.[4] Conceivably, factors involved in conscious or unconscious groupings are discernable in biographical information about individual deputies and these, in turn, reflect wider societal phenomena.

Political struggles in the *Sejm* during the 1780s had pitted the king and his grouping against the magnates. The main dispute had been control over the armed forces which in 1776 had been transferred from the *hetman*—invariably a leading magnate—to the Department of the Army in the Permanent Council. The army had for centuries been perceived as the main instrument by which royal power could effect its natural—and in the eyes of the nobility, dangerous—predilection towards absolutism. The constitution from 1776 appeared to many to have taken a major step in this direction and as the central government extended its activities the army provided the only means of law enforcement in the absence of local police or militia forces. To make the situation more odious and dangerous, behind royal authority and the new Permanent Council stood the Russian ambassador and Empress. Ironically through the middle 1780s the magnate "patriotic" grouping itself sought favors from Stackelberg, Catherine and/or Potemkin without understanding Russia's duplicity towards the "nation" and its firm support for Stanisław August. After Catherine's 1787 visit to Kiev and nearby Kaniów on the Polish bank of the Dnieper, one of the leading magnates and a prominent member of the exceptionally large Potocki clan, Ignacy Potocki, realized the Russian commitment to the king and swiftly reoriented his position towards Prussia. Thus, on the eve of the Four Years' *Sejm* the royal grouping faced a divided opposition.

Four groupings with different political orientations and sensibilities functioned by the convening of the *Sejm* in October 1788. The royal grouping, bound together by royal patronage and reliant on support from Russia, sought a strengthening of royal power and a more efficient government. The magnate opposition splintered further. The Puławy group, centered around the brothers Ignacy and Stanisław Kostka Potocki and exhibiting a fine sensitivity for popular opinion among the nobility, was the only pro-Prussian group. It aimed at strengthening the parliamentary system and focussing power on the ministries. The other two were closely associated and pro-Russian.

From his Ukrainian residence in Białocerkiew, Hetman Ksawery Branicki led a reactionary grouping cherishing the "golden freedom" of the Polish system, and using effective traditional demogoguery and misperceived Russian support in the hope of reestablishing the hetmanship as an intermediary authority between the king and the nation. Finally, Szczęsny Potocki (cousin of Ignacy and Stanisław), based in his Wołynian holding of Tulczyn, stubbornly sought to abolish the monarchy and establish a popular "republican" dictatorship.[5]

At the opening of the Four Years' *Sejm* control over the army was once again shifted, this time to the *Sejm* itself as the instrument of the broader *szlachta* nation. By late 1790, the royal grouping and Potocki's "patriots" allied into the reform group that produced the May Third Constitution and by 1792 Hetman Branicki and Szczęsny Potocki travelled to St. Petersburg to organize a counterrevolution backed by the Russian army and ostensively headquartered in the border town of Targowica.

Such is the simple generally accepted outline. Another opportunity for analysis is provided by the roll call votes examined in chapter four. Cluster analysis provides a means to discern political groupings on this most fundamental level. A widely used technique from the social sciences cluster analysis can measure actual political groupings, as opposed to reputations. This in turn provides a view into the political and ideological climate of the Four Years' *Sejm*.[6] A limitation that must be kept in mind is the difference between voting in divisions and participation in debates or other interaction among deputies.

Of the 120 roll calls that were conducted during the Four Years' *Sejm* tally sheets for at least 53 have been preserved for the Chamber of Deputies: 17 from the first term and 36 from the second.[7] The initial approach in this study was to analyze the voting patterns of all 359 deputies who participated at anytime during the *Sejm*.[8] The cluster analysis program examined each pair of voting patterns, assigning each pair of deputies a similarity coefficient. These similarity coefficients were then put into a matrix on the basis of which an icicle plot was generated. The numerous instances of absences necessitated the conversion of essentially binary data into data with three variables. Thus, while ideally the analysis should have dealt with only two types of answers—"1" for affirmative and "0" for negative, with absences left blank and ignored—the SPSSx cluster program blocked such an analysis because of numerous blanks. This obstacle was circumvented by recoding the information: "2" for an affirmative vote, "0" for a negative vote and "1" for an absence or abstention. Presumably, the lack of an opinion can be considered to lie somewhere between the two definite opinions. The presence of numerous absences did, however, cause problems, as will be seen shortly.

The initial cluster analysis produced a massive icicle graph characterized by numerous "thin" icicles with a general upper left-hand to lower right-hand trend. Two tendencies were evident. First, members did not form large groups. The individual deputies, more often than not, seem to have acted alone. Second, the deputies who clustered latest clustered precisely because of their sparse voting records. More active members tended to cluster early. Interestingly, the two leaders of the *Sejm*, Stanisław Małachowski and Kazimierz Nestor Sapieha, voted on 94 percent of the issues; they formed a separate cluster early in the analysis and with no other member joining their group. In this

Table 48

First Term Clusters

Clusters

Roll Call Issues	1	2	3	4	5	6	7	8	9
abolish Permanent Council	1	1	1	*	1	(1)	(1)	1	1
increase tax: mortgaged royal land	0	1	0	0	(1)	0	0	1	1
temporary recruit in Crown	0	1	0	(1)	1	0	1/0	(0/1)	-
establish Kommissaryat	1	1	1	1	1	(1)	(1)	(1)	(1)
new title: Great Deputy to Port	(0)	1	(0)	1	(1)	1	(1/0)	1	0
keep noble tax on Kowel starostwo	-	-	-	-	(0)	-	(1)	-	-
neighboring royalty electable	1	*	1	1/0	0	0	(1/0)	1	1
exception	0	*	0	1	1	1	*	0	1
elect deputies: 16 November 1790	1	(1)	1	1	0/1	1/0	1/0	1	0
amendment	0	0	0	0	1	0	1/0	0	0
secret ballot: instructions/deputies	0	0	1	0	0	0	1/0	0	-
delay Belz issue/Chelm representation	1	0	0	0/1	(0)	1	0/1	1	(1)
decide issue annexed area represent.	0	1	1	1/0	1	0	0/1	0	-
total abolition of waivers for MPs	(1)	1	1	1/0	(*)	1	(*)	(1)	-
keep tax on church, Malta, stolowe	1	1	*	0	0	1	1	(1)	-
officers share in grain collection	1	1	1	(0)	0	1	1	(1)	-
new date post-Sejm sejmik	1	1	1	1	1	1	(1/0)	0	-

( ) less than half responding
1/0 no clear majority, positives dominate
0/1 no clear majority, negatives dominate
*tie

instance, the analysis was meaningful since the variables being compared were yes and no votes, not absences. Clearly, there was genuine cooperation between the two marshals throughout the Four Years' *Sejm*.

But cluster analysis of the entire Four Years' *Sejm*, with absence as one of the examined variables, was not entirely satisfactory. Second term deputies were, of necessity, absent for the first 17 roll calls and since this was indistinguishable from the absenteeism of first term deputies, it produced profound distortions. Separate cluster analyses of each term partially alleviated this problem. The next set to be clustered consisted of first term deputies by themselves. Since no vote was still a variable, there was a general tendency for more active deputies to cluster early. The sample quality of the available roll calls was good. Though most of the 17 results recovered out of the total seventy roll calls come from late 1790, they do include such important issues as the vote over the Permanent Council in January 1789. The Table 48 shows the results for the 17 first term *turni* according to the typical responses of 9 clusters from the high attendance end of the icicle plot.

The following are brief descriptions and comparisons of the nine clusters:

Cluster One

Stanisław Małachowski	Eydziatowicz
Chrapowicki	

At the upper left-hand corner of the icicle plot the speaker of the Chamber of Deputies formed a distinct cluster with two representatives of annexed territories. This group supported political reforms (abolition of Permanent Council, early elections) and military reform (creation of the Commissariat); it opposed other political reforms (exclusion of foreign royalty in elections, secret ballots in *sejmiki*) and increased taxes (some royal estates taxed no more than noble estates, no temporary recruits). With Małachowski's reputation this group can be considered mainstream for the first term.

Cluster Two

Jerzmanowski	Sapieha
Gaiewski	Dłuski
—	—
Suchodolski (Smoleńsk)	"—" indicates a subcluster

This grouping of three Wielkopolska representatives, the marshal of the Lithuanian confederation and a deputy from Lublin differs from the Małachowski cluster in several non-political respects: approval of higher taxes on mortgaged royal estates, temporary recruits, opposition to a new title for the Republic's ambassador to Istanbul, support for exceptions to the candidacy of foreign royalty to the Polish throne, and on the issue of representation for ceded territories.

Cluster Three

Czacki	—
Rostworowski	Radziñowski, J.

Three Crown deputies voted almost identically to the Małachowski group except for their approval of the secret ballot, the issue of annexed territories and weaker support for increased taxes on church lands.

Cluster Four

Czetwertyński	—
Sokolnicki	Oborski
—	Szymanowski
Zakrzewski	

This group differed substantially from Małachowski's. With the only strong opposition to the abolition of the Permanent Council (in accord with Stanisław August's strategy of avoiding a break with Russia) these Wielkopolanians and a future senator from Małopolska (Czetwertyński) tended to support somewhat more radical reforms such as exclusion of foreign candidates to the throne and increased taxes. They also differed from Małachowski's cluster on the issue of representation for ceded territories and a new title for the ambassador to the Ottoman Empire.

Cluster Five

Suchodolski (Chełm)	Karwicki
Minorski	Stroynowski
Wybranowski	
—	Świętosławski
Chołoniewski	Jordan
Radoliński	

The second largest of the nine significant clusters in the first term, this group of Crown deputies showed the most variation from Małachowski's line. In fact, the two groups agreed on only two issues: the abolition of the Permanent Council and the establishment of definite dates for the rescheduled post-*Sejm sejmiki*. This group probably was the core of the reactionary opposition in the Chamber of Deputies—those most opposed to the changes advocated by Stanisław August and Ignacy Potocki.

Cluster Six

Gorski Wawrzecki
Skorkowski Gorzeński
—

Drawn from throughout the *Rzeczpospolita* this group differed from Małachowski only on the issue of foreign candidates and a new title for the ambassador to Turkey.

Cluster Seven

Grocholski Jabłonowski
Czartoryski —
— Kwilecki
Moszyński
— Gutakowski
Krasicki Sołtan
Zabiełło —
  Wilczewski
Jozofowicz Zaleski
Leszczyński Działyński
Kicki

The largest cluster approached cluster five in its variation from the Małachowski reforms except on two volatile issues: the Permanent Council which it opposed and temporary recruits which it tended to support. This group was, therefore, somewhat less averse to the trend of reform.

Cluster Eight

Weyssenhoff —
— Morawski
Kublicki Kościałkowski

Butrymowicz   —
—   Morikoni
Grabowski

Extremely coherent in composition and voting, this fairly large cluster of five Lithuanians and the two Livonians associated with Lithuania voted very closely to Małachowski's group and acted as a moderate reform group. These deputies differed from the *Sejm* marshals by supporting higher taxes on mortgaged royal lands, favoring a new title for the ambassador to the Porte and arguing for a rescheduling of the post-*Sejm sejmiki*.

Cluster Nine

Godlewski   Cholewski
Oborski   Wereszczyński
—

Substantively close to clusters one and eight, this group differed from the first on the issue of higher taxes for rented royal estates, on exceptions to foreign candidates and on the issue of November 16, 1790 local assemblies. From the latter it differed only on the issue of title for ambassador to the Porte and on exceptions for foreign candidates.

These nine clusters based on the voting records of all first term deputies for all the available first term *turni* can be scaled according to the "progressive" character of their votes. The mild reforming attitude of Małachowski and his reputation for fairness have made him the norm as cluster number one:

Figure 2: First Term Clusters

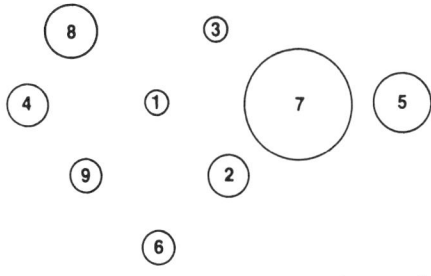

most radical change   least radical change

With the great variety of multifaceted issues and the large number of deputies, clustering could continue almost ad infinitum. But the crucial problem for this study is the behavior of the deputies during the second term which brought the most important constitutional changes. A clustering of all deputies for all available divisions during the second term produced at least two substantial and related clusters:[9]

Table 49

Second Term Clusters

Cluster One	Cluster Two
Rzetkowski	Lemnicki
Gutakowski	Kaczanowski
Szymanowski	Niemcewicz
Sobolewski	Zaiączek
Chrzeptowicz	Potocki, S. K.
Puzyna	Weyssenhoff
Eydziatowski	Zabiełło
Niemcewicz	Batowski
Sapieha (marshal)	Leżeńki
Małachowski (marshal)	Byszewski
	Potocki, Jo.
	Kublicki
	Gorzeński
	Działyński, I.
	Działyński, K.
	Ośniałowski
	Zboiński
	Wawrzecki
	Linowski

Several interesting contrasts appear in the backgrounds of these two groups. The geographic distribution was different: 60 percent of the first grouping represented Lithuania, 30 percent Wielkopolska and 10 percent Małopolska while 36.8 percent of the second grouping represented Wielkopolska, 26.3 percent Livonia, 26.3 percent Małopolska and only 10.5 percent Lithuania. Though the information is thin, it seems that the second group had a greater variety of education; a fifth of each had attended the Collegium Nobilium. In political experience, the first, predominantly Lithuanian grouping which also included the two marshals, had a *Sejm* attendance rate of 2.5 compared to the 1.385 rate of the other. Interestingly, though each had about 50 percent novices, the marshals' and Lithuanian delegates were either novices or veterans of at least three *Sejmy*; the distribution of experience was more even for the other grouping. The latter also included the sole veteran of the Bar Confederation. From the available information, both groups were comprised solely of adherents and converts to the Constitution, the overwhelming majority of each group belonged to the Zgromadzenie and opposed Targowica. Each had an unusually high rate of masons (40 and 30 percent respectively) but they differed in respect to military experience; 20 percent of the marshals' and Lithuanian grouping had had at least some while for the second grouping the figure was 64.3 percent of those for whom there is information, including 21.4 percent who were professional officers. The age difference was significant, 41.3 years compared to 36.5, as was the difference in economic positions:

Wealth

	First Cluster	Second Cluster
poor	–	22.2%
middle	–	11.1%
wealthy	66.7%	55.6%
magnate	33.3%	11.1%

Arguably the first cluster consisted of mainstream reformers: wealthy, Lithuanians with extensive parliamentary experience while the second cluster was comprised of less wealthy reformers from the other two provinces and Livonia with a variety of education, a strong military influence and less parliamentary experience.

A single issue accounted for the major difference between these two clusters: the bill on local assemblies (*sejmiki*) sent for revisions by a 155 to 41 vote on 14 March 1791. Małachowski and Sapieha wanted revisions but the other group, especially active Livonian deputies, who otherwise generally supported the marshals, was content with the bill as it stood.[10] This could present a promising association between socioeconomic factors and political issues. Moreover, this controversy was part of the split over the Constitution and thus had a powerful quality in historical hindsight.

Central to the constitutional controversy is the clustering of deputies according to constitutional issues and, more strictly, those issues most clearly identified with the new system. Three sets of divisions (roll call votes) have been chosen for this purpose: those that defined voting rights, those that created central governmental institutions and the one division most directly connected with the defense of the constitutional system.[11] This approach produced substantial clusters. In all three, the voting records of the two marshals, Małachowski and Sapieha, clung together, thus indicating again a unified leadership in the *Sejm*. But two problems became evident in the analysis. While numerous deputies moved around the marshals in neighboring clusters, only one, Zboiński was in the same cluster with Małachowski and Sapieha in all three cases. Would this indicate a lack of stable groupings? Or was this due to data's imperfections?

A more serious complication occurred with the association in one cluster of Mierzejewski, Eydziatowicz, and Puzyna for the divisions covering voting rights, institutions and the censure vote. All three had very similar voting patterns for the specified divisions through April 1791 and all three were absent from April through the July-August recess. But Eydziatowicz and Puzyna both returned in September and voted along with the marshals on constitutional issues through the end of the *Sejm* the following May. Mierzejewski never did return. It is known from secondary sources that Mierzejewski was a client of Hetman Branicki who opposed the Constitution. Mierzejewski's absence from April 1791 was, therefore, hostile while that of Eydziatowicz and Puzyna, which overlapped his until September, must have had other causes.[12] The association of the three in the same cluster is next to meaningless except for the possibility that May Third brought a parting of the ways by accentuated differences in the *Sejm*.

This points to a fundamental flaw in clustering deputies' votes. To avoid clustering problems with missing values, each absence of a vote has been given equal weight to a positive vote and a negative vote. Such cases could have significance if absences could always be identified with opposition but that clearly cannot be assumed. Abstentions were recorded only early in the *Sejm*, subsequently, the lack of a vote could have been due to an abstention or to an absence. In instances where a deputy was frequently absent or present but did not vote, comparisons lose their expected meaning. Thus, only those clusters which mainly include active members are useful. To a large extent this corresponds to the two sets of institutional/censure divisions and institutional votes alone and eliminates the four votes on political rights prior to the summer 1791 recess.

The marshals' clusters in these sets were:

Table 50

Marshals' Cluster		
Institutional	(Core)	Institutional/Censure
	Małachowski	
	Sapieha	
	Zboiński	
	Byszewski	
	Szymanowski	
	Sobolewski	
	Gutakowski	
Kaczanowski		Chreptowicz
Zabiełło		Sokolnicki
Rzetkowski		Wawrzecki
Zaiączek		

Except for Rzetkowski, who was absent for the censure vote (27 January 1792), the difference between the two clusters was precisely the censure vote. The censure and demotions of Szczęsny Potocki and Adam Rzewuski for failing to take an oath to the Constitution were extremely controversial: they were initially defeated in a roll call vote 39 to 58 but then passed in secret ballot 51 to 43. The marshals were themselves split on the issue with Małachowski pressing for the unprecedented, and in the end, uniquely harsh treatment of the opposition. Kaczanowski, Zabiełło and Zaiączek backed the censure; Chreptowicz, Sokolnicki and Wawrzecki joined the entire common group, except for Małachowski, in opposing this strong action. The essential difference between these two groups within the marshals' cluster seems to have been in the degree of zeal or in the confidence of the new order's strength.

Due to the nature of the voting data, clustering has limited value for examining parliamentary procedure in the Four Years' *Sejm*. More useful is a much less sophisticated method. Except for a rare absence and the censure issue, Małachowski and Sapieha had identical voting records for the fourteen divisions that have survived from the final phase of the Four Years' *Sejm* (September 1791 through May 1792). Presumably, those who voted in a similar manner were in agreement with the *Sejm* leadership and formed a grouping, if only unconsciously. The cutoff point for inclusion has been set at 50 percent agreement. This is perhaps overly generous but it seems justified by the high frequency and the political ambiguity of absenteeism. Fifty-nine deputies belonged to this "Marshals' Group."[13] Only six deputies voted consistently against the marshals at the same 50 percent level.[14] Nonetheless, at least 214 deputies and senators would attend any single session during this period.[15] The inconsistent activity and differences in voting for the balance of the deputies could have been due to a variety of motives, not all of them political. The "Marshals' Group" did behave consistently and formed a kind of pro-Constitution group.

The socioeconomic context of the May Third Constitution can be illustrated with a comparison of the biographical information of three concentric groups: all the deputies, those deputies who supported the Constitution and those who actively backed the new system as members of the Marshals' Group.[16] The relationship of the last two groups is not perfect. Biographical information does not supply the stance of twenty-two of the fifty-nine members of the Marshals' Group with regard to the Constitution. Conceivably, these twenty-two were all supporters and should be added to the list of eighty-nine adherents identified earlier. Conceivable some or most may not, in fact, have been supporters despite their voting record. Until more information is obtained these, however, will be considered part of the pro-Constitution grouping.[17]

Following the order used in previous chapters, the following factors have been examined: geography, age, education, travels abroad, political experience, offices, wealth, future careers, and lesser factors. The geographic distribution of the three groups was:

Province	Sejm	Supporters	Marshals' Group
Wielkopolska	37.0%	32.9%	33.9%
Małopolska	32.6%	32.9%	20.9%

Lithunaia	27.0%	27.1%	32.2%
Livonia	3.3%	7.7%	13.6%

Geographically, supporters, as a whole, were typical of the *Sejm*—with slight allowances made for Wielkopolska and Livonia—but the politically active supporters, (the Marshals' Group) were atypical. The percentage of membership in the Marshals' Group in comparison to the *Sejm* norm was only 62.3 percent of the norm for Małopolanians, 91.6 percent for Wielkopolanians, 119 percent for Lithuanians and a startling 412 percent for Livonians. Comparable figures for opponents were 158 percent for Małopolanians, 96.6 percent for Wielkopolanians, 58.7 percent for Lithuanians and 0 percent for Livonians. The popularity of the May Third Constitution among parliamentary activists was, therefore, highest among the at large deputies representing Livonia and in descending order among the provinces: Lithuania, Wielkopolska, and Małopolska.

There does not seem to have been a single Republic-wide pattern distinguishing members of the Marshals' Group from other deputies in their respective provinces. But some differences did exist. In Wielkopolska, the contrasts were strong. Supporters of the Constitution had less of a Jesuit education and more schooling abroad than the average Wielkopolanian deputy; Marshals' Group members differed from other supporters because of an even weaker Jesuit influence. There was a progressively positive influence of the Collegium Nobilium from the average Wielkopolanian deputy to a supporter of the Constitution to a member of the Marshals' Group but the numbers are very low. Attendance at the Szkoła Rycerska was irrelevant, at least by itself. Members of the Marshals' Group were more travelled than the average Wielkopolanian supporter of the new system but less so than the average Wielkopolanian deputy. On the whole, increased experience in the *Sejm* was associated with support for the Constitution and even more for inclusion in the Marshals' Group but involvement in the Confederation of Bar was not a factor. Wielkopolanians in the Marshals' Group were the same as regular Wielkopolanian supporters in respect to the Society of Friends of the Constitution, Targowica, the Kościuszko Uprising and officeholding in the Duchy of Warsaw but not in Congress Poland. The Wielkopolanians included in the Marshals' Group were notably less affluent as shown below.

While support had come mainly from the wealthy, with the exception of Wielkopolanian magnates, active support seems to have been associated with even generally more limited means. The association was not because poor or middling nobles made up a majority of the Marshals' Group but rather because they appeared in conspicuously larger numbers. The Marshals' Group, compared to all Wielkopolanian supporters, had a higher likelihood of masonry but in contrast to all other deputies from their province, they had more

Wealth

	All Wielko-polanians	Supporters	Marshals' Group
poor	5.9%	4.2%	12.5%
middle	14.7%	16.7%	25.0%
wealthy	73.5%	79.2%	62.5%
magnate	5.9%	–	–

military experience (20 percent). Finally, the politically active group was the same age as the entire delegation which then, on average, was three-and-a-half years *older* than the supporters taken as a whole. The Wielkopolanians in the Marshals' Group were individuals of slightly above average age and below average wealth who had been less influenced by the Jesuits but had had more political experience, military experience, and a higher instance of membership in Freemasonry.

Differences were sharper among the Małopolanians. Education seems to have been a deciding factor. Małopolanians in the Marshals' Group had twice the rate of attendance at Piarists schools exclusively (60 percent) as opposed to all Małopolanian supporters (31.5 percent) and all Małopolanian deputies (26.9 percent). Attendance at the Collegium Nobilium had a similar, though much less important, effect. Twice as many Małopolanians in the Marshals' Group had travelled abroad as had either of the two other groups. The politically active group also had more parliamentary experience. The wealth factor had a different effect among the Małopolanians than their Wielkopolanian colleagues:

Wealth

	All Mało-polanians	Supporters	Marshals' Group
poor	4.7%	0.0%	0.0%
middle	7.0%	5.3%	20.0%
wealthy	65.1%	63.2%	40.0%
magnate	23.3%	31.6%	40.0%

The Małopolanians in the Marshals' Group were both poorer and wealthier than others from their province. This obscure picture does indicate that magnates were not necessarily averse to the new system. Active support in Małopolska came from the middle *szlachta* and especially the very rich nobles *and* magnates. The Marshals' Group also had higher instances of membership in Freemasonry and military experience. With a mean age of 37.3 years, these deputies were three years younger than supporters and four years younger than the average Małopolanian deputy. Young, well travelled, Piarist educated magnates and wealthy nobles were, therefore, typical of Małopolanian deputies actively supporting the new system.

Among the Lithuanians in the Marshals' Group the combination of factors was different still. Interestingly, these active deputies had the same Piarist background as all Lithuanian supporters (66.7 percent) but also the same level of Jesuit background as the entire Lithuanian delegation (33.3 percent). Missing were other forms of education, including schooling abroad. Similarly, the Marshals' Group was less well travelled than were Lithuanian supporters taken as a whole. The Collegium Nobilium seemed to have had the same influence as in other provinces. Lithuanians in the Marshals' Group were also polarized in respect to parliamentary experience; they included more inexperienced individuals and more experienced veterans of the *Sejm* than the set of all Lithuanian supporters. More of them were Freemasons (41.7 percent) compared to all Lithuanian supporters (15 percent) and all Lithuanian deputies (11.6 percent). The military was not a factor in Lithuania but wealth definitely seems to have been:

Wealth

	All Lithuanians	Supporters	Marshals' Group
poor	0.0%	0.0%	0.0%
middle	14.3%	9.1%	0.0%
wealthy	64.3%	81.8%	100.0%
magnate	21.4%	9.1%	0.0%

Among the Lithuanians, a high level of wealth but not magnatorial fortunes seemed to have predisposed a person first towards supporting the *Ustawa Rządowa* and then towards actively developing the Constitution in the *Sejm*. Another explanation is that the May Third Constitution unequivocally appealed only to the wealthy strata of Lithuanian nobles and satisfaction was quite thin among other strata.

Finally on the province level, the Marshals' Group of Livonians is actually larger than the set of Livonian supporters gathered from the *Polski słownik biograficzny*. The only variations among the three sets of Livonians are the absence in the Marshals' Group of the only known "wealthy" Livonian and the higher instance of Freemasonry and military service. Apparently, these were career politicians from an at large district, distinctively poor and ambitious.

The general geographic distribution of activism among the provinces extends to the subprovince level. Only two *województwa* had a 75 percent approval rate among their deputies: Livonia (Crown) and Wieluń (Sieradz) in Wielkopolska and four had 75 percent of their representatives as members of the Marshals' Group. Livonia (Lithuania), Smoleńsk and Brześć Litewski in Lithuania and Mazowsze (Warsaw) in Wielkopolska. Support was also more widely distributed throughout the entire Republic than was the opposition. More than half of the opposition came from Małopolska and especially from Wołyń (as illustrated by Nanke) and Podole. Not surprisingly, none of the Wołynians belonged to the Marshals' Group though they did comprise about a fourth of the known opposition among the deputies.

The Marshals' Group on the Republic level had the same average age as all supporters (39.4 years) which was less than the *Sejm* norm (41.2 years) and the average for opponents (42.8 years), though the differences were small. Education was, however, a stronger factor:

Education

	Sejm	Supporters	Marshals' Group
Piarist	24.6%	28.2%	35.7%
Jesuit	32.8%	23.1%	21.4%
abroad	11.5%	17.9%	14.3%
private	11.5%	12.8%	14.3%

Education by the Piarists seems to have inclined a person not only towards the reforms but also into active support of the Constitution— 60 percent of the activists from Lithuania and Małopolska, for whom there is evidence, were Piarist educated. Attendance at the Collegium Nobilium had a similar but less powerful effect. Seven percent of all deputies for whom there is information had attended this school; the figures for the Constitution's supporters and the Marshals' Group were 11.7 percent and 22.9 percent respectively. Thus, innovative domestic education was a factor but exposure to the rest of Europe was somewhat less important. Twenty-three percent of the deputies had travelled abroad, 31.2 percent of the supporters and 32.4 percent of the Marshals' Group had. Interestingly, the rate of extensive travel abroad for the Marshals' Group was only half, percentage wise, of that of all supporters. Apparently, innovative education and a hint of the outside world may have been tied to political activism in favor of reform.

Past political experience varied in only one respect. Past experience in the *Sejm* hovered around 50 percent for all three sets of deputies. The Marshals' Group had a lower rate of participation in the Confederation of Bar than the other two sets of representatives. The rates were 2.8 percent for the Marshals' Group versus 13.9 percent and 11.7 percent for the other two respectively. Age was a factor but the Confederation of Bar may have made active participants reticent to support change. Not surprisingly, only one of the Marshals' Group had laid his property and life on the line in the previous generation's revolt. The others took the gamble with the May Third Constitution.

Orders and offices were associated with reform and the Marshals' Group. As shown previously, opponents seem to have been passed over for orders and the semi-honorific, semi-functional local offices. The Marshals' Group followed the norm for the Constitution's supporters. The lifelong advancement in traditional local offices for members of the Marshals' Group who came from the Crown corresponded exactly to the norm for all Crown supporters but it was lower for those who came from Lithuania. This observation is, however, based on very limited information and probably is of dubious value.[18]

The Marshals' Group had a striking association with the Society of Friends of the Constitution. Just as supporters taken together tended to be members of the nascent political party, those deputies who voted with the marshals in the final phase of the Four Years' *Sejm* were organized in the Society. For those deputies for whom there is information, the figures for the Marshals' Group and all supporters as a whole were 93.5 percent and 87.5 percent respectively.[19] Participation rates are similar for the two groups with respect to Targowica and the Kościuszko Uprising. The Marshals' Group also had relatively high rates of officeholding in the Duchy of Warsaw and Congress Poland.

Military experience had a positive relationship with support for the Constitution and inclusion in the Marshals' Group:

Military

	Sejm	Supporters	Opponents	Marshals' Group
some experience	16.4%	20.5%	11.8%	30.6%
career officers	9.4%	10.3%	2.9%	8.3%
total	25.8%	30.8%	14.7%	38.9%

Minor characteristics such as contacts with other countries and diplomatic experience were insignificant for the Marshals' Group—with one exception. Deputies who formed the Marshals' Group had an unusually high rate of membership in the Freemasonry. The rate was similar for the *Sejm* and for supporters—12.9 percent and 18.2 percent respectively—but for the Marshals' Group it was 37.1 percent.

But perhaps the most significant characteristic of the Marshals' Group was its economic composition. Intra-*szlachta* stratification did vary for the four groups discussed:

Wealth

	Sejm	Supporters	Opponents	Marshals' Group
poor	5.5%	3.8%	11.5%	14.3%
middle	11.9%	11.5%	7.7%	19.0%
wealthy	66.1%	71.2%	53.8%	57.1%
magnates	16.5%	13.5%	26.9%	9.5%

The Marshals' Group included an unusually high number of middle and poor nobles at the expense of both the wealthy and magnate strata. While supporters, as a whole, were more or less typical of the entire *Sejm* with a tendency to include more wealthy *szlachta*, the activist supporters, who remained in the *Sejm* after the May Third Revolution and backed the parliament's leadership, were much poorer. This must have been striking to contemporaries and this may be one of the reasons the May Third Constitution has been associated with the middle nobility despite the fact that its most characteristic backers were actually somewhat wealthier.

Cumulative Observations

In conclusion, deputies who were the most active after the *Sejm* reconvened in September 1791, subsequent to the adoption of the May Third Constitution, exhibited characteristics that distinguished them not only from the Four Years' *Sejm* as a whole but also from the entire set of deputies who supported the Constitution. Real and perceived support, therefore, could have been different. Bearing in mind the imperfections of the data—the incompleteness and inevitable subjectivity of the biographical information, the disruptive role of absences in the voting information and the imperfect correlation between activity in the *Sejm* and *turni* behavior—composite portraits have been constructed over the last three chapters for supporters/opponents and for political groupings in 1791-92.

Conclusions are, moreover, dependent on the angle of observation. The attempt in an earlier chapter to directly correlate a group of biographical factors for all the deputies with support or opposition to the Constitution brought only one statistically significant relationship, provided such measures are appropriate. Supporters tended to be members of the Society of Friends of the Constitution (the *Zgromadzenie*); opponents were not. While this has an element of the obvious to it, the relationship could also mean that not only was parliamentary support for the new system well organized but perhaps that organization had existed before May 3, 1791 and the opponents' charges of conspiracy were valid. An equivalent organization of opponents did not exist before the Targowica Confederation a year later.

But the lack of other readily visible relationships did not mean that relationships did not exist. By taking into account two dimensions according to which the deputies naturally cleaved, geography and terms, additional relationships were discovered. Some were weak, almost hints of possible influences. Others were much stronger. From this angle it became evident that support was strongest in Lithuania and among the Livonian at large delegation while it was weakest in Małopolska. This was magnified among first term Lithuanians and first term Małopolanians. The members of the first group, with an 85 percent approval rate for the Constitution, were of above average wealth (wealthy and magnates), with evident influence from the Piarists and unusual advancement in orders. The second group, with only a 53.8 percent approval rate for the Constitution, included more magnates and poor nobles and had a higher Jesuit influence.

250 Fateful Transformations

There were also some additional patterns that appeared when viewing all the deputies together at a closer distance. A slight majority of supporters had previous experience in the *Sejm* while a slight majority of opponents were novices. Supporters had a noticeably higher rate of acquiring prestigeous national orders. And finally, the wealth profile of supporters seemed closer to the general norm than did that of opponents.

The use of a different measurement of statistical significance pointed to additional examination of geography, age, and careers. On the basis of this biographical information, it had been concluded that:

1. Geographically, the strongest support seems to have been along the northern ethnic borderland regions of Podlasie, Brześć Litewski, and Wilno, in the Smoleńsk, at large, delegation from Lithuania and in the Małopolanian area of Sandomierz.

2. Geographically the strongest opposition was in the southern Ruthenia *województwa* of Wołyń and Podole, the at large Ruthenian delegation of Czernichów (Chernihiv) and the Wielkopolanian area of Łęczyca.

3. A composite portrait of deputies from these extreme *województwa* indicates that at least in these areas:
    a. delegations with greater unanimity for or against the Constitution tended to be younger than the *Sejm*'s norms,
    b. the amount of travel abroad by deputies was irrelevant,
    c. Jesuit education tended to disincline deputies toward the Constitution,
    d. greater parliamentary experience was associated with support for the reforms,
    e. participation in the Confederation of Bar was associated with opposition to the new system,
    f. supporters acquired more of the prestigious medals during the Four Years' *Sejm*,
    g. deputies with more regular military experience tended to support the new Constitution,
    h. supporters were limited to very wealthy nobles and some magnates while opponents came more evenly from all strata of nobles.

4. The most active deputies in the months leading up to the May Third Constitution were, by far, second term deputies between

the ages of 35 and 39, inclusive. These, however, were not unanimously inclined to support the revolution.

5. The second and third most active groups of deputies by age in this period consisted of 30 to 34-year-olds from each terms. Taken as a whole, this group showed extraordinary zeal for the May Third Constitution. They and the second term 35 to 39-year-olds were highly visible, creating the impression that in the months up to May 3, 1791 there was a strong presence of young wealthy nobles or sons of senators advocating change.

6. Overall, supporters of the new system were slightly younger than were opponents. While there may not be a statistically significant difference between their ages, the average difference of five years between second term supporters and second term opponents may have been enough to separate those who had matured before or during the Confederation of Bar and those whose maturation came later. The latter group seemed more inclined to support the May Third Constitution.

7. The Constitution's supporters in the Chamber of Deputies had fewer traditional local offices than had the Constitution's opponents. Those supporters in the Crown who did, however, hold traditional offices tended to have received them at a younger age and their careers had been more rapid and hence probably more satisfying before May 3, 1791. Opponents with traditional offices, on the other hand, received them later and then tended to stagnate in a particular office.

The biographical data may be considered as the entire universe of available information and measurements of statistical significance would therefore be unnecessary. In this case these observations would carry greater importance.

Cluster analysis of the active deputies in the closing phase of the Four Years' *Sejm* shows that the *Sejm* leadership was united—as it had been through much of the *Sejm*—and that the May Third Revolution probably formed a party based on attendance and voting, if not on a conscious choice to act in unison. Cluster analysis had its limitation, however.

While earlier analysis had examined the young deputies who proved most active in the months leading up to May 3, 1791, this chapter contained an analysis of the most active group after the summer recess. A large, active opposition made up of deputies did not remain in the *Sejm* after the adoption of May Third Constitution, though it is possible that malcontents were active on the floor but did not vote. The role of senators is much less clear from division records.[20] A group of 59 deputies comprised the main support for reform between September 1791 to May 1792, though, at times, attendance in this period did reach a total of 214 deputies and senators. Almost all these activists supported the new Constitution and some had been among the pre-May activists. This group of supporters, which has been given the arbitrary name "the Marshals' Group" because it voted closely with Małachowski and Sapieha, included five deputies who had been among the most active earlier in the year (41.6 percent of the second term deputies between the ages of 35 and 39) and nine from the second most active age group (50 percent of the 30 to 34-year-olds of both terms).[21] Only six deputies voted consistently against the Marshals in the last phase of the Four Years' *Sejm*.

The set of deputies, called in historical hindsight the Marshals' Group and arguably identifiable with the group called "the patriots" in secondary sources, exhibited characteristics that distinguished it both from the Constitution's opponents and from other supporters. The distinctive characteristics of these activists were geographic (strongest support from Livonia and Lithuania), educational (strong influence from the Piarists and to a lesser degree from the Collegium Nobilium), political (less than average participation in the Bar Confederation) and socioeconomic (high instance of military service and Freemasonry and less economic security or power).

These broad observations were supplemented by variations among the provincial delegations. In Wielkopolska, compared to the average deputy from the province or the average supporter, those in the Marshals' Group showed a weaker Jesuit influence, greater attendance at the Collegium Nobilium, more political experience, somewhat more limited material means and greater membership in the military and Freemasonry; this activist group was more travelled than the average Wielkopolanian supporter but less than all Wielkopolanian taken together. In Małopolska, the activists of the Marshals' Group were younger, more travelled, Piarist educated and more politically experienced magnates and wealthy nobles. In Lithuania, the Marshals' Group included only wealthy nobles with a higher instance of Piarist education and attendance at the Collegium Nobilium, polarized parliamentary experience, and more frequent membership in Freemasonry. Finally, the Livonians were simply atypical. They seem to have been career politicians with limited means.

The multiplicity of factors that may have contributed to a deputy's stance *vis-à-vis* the new Constitution and the shifting combinations of factors according to province, support/opposition or activism indicate a complexity to life, evident to most. It is unlikely that an individual acted according to solely one interest or because of a single influence. Incomplete and faulty data, imperfect conceptualization add to the inevitable and incalculable distortions in perception. And yet some tendencies, hopefully real, have emerged to distinguish behavior in the Four Years' *Sejm* in respect to the May Third Constitution. Education, local influences and to some extent wealth affected the different visions of political organization held by the representatives of the szlachta. Piarist reform, economic self-sufficiency, military discipline, successful careers in traditional offices for those for whom it was important, and the innocence of idealism seemed to have predisposed a person to support the reforms.

CONCLUDING CONSIDERATIONS

Time often appears to narrow the gap between knowledge and reality. As reality becomes less immediate it seems also to become clearer. The theory and practice of the May Third Constitution, and the Four Years' *Sejm* which produced it, have been analyzed in many ways. In a specific cultural context, the eighteenth century constitution is politically attractive and has served as a national symbol whose value and, perhaps, whose very nature depended on the subsequent needs of the Polish nation as defined over the last two centuries. This symbolic importance has imparted anachronistic concepts based, in part, on the logical development of ideas contained in the Constitution adapted to the needs of subsequent generations who never lived under its provisions. For instance, democracy is today accepted as good by definition but King Stanisław August and Ignacy Potocki did not see their work as democratic, though in hindsight it did offer such potentials. From the distance of two centuries and adjusted by a critical historical perspective, the May Third Constitution is seen as part of a democratic tradition without itself having been democratic.

From the numerous opinions about the last free parliament of the old Polish-Lithuanian Commonwealth, two add curiously related and refreshing insights. The nineteenth century national poet and émigré activist, Adam Mickiewicz criticized the Four Year's *Sejm* and the May Third Constitution from a classically conservative stance. Law should be historical not rational, organic not mechanical. He saw the reformers as "split off from national history" in an attempt "to deduce from rational principles" a constitution rather than confiding in "the historical wisdom of the people."[1] Mickiewicz's judgment about the Constitution contrasted with the assessment given by Edmund Burke who shared Mickiewicz's analysis of the dangers of legislating an entire system according to a rational schemat. Burke lauded the May Third Constitution precisely because it preserved everything worthwhile and imbued it with new life. From the same classically conservative premise, Mickiewicz and Burke arrived at diametrically opposite conclusions. This paradox provokes speculation. Burke and Mickiewicz each had an "imperfect" relationship to the May Third Constitution. Burke, a contemporary of the Four Years' *Sejm*, used the Polish Revolution as a whip against Whigs who were enamoured with the French Revolution vainly interpreting it as an attempt of the French to reform their system along British lines. Mickiewicz was temporally removed from the Constitution. At least one generation, froth with the drama and shock of Targowica, the Second Partition, the Kościuszko Uprising, the Third Partition, the Duchy experiment and the collapsed hopes associated with Napoleon, separated him from the dimension of currency. Yet, neither conservative was completely divorced from the reality he evaluated. Burke did not use simple, empty political slogans; his convictions were based on intellectual analyses. Mickiewicz expressed the culture and heritage of his beloved Black Rus' and the lost Commonwealth. One may wonder how many of the *szlachta* in 1791 shared the analysis of the future national poet from Nowogródek or that of the contemporary founder of modern British conservatism.

The conflicts within the Four Years' *Sejm*, and throughout the Republic concerning the May Third Constitution, were controversies among differing constitutional visions. The conservative political attitude in the Commonwealth was constitutionalism; the ideology of reform was also constitutionalism. The conflicts were not between "absolutism" and constitutional government, nor between the arbitrariness of despotism and the rule of law. Though most of the *szlachta* feared *absolutum dominium*—tsarist despotism and French ideals of absolutism were the same to them—there was no one in the Republic who actually advocated it. A government emanating from the political nation (limited to the nobility) and answerable to it was the commonly accepted ideal. Only some of the magnates behaved like *króliki* ("little kings") in their arbitrary overshadowing of large regions, especially in the southeast. But even among the magnates, there were those who restrained their own power and all felt a need to dress their motives and actions in the traditional republican, constitutional language of "golden freedom." The political habits, institutions and ideals that had developed over the centuries had a living presence in the idea of *Rzeczpospolita* which would bind together enemies even after the controversy over the May Third Constitution. Many of the opponents of the Constitution and many of the supporters of the reactionary Targowica Confederation joined to defend the Republic in the Kościuszko Uprising. This even applied to the center of opposition in the Ruthenian lands of Małopolska, though geographically they were removed from the events of 1794.

The competing constitutional visions partly resulted from different perceptions of the past. Each looked to the old system as to an ideal but each saw a different past reality. Both essentially approved of the institutions that had existed, basically unchanged, from the late sixteenth century. But the old conservatives held that this was the best of all systems—the incarnation of the golden freedoms—that still functioned effectively and should not be changed. The newer constitutionalists, those who advocated substantial reform, realized that the old political system had malfunctioned both internally and externally. For the reformers, some magnates had distorted the democracy of the nobility into an oligarchy of strong individuals over the rest of the *szlachta*, thus perverting the very spirit of the system. For the reformers too, the theoretically best of all systems had failed miserably in defending the body politic. True, the territorial losses had been relatively small in the half century of troubles beginning with the Khmelnytsky Uprising. Ducal Prussia had been lost to the Hohenzollerns and the Left Bank of the Dniepr to Russia, but Podole had been wrestled back from the Turks while the heroism and marshal skills of the free nation had saved Vienna—and Europe—from the Turks. But the Partition was another matter. The old strategy of ensuring the *Rzeczpospolita*'s continued existence by making the Republic harmless to its neighbors had failed. Almost all agreed that the Republic's defenses must be improved. Thus, the first major measure of the Four Years' *Sejm* was to levy a 100,000 strong army. The split came in the working out of the consequences of this move. Some thought that the enlarged army would be sufficient—provided, of course, that it were kept firmly in the hands of the *Sejm* to prevent it from becoming a tool to impose *absolutum dominium*. Some magnates and their supporters wanted to put the army under the control of independent hetmen. Others were convinced that the reforms had to be more comprehensive, that an efficient government and prosperous, well-ordered society were indispensible for an effective defense. Various members of the *Sejm* saw various limits to these reforms. The constitution which eventually was adopted resulted from the cooperation of two groups, one led by King Stanisław August and the other by the magnate, Ignacy Potocki.

The institutions of the old *Rzeczpospolita* were transformed but not discarded by the May Third Constitution. The old system had come into being from the mid-fourteenth through the sixteenth centuries. Beginning with limits on noble service to the king, extending to guarantees on noble property and subsequently the noble person in the *neminem captivabimus* law, the ever expanding privileges of the new *szlachta* eventually produced the *nihil novi* provision making the *Sejm* indispensible in an uncodified constitutional arrangement of power sharing among king, senators and knights. Starowolski's oft mentioned quote describes this ideal. The historical accidents of the extinction of the Jagiellonian dynasty and abandonment by the Valois king made the monarchy elective, in fact and not just theory, and formalized the main privileges in the Henrician Articles as a permanent part of the polity. This same act of fortune established an explicitly contractual relationship between king and *szlachta* in the *pacta conventa*. Each noble also had the right to participate directly or indirectly in the only legal lawmaking process and to join all other nobles in the election of the king and the arrangement of the contract.

Separated by geography and economy, the old Polish-Lithuanian system nonetheless paralleled the British in many ways. The centuries' long growth of parliamentarianism may have resulted from an imperfect development of feudalism in each. On both institutional and ideological levels the similarities are striking. The *Sejm* became indispensable by 1505, the English Parliament with the 1660 Stuart restoration. The ideology of mixed government current in sixteenth century Poland was formulated in its English version at the time of the Glorious Revolution. "*Król, senat i sejm*" anticipated "king, lords and commons." The practice of *pacta conventa* foreshadowed the explicit concept of contract at the base of a state. The *Rzeczpospolita*'s practice of contract was contemporary with Hobbes' theory of the social contract and the Polish dissolvability of the state-society agreement anticipated the more optimistic Lockean interpretation of the relationship between society and government. Not surprisingly, as the system was preserved in altered form by the May Third Constitution, Edmund Burke became one of its admirers.

But the system created up to the end of the sixteenth century had changed in character, if not in form, before 1791. The guarantee against tyranny of the majority, the cherished "free voice" or infamous *liberum veto*, came to be used, in a declining political culture, to execute the will of magnates. The central lawmaking body became paralyzed while the central administration continued to be restrained to prevent the perceived danger of absolutism. Despite odds, or because of them, as the eighteenth century adage held, "Poland stood because it lacked a government."

While the confederation provided an immediate emergency measure to overcome systemic paralysis resulting from the right of even a single individual noblemen not to be oppressed, significant reform came with the election of Stanisław August in 1764. Before and after the First Partition, the "free voice" was limited to the most fundamental matters while other issues were decided by majorities of varying sizes. The central administration was revitalized with the creation of the Permanent Council and executive commissions. Most importantly, the shock of the Partition, the confidence of the Enlightenment and an awareness of sixteenth century realities and subsequent political traditions sparked a wide debate on reform of the political system.

The Four Years' *Sejm* became a prolonged effort to forge together the many proposals for reform. The struggle between the king and magnates continued but, in this historic parliament, deputies, representating the broader nobility and enlivened by the intense polemics of the 1780s, interacted under the majority rule of a confederation, bound by local instructions and a *Sejm* oath to expand the armed forces and to do whatever was needed to improve the country's well-being. Under favorable international conditions and in a whirlwind of patriotism, the *Sejm* voted for an internationally competitive army under its control and swept away the government guaranteed by the partitioners.

But the need to follow the logic of this reform tapped the popular debate of the preceding decade and made the normally six weeks' *Sejm* into the Four Years' *Sejm*. The reforms congealed, or were forced through, in the *Ustawa Rządowa* and the wider, developing, Constitution brought important changes in traditional institutions and ideology. At least in theory, the balance of the three *stany* was struck once again by strengthening the king. More radically oligarchic forces were tamed by reducing the powers and prestige of the senate—part of a process that had already been under way—and by disenfranchising the landless nobility as a group inclined to magnaterial subservience. Sovereignty lay with the nation which presented a problem: mixed government implied divided sovereignty. In 1791 the old tripartite quality of sovereignty was transferred to a triad of authorities or powers in government—the division of powers typical of emerging liberalism—with ultimate authority resting in the nation. The Constitution also partially crystallized the reform efforts throughout the Four Years' *Sejm* to redefine the nation. To strengthen the political elite, the Constitution disenfranchised the landless nobles and grafted onto the remainder, rather imperfectly, the more vital, i.e., wealthier, segments of the townspeople. The result was not strictly speaking a class, since differences in agricultural and commercial interests were magnified by ethnic distinctions, but rather a stratum of individuals judged to have a stake in society. The traditional value of social utility based on inherited virtue through service to the Republic was resurrected and redefined on a more materialistic basis, with the main criterion being ownership of land or possession of property. Wealth and virtue became less distinguishable. A three tier system was created: men with all the rights of citizens including the franchise, men with civil rights but no political rights and men vaguely under the protection of the law. Traditional Polish political ideology was being blended with a modernity emerging from the outmoded old regime. The nation was greater than the *szlachta*. Thus, the old *nihil novi* became, in the *Ustawa Rządowa*, the modern liberal principle: "sovereignty lies in the nation."

This was not democracy but was it was a kind of representative government? The discussion of the noble republic transforming itself into a more modern constitutional, parliamentary system with many characteristics of emerging liberalism raises several legitimate and serious questions. When is a system oligarchic and when is it representative with a limited franchise? Was the perceived transformation nothing more than a circulation of elites? Can a system be representative and still permit the bondage of serfdom? From the end of the fifteenth century, roughly 10 percent of the Commonwealth belonged to the *szlachta* which secured a guarantee of property and person, made laws through a parliament, held equality as one of its central ideals, and regarded themselves as real citizens. At the same time serfdom continued to exist, creating a sharp contrast between intra-estate equality and widespread bondage. But the Four Years' *Sejm* and in particular the members analyzed in this study redefined the political nation and began to univeralize the intra-estate ideology of equality and citizenship. With these considerations, can the reformed governmental mechanism introduced by the May Third Constitution be considered a modern representative system?

Perhaps an effective way to answer these questions is with two other questions. How representative was the "democracy" of an ancient Greek city which has become the symbol of Western democracy when it restricted political rights not only by gender but by geographic origin and its entire civilization was based on a slave economy? Does the 1791 Commonwealth differ greatly from a republic founded on the "self-evident truths" of the "rights of man," equality, and representative government but which limited suffrage by property qualifications and continued to keep a significant part of its population in slavery till the 1860s? In all three cases a basic principle of representation was at the heart of the political system, though political rights and equality were most definitely restricted. Oligarchy or limited representation? The further development of the systems seems to have determined their reputations.

The conservative Burke applauded the May Third Constitution but some of the political nation in Poland did not. The patriotic but landless nobility (some undoubtedly Mickiewicz's neighbors), who literally possessed only their non-material virtue, were left dumbfounded by their exclusion from the political process. Enfranchised townspeople were genuinely enthusiastic but they also demanded fuller equality. Some agitated to extend more rights to peasants and Jews. Even if the old system had become ineffective, the reintroduction of a hereditary monarchy, albeit elected by dynasty, appeared to many to be an intolerable departure from the old system, the first step towards the "absolutism" dominating Europe. Broad, genuine support mixed with insincere public pronouncements and relatively isolated manifestations of outrage. The divisions were clearer and more easily grasped in the parliamentary interplay, members themselves and through them the nobility as a whole.

Though the *Sejm*'s leadership was united, the deputies did not seem to have voted in clear blocks during the *Sejm*'s first two years. The Parliament's productivity was further hindered by rather complex procedures, traditionally verbose speech-making and the lingering ideal of unanimity. Deputies were most united on military reform and least about how to pay for them. The small number of senators who continued to attend were most divided on fundamental constitutional issues—an indication of divisions among the magnates. Extension of the *Sejm* through the next scheduled biennial elections became necessary.

Progress had been very slow for two years. The concluding

months of the first term, however, brought a reexamination of the purpose and nature of the 1788 confederation. For a while, the lengthy attempts at perfect consensus were replaced by frequent roll call votes. More importantly, part of the magnatorial opposition approached the king and began the cooperation that would yield fundamental reforms after the arrival of the second set of deputies in December 1790.

The early months of the second term brought increasingly effective parliamentary work, such as passage of new house rules, a law on local assemblies and revolutionary reform of formerly royal cities. The most active deputies in this period were in their thirties, especially 35 to 39-year-olds recently elected. These had matured amidst the intellectual and publicistic ferment following the Bar Confederation and Partition disasters. These young active deputies also reflected a geographic cross section of the Republic as well as a variety of educational backgrounds. Their economic foundation was, however, distinctive. Almost three-fourths were very wealthy but few were true magnates or true middle nobility. This group seemed to have vitalized the *Sejm*.

Nonetheless, the king and Ignacy Potocki, along with the *Sejm* leadership, did not think that the *Sejm* would adopt a new constitution under normal conditions. On a day when most members still had not returned from Easter recess, and in flagrant disregard of the house rules recently adopted, the *Ustawa Rządowa* was passed without a roll call. Marshal Małachowski, representing the mainstream and genuinely respected for his high standards of fairness, declared that revolutionary times required revolutionary methods.

This line of thinking seems to have been generally accepted. As the *Ustawa Rządowa* was expanded into a full constitution, support among the deputies and the wide masses of nobility and townspeople increased. The biographical profiles of supporters did not vary significantly from the deputies taken as a whole. Yet, in each province factors of wealth, education, political and military experience, travels abroad and membership in Freemasonry distinguished supporters from opponents to varying degrees and in varying combinations. Particularly striking was the support of young, Piarist educated, wealthy nobles from Lithuania and the presence of a smaller group of reform minded magnates.

The general body of supporters was distinct, however, from the deputies who formed a group of activists supporting the *Sejm* leadership after the summer recess in the continuing construction of the May

Third system. These deputies seemed to have possessed those characteristics which in some combinations of term and geography had distinguished supporters from the average deputy—with one significant difference: they seem to have been less wealthy and less prominent. Most active were the Livonians. The characteristics of this "Marshals' Group" may have been the qualities which in historians' eyes made them "patriots" but which for Mickiewicz had split them off from national history. These too were most attracted to the redefinition of political rights and the reconstruction of an effective central government.

The socioeconomic backgrounds of the participants in the Four Years' *Sejm* also shed some light on the internal conflicts within the noble estate and its relationship to reform. The reform movement in the Four Years' *Sejm* was not a ground swell of middle stratum nobles endeavoring to place limits on the magnates. The anti-magnate measures that reduced the large landowners' influence in the local assemblies and which reduced the Senate to a more passive check on the Chamber of Deputies were spearheaded by reform minded, very wealthy nobles and by some of the magnates themselves and supported by a cross section of the *Sejm*. The movement associated with the interests of the middle *szlachta* was not led by the middle *szlachta*; the mistaken impression was fostered in large part by the composition of the group of deputies who cooperated with the marshals in the last phase of the Four Years' *Sejm* and in notable exceptions such as Kołłątaj, a noble originally of modest means from Wołyń. Otherwise, the leadership and support came from an elite within the elite (if such the nobility could be considered).

It seems not only feasible but likely that the reforming, very wealthy nobles thought of their own economic and status interests as part of, and subordinate to, the interests of the entire polity. They sought remedies to correct the faults which endangered the state. Indeed the *Ustawa Rządowa* begins with a statement of intent: the salvation of the Polish-Lithuanian polity during this most unusual opportunity. There is no compelling reason not to take this at face value. The appeal of non-class, non-economic ideals, the appeal of solutions for governmental dysfunction had attracted individual magnates to the law and order/due process ideals of the execution of the law movement and to the Husitism of the Spytko revolt. This phenomenon was repeated in the 1790s.

A gap in many historians' understanding of this phenomenon is the assumption that nationalism, or to purify the term of negative connotations, national loyalty formed under medieval monarchies and emerged in the crucible of the English and French Revolutions within a society about to be bourgeois. From there it spread to the more exclusively agrarian regions of the continent where it became ethnocentric. But national loyalty had already been quite strong in the *Rzeczpospolita* before its supposed exportation by the French Revolution and that feeling of nationality was not the narrowly cultural and linguistic nationalism simplistically attributed to the "East" by the commonly accepted Hans Kohn dichotomy. The noble culture in Poland-Lithuania espoused a political national loyalty—not simply a ethno-linguistic consciousness—as a basic tenet of honor because the centuries old political system was perceived as uniquely "free." The *Rzeczpospolita* for centuries had been seen by the nobility as truly their *res publica*. The system that made the nobility masters of the state and which consequently emasculated the monarchy, the central administration and the armed forces produced a state that was a feeble competitor in "absolutist" dominated Europe but one from which the nobility was not alienated, one which, on the contrary, elicited passionate loyalty. The conservative mind remained loyal to this form of constitutionalism. Others, perhaps due to reformed education, economic self-reliance or well-being and a whiff of the broader world, favored a transformed constitutional vision.

But did not the feelings of loyalty to the fatherland so evident in the 1780s and 1790s seem like a novelty in eighteenth century Poland-Lithuania? Had not the political elite remained conspicuously dormant during the Saxon night and had not the Sejm of 1773–75 ratified the First Partition in large part for the individual profit of its members? Indeed, the ineffective resistance to the Russian invasion in 1792 prompts second thoughts. But the intensity of the Confederation of Bar, the drama of Reytan's obstructionism, the ardor of the debates in the Four Years' *Sejm* and the tenacity of the Kościuszko Uprising—events which bracket the invasion—are convincing examples of patriotism.

Something crucial had happened to the generation that matured politically just before or during the Four Years' Parliament. Smoleński called it "a revolution in mentality," a leap in which modern consciousness was born in the Commonwealth. That breakthrough was not solely caused by the replacement of Sarmatianism with the Enlightenment. Rather, it was quite likely the shock of the First Partition and the penetration of the Enlightenment into Sarmatianism enlivening old traditions and virtues connected with noble-state relations and awakening a new, almost aesthetic taste for national identity and for patriotism. Deputies dispensed with French dress and donned the traditional Polish long coat (*kontusz*) with sash and draping, false sleeves as they reformed the system. The townspeople manifested the same sense of patriotism. The freedoms and privileges of the late Piast and Jagiellonian period were modernized and became the basis for a more modern constitutional monarchy.

The culture of an old nobility began to produce a system with distinctively bourgeois characteristics. A new constitutionalism was being achieved without its early modern negation, "absolutism," as a prerequisite. State building or rebuilding was occurring without a period where royal will ideally was to be law and where medieval representative institutions had atrophied. At the same time the intra-estate equality was restored as the old oligarchy was broken and as the political nation shed its character as an estate. Breaking an exclusive association with the *szlachta*, the representational system presented a principle with broader ramifications as the ideology of equality and guaranteed rights for the *szlachta* could be, and by some was, interpreted as universal. This is more than wishful thinking or biased hindsight. Writers contemporary to the Four Years' *Sejm* took this logical step. And so did radicals and leaders of the Kościuszko Uprising a couple of years later. The May Third Constitution was a conservative compromise with revolutionary potential.

Perceived potential is very important to historical interpretations or evaluations of an idea, an institution or a system. The reputations of Athens, France or the United States rely on the power of two interrelated perceptions: an idea unencumbered by existing political relations and the continued transformation of those systems. In the case of the United States, property qualifications and slavery were eventually eliminated, thus the original ideals of democracy that had operated in a kind of oligarchic system based to a large degree on human bondage were deemed to have been genuine. Subsequent success earns historical remembrance as systemic transformations aid in historical hindsight. The silence of many historians condemns the ideals of the Commonwealth and the May Third Constitution as irrelevant, suspicious or disingenuous.

From the perspective of the late twentieth century, the reality of the Four Years' *Sejm* should seem clearer, however. The most fascinating aspect of the Four Years' *Sejm* and the May Third Constitution was the emergence of a modern state along the Central European model but in the absence of "absolutism." This apparent anomoly is not as severe as it may appear if early modern history is reinterpreted in the light of the totality of the western heritage viewed from the perspective of the revolutions of 1989-1991. This involves the application of contemporary values to the past which is unavoidable in historical writing. A distinguishing feature of the West has been the persistent idea, and the frequent reality, of a social contract between some segment of society and government and the pervasiveness of legalism. The West, more often than not, has developed governments based on some interpretation of popular (or divided) sovereignty and the due process of law distinct from the arbitrary rule of an individual. The Western tradition is the tradition of social contract ranging from the medieval contractual relationship between monarch and nobles (the monarch raised on the shield) through the constitutionalism of the liberal, but not necessarily democratic, state. In this broad view, absolutism—*L'état c'est moi*—and its more modern descendant, totalitarianism—the dictatorship of the party in the name of the people—are the exception.

During periods of "absolutism," regardless of the actual degree of centralization, central authorities penetrated society in most European countries sufficiently to produce the well ordered state that could tap the country's material resources and human loyalties. This was modern state building. But during this process the Polish-Lithuanian state remained contractual with a special quality of legitimacy arising from some degree of popular sovereignty; the state penetrated society during a qualitative leap in conceptualization and reorganization of the constitutional system at the end of the eighteenth century, not during an "absolutist" phase. The combination of strong political traditions, their logical development, international competition, self-interest and humanitarian concerns combined the paternalism of an early modern state with the representative and ideological qualities that resembled much in emergent liberalism. In a sense, then, Polish constitutionalism, embodied in the May Third Constitution, was solidly Western. And Burke's approval seems justified.

The transformation was not complete. The May Third Constitution was a compromise which more radical reformers like Kołłątaj and Staszic had intended to be followed by economic and moral constitutions. Radicalization did come in the Kościuszko Uprising and throughout the nineteenth century the ideology of the Constitution was on the conservative end of the spectrum in the continued political life of the former Commonwealth.

The transformation was also fateful. The May Third Constitution brought agreement between such two divergent minds as Burke and Marx. Moreover, the reformed constitutional system came from the internal logic of long-standing traditions. A viable state was being rebuilt based on principles of representation, guarantees of secure property and person, ideas of nation and national sovereignty when these began to extend beyond their traditional estate limitation and acquire their potential universalization. State-building on principles of estate democracy necessitated a broader application of at least some of its major tenets. The transformation ironically hastened the destruction of the Commonwealth by raising fears among theoretically absolute monarchies and with the unintentionial assistance of the other constitutional vision in the republic manifested by Targowica. Despite Poland's reputation for revolution in the nineteenth century, the elimination of the state relegated these vital constitutional traditions to a growing, stubborn obscurity in Western scholarship. Often hidden in the distant view, the vision of a well-ordered state generated by and answerable to the "nation," nonetheless, remained a natural part of East Central European political values and aspirations.

NOTES

Notes to Introduction

1. Robert R. Palmer, *The Age of Democratic Revolution: A Political History of Europe and America 1760–1800*, 2 vols., (Princeton: Princeton Univerity Press, 1959), Vol. 1, p. 429.
2. Jean Fabre, *Stanislas-Auguste Poniatowski et l'Europe des Lumières*, (Paris: Institut d'Études Slaves, 1952), pp. 526–527.
3. Edmund Burke, "Appeal from the New to the Old Whigs" in *The Works of the Right Honourable Edmund Burke*, new edition, 8 vols., (London: C. and J. Rivington, 1826), Vol. 6, p. 244.
4. Ignacy Potocki, Franciszek Dmochowski and Hugo Kołłątaj, *O ustanowieniu i upadku konstytucyi polskiey 3go maia 1791* (Metz: n.p., 1793), p. 362.
5. Quoted by Leonard Ratajczyk, "Problems of the Defense of Poland" in *Military Techniques, Policy and Strategy in History* (Warsaw: Państwowe Wydawnictwo Naukowe [hereafter, PWN], 1976), p. 295 and by Norman Davies, *God's Playground: A History of Poland in Two Volumes* (New York: Columbia University Press, 1982), Vol. 1, p. 535.
6. This much neglected thread in historical thought is treated in Andrzej Zahorski, *Spór o Stanisława Augusta* (Warsaw: Państwowy Instytut Wydawniczy, [hereafter, PIW], 1988).
7. *Volumina legum*, Vol. 9: I (1788), (Kraków: Akademia Umiejętności, 1889), p. 47.

Notes to Chapter 1

1. Juliusz Bardach, ed., *Historia państwa i prawa Polski do roku 1795* (Warsaw: Polska Akademia Nauk, 1957), Vol. I, pp. 388–391, 447, 493; Vol. II, pp. 41–42, 97. Also, Juliusz Bardach, Bogusław Leśnodorski, Michał Pietrzak, *Historia państwa i prawa polskiego* (Warsaw: PWN, 1976), pp. 89–90.

2. Jaroslaw Pelenski, "The Contest Between Lithuania-Rus' and the Golden Horde in the Fourteenth Century for Supremacy over Eastern Europe" in *Archivum Eurasiae Medii Aevi*, II (1982), (Wiesbaden: Otto Harrasowitz, 1982), p. 307.

3. Henryk Lowmiański, "*Wielkie Księstwo Litewskie: Zagadnienia ustrojowe i prawne*" in Henryk Lowmiański, *Studia nad dziejami Wielkiego Księstwa Litewskiego* (Poznań: Wydawnictwo Uniwersytetu im. Adama Mickiewicza, 1983), Seria Historia number 108, p. 353 originally *Kwartalnik Historyczny*, 79 (1972): 4, pp. 885–896. The debate over the intent of the phrase "*perpetuo applicare*" continued for almost two centuries.

4. Norman Davies, *God's Playground: A History of Poland in Two Volumes* (New York: Columbia University Press, 1982), Vol. 1, p. 322.

5. See "*Zaręczenie wzaiemne oboyga narodów*" [Reciprocal declaration of both nations], *Volumina legum*, 9:CCCLVI, pp. 316–317.

6. Bardach *et al.*, p. 90.

7. See Aleksander Brückner, *Słownik etymologiczny języka polskiego*, 2nd. ed. (Warsaw: Wiedza Powszechna, 1970). The term's interesting kinship to words for market or congregation in other Slavic languages is found in M. Samuel Bogumił Linde, *Słownik języka polskiego*, 2nd ed. (Lwów: Ossolineum, 1859; reprint, Warsaw: PIW, 1951).

8. Eventually six different types of *sejmiki* functioned in the Polish-Lithuanian state: a *sejmik* to elect deputies to the *Sejm*, another at which the deputies were confronted by their constituencies after the adjournment of the *Sejm*, a third for the election of local officials, a fourth to maintain unity during interregna, a fifth to elect judges for the Tribunals after 1578 and finally, a sixth to maintain essential governmental functions when the *Sejm* became paralyzed. For further discussion including the dates for the origin of each, see Bardach, (1976), pp. 228–230.

9. Stanisław Kutrzeba, *Historya ustroju Polski w zarysie*, 5th ed. Vol. 1 *Korona* (Lwów: Połoniecki, 1920), p. 105.

10. Kutrzeba describes the rise of *sejmiki* and the *Sejm* differently. While acknowledging a distinction between the *rada królewska* [king's council] and representatives from the *sejmiki*, Kutrzeba calls the expanded royal council a *sejm* and explains that later the term *senat* was used. The *Sejm* in this usage included representatives from

the local *sejmiki* only in those, apparently, rare instances when the consent of the entire *szlachta* was deemed necessary. Thus, at this stage the *Sejm* was still limited essentially to dignitaries. Kutrzeba further concludes that this early *Sejm* was a union of the various *wiece* and that within the latter a distinction was arising between a council of dignitaries limited to functionaries and the assembly of nobles. Eventually, it is assumed, parts of the *wiece* began to be called *sejmiki* and to send delegates to each other and to the *Sejm*. As the needs of the king and the interests of the *szlachta* increased, so did the habit of sending delegations. Thus arose the *izba poselska* [Chamber of Deputies]; ibid., pp. 103–107.

11. Władysław Czapliński, ed., *The Polish Parliament at the Summit of Its Development (16th-17th Centuries) Anthologies* (Wrocław: Ossolineum, 1985). The independence of the *Sejm* was, in a sense, best seen in the requirement that the *Sejm* would have to meet every two years whether or not the king convened it.

12. Bardach, *et al.*, pp. 94–96.

13. Henryk Łowmiański, *Uwagi w sprawie podłoża społecznego i gospodarskiego unii jagiellońskiej*, in *op. cit.*, pp. 406, 409.

14. Bardach points out that the source of this information was the fifteenth century chronicle *Historia Poloniae* by Długosz. Bardach ed., Vol. I, p. 428. The absence of an official name for these privileges is telling.

15. Jaroslaw Pelenski, "The Incorporation of the Ukrainian Lands of Old Rus' into Crown Poland (1569) (Socio-material Interests and Ideology - A Reexamination)," pp. 47–48 in Anna Cienciala, ed., *American Contributions to the Seventh International Congress of Slavists* (Warsaw, 21–27 August 1973), Vol. III *History* (The Hague: Mouton, 1973), pp. 19–52.

16. This was out of 133 senators, 58 of whom were Protestants. W. F. Reddaway, J. H. Penson, O. Halecki and R. Dyboski, eds., *The Cambridge History of Poland* (New York: Octagon, 1978), Vol. 1, pp. 344–345.

17. The nature of the Uniate church in the Polish-Lithuanian Commonwealth has long been disputed, with the Roman hierarchy regarding it as a union of Roman and Orthodox Churches and the Uniates considering themselves as a new body with a separate status analogous to that of the Armenian church whose presence in the eastern part of the Commonwealth was also quite visible. Today the Uniates are usually referred to as Ukrainian Catholics.

18. These restrictions were contained in a separate act to the treaty between the *Rzeczpospolita* and the partitioning powers in 1775, article 1, par. 1 and 2., *Volumina legum*, 8, pp. 47–48. These were in marked contrast to the provisions of the 1788 treaty between Poland and Russia, separate act, article 2, par. 16, *Volumina legum*, 7, p. 269. The political history of the Uniate and Orthodox *szlachta* during the Four Years' *Sejm* has yet to be written.

19. Scholars differ even on the inauguration of the council: Kutrzeba argues for 1576; Bardach for 1607. Neither is sure about the precise date *senatorowie-residenci* stopped functioning except that it was sometime in the early eighteenth century. Kutrzeba, Vol. 1, pp. 161–162; Bardach, Vol. 2, p. 122. See also, Władysław Konopczyński, *Geneza Rady Nieustającej* (Kraków: Akademia Umiejętności, 1917).

20. For an excellent and overdue treatment of administrative offices see, Zbigniew Góralski, *Urzędy i godności w dawnej Polsce* (Warsaw: Ludowa Spółdzielnia Wydawnicza, 1983).

21. Norman Davies best summarizes these in his book, *God's Playground, A History of Poland in Two Volumes* (New York: Columbia University Press, 1982). Occasional factual inaccuracies do not mar the breadth of view and conceptual depth of this currently most definitive synthesis of Polish history.

22. Hans Koenigsberger, "*Dominium regale* or *dominium politicum et regale*? Monarchies and parliaments in early modern Europe," in *Human Figurations: Essays for Norbert Elias*, Peter R. Gleichman, ed. (Amsterdam: Amsterdams Sociologisch Tijshrift, 1977), p. 298.

23. Ibid., p. 302.

24. Aleksander Gieysztor, ed., *History of Poland*, 2nd ed. (Warsaw: Polskie Wydawnictwo Naukowe, 1979), p. 185.

25. A rarely noticed piece of evidence supporting the idea of an early and effective consolidation of the Polish monarchy is the successful quarantine efforts undertaken by royal authorities which spared most of Poland controlled by Kazimierz Wielki from the Black Death. The spread of epidemic is not, however, well understood.

26. In a sense, the debate was a continuation of the optimist/pessimist Polish historical polemics between the Warsaw and Kraków tendencies in writing, with Lwów replacing Warsaw, due in part to the First World War and the participation of other non-Polish Austro-Hungarian historians such as Kadlec, Diveky, and Leonhard. The

Poles included Zakrzewski, Kutrzeba, and Brückner. The intensity of the debate was great. Balzer's book eventually had three editions and at least five printings between 1915 and 1920.

27. *Volumina legum*, 9:CCLXVII, article II, p. 220.

28. Joachim Lelewel, "*Plan Historii Polski podany przez kolegę Joachima Lelewela nad którą pracuje w marcu 1815 roku do archiwum oddano*," cited in Zygmunt Kolankowski, ed., *Historia Polski do końca panowania Stefana Batorego*, Vol. VI of Joachim Lelewel, *Dzieła*, J. Adamus, ed. (Warsaw: Instytut Historii Polskiej Akademii Nauk and PWN, 1962), pp. 483-484. A complete archival citation is included.

29. Wacław W. Soroka, "Historical Studies of Polish Law," in *Polish Law Throughout the Ages*, Wenceslas J. Wagner, ed. (Stanford: Hoover Institution Press), p. 24. This collected work contains numerous lucid articles on the subject.

30. Jaroslaw Pelenski, "Poland-Lithuania (1454-1573): Nobility Democracy or Tripartite Mixed Government?," an unpublished paper presented at the Third Conference of Polish and American Historians held in Poznań, Poland, 28 May-2 June 1979.

31. Bardach, ed., Vol. 2, Zbigniew Kaczmarek, "*Od połowy XV wieku do roku 1795*," p. 35.

32. Engels regarded the democracy of the nobility as "one of the most primitive forms of society." Friedrich Engels, "Peasant War in Germany" as quoted in Jaroslaw Pelenski, "V. Lypyns'kyj and the Problem of the Elite," *Harvard Ukrainian Studies*, IX (December 1985) 3/4, p. 334, n. 27.

33. Bardach, ed., Vol. I, p. 229.

34. Oswald Balzer, *Z zagadnień ustrojowych Polski*, 2nd ed. (Lwów.: Towarzystwo dla Popieranie Nauki Polskiej, 1917), pp. 8-9.

35. Szymon Starowolski, *Polska albo opisanie położenia Królestwa Polskiego*, translated into Polish from the Latin by Antoni Piskadło (Warsaw: Wydawnictwo Literackie, 1976), p. 130. Piskadło provides an excellent translation into Polish and a very scholarly and useful commentary.

36. These magnates were not, of course, the old medieval magnates but scions of new fortunes accumulated in the general prosperity and expansion of the *Rzeczpospolita* after 1569.

37. Jarema Maciszewski, *Szlachta polska i jej państwo* (Warsaw: Wiedza Powszechna, 1969), pp. 138-139.

Notes to Chapter 2

1. Numerous original printed copies and some handwritten ver-

sions of the *Ustawa Rządowa* have survived. For the authoritative discussion of these texts see, Jerzy Kowecki, "Rękopisy i pierwsze druki," in Jerzy Kowecki, ed. *Konstytucja 3 maja 1791. Statut zgromadzenia Przyjaciół Konstytucji*, with an introduction by the foremost post-war expert on the subject, Bolesław Leśnodorski (Warsaw: PWN, 1981). The printing of this latest edition of the Constitution was ready in 1970 but delayed until 1981 "by causes not dependent on the academic world." Andrzej Ajnenkiel, *Polskie konstytucje* (Warsaw: Wiedza Powszechna, 1983), p. 9. Since that time at least two popular editions have appeared: Jerzy Łojek, ed. *Konstytucja 3 maja* in the "*Dokumenty naszej tradycji*" series, (Lublin: Wydawnictwo Lubelskie, 1984). The very lengthy introduction foreshadows Łojek's *Geneza i obalenie Konstytucji 3 Maja* [Warsaw, 1986]. For over a century, the standard version of the *Ustawa Rządowa* has been in the *Volumina legum*, the compilation of Polish laws from 1347 through 1792 whose publication was initiated by the Kolegium Pijarskie in 1732 and completed in 1889 by the Komisya Prawnicza of the Akademia Umiejętności. This ten volume work with two appendices but without volume 10 was reprinted in 1980 in limited edition (800 copies). All citations from the *Ustawa Rządowa* and other statutes used in this study are taken from the *Volumina legum* 1980 reprint, unless otherwise indicated.

A recently recovered English translation from 1791 has been reprinted: *New Constitution of the Government of Poland Established by the Revolution, the Third of May, 1791*. 2nd ed. (London, 1791) reprinted in 1991 by Zamek Królewski w Warszawie.

2. The most recent formulation of this idea appears in Jerzy Michalski, *Historia sejmu polskiego*, 2 vols. (Warsaw: PWN, 1984) Vol. 1, p. 407. An earlier description called the *Ustawa Rządowa* a "statute of principles," see Zdzisław Kaczmarek and Bolesław Leśnodorski, *Historia państwa i prawa polskiego do roku 1795*, Vol. 2, *Od połowy XV wieku do r. 1795* (Warsaw: Polska Akademia Nauk, 1957), pp. 428–429. Kaczmarek and Leśnodorski further state that in contemporary language the term *rząd* [government] meant *ustrój* [political system].

3. *Volumina legum*, 9:CCLXVII, pp. 220–225.

4. Ibid.

5. *Uznaiąc, iż los nas wszystkich od ugruntowania i wydoskonale-*

nia konstytucyi narodowey iedynie zawisł . . . Ibid., p. 220.

6. *Zapobiegaiąc z iedney strony gwałtownym i częstym odmianom konstytucyi narodowey, z drugiey uznaiąc potrzebę wydoskonalenia oney, po doświadczeniu iey skutków, co do pomyślności puhliczney; porę i czas rewizyi i poprawy konstytucyi co lat dwadzieścia pięć naznaczamy.*

Ibid., p. 222.

7. *Kommisyi zaś edukacyiney powinnością będzie, podać układ instrukcyi i edukacyi synów królewskich, do potwierdzenia seymowi, a to, aby iednostayne w wychowaniu ich prawidła wpaiały ciągle i wcześnie w umysły przyszłych następców tronu, religią, miłość cnoty, oyczyzny, wolności, i konstytucyi kraiowey.*

Ibid., p. 225.

8. *. . . dla dobra powszechnego, dla ugruntowania wolności, dla ocalenia ojczyzny naszey, i iey granic, z naywieksza stałoscią ducha, ninieysza konstytucya uchwalamy. . . .*

Ibid., p. 220.

9. *. . . y tę całkowicie za świętą, za niewzruszoną deklaruiemy, dopókiby naród w czasie prawem przepisanym wyraźną wolą swoią nie uznał potrzeby odmienienia w niey iakiego artykułu. Do którey to konstytucyi dalsze ustawy seymu teraźnieyszego, we wszystkim stosować się maią.*

Ibid.

10. Ibid., ". . . *[S]zczególniey zaś prawa, statuta i prywileie temu stanowi od Kazimierza Wielkiego, Ludwika Węgierskiego, Władysława Jagiełły i Witolda brata iego, Wielkiego Xiążęcia Litewskiego, niemniey od Władysława i Kaziemierza Jagiellończyków, od Jana Alberta, Alexandra i Zygmunta Pierwszego braci, od Zygmunta Augusta ostatniego z linii Jagiellonskiey sprawiedliwie i prawnie nadane, utwierdzamy, zapewniamy i za niewzruszone uznaiemy.*" The absence of any mention of rulers after the extinction of the Jagiellonian dynasty would seem to indicate an exclusion of similar privileges bestowed after 1572. If this was the case, the omission could have been of fundamental significance. Another possible interpretation would argue that only those rulers were mentioned who were deemed worthy of special note but that all past privileges of the nobility were confirmed.

11. Ibid., p. 221. A separate, brief article devoted to this law is provided.

12. *Prawo o sejmikach na teraźnieyszym seymie ustawione, iako nayistotnieyszą zasadę wolności obywatelskiey, uroczyście zabeśpieczamy.* Ibid., p. 222.

13. There is another curiosity connected with this law. Though passed on 24 March 1791 (*Dyaryusz* . . .) it appears in the *Volumina legum* as CCXCIV, dated 28 May 1791. Whether this was due to an error on the part of the compilers of the *Volumina* or to an actual delay in registration is not clear. Such a delay would not have been unprecedented. The "*Prawa kardynalne niezwruszone*" [Cardinal laws unchanged] was passed in November 1790 but registered by the *marszałek* [marshal] of the *Sejm*, Stanisław Małachowski, only the following January.

14. *Dla porządnego władzy wykonawczey dopełnienia, ustanawiamy oddzielne kommissye, maiące związek ze strażą, i obowiązane do posłuszeństwa teyże straży. Kommissarze do nich wybierani będą przez seym do sprawowania urzędów swoich w przeciągu czasu prawem opisanego. Kommissye te są. 1mo. Edukacyi. 2do. Policyi. 3tio. Woyska. 4to. Skarbu.* Ibid. p. 224.

15. Ibid., article VIII.

16. *Wszystkie prawa dawne i teraźnieysze, przeciwne ninieyszey konstytucyi lub któremukolwiek iey artykulowi, znosiemy; a opisy szczególne do artykulów i każdey materyi w ninieyszey konstytucyi zamkniętnych potrzebne, iako dokładniey wyszczególniaiące obowiązki i układ rządu, za część składaiącą tęż konstytucyą deklaruiemy.* Ibid., 9:CCLXVIII, p. 225.

17. *Porządek seymów, i wszelkie ich odrządki tak iak są w teraźniejszym prawie, w całey rozciągłości przepisane, iednym odtąd prawidłem seymowania na zawsze będą, które całe prawo teraźnieysze o seymach za prawo konstytucyine postanawiamy; a wszelkie inne prawa porządku seymowania dawniey ustanowione, uchylamy.* Ibid., 9:CCXCIX, p. 265.

18. Ibid., article VII "*O czynieniu zarzutów senatorów, ministrom, i posłom,*" point 2, p. 252.

19. Ibid., 9:CCLXVII, p. 221.
20. Ibid., 9:CCXCVI, pp. 241–242.
21. Ibid., 9:CCLXVII, p. 221.
22. . . . *Dzielić zaś będzie deputacya seymowa proiekta na prawodawcze i uchwały sejmowe. 2do. W rzędie proiektów prawodawczych umieszczać będzie deputacya seymowa 1mo. Proiekta do praw politycznych. 2do Do praw cywilnych. 3tio Do praw kryminalnych. 4to Do podaktów wieczystych.*

and

cokolwiek ściągać się do udoskonalenia w odmianie lub poprawie szczególnych opisów formy rządowey, zawsze iednak bez naruszenia fundamentalnego prawa pod tytulem: Ustawa Rządowa.

Ibid., 9:CCXCIX, p. 258.

23. *Diariusz sejmowy*, 5 May 1791, *Archiwum Sejmu Wielkiego (Czteroletniego)* (hereafter, ASW) 19:78r. (The reverse of each page in ASW does not have a separate number; here it is indicated by the number from the front side of the page plus an "r.")

24. Ibid., ASW 19:75r.

25. Printed speech dated 9 May 1791, ASW 19: 68r-70r.

26. Parts of two printed copies of the proposed constitution have been preserved in the *Archiwum Sejmu Czteroletniego*: ASW 16: 381–393r, 395–407r, 435–498r, 492–535.

27. The members of the Constitutional Committee (*Deputacja do ułożenia projektu formy rządu*) were: Krasiński bishop of Krzemieniec, Ogiński Great Hetman of Lithuania, Chreptowicz Vice Chancellor of Lithuania, Ignacy Potocki Court Marshal of the Grand Duchy of Lithuania, Kossowski Crown Under-Treasurer, Suchodolski deputy from Chełm, Moszyński secretary of the Grand Duchy of Lithuania, Działyński deputy from Poznań, Sokołowski deputy from Inowrocław, Wawrzecki chamberlain of Kowno and deputy from Bracław, and Weyssenhoff deputy from Livonia. ASW 16: 385r, 386r-387, *Volumina legum* 9:LXXXIII, pp. 107–108. Nowakowski and Kossakowski seem to have been added later or they may have been misidentified in the minutes. For the relationship between the constitutional committee and the actual, secret preparation of the May Third Constitution, see, Emanuel Rostworowski, *Ostatni król Rzeczypospolitej* (Warsaw: Wiedza Powszechna, 1966).

28. "*Urządzenie wewnętrzne miast wolnych Rzeczypospolitey w Koronie i w Wielkim Xięstwie Litewskim*," *Volumina legum*, 9:CCCXXXVII, pp. 291–297 and "*Ostrzeżenie względem exekucyi prawa o miastach Naszych, dawniey Królewskich, a teraz wolnych Rzeczypospolitey*," ibid., 9:CCCXXXVIII, pp. 297–298.

29. See, *Dyariusz sejmowy*, 26 May 1791, ASW 19:342–352r.

30. Ibid., 9:CCLXVII, article V "*Rząd czyli oznaczenie władz politycznych*," p. 221.

31. Ibid., 9:CDV, p. 401.

32. Juliusz Bardach, *Historia państwa i prawa polskiego* (Warsaw. PWN, 1957), Vol. 2, pp. 22 23.

33. Zbigniew Radwański, *Prawa kardinalne w Polsce*, Zygmunt Wojciechowski, ed., *Studia nad historią prawa polskim*, Vol. 21 no. 1 (Poznań: Towarzystwo Przyjaciół Nauk, 1952).

34. The two laws are found in *Volumina legum*, 9:CXVIII, pp. 157–159 and 9:CCXXXV, pp. 202–203, respectively.

35. These two handwritten documents are found in ASW 16:413–414r and 16:415–416r. The wording and frequent corrections indicate these to be rough drafts of a presentation by a member of the Constitutional Committee before the entire body. Another clue to their identity is found in Stanisław August's letter dated 4 September 1790 to his ambassador in St. Petersburg, Deboli. The king mentions a printed bill on cardinal laws in which the wording of the first article caused stiff opposition from Lithuanian deputies. Sołtan objected to "Catholic faith in the Republic and the provinces which belong to it" preferring instead "Catholic faith in Poland and Lithuania." See, *Zbiór Popielów* 20: 962–963. Since the objectionable phrase is written in as an addition to the handwritten documents, it is likely that the latter are a draft of a bill discussed in the *Sejm* at the beginning of September 1790 and an accompanying explanation.

36. The original "*człowiek*" (person) had been crossed out.

37. Parts of two printed copies of the proposed law have been preserved in ASW 16: 381–393r, 395–407r, 435–489r, 492–535.

38. ASW 16: 384–393r and an earlier working version during deliberations, ASW 25:155–157 eleven articles plus additions.

39. The ideal of equality within the *szlachta* was an ancient and prominent part of noble culture. Both in everyday life and in formal address nobles called each other "brother" and even the diminutive "*braciszek*" [little brother] was considered an affront. Nobles could

travel the length and breadth of the Commonwealth and be assured of lodging at any noble house along the way. The prevelant ideology held that the nation, i.e., the nobility was literally an extended family. This organic unity lent a consciously democratic quality to *szlachta* ideology. Reality contrasted with the ideal, however. While the Union of Lublin (1569) outlawed the bestowing of additional hereditary titles in the Commonwealth and this was confirmed by legislation in 1638, by the eighteenth century a virtual titlemania prevailed in which almost all nobles sought distinctive titles of almost any kind. Medieval purely fictional titles such as cup bearer were eagerly sought and easily obtained from the king and his reduced administration. New titles such as member of the Order of the White Eagle and member of the Order of St. Stanisław were created by the Saxon kings and Stanisław August. The egalitarian ideology accommodated this titlemania by maintaining the existence of differences in degree but not in kind. This will be discussed in chapter 6. See, Jan Stanisław Bystroń, *Dzieje obyczajów w dawnej Polsce, wiek XVI-XVIII*, 2 vols. (Warsaw: PIW, 1960) reprint of 1932 edition, Vol. 1, pp. 157–166 and the exceptionally interesting study by Andrzej Zajączkowski, *Główne elementy kultury szlacheckiej w Polsce*, (Wrocław-Warsaw-Kraków: Ossolineum, 1961) especially pp. 57–59.

40. *Volumina legum*, 9:CCLXVII, article II, p. 220.

41. A printed copy of Korsak's speech has been preserved. ASW 19: 45–47r.

42. *Volumina legum*, 9:CCXCIV, "*Seymiki*," p. 234.

43. According to Korzon the number of *szaraczkowie* [yeoman], i.e., landless nobles in 1791 was approximately 407,000 as compared to 318,000 *possesyoniatów* [hereditary landowners]. The number of landless nobles represented about 3.5 percent of the total population and 56 percent of the *szlachta*. See, Tadeusz Korzon, *Wewnętrzne dzieje Polski za Stanisława Augusta 1764-1794*, 6 vols. (Kraków and Warsaw: Zwoliński, 1897) Vol. 1, table after p. 320.

44. Ibid., 9:CCLXVII, article V, p. 221.

45. Ibid., article II, p. 221.

46. *Diariusz seymowy*, ASW 23: 316–319r.

47. Ibid, 9:CCLXIII, *Miasta nasze królewskie wolne w państwach Rzeczypospolitej*, article I, "*O prerogatywach mieszczań*," paragraph 1, p. 216. This was called a cardinal law. The original *neminem captivabimus* arose through a series of concessions made by the king:

Privileges of Czerwińsk (1422), Privileges of Jedlno (1430) and the Privileges of Kraków (1433). See, Juliusz Bardach, *Historia państwa i prawa polskiego* (Warsaw: PIW, 1957), Vol. 1, pp. 427-428.

48. Compare *Volumina legum*, 9:CCXCV, "*Xięga ziemiańska*"(28 May (1791), pp. 240-241 with ibid., 9:CCCXXXVII, "*Urządzenie wewnętrzne miast wolnych Rzeczypospolitej w Koronie i w Wielkim Xięstwie Litewskim*" (30 June 1791) article I, p. 291 and ibid., 9:CCCLVII, "*Przedłużenie gotowości i ksiąg ziemiańskich*," p. 317.

49. Ibid., 9:CCCXXXVII, "*Urządzenie . . .,*" p. 291.

50. See ibid., 9:CCLXIII, "*Miasta . . .,*" article II, p. 216, ibid., 9:CCXCIX, "*Seymy*," pp. 250-266 and ibid., CCLXII, "*Zasady do proiektu o miastach*", pp. 214-219.

51. *Diariusz seymowy*, ASW 9:586r and a printed copy of Saparski's speech, ASW 9:589-590r.

52. Ibid., 9:CCLXIII, "*Miasta . . .*"

53. Ibid., 9:CCLXVII, article III, p. 221.

54. Ibid., article IV, p. 221.

55. The stratification of the peasantry in eighteenth century Poland-Lithuania has not been determined. W. Urban discerned 28 categories of peasants in the Kraków *województwo* alone. Jerzy Kowecki justifiably points out that this amount would have to be multiplied by geography but he does not supply an answer. Concerning the number of free peasants and the percentage of the population they comprised, the second edition of *Historia państwa i prawa polskiego* gives 2 percent or 170,000. The name given is "*osadnicy*" [settlers]. Tadeusz Korzon, on whose work the authors of *Historia państwa i prawa* rely, lists many more. Basing his information on Tsarist statistics from the Wilno region in Lithuania compiled in 1806, he concludes that for the entire Commonwealth one million peasants or 11 percent of the population were free peasants. This is a surprising but as yet unrefuted conclusion. Tadeusz Korzon, *Wewnętrzne dzieje* (Kraków: Księgarnia Zwolińskiego, 1899), Vol. 1, pp. 314-320 + table.

56. Letter from Deboli (Polish ambassador to St. Petersburg) to King Stanisław August (5 March 1792) quoted in Łojek, *Rok nadziei* (Warsaw: Czytelnik, 1964), p. 115 and Łojek, *Geneza i obalenie Konstytucji 3 maja* (Lublin: Wydawnictwo Lubelskie, 1986), p. 223.

57. *Volumina legum*, 9: CCLXVII, article I. p. 220.

58. *Diariusz* in ASW and "Załatwienie żądań obywatełów Pol-

skich Greko-nieunitów i Dyssydentów," *Volumina legum*, 9:CDLXII, p. 447.

59. For an extensive treatment of the "*dysunici*" see Tadeusz Korzon, *Wewnętrzne dzieje* (Kraków: Księgarnia Zwolińskiego, 1897–98), Vol. 1, pp. 170–216 and table on p. 320. The *Sejm* passed eight laws concerning "*Greko-nieunici*: 9:XLIV, LXI, CCXXXIII, CCLII, CCLIII, CCLV, CCLXXVIII, CCCLXXXIX, and CDLXII.

60. Jerzy Kowecki, "*U początków nowoczesnego narodu*" in Bolesław Leśnodorski, ed., *Polska w epoce Oświecenia: państwo, społeczeństwo kultura*, Konfrontacje historyczne series, (Warsaw: Wiedza Powszechna, 1971), pp. 106–170.

61. The landmark and essentially Marxist interpretation of the May Third system is Leśnordorski's *Dzieło Sejmu Czteroletniego* (Wrocław: Osolineum, 1951) which contained as its most valuable synthetic insight the conclusion that the reforms were intended to preserve the feudal system and were only pseudobourgeois.

62. *Volumina legum*, 9:CCLXVII, article V, p. 221.

63. The most exhaustive treatment is in the impressive positivistic work by Tadeusz Korzon, *Wewnętrzne dzieje Polski za Stanisława Augusta (1764–1794)*, 6 vols. (Kraków-Warsaw: Zwoliński, 1897), Vol. 5, pp. 1–132. Other extensive descriptions are presented in: Waleryan Kalinka, *Sejm Czteroletni*, 3 vols., 4th ed. (Kraków: Księgarnia Spółki Wydawniczej Polskiej, 1895–96); Stanisław Kutrzeba, *Historya ustroju polskiego w zarysie*, 2 vols., 5th ed., Vol. 1 (Lwów: Księgarnia Polska Bernarda Połonieckiego, 1920), pp. 175–196, Vol. 2 (Lwów: 1921), pp. 144–146, 151–160 (Kutrzeba gives the Crown and the Grand Duchy each a separate volume.); Kaczmarek and Leśnodorski, *Historia państwa i praw polskiego* (Wrocław: Ossolineum, 1951), Vol. 2, pp. 436–451; Bardach, Leśnodorski and Pietrzak, *Historia państwa i prawa polskiego*, 2nd ed. (Warsaw: PWN, 1957), pp. 318–327.

64. *Volumina legum*, 9:CCCLVI, "*Zaręczenie wzaiemne oboyga narodów*," pp. 316–317. *Zaręczenie* may also mean engagement; 9:CCCLXIV, "*Rozkład woiewództw, ziem, i powiatów, z oznaczeniem miast, a w nich mieysc konstytucyinych dla seymików w prowincyach Koronnych i Wielkiego Xięstwa Litewskiego*," pp. 326–338.

65. Łukasz Kądziela, "Local Administration Reforms during the Four Years' *Sejm*," an unpublished paper presented at the Conference

entitled, "The Bicentennial of the Polish Constitution of May 3, 1791 and the Tradition of Polish Democracy," Indiana University, October 7-8, 1991.

66. Ibid., 9:CCLXVII, article V, p. 221.

67. Ibid., 9:CCXCIX, article III, pts. 3 and 4, p. 251.

68. Ibid., 9:CCLXVII, article VII, p. 222.

69. An entire monograph has been devoted to the institution: Józef Wojakowski, *Straż Praw*, (Warsaw: Uniwersytet Warszawski, 1982). See also Lojek, *Geneza i obalenie Konstytucji 3 Maja. Polityka zagraniczna Rzeczypospolitej 1787-1792* (Lublin: Wydawnictwo Lubelskie, 1986).

70. The excerpt is taken from a report by the Committee for the Rectification of the Form of Government delegated by the *Sejm* and cited in Władysław Smoleński, *Przewrót umysłowy a Polsce wieku XVIII* (Warsaw: Ossolineum, 1949), pp. 344-345.

71. Michał Bobrzyński, *Dzieje Polski w zarysie*, 3 vols. 4th ed., (Warsaw: Gebethner, 1927), Vol. 2, p. 264.

72. Unlike the other Great Commissions, the Commission of National Education was sometimes called the *izba edukacyjna* [educational chamber]. See *Volumina legum*, 9:CCCI, "*Straż*," p. 266. *Izba* usually referred to a component part of the *Sejm*.

73. *Volumina legum*, 9:CCCLXIII, "*Kommissya skarbowa Rzeczypospolitey oboyga narodów*" articles III-V, pp. 319-326.

74. Ibid., 9:CCCXXVI, "Kommissya policyi" articles II-VIII, pp. 277-287.

75. This stipulation is repeated in very similar language for these two commissions, Treasury: article VIII.4; Police: article X.4 as well as for the Army Commission: article VIII.8.

76. The commissions had a mandate to establish parish schools throughout the Republic. In this area there were variations written into the law. In Lithuania, the schools were for peasants, in the Crown they were for peasants and impoverished nobles. But the variations also extended into the realm of religion. The statute on commissions in the Crown stipulates that members could practice either rite of Catholicism: Roman or Greek. Yet, the same statute specifies that the parish schools should be established for Latin parishes, implying their nonexistence in Uniate parishes. The Lithuanian statute, passed before the Crown law, remained silent on both issues and as a result was perhaps not as exclusive. This discrimination runs contrary to the democracy perceived in hindsight.

77. The operation of one of these commissions has been treated in a master's essay by the present author entitled, "The Great Reforms and the Civil-Military Administrative Commission for the Palatinate of Kraków (Districts of Kraków and Proszowice)," University of Iowa, 1980.

78. Szymon Starowolski, *Polska albo opisanie położenia Królestwa Polskiego*, translated into Polish from the Latin by Antoni Piskadło, (Warsaw: Wydawnictwo Literackie, 1976), p. 130.

79. Edmund Burke, "Appeal from the New to the Old Whigs" in *The Works and Correspondence of the Right Honourable Edmund Burke*, new edition, 8 vols., (London: Francis and John Rivington, 1852), Vol. 4, pp. 432, 479.

80. Scholars have tried to reconstruct these from the writings of the major reformers in the Four Years' *Sejm*. The most ambitious attempt proved less than satisfactory, see Jan Dihm, *Sprawa konstytucji ekonomicznej z 1791 r. na tle wewnętrznej i zagranicznej sytuacji Polski* (Wrocław: Ossolineum, 1959).

81. Franciszek Dmochowski, Ignacy Potocki and Hugo Kołłątaj, *O ustanowieniu i upadku polskiej Konstytucji 3 Maja* (Leipzig-Lwów: n.p., 1793), part 2, p. 362.

Notes to Chapter 3

1. Komisja Prawnicza Akademii Umiejętności w Krakowie, Volumina legum (Kraków: Akademia Umiejętności, 1889) 9: I, p. 47. A slightly different version is found in the parliamentary minutes, see Jan Łuszczewski, *Dyaryusz Sejmu ordynaryinego pod Związkiem Konfederacji Generalney Oboyga Narodow w Warszawie rozpoczętego roku Pańskiego 1788*, 2 vols., 2 parts each (Warsaw: Drukarnia Narodowa JKMci i Prześwietney Kommisyi Edukacyi Narodowey, 1788–90), Vol. 1, part 1, pp. 21–22.

2. The definitive study of the *liberum veto* is Władysław Konopczyński, *Liberum veto. Studium porównawczo-historyczne* (Kraków: Akademia Umiejętności, 1917). There is a French translation of the book and an English translation of the chapter concerning the principle of unanimity during the Renaissance has been printed in, Władysław Czapliński ed., *The Polish Parliament at the Summit of Its Development (16th-17th Centuries) Anthologies* (Wrocław: Ossolineum, 1985).

3. Edmund Burke, "The War with Jacobin France" in Ross J. S. Hoffman and Paul Levack, eds., *Burke's Politics: Selected Writings and Speeches of Edmund Burke on Reform, Revolution and War* (New York: Knopf, 1967), p. 418.

4. But the deputy, Władysław Siciński, from Upita in Lithuania was not left in peace. Not only did the *Sejm* members curse him as he left but when he died thirteen years later in 1664, the local *szlachta* dug up his casket and placed it with the lid open and the hapless ex-deputy still inside into the local inn/saloon. His fellow noblemen held that the sacred soil of the Republic had expelled its villainous son. In the early nineteenth century, Adam Mickiewicz, viewed the body still on display and wrote a poem about Siciński entitled, "*Popas w Upicie*" [A Stop in Upita]. In 1860 the local pastor brought Siciński's remains inside the Roman Catholic Church in Upita but did not bury them. The originator of abusive *liberum veto* was left propped up in the main nave for all to see. Zygmunt Gloger, *Encyklopedia staropolska ilustrowana*, (originally published in 1897) (Warsaw: Wiedza Powszechna, 1972), Vol. 3, pp. 407-408.

5. Józef Andrej Gierowski, *Historia Polski 1505-1764* (Warsaw: PWN, 1984) p. 253. Confederations are still awaiting more than just brief treatments in larger studies. Research on these institutions which predate the parliament are being conducted by doctoral candidates at the Historical Institute of the Polish Academy of Science in Warsaw.

6. Władysław Konopczyński provides the most informative analysis of the institution in his exhaustive narrative of the Confederation of Bar. See his, *Konfederacja Barska* (Warsaw: Instytut Popierania Nauki, 1938) Vol. 2, section entitled "*Prawo*," pp. 411-464.

7. Jerzy Michalski disagrees. "In these *Sejmy* the majority principle was not obligatory but the *liberum veto* was rather strongly limited." Michalski's observations applied not only to ordinary confederated *Sejmy* but also to convocational *Sejmy* convened during interregna and regularly confederated since the beginning of the sixteenth century; undoubtedly this could alter the sense of his assertion. Michalski also observed that during the Saxon period two opposite views coexisted: one favored the prohibition of a *veto* dissolving a *Sejm* and the other cherished the *liberum veto* as the final safeguard of freedom. Michalski, however, is not concerned with providing evidence that a confederated *Sejm* was at any time actually exploded by this infamous prerogative. Jerzy Michalski, "*Sejm w czasach sas-*

kich" esp. pp. 331-332 in Jerzy Michalski, ed., *Historia Sejmu polskiego*, Vol. 1, *Do schyłku szlacheckiej Rzeczpospolitej* (Warsaw: PWN, 1984).

8. Among the works that convey the forced nature of this confederation and the accompanying resentment is Wanda Konczyńska's *Rejtan, Korsak i Bohuszewicz. Materiały do monografji posła nowogrodzkiego* (Wilno, 1935). A published account of the proceedings is found in Stanisław August's incomplete memoirs, *Pamiętniki*, edited by Bronisław Zaleski (Dresden, 1870). The full memoirs were in the possession of the Soviet Academy of Science, see Andrzej Zahorski, *Spór o Stanisława Augusta*, (Warsaw: PIW, 1988).

9. Bracław (1764) *Volumina legum*, 7, p. 34; Poznań, Kalisz and Ziemia Wschowska (1766) *Volumina legum*, 7, p. 155.

10. *Volumina legum*, 5, p. 371.

11. "*Porządek sejmowania*," *Volumina legum*, 7, pp. 288-292. The previous parliamentary procedure law entitled, "O porządku Seymowania," *Volumina legum*, 7, pp. 17-18 was passed by the convocational *Sejm* in 1764 prior to the election of Stanisław August Poniatowski. Its provisions were used in three *Sejmy*: the electoral and regular *Sejmy* of 1764 and the *Sejm* of 1766. Earlier laws on parliamentary procedure had been passed in 1736 (*Volumina legum*, 6, p. 323), 1690 (*Volumina legum*, 5, pp. 371-372), and 1673 (*Volumina legum*, 5, p. 106).

12. The most comprehensive, recent treatment of procedural regulations is in Jerzy Michalski, ed., *Historia sejmu polskiego*, Vol. 1, *Do schyłku szlacheckiej Rzeczypospolitej* (Warszawa: PWN, 1984). Somewhat earlier and chronologically more restricted studies include Henryk Olszewski, *Sejm Rzeczpospolitej epoki oligarchii 1652-1763: Prawo-praktyka-teoria-programy*, (Poznań: PWN, 1966); Juliusz Bardach, "*Sejm szlachecki doby oligarchii*" *Kwartalnik Historyczny*, Vol. 74 (1966) number 2; Ryszard Łaszewski, *Sejm Polski w latach 1764-93: Studium historyczno-prawne*, *Studia Iuridica*, Vol. 3, notebook 3 (Warsaw-Poznań: Towarzystwo Naukowe w Toruniu, 1973). The Four Years' *Sejm* is specifically examined in Bogusław Leśnodorski, *Dzieło Sejmu Czteroletniego (1788-1792). Studium historyczno-prawne* (Wrocław: Ossolineum, 1951). Waleryan Kalinka includes a very general treatment in his classic, *Sejm Czteroletni*, 4th ed. (Kraków: Księgarnia Spółki Wydawniczej Polskiej, 1895), Vol. 1, book 3, pp. 525-532. Parliamentary procedures are also discussed throughout

the first survey history of the Polish parliament to be published in English. The treatment of procedures in the old Commonwealth is interesting but general, relying mainly on a 1678 account by the Englishman Moses Pitt; eighteenth century changes are presented even more sketchily. Jacek Jedruch, *Constitutions, Elections and Legislatures of Poland 1493-1977: A Guide to Their History* (Washington, D.C.: University Press of America, 1982), pp. 46-47, 140-151, 187.

13. Article 17 of the "*Akt Osobny Drugi zamykaiący w sobie Nayiaśnieyszey Rzeczypospolitey Polskiey prawa kardinalne, wieczyście trwałe, y odmienne być nigdy nie mogące, et materias Status, które tylko unanimitate na Seymach wolnych decydowane być powinny.*" of the "*Traktat Wieczysty Między Rzecząpospolitą Polską, y Imperium caley Rossyi, Volumina legum,* 7, p. 280.

14. The regular *Sejm* had often been called *walny* or general but the term *wolne* was not a misprint. Sapieha used the term when quoting this law in the parliamentary debate of 26 May 1789. ASW 2:246.

15. As the term implies, *possessionitatis* meant holding hereditary title to land. Significantly the law was double-edged. Coming after the end of a generation of absentee monarchial rule and administrations dominated by foreigners the provision probably was aimed, in part, at assuring greater responsibility and patriotism in public service. The vague designation "*dobrze* [well] *possessionitatis,*" however, also delineated minimum qualifications applicable to native office-holders. While some kind of property requirements had been a longstanding unspoken practice its enunciation in this new reform law gave it new explicit meaning and may have made the eventual equating of land ownership and full citizenship more familiar and acceptable.

16. *Volumina legum,* 7, pp. 282-284.

17. The most dramatic attempt at a *liberum veto* occurred in this *Sejm*. The deputy Reytan prostrated himself before the *Sejm* chambers to prevent the ratification of the First Partition. His corporal *nie pozwalam* was uncomfortably ignored with regrettable consequences for the Commonwealth. Though the new order established by the Four Years' *Sejm* outlawed the *liberum veto* it also rewarded the descendents of the author of this famous act. Ironically, the 1776 incident confirmed the conviction of many conservatives that the *liberum veto* was the prized, time-proven and revered safeguard against the

tyranny or foolishness of the majority. At times, it seemed that only one person might have the correct interest of the community in mind and he must therefore have a particularly powerful instrument to restrain all his colleagues.

18. These artificial categories are imperfect with some laws rightly falling into at least two. The 1780 measure freeing Antoni Chmielewski from censure by the Army Department is classified as "other" private case though it could also arguably be viewed as a directive to an executive office. The 1786 settlement of boundary disputes between Prussia and individual Polish landowners is considered a diplomatic agreement and as such *materia status*.

19. Evidently a complex long term dispute involving numerous parties, the Walewski-Herburtowski case was sent to the Crown Tribunal in Lublin for an immediate decision. *Volumina legum*, 7, pp. 580–581.

20. For an earlier period, this question is tangentially treated in Konstanty Grzybowski, *Teoria reprezentacji w Polsce w epoce odrodzenia* [The theory of representation in Renaissance Poland] (Warsaw: PWN, 1959).

21. *Volumina legum*, 9: CCLXVI, p. 222.

22. Franciszek Antoni Kwilecki, *starosta* of Wschowa, was the "first" of the Wielkopolanian deputies. Normally the *marszałek* of the previous Sejm gave the keynote address as the temporary *marszałek* of the new Parliament. In the interim, however, the 1786 *marszałek* Stanisław Gadomski, *podkomorzy* of Sochaczew, had been "raised" to the status of *wojewoda* of Łęczyca and, thus, no longer belonged to the knightly estate. The distinctions between the deputies and the senators as well as among the deputies according to a hierarchy of provincial and local offices remained more than an old custom. Though titles were forbidden since 1569, except for a few cases, new formalities connected with actual or titular local offices produced a veritable titlemania in the eighteenth century. Such ranking affected procedures in the *Sejm* such as the order of voting.

23. Luszczewski, *Dyaryusz*, Vol. 1, part 1, p. 4.

24. *Dziennik Czynności Sejmu Głównego Ordynaryinego Warszawskiego pod związkiem Konfederacyi Oboyga Narodów agituiącego się 1789* (Warsaw: Zawadzki, 1789), Vol. 5, 22 December 1789.

25. The *Ustawa Rządowa* granted the Infanta of Saxony title to the Polish throne. The arrangement was peculiar. The Wettins had

been popular among the nobility when they ruled as elected monarchs from 1696 to 1764 mainly because of the failure of their plans to establish absolutism. But the Polish crown was to go to whomever the daughter of the Elector might marry. This *carte blanche* seemed reckless. As matters developed, the offer was never accepted.

26. A copy of the letter has been preserved in ASW 22:69-70r. Stanisław August further argued that the Constitution was legal because of this unanimity and the fact that "hardly any civil military administrative commission has not expressed either in writing or through a delegation the most eager and liveliest approval of this Constitution. I, therefore, repeat that whoever would wish to carefully consider the matter he could not deny or fail to see that the nation is willingly inclined to the May Third Constitution and on this basis will not deny its legality." The king's confidence extended to the reaction of neighboring governments: "we not only have no cause to fear any dangerous consequences but two neighboring courts have strongly assured (us) that not only do they not desire to harm or subvert our constitution but even that they are ready to save our borders should some other power attempt an attack."

27. *Volumina legum*, 9: CCCLXXX, p. 367.

28. "*Uroczyste zaręczenie porządku Izby na teraźniejszym sejmie*," *Volumina legum*, 9: CCXXXIV, pp. 202-203; "*Uchylenie konstytucji 1768, titt: 'Porządek sejmowania' co do punktu decydowania projektów kategorjami opisującego*," ibid., 9: CCXLVI, p. 210; "*Sejmy*," ibid., 9: CCXCLX, p. 250-266.

29. Łuszczewski, *Dyaryusz*, Vol. 1, part 1, p. 5.

30. The events just prior to this are unclear. The text reads: "*Izba zatym poselska po zaszłych, według dawnego zwyczaju od siebie do Senatu i od Senatu do Izby Poselskiej Poselstwach, oddawszy na piśmie przez Województwa, Ziemia, y Powiaty każde w szczegulności zaleczenie osób do rozdawnictwa wakansow w ręce Sejmowego Marszałka . . .*" *Volumina legum* 7, p. 289.

31. The text reads, "*z wolnym domawieniem się do tychże paktów.*"

32. The term actually referred to the municipal archives of the town (*gród*) in which the *Sejm* was held.

33. It is not entirely clear what determined the order of deputies. The sequence of *województwa* and *powiaty* was not the same as the order of senators, the latter being established by law in 1768. Within

each *województwo* and *powiat* the order of deputies was apparently set by the deputy *sejmik* according to local titles, to be explained in chapter 6.

34. *Walne*, or general, *Sejmy* were limited to six weeks; therefore the final period in which the approved laws were confirmed and signed could last up to one week. Interestingly these *Seymy* are sometimes also called *wolne* or free.

35. As a conclusion to the lengthy statute a phrase is included prohibiting the taking of members' places or the center area by spectators. This, however, continued to be a problem.

36. The war with Russia brought the adjournment date to 31 May 1792.

37. "*Akt konfederacji generalnej w sejmuiących stanach oboyga narodów*," *Volumina legum*, 9: I, p. 46.

38. The consensus is evident in the surviving handwritten drafts of the bills in ASW 25: "*Deputacyi Porządku Izby Seymowey*" (120–126r), "*Na Sessyi Prowincyi Małopolskiey Uroczyste zaręczenie porządku Izby teraźnieyszym Seymu 28 Octobra 1790*" (127–127r), J. W. Mostowski: *Kasztelan Raciążki* "*Ordynacya Seymowa*" (128–129r), J. W. Stroynowski Poseł Wołyński "*Porządek Izby Seymowey*" (130–131), J. W. Wołyński Ex. Pod. Star. Poseł Krakowski "*Porządek Izby Seymowey*" (132–132r), "*Od Prowincyi Litt. Uroczyste Zaręczenie Porządku Izby na Teraźnieyszym Seymie 28 Octobra 1790 czytany*" (133–134), J. W. Walewski, *Porządek i Poseł Sieradzki* "*Deklaracya Porządku Seymowania*" (135–135r), untitled (136–136r) with internal numbers 389–393. The draft from Małopolska formed the basis of the new law. Somewhat different from the rest of the projects were the proposals from Sołtyk and Walewski, both of whom believed the sufficiency of previous laws (from 1673, 1736, 1764, 1768 and for Sołtyk alone 1690).

39. The article also stipulates that no member can waiver his turn in favor of someone who has already spoken.

40. "There is a rule that no decision can be made on a matter of public business unless it has been discussed in the senate for three separate days." Thomas More, *Utopia*, Robert M. Adams, trans. (New York: Norton, 1974), p. 39. The precise relationship between this sixteenth century idea and the reform of 1791 is unclear, though the structural similarity is striking.

41. Of interest is the heated debate on this topic which took place on 14 October 1790, *Dyaryusz Seymowy*, ASW 22: 266r.
42. Ibid., 21 February 1791, ASW 19: 662-671r.
43. See the description below.
44. "*Uroczyste zaręczenie porządku Izby na teraźnieyszym sejmie*," *Volumina legum*, 9:CCXXXIV, pp. 202-203.
45. *Zbiór Popielów*, 413 (1 January 1791).
46. *Dyaryusz Seymowy*, ASW 5:633-637.
47. 21 February 1791, ASW 19: 664r-665r.
48. "*Uchylenie konstytucji 1768. titl.: 'Porządek sejmowania' co do punktu decydowania proiektów kategoryami opisanego*," *Volumina legum* 9: CCXLVI, p. 210.
49. *Dyaryusz Seymowy*, ASW 22:281r.
50. One deputy, Ignacy Siwicki, deputy from Troki, judged the opposite. See his speech given on 9 May 1791. ASW 19:101r.
51. "*Seymy*" *Volumina legum*, 9: CCXCIX, pp. 250-266; see article XI "*Co do czynów seymowych po złączeniu izb aż do rozłączenia*," p. 255.
52. The law, "*Seymy*," neglected to designate the required majority for *dezyderia*. Moreover, the *dezyderia* are not mentioned in the *Ustawa Rządowa* although all other types of bills are described in the section, "*Seym czyli władza prawodawcza*" *Volumina legum*, 9: CCLXVII, article VI, pp. 221-222. Furthermore, there are variations in the definitions of the categories of bills in articles XVI and XVII of the "*Seymy*" statute and throughout the May Third Constitution.
53. The difference in terminology is not as great in Polish: formerly, "*Deputacja do konstytucji*"; beginning in June 1791, "*deputacja sejmowa*."
54. Luszczewski, *Dyaryusz*, Vol. 1, part 1, p. 59 (16 October 1788).
55. In addition, article XVI reiterated the crucial modification in the composition of the *Sejm* stated in article XIV as well as in the original *Ustawa Rządowa*. The reformed Chamber of Deputies included "*assessorowie* and municipal commissioners sitting in the *assessorye* [courts], police and treasury commissions [who] will take their places in the chamber after the delegates of the governmental commissions for the presentation of the cities' *dezyderye*. . . ." *Volumina legum*, 9: CCXCIX, article XVI, paragraph 3, p. 259.
56. Every third *Sejm* was held in the Lithuanian town of Grodno.

57. Spelled variously, the *scartabellus, schartabel, skartabell, skartabellus* or *skartabelat* referred to an internship from newly ennobled *szlachta* that originally would last for three generations. Gloger confirmed Lelewel's identification of the term with the German *Papieradel*. Traditionally, membership in the nobility was viewed as the just reward for service rendered the kingdom and later the Commonwealth. Noble deeds accumulated with time in noble families; consequently new members needed extra service and sacrifices (mainly taxes) to reach the norm of the older *szlachta* and in this time of internship the younger nobility could not exercise full noble privileges. Gloger stated that as late as 1736 a law was passed prohibiting tenure of Crown offices by the *skartabell* (the term also referred to the new nobility itself and to its individual members). Zygmunt Gloger, *Encyklopedia staropolska ilustrowana* (Warsaw: Wiedza Powszechna, 1972) 4:243. Balzer more specifically emphasized the waning of restrictions mentioned only in passing by Gloger. According to him the formerly numerous obligations of the *skartabelat* had fallen into disuse by 1685. In their place eighteenth century parliaments set down new requirements: conversion to Roman Catholicism if the new noble came from outside the Church of Rome, an oath of loyalty initially to the king and beginning in 1790 to the Commonwealth, purchase of hereditary land worth at least 50,000 *złoty* within a year (after 1790 within three years) and payment of a special stamp tax within a year and six weeks. Oswald Balzer, *Skartabelat w ustroju szlachectwa polskiego* (Kraków: Akademia Umiejętności, 1911), pp. 314–315.

58. *Volumina legum*, 9:CCXCIX, article XXI, paragraph 13, pp. 263–264.

59. These were the respective opinions of Ignacy Krzucki (Wołyń) and Celestyn Sokolnicki (Poznań). The Wołynian argued against a proposed *turnus* on the Treasury Commission since the new law stipulated that once a project had been rejected it could not be discussed again in the same parliament. The deputy from Poznań, however, argued that "the cited clause from the Law on *Sejmy* cannot be applied to the present *Sejm* which is confederated and [thus] regulated like past *sejmy*." *Dyaryusz Seymowy*, ASW 22: 279–280.

Notes to Chapter 4

1. The notable exception is Jerzy Kowecki. See, for instance, his

"*Od klubów do stronnictwa politycznego w Warszawie stanisławowskiej*" *Rocznik Warszawski*, 19 (1987): 43–70.

2. In addition, a handwritten record of part of the first term was used; this filled a gap in the printed record. Czartoryski Archives (Kraków), 884IV "*Codice hoc continentuo diaria canitiorum generalium Regni Poloniae et N.D. Lithuaniae inde a die sexta Octobris a 1788 usque ad diem decimam octavam Maia 1789 Varsoviae habitorum.*"

3. Two handwritten documents with listings of roll call propositions exist in the *Archiwum Sejmu Wielkiego* (14: 588–588r (589r); 590–592). The lists do not vary in content and enable verification of some of the roll call information though they do not provide any results. Two odd features invite speculation: most of the dates are off by one or two days and the lists include one vote from 1788 and 1789 each, none from 1790, but they are complete for 1791 and 1792. The lists have been archived among copies of bills and may have been used by the *Sejm* secretary or some other individual after the suspension of the *Sejm* in May 1792. The discrepency of dates may be connected with the publishing date of the material in the *Dziennik*. The two pre-1791 propositions may have been corrections of oversights on some earlier lists or they may have been indicative of the political concerns of the compiler. If the latter is the case, at least one contemporary thought that the issue of an Army Commission versus a Department of the Army and the overthow of the Permanent Council were more vital than any other political controversy voted upon before 1791.

4. The most comprehensive study of the Partition *Sejm* is found in Władysław Konopczyński's *Geneza i ustanowienie Rady Nieustającej*, (Kraków: Akademia Umiejętności, 1917).

5. Łukasz Kądziela, *Narodziny Konstytucji 3 Maja* (Warsaw: Agencja Omnipress, 1991), p. 20–22.

6. The graph was made possible through the generous assistance of Sharon Anderson at the Weeg Computing Center of the University of Iowa.

7. *Dziennik*, 25 October 1790.

8. The *Sejm* Committee which screened bills before they were debated probably had a categorization system but the committee's records, if they ever existed, have not been located. In this study, "constitutional" refers to permanent systemic changes, "military" to those issues whose primary concern was the armed forces, "taxes" to

permanent levies, "fiscal" to expenditures or temporary levies and "political" to limited policies or actions.

Notes to Chapter 5

1. In a sense, the king also represented the nation since in old terminology, he, the senators and the knights each constituted a separate *stan* or estate. Population figures are found in Tadeusz Korzon, *Wewnętrzne dzieje za Stanisława Augusta*, (Kraków: Zwoliński, 1897), Vol. 1, pp. 160–163 and Władysław Czapliński and Tadeusz Ładogórski, eds., *The Historical Atlas of Poland*, (Warsaw-Wrocław: Państwowe Przedsiębiorstwo Wydawnictw Kartograficznych, 1986), p. 14.

2. These sources consist of minutes in manuscript form and other varia in the *Archiwum Sejmu Czteroletniego*, the printed but incomplete *Dyaryusz czynności*, the *Dziennik*, the *Volumina legum*, and the annual *Serie* and *Kalendarzyk polityczny* over the course of the Four Years' *Sejm*.

3. Mazowsze was joined to the Crown in 1526 and in many respects it remained economically and socially distinct. It has been estimated that a quarter of the population in Mazowsze belonged to the *szlachta*, two and half times the Republic's average.

4. The seizure of territories in the first partition came in 1772 but they were not formally approved by the *Sejm* until three years later.

5. The first law tightened the union of the Crown and the Grand Duchy into a nearly unitary state with a single treasury, army and set of ministers. The legislative organ had already been fused in 1569. "*Zaręczenie wzaiemne oboyga narodów*," *Volumina legum*, 9:CCCLVI, 22 October 1791. The second statute standardized representation in the *Sejm*. The three provinces were defined as Wielkopolska, Małopolska and the Grand Duchy and each was divided into thirty-four *powiaty*. *Województwa* and the occasional *ziemia* ("lands," remnants of older units) were preserved but they were not the focus of attention since they were not standardized. Since each *powiat* had two representatives, each province had 68 deputies in the *Sejm*. This meant a real redistribution of power: Wielkopolska gained two representatives, Małopolska 10 and Lithuania 19. Part of the gain for Lithuania came from the attachment of Livonia to the Grand Duchy. "*Rozkład województw, ziem, i powiatów z oznaczeniem miast,*

a nich mieysc konstytucyinych dla seymików w prowincyach Koronnych i Wielkiego Xięstwa Litewskiego," *Volumina legum,* 9:CCCLXIV, 2 November 1791. The reduction of the Grand Duchy to one of three equal provinces was not complete nor was it necessarily to Lithuania's disadvantage. In addition to an increased share in the *Sejm,* the Grand Duchy exchanged separate treasury and army commissions for half the membership of the joint commissions and their alternate presidencies. As a province, Lithuania still had a special status.

6. Gdańsk and Toruń had a special status and did sent observers.

7. Property assessments for the 10 percent income tax on agricultural land have been preserved for Płock and Łęczyca, Archiwum Główne Akt Dawnych, Księgi Ziemskie, Płock (95) and Łęczyca (133). The materials for the historical and geographic atlas have been published in Władysław Semkowicz ed., *Materiały do słownika historyczno-geograficznego województwa krakowskiego w dobie Sejmu Czteroletniego (1788-1792)* (Kraków: Akademia Umiejętności, 1939-1960).

8. Janina Leskiewicz provides a brief but lucid discussion of this issue in her introduction to *Ziemiaństwo polskie 1795-1945: Zbiór prac o dziejach warstwy i ludzi,* (Warsaw: PWN, 1985). The discussion of this issue is continued in the section on stratification in chapter 6.

Notes to Chapter 6

1. Podlasie was on the eastern edge of the Polish Mazowsze region, shading into Black Rus' in the Grand Duchy. The Brześć Litewski *województwo* was divided into two areas. Brześć Litewski itself was in a sense a continuation of Podlasie but with the shading of Polish and Ukrainian speaking peasant populations while the other half of the *województwo* consisted of Pińsk or roughly Polesie on the border of Black Rus' and the Ukrainian lands to the south. The border quality of these regions may have been a factor though ethnic distinctions might be irrelevant because of the unified Polish culture of the *szlachta*.

2. Three authors have classified additional Wołynians not found in the *Polski słownik biograficzny* and *Encyklopedia powszechna*. Smoleński and Dihm included Walenty Stroynowski and Jan Zagurski among the Wołynian opponents of the Constitution. Nanke presented the most complete and authoritative analysis of the Wołynian

deputies in his *Szlachta wołyńska wobec Konstytucji Trzeciego Maja* (Lwów: Towarzystwo dla Popierania Nauki Polskiej, 1907). Nanke showed that five deputies from Wołyń entered a condemnation into the Warsaw *gród* against the revolution the day before: Aksak, B. Hulewicz, Krzucki, Stroynowski and Jan Zagórski. (p. 23) Another manifesto was registered in Lublin on 13 May by J. K. Czartoryski, S. Hulewicz and J. Piniński. (p. 25) Additionally, Kalasanty Olizar and Wojciech August Świętosławski are discussed as opposing deputies. (p. 28) Kalasanty Olizar is undoubtedly Józef Kalasanty Olizar. Nanke also concluded that both Krzucki and Stroynowski were eventually won over by the king. (p. 33) No mention is made anywhere of the two remaining deputies, Stanisław Paweł Jabłonowski and Dunin Krzysztof Karwicki. In sum, Nanke identified eight diehard opponents and two converts. The rating for Wołyń, therefore, would have been initially a 0.0 percent approval rate and ultimately 20 percent as opposed to the 14.29 percent accorded it in this study. This would not change Wołyń's relative standing among the *województwa*. Moreover, this instance of comparison between the information in the PSB and EP with the fuller data in Nanke's monograph tends to confirm the assumption that the incompleteness of the data does in fact carry an element of random chance. For the sake of consistency and considering the lack of biographical information, neither Stroynowski and Świętosławski are included in this analysis.

3. Variations in the sources do have an influence on the breakdown of the Podolian delegation. While all available secondary sources agree on the identity of the opponents, there is disagreement on the supporters:

SUPPORTERS		OPPONENTS
PSB and EP	Smoleński/Dihm	PSB/EP/Smoleński/Dihm
Boreyko		Kosecki
	Grabiński	Mierzejewski
Morski		Orłowski
	Rzewuski	Złotnicki
	Witosławski	
Zajączek	Zajączek	

Should Smoleński and Dihm have been correct, the approval rate for the Podolian delegation would rise to 50 percent; if all sources were combined the rate would be 60 percent and Podole would fit into the mainstream of the Four Years' *Sejm*. The lack of overlapping among the sources identifying supporters is disturbing; they agree only on one individual. To maintain consistency only PSB and EP have been used but the questionable categorization of Podole should be kept in mind.

4. Stanisław August did use orders and the promise of orders to create a group of supporters for the new Constitution. Feelings of obligation stemming from gratitude or the hope for additional favors were used by the King and Hugo Kołłątaj to counter Wołynian opposition. The two "showered . . . medals on Wołyń in an abundance that none of the *szlachta* could remember." Nanke, *op. cit.*, pp. 45-48. The figures for order distribution among deputies opposing the Constitution would indicate that the treatment accorded Wołyń was atypical and perhaps adapted to the special mentality of the local nobility. The King's strategy was only partly successful; gratitude faded quickly and hope for gain followed momentary acquiescence.

5. The difference in the number of cases for the two terms has several logical explanations. First term deputies had twice as much time as their second term colleagues to become known during the Four Years' *Sejm*. Considering the doubling of deputies, another explanation might be that the local dietines chose their most effective members as deputies in the 1788 elections rather than in the unexpected elections of 1790. Second term deputies had less time to pursue careers before the destruction of the state in 1795. This, however, would not preclude the possibility of careers, and hence historical remembrance, in the Duchy of Warsaw or the Congress Kingdom.

6. The outright supporters were the Małopolanians, Ignacy Dembiński (Kraków), Jan Nepomucin Dunin Karwicki (Sandomierz), Antoni Ledóchowski (Czernichów), Stanisław Sołtyk (Kraków), and Józef Zaiączek (Podole) and the Wielkopolanians, Stanisław Breza (Gniezno), Ignacy Działyński (Dobrzyń). Two were converts, the Wielkopolanian Jan Dołęga Nosarzewski (Mazowsze - Ciechanów) and the Lithuanian Stanisław Niemcewicz (Brześć Litewski). The opponents were the Wielkopolanian, Felix Kretkowski (Łęczyca) and the Małopolanian, Józef Piniński (Wołyń). The Wielkopolanian Karol Jezierski (Mazowsze - Czersk) apparently took an ambivalent stance towards the Constitution as did his father the Kasztelan of Łuków. It should be noted that the support of one of the deputies was deduced: Sołtyk

as a member of the Society of Friends of the Constitution was at the least a convert.

7. The coverts and their ages in 1791 were: Korsak (50), Krzucki (41), S. Niemcewicz (38), J. D. Nosarzewski (36) and Pawlikowski (unknown).

8. The stalwart opponent had been discussed earlier, Piniński from Wołyń, and the "moderate" opponent was Kretkowski from Łęczyca.

9. The very wealthy were Działyński, Karwicki, Ledóchowski, Niemcewicz, Nosarzewski and Piniński; those from the "middle nobility" were Breza and Dembiński.

10. The information is strangely skewed geographically:

	% of Confederates	% of Deputies
Livonia	7.4	3.3
Lithuania	7.4	27.0
Małopolska	37.0	32.6
Wielkopolska	48.1	37.0

A probable factor in this distribution is the survival of biographical information.

11. But the usefulness of class categories fails in the case of the *Rzeczpospolita*. As Stanisław August strenuously argued the Polish reform differed from the French Revolution and his conviction was shared by Edmund Burke.

12. Bogusław Leśnodorski, *Dzieło Sejmu Czteroletniego (1788-1792) Studium Historyczno-prawny* (Wrocław: Ossolineum, 1951) pp. 366-369, 372-375.

13. In this discussion, Leśnodorski seems not to have distinquished between medieval and modern modes of thought. The collective was quite common in the medieval worldview ranging from the concept of no salvation outside the church to the legal categories of estate and estate prerogatives. Rather than a geographical phenomenon the preference of the individual over the collective was a process over time, probably associated with the rise of the individualistic hero in chivalry, the independent person of the Renaissance and the self-made capitalist.

14. The May Third Constitution's treatment of the peasantry received interesting evaluations from political figures in the decades immediately after the Republic's demise. Some of these views were

recorded in a survey conducted by the Committee on Civilian Reform (*Komitet Cywilnego Reformu*) while the Duchy of Warsaw was under Russian occupation in 1814. On the issue of agrarian reform, public officials and prominent citizens often looked to the 1791 Constitution for precedence. Some found in the Constitution proof that, contrary to the opinion of Poland's neighbors, the peasantry had not been ignored. Wojciech Grzymała, prefect of the Lublin Department, observed that it would have been impossible for the Four Years' *Sejm* to have done anymore. "It did not do everything in this area that should have been because, if we can only do it gradually today, far less could it have done so openly and boldly in this field in those days." Zbigniew Stankiewicz, "*Szlachta-ziemianie w świetle ankiety włościanskiej 1814 r.*" in Janina Leskiewicz, ed., *Ziemiaństwo polskie 1795–1945: zbiór prac z dziejów warstw i ludzi* (Warsaw: PWN, 1985), pp. 85–120, esp. 95–96.

15. Andrzej Wyczański, *Uwarstwienie społeczne w Polsce XVI wieku: studia* [Social Stratification in Sixteenth Century Poland: Studies] (Wrocław: Ossolineum, 1977), pp. 68–69.

16. Ibid., pp. 253–254.

17. Andrzej Zajączkowski, *Główne elementy kultury szlachty polskiej: ideologia a struktury społeczne* (Wrocław: Ossolineum, 1961), p. 58.

18. Quoted in Walerjan Kalinka, *Sejm Czteroletni*, Vol. 2, part 2, pp. 568–569 and Krystyna Zieńkowska, *Jacek Jezierski, kasztelan łukowski 1772–1805* (Warsaw: PWN, 1963), pp. 135–136.

19. Władysław Konopczyński, *Konfederacja Barska* (Warsaw: Towarzystwo dla Popieranie Nauki, 1938), 2 vols., pp. 388–391. This a part of a fascinating analysis of social support for the uprising, "*Społeczeństwo*" Vol. 2, pp. 375–410.

20. Szymon Starowolski, *Polska albo opisanie położenia królestwa polskiego*, (reprint: Kraków: Wydawnictwo Literackie, 1977) pp. 130–133. The section, "*Władza Polityczna*" [political authority] gives a succinct description of the political institutions and dominant ideology of the *Rzeczpospolita* that in many respects remained valid 150 years later. The government was explicitly characterized as mixed to ensure a balanced rule of law. Originally: Simonis Starovolsci, *Polonia sive status Regni Poloniae descriptio*, (Cologne: Henricum Crithium, 1632).

21. The basic order and description of the plethora of offices is

provided in Zbigniew Góralski, *Urzędy i godności w dawnej Polsce*, (Warsaw: Ludowa Spółdzielnia Wydawnicza, 1983). Other valuable sources include: Gloger, *Encyclopedia staropolska*, Antoni Piskadło's impressive appendix to the reprint of Starowolski's *Polonia*, and Boniecki's *Herbarz polski*.

22. Teresa Zielińska, *Magnateria polska w epoce saskiej. Funkcja urzędów i królewszczyzn w procesie przeobrażeń warstwy społecznej* (Wrocław: Polska Akademia Nauk and Ossolineum, 1977). The same commonly accepted position was expressed in Krystyna Zieńkowska, *Jacek Jezierski, kasztelan łukowski (1722-1805), Z dziejów szlachty polskiej XVIII w.* (Warsaw: PWN, 1963).

23. The sons of *wojewodowie* were Ksawery Działyński (Wschow, Poznań) and Antoni Ledóchowski (Czernichów); the sons of *kasztelanie* were Karol Jezierski (Mazowsze-Czersk), and Jan Karwicki (Sandomierz).

24. Zbigniew Góralski, *Urzędy i godności w dawnej Polsce* [Offices and Titles in Old Poland] (Warsaw: Ludowa Społdzielnia Wydawnicza, 1983), chapter 7 "*Urzędy ziemskie*" [Land offices], pp. 184-207.

25. No record known to the author exists listing the *grodowe starostwa*. The thirteen were identified on the basis of recognizability of city names. But since the offices were old and the decline of Polish cities since the sixteenth century great, it is likely that some *grodowe starostwa* have remained unrecognized.

26. The ratios of support to opposition in these smaller groups are quite similar to the ratio for the *Sejm* as a whole. Thus, the 45 known careers appear to be an accurate sample, as are the deputies' biograms.

Notes to Chapter 7

1. Władysław Czapliński and Tadeusz Ladogórski, *The Historical Atlas of Poland* (Warsaw-Wrocław: Państwowe Przedsiębiorstwo Wydawnictw Kartograficznych, 1986), p. 18.

2. The provincial sessions had grown out of provincial gatherings that had once met prior to the *Sejm*. In 1788–1792 they took place simultaneously with the *Sejm*, usually on Wednesdays when plenum sessions were not held. Little is known about them, the records seem to have been lost, but their existence is quite evident in the coordinated voting of deputies from particular provinces and from references in parliamentary records. Some discussion is offered in Ryszard Laszewski, *Sejm polski w latach 1764–1793. Studium historycznoprawne* (Warsaw - Poznań: Towarzystwo Naukowe w Toruniu, 1973), pp. 103–106.

3. See, for instance, the law on the Treasury Commission, *Volumina legum*, 9: CCCLXIII, pp. 319–326.

4. Human activity is seldom completely accidental. The results of the elections to the Four Years' *Sejm*, no doubt, were at least in part the effects of numerous conscious efforts.

5. Emanuel Rostworowski, *Sprawa aukcji wojska na tle sytuacji politycznej przed Sejmem Czteroletnim* (Warsaw: PWN, 1957). See especially pp. 134–135.

6. The SPSSx statistical package has been used in the following cluster analyses. Dr. Chia-Hsing Lu's help has been indispensible and Prof. George Boynton has provided general but essential advice on appropriate quantitative techniques.

7. Only eighteen *turni* sheets for the Senate have been preserved in the Archiwum Sejmu Wielkiego, the earliest dating from 10 February 1791. This serious handicap might be overcome by further examination of the Fryderyk Moszyński files at the Catholic University of Lublin and the State Archives at Kórniki.

8. A similar analysis of the Senate was impossible due to the paucity of materials.

9. The clustering used the 36 division tallies that were available from the 50 divisions conducted during the second term. It is not clear how the lack of clusters could be reconciled to the higher "c" value for the second term except that the difference may arise from the difference between *turni* tallies and the intact *turni* sheets used for clustering.

10. These were Batowski, Niemcewicz, Weyssenhoff, and Kublicki. Two others, Pągowski and Trembicki, supported the marshals while the rest were absent or did not vote.

11. The specific dates and topics for these are:

voting rights

10 February 1791	limiting participation in local assemblies to hereditary landowners
10 February 1791	protecting political rights of hereditary landowners who are in another's service
11 February 1791	prohibiting income qualifications for hereditary landowners seeking public office
14 February 1791	permitting military personnel excluded from other civilian offices to be deputies

creation of institutions

14 February 1791	two procedural divisions concerning local assemblies
14 March 1791	correction of local assemblies bill
5 April 1791	procedural division to debate Towns bill before the *Sejmy* bill
12 April 1791	passage of Towns law
12 May 1791	passage of *Sejmy* law
17 June 1791	passage of Police Commission law
3 October 1791	passage of *Assessorye* (Appellate Court) law
18 May 1792	passage of Army Commission law

defense of system

27 January 1792	censure and dismissal of Szczęsny Potocki and Adam Rzewuski from high military offices for not taking an oath to the Constitution

A full record of these divisions appears in chapter 4.

12. Distance could have been a factor. Once Eydziatowicz left for his estates, presumably in the eastern boundary lands of the Lithuanian Ruthenian lands, it would have been costly for him to return to Warsaw after Easter, and then to leave once again for the St. John's Fairs and the harvest.

13. These were Batowski (Livonia), Bernowicz (Nowogródek), Breza (Gniezno), Bronikowski (Gniezno), Butrymowicz (Brześć Litewski), T. Byszewski (Łęczyca), A. Byszewski (Mazowsze), Chrapowiecki (Smoleńsk), Chreptowicz (Nowogródek), Dembiński (Kraków), Działyński (Poznań), Ejdziatowicz (Smoleńsk), Gieysztor (Troki), Gliszczyński (Poznań), Gorzeński (Poznań), Grabowski (Wilkomierz), Grotowski (Rawa), Gutakowski (Orsza), Jelski (Smoleńsk), Kaczanowski (Livonia), Kiciński (Mazowsze), Kochanowski (Sandomierz), Kościałkowski (Wilno), Kublicki (Livonia), Lappa (Starodub), Lemnicki (Lublin), Leżeński (Bracław), Linowski (Kraków), Małachowski (Sandomierz), Miaskowski (Kalisz), D. Narbutt (Wilno), W. Narbutt (Wilno), Niemcewicz (Brześć Litewski), J. O. Ossoliński (Podlasie), J. K. Ossoliński (Podlasie), Pągowski (Livonia), Niemcewicz (Livonia), Ośniałowski (Dobrzyń), Pomarnacki (Wilno), Potocki (Lublin), Psarski (Wieluń), Puzyna (Smoleńsk), Radoliński (Kalisz), Radzicki (Mazowsze-Zakroczym), Rogowski (Mazowsze), Russocki (Kraków), Sapieha (Brześć Litewski), Sobolewski (Mazowsze), Sołtyk (Kraków), Szymanowski (Rawa), Trembicki (Livonia), Wawrzecki (Wilno), Weyssenhoff (Livonia), Wysłouch (Brześć Litewski), Zabiełło (Livonia), Zaiączek (Podole), Zambrzycki (Mazowsze-Nur), Zawisza (Rawa), Zboiński (Dobrzyń). The Marshals' Group includes the two earlier marshals' clusters with the exception of Rzetkowski. Further examinations of specific roll call votes would probably reveal subgroups.

14. The oppositional anti-Marshals' deputies who voted at least half of the time against the marshals were Krzucki (Wołyń), Meżeński (Sandomierz), Radzimiński (Czernichów), Stoiński (Lublin), Zagurski (Wołyń), and Zieliński (Mazowsze - Nur).

15. Senators have been excluded from this study because only five complete *turni* during the subperiod are known: 27 September, 19 October, 31 October, 7 November, 27 January; the only one of interest was the censure vote.

16. The biographical information is too incomplete for an analysis of the oppositional deputies. Only three characteristics are known for each. All had been elected in the second term (1790); five were from Małopolska (two from Wołyń), one (Zieliński) came from Wielkopolska; and only two held traditional local offices.

17. In addition, one member of the Marshal's Group, Radzicki, voted with Małachowski and Sapieha 50 percent of the time, yet, in the biographical information he is identified as an opponent. He

was also the only one from the Marshal's Group to accede to the Targowica Confederation before the king. The exact circumstances are unknown. Perhaps, Radzicki had been an opponent throughout the final phase of the *Sejm* despite his voting record. Perhaps, he became a convinced opponent after the suspension of parliament in May 1792. Or perhaps he joined under real or perceived pressure despite his convictions.

18. The career slopes are known for seven of the Marshals' Group: five from the Crown (Dembiński, S. Małachowski, Ossoliński, Psarski and Rogowski) and two from the Grand Duchy (Gieysztor and Niemcewicz). The comparative rates are .292 versus .298 and .261 versus .370.

19. Membership information is known for 55.9 percent of the Marshals' Group and 75.3 percent of supporters taken together. The rate for the *Sejm* as a whole was 31.8 percent. It would seem that history, or historians, have remembered the broad set of supporters better than the average deputy to the Four Years' *Sejm*. But while the Marshals' Group had strongly supported the Constitution, its biographical information is less complete. The Marshals' Group seems, therefore, to have included more individuals subsequently judged by history as non-entities.

20. Senators undoubtedly played a role. Ignacy Potocki, Lithuanian Grand Marshal, clearly led the members supporting the Constitution as did Hugo Kołłątaj who had recently been elevated to the post of Crown Vice Chancellor. Further research can be conducted on the role of senators through examination of the *Dziennik*.

21. Those who had belonged to the most active age group (35 to 39-year-olds) just prior to May Third and who also were part of the Marshals' Group were Breza, Działyński (Poznań), Niemcewicz (Brześć Litewski) and Zaiączek. Those who were in the second most active age group (30 to 34-year-olds) and who also belonged to the Marshals' Group were Batowski, Bronikowski, Grabowski, Kaczanowski, Kochanowski, Linowski, Niemcewicz (Livonia), both Ossolińskis and Wawrzecki.

Notes to Chapter 8

1. Andrzej Walicki, *Philosophical and Romantic Nationalism: The Case of Poland* (Oxford: Clarendon, 1982), p. 273.

GLOSSARY OF FOREIGN TERMS

assessorya - courts for royal cities, later free cities
asesor sądu nadwornego - associate judge at the king's court
chorąży - standard bearer
ciwuń - bailiff (in Lithuania)
corona regnum poloniae - "Crown of the Polish Kingdom," term indicating the separation of the state from the person of the rule in the fourteenth century
cześnik - cupbearer
demokracja szlachecka - democracy of the nobility
dezyderia - requests issued by electional local assemblies to the *Sejm*; roughly equivalent to the *cahier de doléance*
gród - a town; usually refers to the archives of the town's court where all laws had to be registered. Laws passed by the *Sejm* were not valid until they were entered into the Warsaw *gród*
hetman - chief military leader of which there were two kinds (*wielki* [great] and *polny* [field]) in the Crown and the Grand Duchy
instrukcje - detailed instructions from local assemblies for their representatives to the *Sejm*
instygator - prosecutor
Inflanty - Livonia; southwestern part of present-day Latvia
izba poselska - Chamber of Deputies
kasztelan - (pl. *kasztelanowie*) senators who ranked below the *wojewódowie*, formerly known as *comites, castellans*
konfederacja - confederation
koniuszy - equerry
Korona - the Crown; lands of the Polish Crown, one of the two components of the Polish-Lithuanian Commonwealth subdi-

vided into *Wielkopolska* and *Małopolska*
krajczy - carver
liberum veto - "free voice"; the right of each member of the *Sejm* to dissent
Litwa - Lithuania
łowczy - master of the royal hunt
Małopolska - Little Poland; southern territories of the Commonwealth between the rivers Pilica and Dniepr; present-day southeastern Poland and most of Right Bank Ukraine
marszałek - marshal; chief executive officer at the *sejmiki*, *Sejmy*, king's court, etc.
materia aeconomica - "economic matters"; those issues which beginning with 1768 could be passed by a majority of votes in the *Sejm*
materia status - "matters of state"; those issues which after 1768 still required unanimity in the *Sejm*
naród - nation
nec bona recipiantur - 1422 privilege protecting noble's property from confiscation by the king
neminem captivabimus nisi jure victum - 1433 privilege equivalent to the English and Hungarian *habeas corpus* requiring due process of law for the arrest of a nobleman except when caught in the act of rape, arson, theft or murder
nie pozwalam - "I do not allow," the Polish language equivalent of *liberum veto*
nihil novi nisi commune consensu - 1505 law requiring the consent of the *Sejm* for any new law
oboźny - camp leader
pacta conventa - contract between the elected monarch and the nobility
pisarz grodzki - city clerk
pisarz wielki - great clerk
pisarz ziemski - land clerk
podczasy - cupbearer
podkomorzy - chamberlain
podsędek - vice-judge
podskarbi nadworny - court vice-treasurer
podstarosta - vice-elder

podstoli - steward
podwojewoda - vice-*wojewoda*
poseł - deputy to the *Sejm*
pospolite ruszenie - "general mobilization" of the nobility
powiat - (pl. *powiaty*) district; subunit of a *województwo*
Rada Nieustająca - Permanent Council; council of ministers created in 1776
referendarz duchowny - clerical law clerk (*referendary*) who accepted complaints to the king and later to the *Sejm*; eventually he came to settle many of these cases
refendarz świecki - lay equivalent of above
regnum poloniae - the concept of the kingdom of Poland used historically before the full separation of the state from the person of the monarch
Rzeczpospolita - *res publica*; Republic; term used for the Polish-Lithuanian Commonwealth beginning with the Union of Lublin in 1569
sędzia grodzki - city judge
sędzia ziemski - land judge
Sejm - (pl. *Sejmy*) Parliament
sejmik - (pl. *sejmiki*) one of several kinds of local assemblies limited to the *szlachta: elekcyjny* (electional) which elect deputies to the *Sejm* and drew up a statement on current issues to be considered; *relacyjny* at which depu-reported back to their constituencies; *deputacki* which elected local officials; *gospodarski* which attended to various local "economic" needs
sekretarz - secretary
senatorowie-rezidenci - a council of senators who "resided" with the king from the early seventeenth century to prevent any abuse of royal power
skarbnik - treasurer
starosta grodowy - city elder
stolnik - esquire carver
Straż Praw - "Guardians of the Laws," new council of ministers created in 1791
strażnik - guard
szambelan - older term for chamberlain
szlachcic - an adult male nobleperson; *szlachcianka* referred to

a noble woman

szlachta - the nobility of the Polish-Lithuanian Commonwealth

turnus - (pl. *turni*) roll call votes or divisions

Ustawa Rządowa - Statute of Government, core of the May Third Constitution

Wielkie Xięstwo - the Grand Duchy, that is, Lithuania; northeastern territories of the Commonwealth; present-day Lithuania, Belarus and extreme northeastern Poland

Wielkopolska - Great Poland; western territories of the Commonwealth west of the river Pilica and including the duchy of Mazowsze with Warsaw; present-day central Poland

wojewoda - (pl. *wojewódowie*) literally a military or war leader this was the highest position in the Senate and the head of the officials in the *województwa*

województwo - (pl. *województwa*) subdivision of the province further divided into *powiaty*

wojski - nobleman left in charge of noble families who had taken refuge in a regional castle during wartime

Wołyń - old Ruthenian *województwo* whose *szlachta* was particularly traditionalist politically

ziemia - land, a political unit of ancient origin predating the *województwo*

złoty - golden; Polish monetary unit and coin

złoty czerwony - ducat

BIBLIOGRAPHY

Unpublished Sources

Archiwum Główne Akt Dawnych

Archiwum Sejmu Czteroletniego (ASW 1-25)
Archiwum Królestwa Polskiego
Archiwum Publiczny Potockich
96 - Niektóre pisma z czynności Sejmu Czteroletniego (1788-1792) pozostałe
97 - Pisma diplomatyczne ze czasów Sejmu Czteroletniego (1788-1792)
98 - Rękopisma statystyczno-polityczne w czasach Sejmu Czteroletniego ku polepszenia rządu i mienia Rptlej wydane

Księgi Grodzkie

Płock, Grodzkie Oblaty 35
Łęczyca, Grodzkie Varia 11

Zbiór Popiełów

413 - Korespondencja Stanisława Augusta z Debolim 1791-93
414 - Korespondencja Stanisława Augusta z Debolim 1789

Biblioteka Muzeum X.X. Czartoryskich

884 IV "Codice hoc continentuo diaria canitiorum generalium Regni Poloniae et N.D. Lithuaniae inde a die sexta Octobris a 1788 usque ad diem decimam octavam Maia 1789 Varsoviae habitorum."

2348 "Szczególnieysze Rzeczy Sejmu Blisko Czteroletniego

który R. 1788 zaczął się pod konfederacją zalimitował pod Rewolucje i R 1792 obalony przez konfederaję Targowicką jak niektórzy zwali"

1789 III "Propozycya"

Biblioteka Katolickiego Uniwersytetu w Lublinie
70 - 71 Teki Fryderyka Moszyńskiego

Biblioteka Ossolińskich
XVIII 17089-IV Adl - "Propozycya"

Biblioteka Uniwersytetu Warszawskiego - Stare Druki
items entitled, "Propozycya" with these signatures:
4.18.1.260-265.
4.18.2.94,95,98,100-103,105-108,110-116,529-531.

Published Primary Sources

Dziennik Czynności Sejmu Głównego Ordynaryinego Warszawskiego pod związkiem Konfederacyi Oboyga Narodow agituiącego się 1789. Warsaw: Zawadzki, 1789-1792.

Dyaryusz krótko zebrany Sejmu głównego Ordynarynego Warszawskiego pod związkiem Konfederacji Oboyga Narodow roku 1788 zaczętego, Warsaw: Dufour, 1789-1792.

Gazeta Warszawska. Warsaw, 1788-1792.

Kalendarz polityczny dla Królestwa Polskiego i Wielkiego Księstwa Litewskiego. Warsaw: Drukarnia Pijarów, 1788-1792.

Kalendarzyk narodowy i obcy. Warsaw: Zawadzki, 1791-92.

Łuszczewski Jan. *Dyaryusz Sejmu ordynaryinego pod Związkiem Konfederacji Generalney Oboyga Narodow w Warszawie Rozpoczętego Roku Pańskiego 1788.* 2 vols. 2 parts each. Warsaw: Drukarnia Narodowa JKMci i Przeświętney Kommisyi Edukacyi Narodowey, 1789.

Potocki, Ignacy, Franciszek Dmochowski, and Hugo Kołłątaj. *O ustanowieniu i upadku Konstytucji 3 maja 1791 roku.* Metz: n.p., 1793.

Serie. n.p., (1788-1792)

Siarczyński, Antoni. *Dyaryusz Sejmu ordynaryinego pod Związkiem Konfederacji Generalney Oboyga Narodow w Podwóynym Składzie* zgromadzonego w Warszawie od Dnia 16 Grudnia Roku 1790. Warsaw: Michał Gröll, 1791. "Ustawa Rządowa" Warsaw: Gröll, 1791.

Reprinted Primary Sources

Burke, Edmund. "Appeal from the New to the Old Whigs" in *The Works and Correspondence of the Right Honourable Edmund Burke*. new edition. 8 vols. London: Francis and John Rivington, 1852.

Czacki, Michał, *Wspomnienia z roku 1788 po 1792*. Poznań: n.p., 1862.

Kitowicz, Jędrzej. *Pamiętniki księdza J. Kitowicza do panowania Stanisława Poniatowskiego*. Poznań: Simon, 1845.

Konstytucja 3 Maja, reprint of "*Ustawa Rządowa. Prawa uchwalone dniu 3 Maia, Roku 1791.*" Warsaw: Gröll, 1791. Warsaw: Instytut Wydawniczy Związków Zawodowych, 1981.

Konstytucja 3 Maja, Jerzy Łojek critical editor and introduction. "Dokumenty naszej tradycji" series. Lublin: Wydawnictwo Lubelskie, 1981.

Konstytucia 3 Maja 1791, Statut Zgromadzenia Przyjaciół Konstytucji, Jerzy Kowecki critical editor, Bogusław Leśnodorski introduction. Warsaw: Państwowe Wydawnictwo Naukowe (hereafter: PWN), 1981; reprint 1983.

New Constitution of the Government of Poland Established by the Revolution, the Third of May, 1791. 2nd ed. London: 1791 reprinted in 1991 by Zamek Królewski w Warszawie.

Rousseau, Jean-Jacques. *The Government of Poland*. translated, with an introduction and notes by Willmoore Kendall. Indianapolis: Bobbs-Merrill, 1972.

Schulz, Fryderyk. *Podróże Inflantczyka z Rygi do Warszawy i po Polsce w latach 1791-1793*. Warszawa: Czytelnik, 1956.

Starowolski, Szymon. *Polska albo opisanie położenia Królestwa Polskiego*, translated from Latin and commentary by Antoni Piskadło. Kraków: Wydawnictwo Literackie w Krakowie, 1976.

Volumina legum. Prawa, konstytucye y przywileie Królestwa Polskiego, Wielkiego Księstwa Litewskiego y wszystkich prowincyi należących na walnych seymiech koronnych od sejmu wiślickiego roku pańskiego 1347 aż do ostatniego seymu uchwalone. 10 vols. plus 2 supplements. Kraków: Polska Akademia Umiejętności,

1889. reprint: Warsaw: Wydawnictwo Artystyczne i Filmowe, 1980.

Woliński, Jerzy, Jerzy Michalski and Emanuel Rostworowski, eds. *Materiały do dziejów Sejmu Czteroletniego*. 4 vols. Wrocław: Ossolineum, 1955, 1959, 1960, 1961.

Auxiliary Sources

Bleszczewski, Julian. *Spis senatorów i dygnitarzy koronnych (świeckich) z XVII wieku według źródeł autentycznych (Metryki Koronnej, Segillat Kanclerskich, Volumina legum i innych)*. Warsaw: n. p., 1862.

Boniecki, B. Adam. *Herbarz polski. Wiadomości historyczno-geneologiczne o rodach szlacheckich*. 17 vols. Warsaw: Gebethner, 1899–1913.

Brückner, Aleksander. *Słownik etymologiczny języka polskiego*, 3rd ed. Warsaw: Wiedza Powszechna, 1970.

Bryndzanacki, W. D. *Poczet imienny senatorów i ministrów królestwa polskiego doprowadzony do r. 1795*. Warsaw: n. p., 1937.

Czapliński, Władysław and Tadeusz Ladogórski, eds., *The Historical Atlas of Poland*. Warsaw-Wrocław: Państwowe Przedsiębiorstwo Wydawnictw Kartograficznych, 1986.

Dworzaczek, Włodzimierz. *Geneologia*. Warsaw: Instytut Historii Polskiej Adademii Nauk and PWN, 1959.

Konopczyński, Władysław. *Chronologia Sejmów Polskich*. Kraków: Archiwum Komisji Historycznej PAU, 1948.

Linde, M. Samuel Bogumił. *Słownik języka polskiego*. 2rd ed. Lwów: Ossolineum, 1859; Warsaw: Państwowy Instytut Wydawniczy (hereafter, PIW), 1951.

Niesiecki, Kasper. *Herbarz Polski*, 10 vols. Leipzig: Brechtkopf und Haertel, 1839–1846.

Olszewski, Henryk. "Nowe materiały do chronologii Sejmów Polskich," *Czasopismo Prawno-Historyczne*. Vol. IX:2 (1957).

Polski Słownik Biograficzny, Kraków: Akademia Umiejętności, 1935–1939, 1945–47. Wrocław: Polska Akademia Nauk, 1947 - present.

Semkowicz, Władysław, ed., *Materiały do słownika historyczno-geograficznego województwa krakowskiego w dobie Sejmu Czteroletniego (1788–92)*, Kraków: Akademia Umiejętności, 1939.

Wolff, Józef. *Senatorowie i dygnitarze Wielkiego Księstwa Litewskiego 1386-1795*. Kraków: Anczyć i Spółka, 1885.

Zychliński, Teodor Szeliga. *Złota księga szlachty polskiej.* 31 vols. Poznań: Chocieszyński, 1879-1908:

Secondary Sources

Ajnenkiel, Andrzej. *Polskie Konstytucje.* Warsaw: Wiedza Powszechna, 1983.
Askenazy, Szymon. *Przymierze polsko-pruskie.* 3rd ed. Kraków: E. Wande i Spółka, 1919.
Assorodobraj, Nina. *Początki klasy robotniczej. Problem rąk robocznych w przemyśle polskim epoki stanisławowskiej.* 2nd ed. Warsaw: PWN, 1966.
Aydelotte, William. "Constituency Influence on the British House of Commons, 1841-1847," in *The History of Parliamentary Behavior*, William Aydelotte, ed. Princeton: Princeton University Press, 1977. pp. 225-246.
Backvis, Claude. *Szkice o kulturze staropolskiej.* Warsaw: PIW, 1975.
Balzer, Oswald. *Konstytucja 3 maja: Reformy społeczne i polityczne Ustawy rządowej z roku 1791.* Lwów: Gebethner i Wolff, 1891.
_____. *Skartabelat w ustroju szlachectwa polskiego.* Kraków: Akademia Umiejętności, 1911.
_____. *Z zagadnień ustrojowych Polski.* 2nd ed. Lwów: Towarzystwo dla Popieranie Nauki Polskiej, 1917.
Bardach, Juliusz, ed. *Historia państwa i prawa polski do roku 1795.* 2 vols. Warsaw: PWN, 1957.
_____, Bogusław Leśnodorski and Michał Pietrzak. *Historia państwa i prawa polskiego.* Warsaw: PWN, 1976.
Bartoszewicz, Kazimierz. *Księga pamiętkowa setnej rocznicy ustanowienia Konstytucji 3 Maja.* 2 vols. Kraków: Koziomski, 1891.
_____. *Konstytucja 3 maja. Kronika dni kwietniowych i majowych w Warszawie w r. 1791.* Warsaw: Jezierski, 1906.
Beard, Charles. *An Economic Interpretation of the Constitution of the United States.* New York: MacMillan, 1925.
Bobrzyński, Michał. *Dzieje Polski w zarysie.* 3 vols. 4th ed. Warsaw: Gebethner, 1927.
Bogucka, Maria and Henryk Samsonowicz. *Dzieje miast i mieszczaństwa w Polsce przedrozbiorej.* Wrocław: Ossolineum, 1986.
Borucki, Marek. *Sejmy i sejmiki szlacheckie.* Warsaw: Książka i Wiedza, 1972.

Bibliography 311

Brückner, Aleksander. *Dzieje kultury polskiej.* 3 vols. Warsaw: Książka i Wiedza, 1958.
Bystroń, Jan Stanisław. *Dzieje obyczajów w dawnej Polsce, wiek XVI-XVIII.* 2 vols. Warsaw: PIW, 1960.
Cegielski, Tadeusz and Łukasz Kądziela. *Rozbiory Polski 1772-1792- 1795.* Warsaw: Wydawnictwo Szkolne i Pedagogiczne, 1990.
Czaja, Aleksander. *Między tronem, buławą a dworem petersburgskim.* Warsaw: PWN, 1988.
Czapliński, Władysław, ed. *The Polish Parliament at the Summit of Its Development (16th-17th Centuries) Anthologies.* Wrocław: Ossolineum, 1985.
Davies, Norman. *God's Playground: A History of Poland in Two Volumes.* New York: Columbia University Press, 1982.
Dembiński, Bronisław. *Polska na przełomie.* Warsaw: H. Altenberg, 1913.
Dembkowski, Harry E. *The Union of Lublin: Polish Federalism in the Golden Age.* East European Monographs, no. CXVI. Boulder: Columbia University Press, 1982.
Dihm, Jan. *Sprawa konstytucji ekonomicznej z 1791 r. na tle wewnętrznej i zagranicznej sytuacji Polski.* Wrocław: Ossolineum, 1959.
_____. *Trzeci maja.* Kraków: Wydawnictwo Literacko-Naukowe, 1932.
Duzinkiewicz, Janusz. *The Great Reforms and the Civil-Military Administrative Commission for the Palatinate of Kraków (Districts of Kraków and Proszowice).* master's essay. University of Iowa, 1980.
Fabre, Jean. *Stanisław-Auguste Poniatowski et l'Europe des Lumières.* Paris: Institut d'Etudes Slaves, 1952.
Fedorowicz, J. K., Maria Bogucka and Henryk Samsonowicz, eds. *A Republic of Nobles: Studies in Polish History to 1864.* Cambridge, London and New York: Columbia, 1982.
Fiszman, Samuel. ed. *The Polish Renaissance in Its European Context.* Bloomington: Indiana University Press, 1988.
Giergielewicz, Edward. *Atmosfera ideologiczna Sejmu Czteroletniego.* Warsaw: Towarzystwo Naukowe Warszawskie, 1938.
Gierowski, Józef Andrzej. ed. *Historia polski.* 4 vols. Warsaw: PWN, 1984.
_____. *Sejmik generalny księstwa Mazowieckiego na tle ustroju sej-*

mowego Mazowsza. Warsaw: Włocławskie Towarzystwo Naukowe, 1948.
Gieysztor, Aleksander, ed. *History of Poland*. 2nd ed. Warsaw: PWN, 1979.
Gieysztorowa, Irena. *Wstęp do demografii staropolskiej*. Warsaw: Instytut Historii Polskiej Academii Nauk and PWN, 1976.
Gloger, Zygmunt. *Encyklopedia staropolska ilustrowana*. (originally published in 1897), Warsaw: Wiedza Powszechna, 1972.
Góralski, Zbigniew. *Urzędy i godności w dawnej Polsce*. Warsaw: Ludowa Spółdzielnia Wydawnicza, 1983.
Grabski, Andrzej Feliks. *Myśl historyczna polskiego Oświeczenia*. Warsaw: PWN, 1976.
———. *Orientacje polskiej myśli historycznej. Studia i rozważania*. Warsaw: PWN, 1972.
Grynwasser, Hipolit. *Demokracja szlachecka*. 2nd ed. Warsaw: PIW, 1948.
Grzybowski, Konstanty. *Teoria reprezentacji w Polsce w epoce Odrodzenia*. Warsaw: PWN, 1959.
Handelsman, Marceli. *Konstytucja 3go Maja*. Kraków: Drukarnia Narodowa, 1907.
Holdys, Sybill. "Sejm polski i parliament angielski w XVI-XVII wieku. Porównanie procedury." *Przegląd Historyczny* 71 (1980) no. 3: 491-514.
Jasienica, Paweł. *Rzeczpospolita Obojga Narodów*. Warsaw: PWN, 1972.
Jedlicki, Jerzy. *Jakiej cywilizacji polacy potrzebują. Studia z dziejów idei i wyobraźni XIX wieku*. Warsaw: PWN, 1988.
———. *Klejnot i bariery społeczne. Przeobrażenie szlachectwa polskiego w schyłkowym okresie feudalizmu*. Warsaw: PWN, 1968.
Jedruch, Jacek. *Constitutions, Elections and Legislatures of Poland, 1493-1977: A Guide to Their History*. Washington: University Press of America, 1982.
Kądziela, Łukasz. *Kołłątaj i inni. Z publicystyki doby Sejmu Czteroletniego*. Warsaw: Wydawnictwo Szkolne i Pedagogiczne, 1990.
Kalinka, Walerjan. *Ostatnie lata panowania Stanisława Augusta*. Kraków: Księgarnia Spółki Wydawniczej Polskiej, 1891.
———. *Sejm Czteroletni*. 4th ed. 3 vols. Kraków: Księgarnia Spółki Wydawniczej Polskiej, 1895-96.
Kaniewska, Irena. *Małopolska reprezentacja sejmowa 1548-1572*.

Kraków: PWN, 1974.

Kasparek-Obst, Joseph. *The Constitutions of Poland and of the United States: Kinships and Genealogy*. Miami: American Institute of Polish Culture, 1980.

Koenigsberger, Hans. "*Dominium regale or dominium politicum et regale?* Monarchies and parliaments in early modern Europe," in Peter R. Gleichman, ed. *Human Figurations: Essays for Norbert Elias*. Amsterdam: Amsterdams Sociologisch Tijshrift, 1977.

Konczyńska, Wanda. *Rejtan, Korsak i Bohuszewicz na sejmie 1773 roku. Materiały do monografii posła nowogrodzkiego*. Wilno: Konczyńska, 1933.

Konopczyński, Władysław. *Geneza i ustanowienie Rady Nieustającej*. Kraków: Akademia Umiejętności, 1917.

———. *Konfederacja Barska*. Warsaw: Towarzystwo dla Popierania Nauki, 1938.

———. *Liberum veto: studyum porównawczo-historyczne*. Kraków: S. A. Krzyżanowski, 1918.

Korzon, Tadeusz. *Wewnętrzne dzieje Polski za Stanisława Augusta*, 2nd ed. 6 vols., Kraków: Księgarnia Zwolińskiego, 1897-98.

———. *Zamknięcie dziejów wewnętrznych Polski za Stanisław Augusta*. Lwów: Towarzystwo Wydawnicze, 1899.

Kowecki, Jerzy. "*Od klubów do stronnictwa politycznego w Warszawie stanisławowskiej*," in *Rocznik Warszawski* 19 (1987) pp. 43-70.

———. "*Posłowie deputanci na Sejmie Czteroletnim*" in *Wiek XVIII. Polska i świat. Księga poświęcona Bogusławowi Leśnodorskiemu*. Warsaw: PWN, 1974.

———, ed. *Sejm Czteroletni i jego tradycye*. Warsaw: PWN, 1991.

Kraszewski, Józef Ignacy. *Polska w czasie trzech rozbiorów 1772-1799*. 3 vols. Warsaw: Gebethner i Wolff, 1902-1903.

Kukiel, Marian. "*Sprawa Stanisława Augusta*," *Teki Historyczne* 17 (1978-1980): 55-82.

Kutrzeba, Stanisław. *Historya ustroju polskiego w zarysie*. 5th ed. 2 vols. Lwów: Księgarnia Polska Bednarda Połonieckiego, 1920.

———. *Konstytucja 3go Maja 1791r*. Kraków: Głos Narodu, 1915.

———. *Sejm walny dawnej Rzeczpospolitej Polskiej*. Warsaw: Polska Składnica Pomocy Skolnej, n.d.

Łaszewski, Ryszard. *Instrukty poselskie w drógiej połowie XVIII wieku*. Toruń: Uniwersytet im. Mikołaja Kopernika, 1973.

———. *Sejm Polski w latach 1764-93: Studium historyczno-prawne*.

Warszawa-Poznań: Towarzystwo Naukowe w Toruniu, 1973.
———. *Sejmiki przedsejmowe w Polsce stanisławowskiej. Problemy organizacji i porządek obrad.* Toruń: Uniwersytet im. Mikołaja Kopernika, 1977.
Lelewel, Joachim. *Dzieje Polski potocznym sposobem opowiedziane.* Warsaw: Drukarnia Weckiego, 1829.
Leskiewicz, Janina, ed. *Ziemiaństwo polskie 1795-1945: Zbiór prac o dziejach warstwy i ludzi.* Warsaw: PWN, 1985.
Leśnodorski, Bogusław. *Dzieło Sejmu Czteroletniego 1788-1792: Studium historyczno-prawne.* Wrocław: Ossolineum, 1951.
———, ed. *Polska w epoce Oświecenia: państwo, społeczeństwo, kultura.* Warsaw: Wiedza Powszechna, 1971.
Lewis-Beck, Michael S., Anne Hildreth, and Alan B. Spitzer. "Was There a Girondist Faction in the National Convention, 1792-1793?" *French Historical Studies.* (and discussion) 15 (1987): 519-548.
Łojek, Jerzy. *Upadek Konstytucji 3go maja.* Wrocław: Ossolineum, 1976.
———. *Geneza i obalenie Konstytucji 3 Maja. Polityka zagraniczna Rzeczypospolitej 1787-1792.* Lublin: Wydawnictwo Lubelskie, 1986.
———. *Rok nadzieji, rok klęski 1791-1792.* Warsaw: Czytelnik, 1964.
Lorence-Kot, Bogna. *Child-Rearing and Reform: A Study of the Nobility in Eighteenth-Century Poland.* Westport, Conn.: Greenwood Press, 1985.
Łowmiański, Henryk. *Studia nad dziejami Wielkiego Księstwa Litewskiego.* Poznań: Uniwersytet im. Adama Mickiewicza, 1983.
Mackiewicz, Stanisław. *Stanisław August.* Warsaw: Pax, 1956.
Maciszewski, Jarema. *Szlachta polska i jej państwo.* Warsaw: Wiedza Powszechna, 1969.
Mączak, Antoni. "Polish Society and Power System in the Renaissance" in Samuel Fiszman, ed. *The Polish Renaissance in Its European Context.* Bloomington and Indianapolis: Indiana University Press, 1988.
McDonald, Forrest. *We the People: The Economic Origins of the Constitution.* Chicago: University of Chicago, 1958.
Michalski, Jerzy. *Rousseau i sarmacki republikanizm.* Warsaw: PWN, 1977.
———. "Sejmiki poselskie 1788 roku," *Przegląd Historyczny* 51 (1960)

no. 1: 52-73; no. 2: 331-367; no. 3: 465-482.

———, ed. *Historia Sejmu Polskiego*. 2 vols. Warsaw: PWN, 1984.

Mikulski, Tadeusz. *Ze studiów nad Oświeceniem. Zagadnienia i fakty*. Warsaw: PIW, 1956.

Mrozowska, Kamilla. *Szkoła Rycerska Stanisława Augusta Poniatowskiego*. Wrocław: Ossolineum, 1961.

Nanke, Czesław. *Szlachta wołyńska wobec Konstytucyi 3 Maja*. Lwów: Towarzystwo dla Popierania Nauki Polskiej, 1907.

Olszewski, Henryk. *Sejm Rzeczypospolitej epoki oligarchii 1652-1763: Prawo-praktyka-teoria-programy*. Poznań: PWN, 1966.

Palmer, R. R. *The Age of the Democratic Revolution: A Political History of Europe and America, 1760-1800*. 2 vols. Princeton: Princeton University Press, 1959.

Pawiński, Adam. *Rządy sejmikowe w Polsce 1572-1795 na tle stosunków województw kujawskich*. 2nd. ed. introduction by Henryk Olszewski. *Klasycy Historiografii Polskiej*. Marian Henryk Serejski and Andrzej Feliks Grabski, eds. Warsaw: PIW, 1978.

Pelenski, Jaroslaw. "The Contest Between Lithuania-Rus' and the Golden Horde in the Fourteenth Century for Supremacy over Eastern Europe" in *Archivum Eurasiae Medii Aevi*. II Wiesbaden: Otto Harrasowitz, 1982.

———. "The Incorporation of the Ukrainian Lands of Old Rus' into Crown Poland (1569). (Socio-Material Interest and Ideology – A Reexamination)" in *American Contributions to the Seventh International Congress of Slavists (Warsaw, August 21-27, 1973)*, Anna Cienciala, ed., Vol. 3: *History*. The Hague: Mouton, 1973.

———. "Muscovite Russia and Poland Lithuania, 1450-1600: State and Society – Some Comparisons in Socio-political Developments" in *State and Society in Europe from the Fifteenth to the Eighteenth Century*. Warsaw: Warsaw University Press, 1985.

———. "Poland-Lithuania (1454-1573): Nobility Democracy or Tripartite Mixed Government?" an unpublished paper presented at the Third Conference of Polish and American Historians held in Poznań, Poland, 28 May - 2 June 1979.

Piekosiński, Franciszek. *Wiece, sejmiki, sejmy i przywileje ziemskie w Polsce wieków średnich. Rozprawa Wydziału Historycznofilozoficzne Akademii Umiejętności*. Vol. 30. Kraków: Akademia Umiejętności, 1900.

Piłat, Roman, *O literaturze Sejmu Czteroletniego (1788-1792)*, Kraków: Paszkowski, 1876.

Radwański, Zbigniew. *Prawa kardinalne w Polsce*. "Studia nad historią prawa polskim" Zygmunt Wojciechowski, ed., Vol. 21 no. 1. Poznań: Towarzystwo Przyjaciół Nauk, 1952.

Ratajczyk, Leonard. *Military Techniques, Policy and Strategy in History*. Warsaw: PWN, 1976.

———. *Wojsko i obronność Rzeczypospolitej, 1788-1792*. Warsaw: Ministerstwo Obrony Narodowej, 1975.

Reddaway, W. F., J. H. Penson, O. Halecki, and R. Dyboski. *The Cambridge History of Poland*. 2 vols. New York: Octogon, 1978.

Rostworowski, Emanuel. *Legendy i fakty XVIII wieku*. Warsaw: PWN, 1963.

———. *Ostatni król Rzeczypospolitej: Geneza i upadek Konstytucji 3 maja*. Warsaw: Wiedza Powszechna, 1966.

———. *Sprawa aukcji wojska na tle sytuacji politycznej przed Sejmem Czteroletnim*. Warsaw: PWN, 1957.

Rutkowski, Jan. *Historia gospodarcza Polski do 1864 r.* Warsaw: Książka i Wiedza, 1953.

Rybarski, Ryszard. *Skarbowość Polski w dobie rozbiorów*. Kraków: Polska Akademia Umiejętności, 1937.

Rychlikowa, Irena. *Ziemiaństwo polskie 1789-1864. Źróźnicowanie społeczne. Polska XIX i XX wieku: dzieje społeczne*. Stanisław Kalabiński, ed. Warsaw: PWN, 1983.

Rymszyna, Maria. *Gabinet Stanisława Augusta*. Warsaw: PWN, 1962.

Schmitt, Henryk. *Dzieje panowania Stanisława Augusta Poniatowskiego*. 3 vols., Lwów: Drukarnia Manieckiego, 1868.

Serejski. Marian Henryk. *Europa a rozbiory Polski. Studium historiograficzne*. Warsaw: PWN, 1970.

Sidorski, Dionizy. "*Panie Kochanku*." Katowice: Śląsk, 1987.

Siemiański, Józef. *Organizacja sejmiku ziemi dobrzyńskiej*. Kraków: 1906. Akademia Umiejętności, 1906.

Skałkowski, Adam. *Towarzystwo Przyjaciół Konstytucji 3 Maja.* "*Pamiętnik Biblioteki Kornickiej*" Series. no. 2. Kórniki, 1930.

Smoleński, Władysław. *Jan Dekert, prezydent starej Warszawy i sprawa miejska podczas Sejmu Wielkiego*. Warsaw: Towarzystwo Miłośników Historii, 1912.

———. *Komisya bonis ordinis warszawska, 1765-89*. Warsaw: Towarzystwo Miłośników Historii, 1913.

_____. *Kuźnia Kołłątajowska. Studium historyczne.* Kraków: Gebethner, 1885; Warsaw: PIW, 1949.

_____. *Ostatni rok Sejmu Wielkiego.* 2nd ed. Kraków: Gebethner, 1897.

_____. *Przewrót umysłowy w Polsce wieku XVIII.* 3rd. ed. Poznań: PIW, 1949.

Śreniowski, Stanisław. *Organizacja sejmiku halickiego.* Lwów: Towarzystwo Naukowe, 1938.

Starzyński, Stanisław. *Konstytucja 3 Maja na tle współczesnego ustroju innych państw europejskich.* Lwów: n.p., 1903.

Stone, Daniel. *Polish Politics and National Reform.* New York: Columbia University Press, 1976.

Stroynowski, Andrzej, *Pozycja społeczna drobnej szlachty Wielkiego Xięstwa Litewskiego w końcu XVIII w.* Zeszyty Naukowe Uniwersytetu Łódźkiego Nauki Humanistyczno-Społeczne. Series 1: 24. Łódź: Uniwersytet Łódźki, 1976.

Tazbir, Janusz. *Kultura szlachecka w Polsce. Rozkwit, upadek, relikty.* Seria Omega. 2nd. ed. Warsaw: Wiedza Powszechna, 1979.

_____, ed. *Polska XVIII wieku: państwo, społeczeństwo, kultura.* Warsaw: Wiedza Powszechna, 1969.

Topolski, Jerzy. "Economic Decline in Poland from the Sixteenth to the Eighteenth Centuries" in *Essays in European Economic History 1500–1800*, Peter Earle, ed. Oxford: Clarendon Press, 1974.

Voise, Waldemar. "Polish Renaissance Political Theory: Andrzej Frycz Modrzewski" in *The Polish Renaissance in Its European Context*, Samuel Fiszman, ed. Bloomington and Indianapolis: Indiana University Press, 1988.

Wagner, Wenceslas J. "Justice for All: Polish Democracy in the Renaissance Period in Historical Perspective" in *The Polish Renaissance in Its European Context*, Samuel Fiszman, ed. Bloomington and Indianapolis: Indiana University Press, 1988.

_____, ed. *Polish Law Throughout the Ages.* Stanford: Hoover Institute Press, 1980.

Walicki, Andrzej. *Philosophy and Romantic Nationalism: The Case of Poland.* Oxford: Clarendon Press, 1982.

_____. "The Political Heritage of the 16th Century and Its Influence on the Nation-building Ideologies of the Polish Enlightenment and Romanticism" in *The Polish Renaissance in Its European*

Context, Samuel Fiszman, ed. Bloomington and Indianapolis: Indiana University Press, 1988.
Wasylewski, Stanisław. *Na dworze króla Stasia*. 3rd ed. Poznań: E. Wegner, 1931.
Wegner, Leon. *Dzieje dnia 3 i 5 maja 1791*. Poznań: Towarzystwo Przyjaciół Nauk Poznańskiego, 1865.
Wojakowski, Józef. *Straż Praw*. Warsaw: Uniwersytet Warszawski, 1982.
Wolff, Larry. *The Vatican and Poland in the Age of the Partitions: Diplomatic and Cultural Encounters at the Warsaw Nunciature*. East European Monographs, no. CCXLV. Boulder: Columbia University Press, 1988.
Wyczański, Andrzej. *Uwarstwienie społeczne w Polsce XVI wieku*. Wrocław: Ossolineum, 1977.
Zahorski, Andrzej. *Centralne instytucje policyjne w Polsce w dobie rozbiorów*. Warsaw: PIW, 1959.
———. *Ignacy Wyssogota Zakrzewski, prezydent Warszawy*. Warsaw: PWN, 1963.
———. *Spór o Stanisława Augusta*. Warsaw: PIW, 1988.
———. *Stanisław August polityk*. Warsaw: Książka i Wiedza, 1966.
Zajączkowski, Andrzej. *Główne elementy kultury szlacheckiej w Polsce. Ideologia a struktury społeczne*. Wrocław-Warsaw-Kraków: Ossolineum, 1961.
Zamoyski, Adam. *The Polish Way. A Thousand Year History of the Poles and Their Culture*. London: John Murray, 1987.
Zielińska, Teresa. *Magnateria polska epoki saskiej. Funkcje urzędów i królewszczyzn w procesie przeobrażeń warstwy społecznej*. Wrocław: Ossolineum, 1977.
Zielińska, Zofia. "Stanisław August, Konstytucja i Targowica" in *Przegląd Historyczny*, 69 (1978) no. 2: 317–336.
Zieńkowska, Krystyna. *Jacek Jezierski kasztelan łukowski (1722–1805). Z dziejów szlachty polskiej XVIII w*. Warsaw: PWN, 1963.
———. *Jan Dekert*. Warsaw, 1982.
Zmuidzinas, Jonas. *Commonwealth polono-lithuanien ou l'Union de Lublin (1569)*. Paris: Mouton, 1978.
Żółtowska, Maria Ewelina. "Epilog działalności politycznej Jana Potockiego: Artykuły w "Journal hebdomadaire de la Diète z 1792 r" in *Przegląd Historyczny* 70 (1979) no. 3: 499–518.

INDEX

absolutism, 4, 5, 14-15, 25-26, 29-30, 69, 78, 86, 231, 255, 258, 260, 263, 264, 265
absolutum dominium, 25-26, 60, 78, 255-256
Act of Confederation (1788), 13, 102, 106, 107-108, 112, 150-151
"age of the democratic revolution," 1, 8
Ajnenkiel, Andrzej, 272
Aksak, Kajetan (deputy from Wołyń) 192, 193, 202
aristocracy, 216
Armenian Church, 269
Army Commission, 14, 44, 49, 52, 53, 72, 79, 81, 82, 83, 85, 98, 104, 107, 122, 123, 130, 143, 151, 280, 289
Army Department, 122, 151, 153, 231, 284, 289
assessorya, 66, 142, 287
Athens, 260, 264
attendance at the Four Years' Sejm, 144-149, 159-160, 161
Austria, 4, 6, 152, 163, 174, 177, 193, 194

Balzer, Oswald, 8, 30, 31, 270, 271, 288
Bardach, Juliusz, 31, 267, 268, 269, 270, 271, 276, 277,

Batory, Stefan (king), 24, 32
Batowski, Alexander (deputy from Livonia) 202, 238
Beard, Charles, 8
Bełz, 134, 153, 154, 219, 220, 233
Białocerkiew, 232
Biecz, castellan of, 110
Bniński, Łukasz (deputy from Poznań) 203
Bobrzyński, Michał, 279
Bohemia, 30
Borch, Józef Kajetan (deputy from Livonia), 202
Boreyko, Pius Franciszek (deputy from Podole), 194
bourgeoisie, 3, 5, 50, 67, 69, 213, 214
  ideology, 70, 263
  (See also towns and townspeople)
Braclaw, 125, 141, 164, 191, 198, 219, 220
Branicki, Franciszek Ksawery (hetman), 100, 232, 240
Brasław, 133, 139
Breza, Stanisław (deputy from Gniezno), 202
Bronikowski, Adam, (deputy from Gniezno), 167, 202
Brückner, Aleksander, 268, 270

Brześć Kujawski, 191, 219, 220
Brześć Litewski, 124, 166, 176, 191, 192, 195, 197, 219, 220, 227, 246, 250, 29
Brzostowski, Michał (deputy from Troki), 131, 202
Buda, privileges of, 19-22
Burke, Edmund, 2, 88, 93, 254-255, 257, 260, 265, 267, 280, 282, 294
Butrymowicz, Mateusz (deputy from Brześć Litewski), 173, 195, 203, 236
Byelarus, 68, 190, 196, 197
Black Rus', 190
Byszewski, 238, 241

Calvinists, 167
cardinal laws, 49, 55-60, 86, 96, 132, 136, 277
Carolingian Empire, 26
Catherine II, 151, 176, 231
Chełm, 123, 133, 135, 153, 164, 191, 219, 220, 235
Chełmno, 219
Chi-square, 189, 190, 212
Chmielewski, Antoni, 284
Choiecki, Jan Nepomucin (deputy from Kijów), 203
Cholewski, Fabian (deputy from Mazowsze), 237
Chołoniewski, Ignacy (deputy from Bracław), 125, 203, 235
Chrapowicki, Antoni (deputy from Smoleńsk), 195, 234
Chreptowicz, Adam (deputy from Nowogródek), 202, 238, 241
Chreptowicz, Joachim (Vice-chancellor of the Grand Duchy of Lithuania), 275
Cienciala, Anna, 269
civic humanism, 64
civil-military administrative commissions, 52, 53, 60, 75, 76, 82, 83, 85, 111, 223, 280
clergy, 14, 27
anticlericism, 168
cluster analysis, 232, 251
Collegium Nobilium, 166-167, 196, 198, 208, 209, 238, 243, 244, 245, 246, 252
Commissions (national), 79, 81, 82, 83, 85, 258, 279-280 (See also individual commissions: Army, National Education, Police and Treasury)
Committee for Foreign Affairs, 130
Confederation of Bar, 93, 163, 176, 177, 178, 179, 184, 189, 192, 193, 194, 195, 196, 197, 199, 210, 211, 212, 217, 228, 239, 243, 247, 250, 251, 252, 261, 263
Confederation of Targowica, 48-49, 89, 111, 154, 163, 186, 189, 192, 193, 194, 195, 196, 197, 200, 208, 209, 232, 239, 243, 247, 249, 255, 256, 266, 299,
Confederation of Warsaw (1573), 22
Congress Kingdom, 163, 208, 243, 247, 293
consensus, measurement of, 155-158, 179

Index

constitutional laws, 46, 47, 48, 49, 57, 59, 60
constitutionalism, 1, 4, 7, 10, 11, 12, 40, 255, 263, 266
corona regni poloniae, 15, 16, 21, 29
Courland, 59, 144, 154
Czacki, Michał (deputy from Czerniechów), 193, 194, 202, 235
Czapliński, Władysław, 269, 281
Czartoryski family, 37, 55, 94
Czartoryski, Prince Adam (deputy from Lublin), 175, 204, 236
Czartoryski, Prince Józef Klemens (deputy from Wołyń), 193, 203
Czerniechów (Chernihiv), 141, 142, 164, 191, 193, 194, 198, 220, 227, 250
Czerwińsk, privileges, 19, 277
Czetwertyński, Prince Antoni Jan Nepomucin (deputy from Bracław; senator), 203, 235
Czyż, Gaspar (deputy from Wilno), 203

Dąmbski, Stanisław (deputy from Brześć Kujawski [elected 1788]), 204
Dąmbski, Stanisław (deputy from Brześć Kujawski [elected 1790]), 202
Davies, Norman, 267, 268, 270
Deklaracyja Stanów Zgromodzonych, 41, 44-45, 47-51, 101
Deklaracja względem manifestów, 101
Deklaracja względem osób woyskowych nieprzysiąglych, 101, 241, 299
Dembiński, Ignacy (deputy from Kraków), 167, 202
democracy, 254, 256, 260, 263, 265, 266
democracy of the nobility (*demokracja szlachecka*), 31-38, 54, 62, 87-88
Department of Foreign Affairs, 97
dezyderja, 66, 75, 77, 106, 113, 114
Dihm, Jan, 8, 280, 292-293
Długosz, 269
Dłuski, Tadeusz, (deputy from Lublin), 165, 173, 204, 234
Dmochowski, Franciszek, 3, 267, 280
Dobrzyń, 143, 175, 220
Duchy of Warsaw, 163, 189, 208, 243, 247, 255, 293, 295
Dyaryusz krótko zebrany..., 121
Dyaryusz Sejmu ordynaryinego..., 121
dyzunici, 22, 144, 270
Działyński, Ignacy (deputy from Inowrocław), 135, 202, 238
Działyński, Ksawery (deputy from Poznań), 202, 236, 238, 275
Dziennik czynności Sejmu Głównego..., 100, 121

economic determinism, 8
Elias, Herbert 27-28, 30
Engels, Friedrich, 271
England, 2, 26-27, 29-30, 255, 257 Parliament, 18, 257
Enlightenment, 1, 5, 37, 64, 68,

70-71, 88, 211, 213, 217, 258, 263
Estreicher, Stanisław, 34
Eydziatowicz, Dominik (deputy from Smoleńsk), 195, 234, 238, 240, 298

Fabre, Jean, 267
France, 1, 2, 6, 29, 66, 69, 89, 161, 163, 174, 194, 264
 cahiers de doléance, 66, 164
 constitution of 1791, 69, 214
 Declaration of the Rights of Man and the Citizen, 217
 French Revolution, 5, 78, 255, 263, 294
Freemasonry, 163, 173, 174, 178, 187, 239, 244, 245, 246, 248, 252, 253

Gadomski, Stanislaw, 285
Gaiewski, Jan Nepomucin (deputy from Łęczyca), 234
Gazeta Warszawska, 122
Gdańsk, 220, 291
Gedymin, 16
Germans and Germany, 9, 68
 East Elbian lands, 26
Gierowski, Józef, 37, 93, 281
Gieysztor, Aleksander, 270
Gieysztor, Dominik (deputy from Troki), 202
Glinka, Mikołaj (deputy from Mazowsze [Różan]), 202
Gliszczyński, Antoni (deputy from Poznań), 202
Gloger, Zygmunt, 281, 288
Gniezno, 135, 138, 167, 191, 219, 220
Godlewski, Antoni Gazdawa (deputy from Mazowsze [Nur]), 237
"golden freedoms," 33, 36, 93, 98, 161, 232
Góralski, Zbigniew, 270
Górski, Stanisław Antoni (deputy from Poznań), 236
Gorzeński, August (deputy from Poznań), 236, 238
Gostyniń, 175
Grabowski, Paweł (deputy from Nowogródek), 167, 202, 236
Grabowski, Zygmunt (deputy from Nowogródek), 167
Grocholski, Franciszek (deputy from Bracław), 204, 236
Grzymała, Wojciech, 296
Gutakowski, Ludwik (deputy from Płock), 203, 236, 238, 241

habias corpus, 20, 59
Halicz (Halič), 21, 22, 220
Henri Valois, 24, 61, 257
Henrician Articles, 23-25, 55, 88, 176, 257
Hinze, Otto, 26-30, 38
Hobbes, Thomas, 257
Holy Roman Empire, 93
Horodło, union of, 21
Hulewicz, Benedict (deputy from Wołyń), 193, 203
Hulewicz, Stanisław Kostka (deputy from Wołyń), 193
Hungary, 26, 30
Husitism, 18, 20, 262

Iliński, Janusz Stanisław (deputy from Kijów), 202
Iliński, Józef August (deputy from Kijów), 202
Inowrocław, 110, 175, 191, 219,

220
instrukcje, 73, 77
Istanbul, 235
Italy, 26
Jabłonowski, Prince Stanisław Paweł (deputy from Wołyń), 202, 236
Jadwiga (queen), 24
Jagiełło, Władysław (king), 16, 24
Jagiellonka, Anna, 24
Janikowski, Konstanty (deputy from Łęczyca), 192
Jaroszyński, Mikołaj (deputy from Bracław), 203
Jaruzelski, Wojciech, 7
Jasieński, Mikołaj (deputy from Sandomierz), 204
Jedlno, privileges, 19, 277
Jelski, Konstanty (deputy from Smoleńsk), 195, 203
Jerzmanowski, Franciszek (deputy from Łęczyca), 192, 203, 234
Jesuits, 28, 36, 165-167, 178, 179, 180, 181, 185, 187, 193, 194, 195, 196, 197, 198, 208, 209, 227, 244, 243, 245, 246, 250, 252
Jews, 19, 68, 81, 260
Jezierski, Jacek (castellan of Luków), 168
Jezierski, Karol (deputy from Mazowsze [Czersk]), 202
Jordan, Jan (deputy from Kraków), 137, 146, 235
Józofowicz, Hlehicki Wincenty (deputy from Płock), 236
Kaczanowski, Grzegorz Nałęcz (deputy from Livonia), 202, 238, 241
Kaczmarek, Zbigniew, 32, 271, 272, 279
Kądziela, Łukasz, 279
Kalendarz polityczny dla królestwa Polskiego i wielkiego Księstwa Litewskiego, 225
Kalendarzyk narodowy i obcy, 122
Kalinka, Waleryan, 6, 56, 279
Kalisz, 125, 127, 130, 131, 132, 136, 152, 191, 219, 220
Kaniów, 231
Karp, Antoni (deputy from Sandomierz), 204
Karp, Maurycy Franciszek (deputy from Żmudź), 203
Karski, Antoni (deputy from Sandomierz), 197, 203
Karski, Kazimierz (deputy from Sandomierz), 197, 203
Karski, Michał (deputy from Mazowsze), 176, 204
Karwicki, Stanisław Dunin, 37
Karwicki, Jan Nepomucin Dunin (dep- uty from Sandomierz), 197, 202
Karwicki, Krzysztof Dunin (deputy from Wołyń), 202, 235
Kazimierz Wielki (king), 18, 21, 29, 30, 43, 50, 61, 213, 270
Kazimierz, Jagiellończyk, 17
Khmelnytsky Uprising, 22, 256
Kiciński, Pius Rogala (deputy from Mazowsze), 202, 215, 219, 223
Kicki, August (deputy from Rus'), 202, 236

Kicki, Onufry (deputy from Mazowsze [Zakroczym]), 203
Kiełczewski, Józef (deputy from Kalisz), 203
Kyyiv (Kiev) city, 231
Kijów (Kyyiv) voivodeship, 164, 191, 198, 219, 220
Kiszynów, 127
Kochanowski, Michał (deputy from Sandomierz), 197, 202
Kocieł, Józef (deputy from Wilno), 196, 202
Koenigsberger, Hans 26-28, 30, 270
Kohn, Hans, 25, 263
Kołłątaj, Hugo, 3, 214, 262, 265, 267, 293
Kommissaryat, 129, 233, 234
Komorowski, Wincenty (deputy from Rus'), 202
Konarski, Stanisław, 37, 166
Konczyńska, Wanda, 282
Konopczyński, Władysław, 217, 270, 281, 282
Korsak, Tadeusz (deputy from Wilno), 61-62, 196, 203, 277, 278
Korzon, Tadeusz, 277
Kościalkowski, Tadeusz (deputy from Wilno), 163, 186, 196, 203, 236
Kościuszko Uprising, 6, 89, 163, 189, 192, 193, 194, 195, 196, 197, 200, 208, 209, 243, 247163, 186, 255, 256, 263, 264, 265
Kosecki, Stanisław (deputy from Podole), 194
Kossakowski, Antoni Korwin (deputy from Troki), 204

Kossakowski, Józef (bishop of Livonia), 48, 275
Kossakowski, Józef Dominik (deputy from Wilno), 164-165, 197, 202
Kossakowski, Michał (deputy from Troki), 202
Kossakowski family, 226
Kossowski, Roch (Crown Under-Treasurer), 275
Koszyce (Košice), privileges of (1373), 17, 19, 21, 22, 31, 32
Kowecki, Jerzy, 9, 272, 278, 289
Kowel, 130l, 233
Kraków, 137, 138, 139, 143, 147, 153, 154, 163, 166, 167, 170, 176, 191, 197, 219, 270, 278
bishops of, 126
privileges of, 19, 277
Krasicki, count Stanisław (deputy from Czerniechów), 236
Krasinski, Bishop, 59, 275
Kretkowski, Felix (deputy from Łęczyca), 192, 202
Krewo, union of (1385), 20, 21
Krzucki, Ignacy (deputy from Wołyń), 192, 193, 203, 288-289
Kublicki, Stanisław (deputy from Livonia), 203, 236, 238
Kuczyński, Ignacy Szymon (deputy from Podlasie), 203
Kuczyński, Wiktoryn (deputy from Podlasie), 204
Kurdwanowski, Kajetan (deputy from Czerniechow), 193
Kutrzeba, Stanisław, 31, 268-

269, 270, 279
Kwilecki, Franciszek Antoni (deputy from Poznań), 100, 204, 236, 284-285

Lasocki, Roch (deputy from Rawa), 203
Law on Constitutional Sejmy, 51
Law on Noble Courts, 52
Law on Sejm Courts, 52
Law on Sejmiki, 43, 45, 51, 62, 63, 76-77, 153
Law on Sejmy, 45, 46, 51, 102, 112, 117, 139, 287, 289
Law on Towns, 41, 43, 45, 46, 48, 50, 51, 64, 66
Łęczyca, 140, 191, 192, 194, 198, 220, 227, 250, 291
Ledóchowski, Antoni (deputy from Czerniechów), 193, 194, 203
legitis curiatae, 102, 108, 110, 118, 196
Lelewel, Joachim, 31-32, 270-271, 288
Lemnicki, Kazimierz (deputy from Lublin), 203, 238
Leśnodorski, Bogusław, 6, 8, 10, 31, 213, 267, 272, 278-279, 294-295
Leszczyński, Dezyderyusz (deputy from Inowrocław), 110, 236
Leszczyński, Stanisław (king), 37
Leżeński, Marcin (deputy from Smolensk), 238
liberalism, 5, 60, 64, 68, 69, 259, 265

liberum veto, 33, 55, 59, 71, 92-95, 98-99, 105-106, 111, 257, 281, 282, 284
Lidz, 196
Linde, Bogusław, 268
Linowski, Aleksander (deputy from Kraków), 202, 238
Lipski, Jan (deputy from Poznań), 203
Livonia, 135, 137, 143, 153, 163-164, 165-167, 168, 172, 173, 174, 175, 176, 177, 179, 180, 187, 188, 190, 191, 193, 209, 212, 219, 220, 227, 239, 242, 243, 245, 246, 249, 252, 253, 262
Locke, John, 257
Łojek, Jerzy, 7, 272, 278, 279
Łokietek, Władysław (king), 18, 29
Łowmiański, Henryk, 20, 268, 269
Lubieński, Feliks Franciszek (deputy from Sieradz), 202
Lublin, 124, 126, 140, 164, 165, 173, 175, 191, 219, 220, 235
Łuck, 219
Ludwig, (king), 17
Łuszczewski, Jan Paweł (deputy from Rawa), 202, 281
Lutherans, 167
Lwów (Lviv), 220, 270

Maciszewski, Jarema, 32, 36, 271
Mączyński, Wojciech (deputy from Wieluń), 202
Madaliński, Antoni (deputy from Gniezno), 203

majority principle, 14, 71, 91-94, 97-102, 107-108, 113, 117-118
Małachowski, Jan (deputy from Sandomierz), 197, 202
Małachowski, Józef (deputy from Kraków), 203
Małachowski, Stanisław, (deputy from Sandomierz and Sejm marshal [Crown]), 48, 91, 103, 107, 110, 135, 138, 139, 142, 143, 175, 176, 197, 204, 233, 234, 235, 236, 237, 238, 239, 240, 241, 252, 261
Malbork, 219
Malta, Order of, 134, 147, 233
Marx, Karl, 2-3
Marxism, 6,
Marxism-Leninism, 3, 7
marxists, 212
"Marshals' Group," 262, 299-300
materiae aeconomica, 96-99, 105, 113, 118, 119
materiae status, 96, 99, 105, 113, 118
Matuszewic, Tadeusz Wiktoryn (deputy from Brześć Litewski), 195, 202
Mazowsze, 72, 163, 176, 190, 191, 219, 220, 246, 290
McDonald, Forrest, 8
Mężeński, Józef (deputy from Sandomierz), 197
Miączyński, Kajetan (deputy from Czerniechów), 193, 194, 203
Michałowski, Antoni (deputy from Kraków), 176

Michalski, Jerzy, 272
Mickiewicz, Adam, 254-255, 260, 262, 281
Miełzyński, Franciszek (deputy from Poznań), 202
Miełzyński, Maksimilian (deputy from Poznań), 203
Mierzejewski, Józef (deputy from Podole), 100, 194, 202, 240
Mikorski, Franciszek Ksawery (deputy from Kalisz), 125, 131, 132, 152, 235
Mikorski, Józef (deputy from Rawa), 175, 176
Mińsk, 191, 219, 220
Mirski, Bogusław (deputy from Wilno), 196
Mirski, Stanisław (deputy from Wilno), 196, 203
Modrzewski, Andrzej Frycz, 35, 87
Mokronoski, Stanisław (deputy from Mazowsze), 202
Montesquieu, 87
Morawski, Mikołaj (deputy from Mińsk), 203, 236
More, Thomas, 109
Morikoni (Morykoni) Ignacy (deputy from Wilno [Wilkomierz]), 236
Morski, Adam (deputy from Lublin), 167
Morski, Onufry (deputy from Podole), 194, 203
Mostowski, Józef (deputy from Livonia), 202
Moszczeński, Adam Nałęcz (deputy from Poznań), 176, 203
Moszyński, Fryderyk (deputy

from Bracław), 122, 203, 236, 275
Mozyr, 224
Mscisław, 219
Mutual Assurance for Both Nations, 71-72

Nakwaski, Cyprian (deputy from Łęczyca), 192, 203
Nanke, Czesław, 9, 246, 292
Napoleon I, 255
Narbutt, Dominik (deputy from Wilno), 196
Narbutt, Wojciech (deputy from Wilno), 196, 202
nation, 82, 84, 85, 161, 214, 231, 232
  concept of, 1, 5, 68, 69, 86, 266
  definition of, 70, 259
National Education Commission, 14, 42, 44, 49, 52, 53, 79, 81-83, 98, 104, 165-167, 185, 208, 209, 279-280
national sovereignty, 4, 5, 20, 70, 73, 78, 85, 112
  concept of, 58, 69
national will, 53, 64, 76, 78, 86, 112
nec bona recipiantur, 19-21, 64-65, 257, 259
neminem captivabimus, 19-21, 33, 59, 64-65, 257, 277
Niechworów, 139, 153
Niemcewicz, Julian Ursyn (deputy from Livonia [Lithuania]), 143, 154, 167, 202, 238
Niemcewicz, Stanisław Ursyn (deputy from Brześć Litewski), 195, 203, 238
Nieszawa, statutes of (1452), 18-20, 32
nihil novi, 18, 23, 32, 54, 60-61, 259
nobility, 5, 8-11, 14-15, 17-28, 30, 32-36, 38, 40, 42, 61-66, 68-70, 77, 84, 87, 90, 97, 99, 104, 151, 167, 168, 171, 172, 173, 176, 178, 180, 185, 186, 187, 214, 258, 263, 276-277
  disenfranchised, 63-64, 213
  foreign, 6
  fusion with townspeople, 66
  hereditary, 62
  landed, 63, 65, 77, 283-284
  landless, 33, 38, 61-62, 65, 100, 259, 260
  lower, 214, 215
  magnates, 5, 8, 10, 20, 24, 27-28, 31-36, 55, 63, 69, 87, 88, 155, 171, 172, 173, 178, 179, 180, 182, 184, 185, 186, 187, 189, 192, 193, 194, 195, 197, 200, 209, 212, 214, 215, 216, 218, 219, 221, 223, 228, 231, 239, 243, 244, 245, 248, 249, 250, 252, 255, 256, 258, 260, 261, 271
  middle, 8, 33, 36, 171, 172, 173, 178, 179, 182, 184, 185, 187, 189, 196, 197, 200, 208, 209, 212, 214, 215, 217, 224, 239, 243, 244, 245, 248, 262
  poor, 69, 171, 172, 173, 178, 179, 180, 182, 184, 185, 192, 193, 196, 200, 209,

213, 214, 239, 243, 244, 245, 246, 248, 250
possessionaci, 171
privileges, 17-25, 43, 50, 51, 61-65, 88
propertied, 65, 73
small, 217
szaraczkowie, 171
upper middle, 173
wealthy, 171, 172, 173, 178, 179, 182, 184, 185, 187, 188, 189, 193, 194, 195, 196, 197, 200, 208, 209, 212, 214, 224, 227, 228, 239, 243, 244, 245, 246, 248, 249, 250, 251, 252
zagrodowa, 171
ziemianie, 171
noble courts, 53
Nowogródek, 191, 219, 220
Nowowieyski, Tomasz (deputy from Mazowsze), 48
Nozarzewski, Jan Dołęga (deputy from Mazowsze), 203
Nur, 136, 141

O ustanowieniu i upadku konstytucji polskiej 3 maja 1791 roku, 89
Oborski, Onufry (deputy from Mazowsze), 203, 235, 237
ofiara dziesiątego grosza, 9, 62, 125, 136, 170
Olędzki, Stanisław (deputy from Żmudź), 202
oligarchy, 26, 30-32, 35-36, 230, 256, 258, 259, 260, 264
Olizar, Józef Kalasanty (deputy from Wołyń), 193
Orders (national awards), 192, 209, 228, 247, 249, 250
Order of St. Stanisław, 168, 169, 170, 178, 182, 184, 192, 193, 194, 200
Order of the White Eagle, 168, 169, 170, 182, 184, 193, 200
Organization of Municipal Courts and Appeals Courts, 52
Orłowski, Jan Onufry (deputy from Podole), 194
Orthodoxy and the Orthodox, 22, 68. 167, 270
deputies, 22
Orzechowski, Stanisław, 35
Oskierko, Jan (deputy from Mińsk), 204
Oskierko family, 224
Ośniałowski, Jan (deputy from Inowrocław), 135, 175-176, 204, 238
Ossoliński, Jan (deputy from Podlasie), 167, 195, 202
Ossoliński, Józef (deputy from Podlasie), 167, 195, 202
Ostrzeżenie względem ezekucji prawa o miastach Naszych, dawniej królewskich, a teraz wolnych Rzeczypospolitej, 50, 51
Oszmiana, 134
Ottoman Empire, 6, 22, 34, 36, 130, 233, 235, 236, 237, 256
Otwinowski, August (deputy from Kraków), 203
Ożarowski, Jerzy (deputy from Kraków), 202
Ożarowski-Ossoliński case, 141

pacta conventa, 23, 25, 78, 88, 104, 257
Palmer, R. R., 8, 267.
panowie, 215, 216, 217
"Parliamentary Order" (1768 law), 94, 96, 98, 102-106, 110-112, 117-118
  abolition, 102, 111, 118
Partitions of Poland, 10, 36, 161
  danger of, 14
  first, 93, 144, 152, 163, 167, 168, 177, 210, 256, 258, 261, 263, 284, 290
  second, 4, 6, 31, 89, 186, 255
  third, 6, 15, 31, 255
Pearson's R, 188, 189, 190
peasantry, 19, 23, 33, 40, 42, 61, 67-70, 81, 84, 88, 171, 260, 278, 295
  Byelorussian, 68
  free, 23, 68,
  royal, 69
  "village folk," 213-214
Pelenski, Jaroslaw, 32, 35, 268, 269, 271
Piarists, 165-167, 178, 181, 180, 185, 186, 187, 188, 193, 195, 196, 197, 198, 209, 227, 244, 245, 246, 249, 252, 253, 261
Pietrzak, Michał, 267, 279
Piłtyński district, 59
Piniński, Józef (deputy from Wołyn), 193, 203
Pińsk, 292
Piotrków, privileges of, 19
Piskadło, Antoni, 271, 296
Pitt, Moses, 283
Plater, Józef (deputy from Żmudź), 202
Płock, 191, 219, 220, 291
Podlasie, 124, 164, 167, 190, 191, 192, 195, 197, 219, 220, 227, 250, 291-292
Podole, 100, 135, 176, 191, 192, 194, 198, 219, 227, 246, 250, 256, 292-293
Polesie, 292
Police Commission, 44, 49, 52-53, 66, 72, 79, 81-83, 85, 141, 143, 280
political controversy at the Four Years' Sejm, 149-160
Połock, 191, 219, 220
Polski słownik biograficzny, 162, 171, 201, 245
Pomorze, 167, 219
pospolite ruszenie, 19, 25, 61
Potocki family, 37, 223, 231
Potocki, Franciszek Pius (deputy from Podlasie), 195, 203, 223
Potocki, Ignacy, 3, 49, 89, 111, 126, 141, 154, 223, 231, 232, 236, 254, 256, 261, 275
Potocki, Jan (deputy from Poznań), 173, 202, 223, 238
Potocki, Jerzy (deputy from Podole), 173, 174, 203, 203
Potocki, Piotr (deputy from Livonia [Crown]), 173, 223
Potocki, Seweryn (deputy from Bracław), 49, 223
Potocki, Stanisław Kostka (deputy from Lublin), 167, 203, 223, 231, 232, 238
Potocki, (Stanisław) Szczęsny

(deputy from Bracław), 101, 153, 203, 223, 232, 241
Poznań, 131, 133, 139, 140, 176, 191, 219, 220
Prawa kardynalne niewzruszone, 56, 59
prawa niewzruszone, 213
Projekt do formy rządu, 49, 53, 59-60
Protestants, 22, 144, 167
senators, 269
szlachta, 28
provincial sessions of the Sejm, 297
Pruski, Jan (deputy from Kalisz), 203
Prussia, 4, 6, 163, 174, 177, 193, 231, 265, 284
Royal, 163
Prussian cities, 17, 23
Przemyśl, 220
Psarski, Fryderyk Jakub (deputy from Wieluń), 204
Pusłowski, Wojciech (deputy from Nowogródek), 173, 202
Puszet, Ksawery (deputy from Kraków), 167, 203, 204
Puzyna, Józef (deputy from Smoleńsk), 204, 238, 240

Rada Nieustająca (Permanent Council), 14, 37, 96, 104, 123, 151, 231, 233, 234, 235, 236, 258, 289
Radoliński, Piotr (deputy from Kalisz), 235
Radwański, Zbigniew, 55, 56, 276
Radzicki, Józef (deputy from Mazowsze), 176, 204

Radzimiński, Józef (deputy from Gniezno), 235
Radzimiński, Michał Ignacy (deputy from Czerniechów), 193
Radziszewski, Michał (deputy from Smoleńsk), 195, 203
Rakowski, Marcin (deputy from Bracław), 204
Ratajczyk, Leonard, 267
Rawa, 141, 175, 191, 219, 220
Renaissance, 37
Repnin, 217
res publica (Rzeczpospolita [republic]), concept of, 16-17
Reytan, 263, 284
Rogowski, Roman (deputy from Mazowsze), 203
Roman Catholic Church, 3, 22, 58, 79, 134, 167, 269, 288
Roman Catholic faith, 13, 60, 276
Roman Catholicism, 28, 58, 68, 168, 280, 288
Rostocki, Teodozy (Metropolitan of Rus'), 22, 68, 167
Rostworowski, Emanuel, 7, 235, 275
Rousseau, Jean-Jacques, 63-64, 99
Rożań, 176
Rożnowski, Antoni (deputy from Gniezno), 135
Rus', 164, 167, 219
Russia, 4, 6, 22, 28, 37, 68, 89, 94, 96, 98, 163, 174, 176, 177, 196, 210, 217, 226, 231, 232, 235, 256, 269
alliance, 14
ambassador, 136
invasion of Poland-Lithuania

(1792), 10, 15, 50, 68, 88, 153, 263, 286
protectorate over Poland-Lithuania, 36, 37
Ruthenia, 193, 194, 198, 215, 227, 243, 250
Rzetkowski, Walenty (deputy from Rawa), 238, 241
Rzewuski, Adam, 101, 143, 154, 203, 241

Sącz, 125
Sandomierz (district), 103, 163, 175, 191, 195, 197, 198, 219, 220, 227, 250
Sapieha, Prince Kazimierz Nestor (deputy from Brześć Litewski), 91, 100, 107, 140, 142, 167, 176, 195, 203, 233, 234, 238, 239, 240, 241, 252, 283
Sarmatianism, 35-36, 37, 211, 217, 263-264
Saxony, 101, 263, 285
Scotland, 93
serfdom, 6, 15, 34, 259
Series, 225
Siciński, Władysław (deputy from Upita [1652]), 281
Siemieński, Hiacynt (deputy from Sieradz), 140
Sieradz, 140, 191, 219, 220, 246
skartabelat, 288
Skorkowski, Kazimierz Albin (deputy from Sandomierz), 236
Smoleńsk, 130, 153, 191, 193, 195, 219, 220, 227, 246, 250
  castellan of, 137

Smoleński, Władysław, 6, 263, 279, 292-293
Sobolewski, Walenty (deputy from Mazowsze), 202, 238, 241
Sokolnicki, Celestyn (deputy from Poznań), 54, 139, 235, 241, 288-289
Sokołowski, Serafin Rafal (deputy from Inowrocław), 49, 275
Solemn Conferral of Order at the Present Sejm (1791), 102, 109-110, 118
Solidarity, 3, 7
Sołtan, Stanisław (deputy from Nowogródek [Słonim]), 236, 276
Sołtyk, Stanisław (deputy from Kraków), 64, 139, 143, 203, 287
Soroka, Wacław, 31, 271
sovereignty, 18, 25, 29, 54, 78, 95, 98-99
  national, 4, 5, 14, 58, 69, 70, 73, 78, 85, 102, 258-259, 266
  popular, 1, 73, 265
Spain, 26
Spytko revolt, 262
Stackelberg, 231
Stanisław August (king), 7, 10, 13, 14, 25, 36-37, 55, 73, 75, 88, 91, 93, 110, 144, 151, 168, 176, 193, 195, 199, 200, 216, 217, 223, 226, 227, 231, 235, 236, 254, 256, 261, 276-277, 282, 285, 293, 294
Starowolski, Szymon, 35, 37, 87, 88, 217, 257, 271, 280

Staszic, Stanisław, 265
Statutes of Nieszawa, 60
Straż Praw, (Guardians of the Laws), 43, 44, 48-49, 51, 53, 60-61, 75, 77-79, 81, 83-85, 112, 114
Stroynowski, Waleryan (deputy from Wołyń), 135, 235
Student's t, 201
Suchodolski, Wojciech (deputy from Rus' [Chełm]), 134, 275
Suchodolski, Antoni (deputy from Smoleńsk), 234, 235
Suchorzewski, Jan (deputy from Kalisz), 128, 131, 152-153
Sweden, 22, 28
Świętosławski, Wojciech August (deputy from Wołyń), 132, 133, 135, 143, 235
Switzerland, 2
Szarmocki, Antoni (deputy from Mazowsze), 49
Szkoła Rycerska, 8, 166-167, 189, 193, 195, 198, 209, 243
szlachta, (see also nobility) 15, 18, 21, 25, 27-29, 32-35, 38, 39, 50, 51, 61-66, 68, 69-70, 82, 86, 88, 156, 161, 167, 168, 170, 171, 174, 176, 186, 187, 194, 232, 245, 248, 253, 255-257, 259, 262, 264, 268-269, 276-277, 288, 292
cząstkowa, 171
drobna, 171
gołota, 171
Orthodox, 22, 270
Protestant, 28

skartabelat, 288
Szymanowski, 235, 238, 241

Tatars, 16, 97
Teutonic Knights, 17, 21
Toruń, 291
totalitarianism, 230, 265
towns and townspeople, 18-19, 34, 40, 61, 64-67, 84, 112-113, 139, 259, 264
plenipotentiaries, 112
Prussian, 23
Transylvania, 22
Treasury Commission, 9, 10, 14, 44, 49, 52, 53, 66, 72, 79, 81-84. 95, 98, 104, 123, 125, 128, 129, 136, 140, 141, 152, 170, 280, 289
Lithuanian, 127, 170
Trembicki, Antoni (deputy from Livonia [Lithuania]), 135
Troki, 110, 131, 191, 219
Trybunał, 23, 52, 53, 95, 105, 143, 154, 268
Tulczyn, 232
turni (roll call votes), 94, 102, 105, 109, 110-111, 114-115, 115, 117, 120-144, 147, 148, 149, 150, 155, 232, 233, 234, 237, 240, 241, 249, 261, 289, 298
listing for the Four Years' Sejm, 122-144

Ukraine, 68, 190, 198, 232, 292 (See also Rus', Ruthenia)
unanimity, 71, 91-102, 105, 119
Uniate (Ukrainian Catholic) Church and Uniates, 22, 58, 68, 167, 168, 269-270, 280

Union of Lublin, 15-16, 21-22, 24, 71, 164, 217, 276
United States, 2, 161, 260, 264
  constitution, 1, 37
  scholarship, 7-8
Urban, W., 278
Urządzenie, 50, 51
Ustawa Rządowa (Statute of Government), 3, 7, 30, 40-54, 55, 56, 61-64, 67-74, 77, 86, 88, 99, 111, 110, 111, 113, 118, 149, 154, 160, 190, 192, 213, 214, 245, 258-259, 261-262, 271-272, 285
Venice, 26
Vienna, 36, 256

Walewski, Kaspar (deputy from Kraków), 287
Walewski-Herburtowski case, 97, 284
Warsaw, 14, 97, 121, 136, 147, 148, 149, 166, 196, 197, 205, 220, 246, 270
Wasa, Zygmunt (king), 28
Wawrzecki, Tomasz (deputy from Wilno), 134, 139, 202, 236, 238, 241, 275
Wereszczyński, Józef (deputy from Troki), 237
Wettins, 36-37, 168
Weyssenhoff, Józef (deputy from Livonia), 236, 238, 275
Wielka encyklopedia, 162, 201
Wieluń, 246
Wilczewski, Franciszek (deputy from Mazowsze), 236
Wilkomierz, 164, 167, 196
Wilno (Vilnius), 10, 97, 166, 170, 191, 195, 196, 197, 219, 227, 250, 278
  diet of (1573), 22
  privileges of, 20-21
Wirtemberg, 130
Wiśniowiecki, Michał Korobut (king), 55
Wojakowski, Józef, 279
Wołkowysk, 167
Wołyń, 132, 133, 135, 143, 164, 191, 192, 193, 194, 198, 219, 220, 227, 232, 246, 250, 262, 292, 293
Woyczyński, Stanisław (deputy from Rawa), 141
Wybranowski, Stanisław (deputy from Lublin), 235
Wyczański, Andrzej, 214, 215

Xięga mieszczan, 65
Xięga ziemianska, 65, 77
Xięgi, 9
  grodzkie, 9
  ziemskie, 9
Zabiełło, 236, 238, 241
Zahorski, Andrzej, 7, 267, 282
Zaiączek, Józef (deputy from Podole), 194, 203, 238, 241
Zajączkowski, Andrzej, 277
Zakroczym, 176
Zakrzewski, Stanisław, 34, 270
Zakrzewski, Ignacy Wyssogota (deputy from Poznań), 131, 133, 203, 235
Zaleski, Michał (deputy from Troki), 110, 236
Załuski Public Library, 97
Zamoyski, Andrzej, 98

Zasady do formu rządu, 56
Zboiński, Jan Nepomucin (deputy from Inowrocław), 142, 238, 240, 241
Zebrzydowski revolt, 28, 32, 55
Zgromadzenie Przyjaciół Konstytucji Rzadowej, (Society of the Friends of the Constitution), 163, 186, 188, 189, 190, 192, 194, 195, 196, 197, 200, 208, 209, 239, 249
Zielińska, Teresa, 219
Zieliński, Aleksander (deputy from Mazowsze), 136
Złotnicki, Antoni (deputy from Podole), 194
Żmudź, 137, 138, 191, 219, 220, 224
Zygmunt August (king), 22, 43, 50, 61, 213